Therap

MW01253022

Therapy and Beyond

Counselling Psychology Contributions to Therapeutic and Social Issues

Edited by Martin Milton

WILEY-BLACKWELL

A John Wiley & Sons, Ltd., Publication

This edition first published 2010
© 2010 John Wiley & Sons Ltd.

All pictures contained within the book were photographed by and belong exclusively to
Dr. Martin Milton.

Wiley-Blackwell is an imprint of John Wiley & Sons, formed by the merger of Wiley's global
Scientific, Technical, and Medical business with Blackwell Publishing.

Registered Office
John Wiley & Sons Ltd, The Atrium, Southern Gate, Chichester, West Sussex, PO19 8SQ, UK

Editorial Offices
The Atrium, Southern Gate, Chichester, West Sussex, PO19 8SQ, UK
9600 Garsington Road, Oxford, OX4 2DQ, UK
350 Main Street, Malden, MA 02148-5020, USA

For details of our global editorial offices, for customer services, and for information about how
to apply for permission to reuse the copyright material in this book please see our website at
www.wiley.com/wiley-blackwell.

Library of Congress Cataloging-in-Publication Data

Therapy and beyond : counselling psychology contributions to therapeutic and social issues /
edited by Martin Milton.
    p. ; cm.
  Includes bibliographical references and index.
  ISBN 978-0-470-71547-5 (cloth) – ISBN 978-0-470-71548-2 (pbk.) 1. Counseling psychology.
I. Milton, Martin.
  [DNLM: 1. Counseling–trends. 2. Psychology, Clinical–methods. WM 55 T398 2010]
  BF636.6.T45 2010
  158′.3–dc22   2010010271

A catalogue record for this book is available from the British Library.

Set in 10.5/13 pt Minion by Thomson Digital, Noida, India
Printed & Bound in Singapore by Ho Printing Singapore Pte Ltd.

1   2010

To Stuart who lets me think and Jordan who stops me...

Contents

Notes on Contributors

The Editor

Dr Martin Milton CPsychol, CSci, AFBPsS, UKCP Reg, is a chartered psychologist, a BPS psychologist specialising in psychotherapy and a UKCP registered psychotherapist. As a practitioner, Martin worked in the British National Health Service for over a decade and now runs his own independent practice.

Martin is Senior Lecturer on the University of Surrey practitioner doctorate in psychotherapeutic and counselling psychology and his research and specialist interests include lesbian and gay affirmative psychology and psychotherapy, and existential psychotherapy and new and burgeoning interests in ecotherapy and the therapeutic aspects of the natural world.

Martin is a former Chair of the BPS Division of Counselling Psychology and served on the Committee of the BPS Lesbian and Gay Psychology section. He remains active in these organisations as a member of the Editorial Board for *Psychology and Sexuality* and *Counselling Psychology Review*, and as a member of the International Advisory Board to *Psychology of Sexualities Review*. Martin is also on the editorial board of the international journal *Ecopsychology* and of *Existential Analysis*.

The Contributors

Dr Heidi Ashley obtained her doctorate in Psychotherapeutic and Counselling Psychology from the University of Surrey in 2005 and works in a secondary care (CMHT) setting with clients who have moderate to severe psychological difficulties. She has interests in supervision and in working therapeutically with people who experience longstanding difficulties with developmental origins. She is presently undertaking further training as an Advanced Schema Therapist.

Dr Lucy Atcheson obtained her doctorate in Psychotherapeutic and Counselling Psychology from the University of Surrey in 2002. As well as working in the NHS and in independent practice, Lucy has presented several television series that made psychological issues and therapy accessible for the public.

Dr Terry Boucher obtained his Practitioner Doctorate in Psychotherapeutic and Counselling Psychology from the University of Surrey in 2005. He works in a specialist pain management service within the NHS and is partner at Vivamus Psychologists in the independent sector.

Dr Adrian Coyle is Director of the MSc in Social Psychology at the University of Surrey, where he worked for 11 years as Research Tutor on the Practitioner Doctorate Programme in Psychotherapeutic and Counselling Psychology. He specialises in qualitative research approaches and his research interests include the psychology of religion and spirituality, identity and loss and bereavement.

Dr Mark Craven obtained his doctorate in Psychotherapeutic and Counselling Psychology from the University of Surrey in 2004. He is interested in social constructionist and collaborative forms of applied practice. He has worked for the NHS in adult acute psychiatric inpatient, community forensic and personality disorder services.

Dr Debora Diamond obtained her doctorate from the University of Surrey. Her areas of specialist interest run across acute care and recovery services and include psychosis, personality disorder, the social positioning of gender and group therapies. Debora is Consultant Counselling Psychologist, Joint Lead in Acute Care and Recovery at NHS Plymouth. She works on an acute psychiatric inpatient ward, in a low secure unit for men and in an open recovery unit for women.

Dr Riccardo Draghi-Lorenz is Director of the Practitioner Doctorate in Psychotherapeutic and Counselling Psychology at the University of Surrey. He is particularly interested in theoretical integration/eclecticism, cultural differences and psychotherapy, the processes underlying intersubjective connectedness and the social and emotional development of infants

Dr Frances Gillies obtained her doctorate in Psychotherapeutic and Counselling Psychology from the University of Surrey in 2004. She works for Devon Partnership Trust (NHS) in adult mental health and has a special interest in developing therapeutic interventions that can help clients with difficult relationship histories foster a sense of wellbeing.

Dr Natalie Hession obtained her doctorate in Psychotherapeutic and Counselling Psychology from the University of Surrey. She currently works in the area of Psycho-oncology and has a special interest in chronic pain. She holds a post as a Senior Psychologist at St Luke's Hospital, Dublin, where she works therapeutically with cancer patients and their families. She is also involved with ongoing research and lectures within affiliated universities and currently serves on the Counselling Psychology Divisional Committee of the Psychological Society of Ireland

Dr Colin Hicks obtained his doctorate in Psychotherapeutic and Counselling Psychology from the University of Surrey in 2006. His area of specialist interest is working with sexual minorities and also psychological distress in university students. He currently has an appointment with Dorset Healthcare Foundation NHS Trust where he works in an Improving Access to Psychological Therapies (IAPT) Service as a counselling psychologist/senior therapist and supervisor. He also works in private practice, where he provides psychological services for individuals and consultancy for businesses.

Dr Joanna Lofthouse obtained her doctorate in Psychotherapeutic and Counselling Psychology from the University of Surrey in 2006. Her area of special interest is psychosocial and cultural phenomena and their implications within the consulting room. She currently has an appointment with North East London Mental Health Trust where she works in a Community Mental Health Team as well as an intermediate psychological service for adult mental health.

Dr Elena Manafi, CPsychol obtained her doctorate from the University of Surrey. She is a Chartered Psychologist registered with the British Psychological Society and an HPC-registered counselling psychologist. She specialises in existential/phenomenological philosophy, psychology and clinical training and is currently the Programme Director on the Professional Doctorate in Counselling Psychology at Regent's College. Elena has also been teaching and supervising at the New School of Psychotherapy and Counselling (NSPC) and runs a private practice in north London.

Dr Donal McAteer obtained his doctorate in Psychotherapeutic and Counselling Psychology from the University of Surrey in 2006. His areas of specialist interest are the therapeutic process and relationship, and the philosophical foundations of counselling psychology. He currently has an appointment with a Psychological Therapies Team in the NHS in Derry, Northern Ireland, where he works with adults experiencing psychological and emotional distress. He is currently acting as Co-Chair of the group working to establish a Northern Ireland Branch of the Division of Counselling Psychology.

Dr Camilla Olsen obtained her doctorate in Psychotherapeutic and Counselling Psychology from the University of Surrey in 2000. Her area of specialist interest is the development of therapeutic relationships with clients suffering from severe and enduring mental ill health. She currently runs her own independent practice and is involved in the training of counselling psychologists as a supervisor and examiner.

Dr Jill Owen, CPsychol obtained her doctorate in Psychotherapeutic and Counselling Psychology from the University of Surrey in 1998 and then returned to the programme as a Professional Tutor for three years. She is an HPC-registered counselling psychologist and an HPC-registered sport and exercise psychologist. She currently runs a private practice and sport psychology consultancy in Guildford, Surrey.

Dr Deborah Rafalin, CPsychol is a practising HPC-registered counselling psychologist. She obtained her Doctorate in Psychotherapeutic and Counselling Psychology from the University of Surrey in 1998. Deborah is a Senior Lecturer on the Practitioner Doctorate in Counselling Psychology at City University, London and her areas of specialist interest include qualitative research methodologies and identity threat. Deborah also works as a consultant to the NHS and the Third Sector on various projects, is a professional member of the fitness to practice and competency panels at the HPC and runs her own private practice

Foreword

Emmy van Deurzen

This book takes a fresh and vigorous look at counselling psychology and invites us to think carefully about the present state and future direction of our profession. It challenges current assumptions that counselling psychologists have to fit in with. It considers and questions the medical, economic and political agendas that oppress contemporary practice. It presents us with the many alternatives that are available and demonstrates the dangers of following a single established model. It sometimes cautiously and sometimes enthusiastically argues the case of pluralism, phenomenology, community, collaboration and ecology as ways of finding interesting new answers to the questions posed by our work with clients of diverse backgrounds and orientations. It proposes alternatives to the categorisation of distress and to the oppressive dichotomies of mental health and illness.

This book provides a stimulating and creative reappraisal of what we usually take for granted. Its chapters are always based in the interaction between theory and practice, drawing new ideas from disciplined thought about experience. It shows that it is only in a continuous exploration of new horizons and by opening a wide range of existential vistas that science and human understanding become validated by life itself. Many of the chapters are a good source of teaching materials to challenge new trainees. But they are even more relevant in the context of continuing professional development. For many of us have become complacent, jaded or battle-fatigued when constantly contending with increasingly tight professional boundaries and regulations. Some of these words will uplift us, some will rattle our cages and all will challenge the status quo.

This is a timely volume. What we are witnessing at the moment is a process of one-dimensional professionalisation which is more interested in quantitative than qualitative outcomes and favours approaches that can be rolled out across the board, tempting us into the shallows. What the contributors to this book are saying is that this short-sighted focus is dangerous and that we need to rethink our values and commitments as counselling psychologists and be true to the principles on which we founded this profession, making sure it remains fit for purpose.

In spite of its serious agenda, the book is light on its feet and easy to read. It will stimulate, intrigue and provoke thought in those who are willing to engage in this important professional debate. Its chapters have been written by the staff and alumni of the well-established doctoral programme in Psychotherapeutic and Counselling Psychology at the University of Surrey, demonstrating the breadth and depth of this school. Here is the rich harvest of fifteen and more years of research and debate. It speaks for itself and will reverberate with other courses, providing many counselling psychology students with new ideas for their own investigations. Each contributor explores the boundaries and borders of the territory of counselling psychology and refocuses the definitions and aspirations of our profession. Together, they formulate a call to our conscience. What is the original mission of our profession and what has become of it? How do we wish to continue to practise our profession in the current climate?

The book helps us to address these and other questions, as it reminds us of the paradigmatic changes our profession has been through and cautions us not to lose the essence of our profession, nor to lose touch with our commitment to help others in understanding their troubled lives. We can get too involved with research and technique and lose sight of what really matters. It is no solution to filter out the best bits of different therapeutic traditions and serve these up in a smorgasbord of tasty titbits, which are not sufficient to satisfy our clients' hunger for real nourishment. The kind of therapeutic integration proposed by low-grade cognitive behavioural therapies may be pragmatically sound but lacks philosophical clarity and depth. The objective should certainly not be simply to integrate established traditions in order to dissolve them. Disciplined pluralism is about working with diversity by holding on to the tensions and by making continuous efforts to creatively juxtapose, maintaining openness and flexibility. It is not about arriving at a dogmatic uniformity that suffocates our responsiveness to clients' predicaments.

As Riccardo Draghi-Lorenz, one of the contributors to this book, argues in his conclusion:

> As is often the case, however, the scientific battle is between reductivists, who fail to understand how little we really comprehend, and those open to the ever-surprising complexity of the human condition. In this situation

theoretical and epistemological differences are to be carefully nurtured, for if science were to proceed by consensus, it would not proceed at all.

Therapy and Beyond shows convincingly that the struggle with different perspectives is more important than reductionist unity of practice. We may be tempted to go along with the easy options and quasi-certainties currently offered us in our field, but we will only ignore the tensions and the perennial need to remain open to doubt and uncertainty at our peril. The entire field of therapy and counselling, and with it the field of counselling psychology, is currently undergoing transformation. We should not assume that change is necessarily change for the better. Important lessons have been learnt over the past decades of careful practice and these can easily be forgotten if we become complacent about homogenisation and too enamoured of evidence-based practices that merely cloak human understanding in an external mantle of knowledge.

This book reminds us that the evidence of good human living is far more complex than some would have us believe. It shows that we need to be prepared to engage with the facts and think about them carefully. Only if we are unafraid of opposing superficially attractive solutions can we develop the multidimensional approach that truly serves our clients. For this to happen we need to have the courage of our conviction that it is our clients' wellbeing that matters most. Then we can maintain a rigorously searching attitude, combine different perspectives and go beyond the quick-fix solutions or the shallow facts of economically driven practice. This book reminds us that life is more complex and precious than what outcome research captures. We owe it to our clients and to ourselves to look beyond the obvious and to keep challenging and renewing our understanding, not just of our profession but of the lives of the clients we set out to serve.

Acknowledgements

On behalf of all the contributors, a heartfelt 'thank you' to everyone who has influenced this book – our clients, research participants, teachers, therapists or supervisors in the field and friends and family in our personal lives. Your contribution to our thinking is very much appreciated.

Martin would like to thank all of the contributors for their hard work and clear thinking. He would particularly like to thank Lucy and Terry who came on board at short notice, excelled at time management and speedy delivery against impossible time-frames. Thanks also to Tania Dolley, Martin Jordan, Dale Judd, Carol Shillito-Clarke and Digby Tantam for your generosity with time and feedback. Thanks to Nickee Higley and Louise Brorstrom for making me think at crucial times in the preparation of this book.

Heidi Ashley would like to thank Veronika Braunton for her valuable feedback in preparing her chapter.

Camilla Olsen would like to thank her 'bacon saver'. Apparently you know who you are.

Introduction

Therapy and Beyond: Counselling Psychology Contributions to Therapeutic and Social Issues

Martin Milton

Counselling Psychology

British counselling psychology is well into its second decade, having formally come into being when the British Psychological Society established the Division of Counselling Psychology in 1994. Counselling psychology is postmodern and multi-modal in nature, with a bent towards a holistic perspective that is attentive to issues as they manifest in psychological therapy, research, individual lives and in the wider world.

During its development, counselling psychology has moved beyond the process of initial definition where much of the initial discourse – our own and that of others – was focused on making distinct its relationship between this discipline and those professions it was similar to or different from, models it used or did not use and contexts with which it engaged. Counselling psychology is now able to elucidate the significant contributions it makes, both to the practice of psychological therapy and to research, policy development and new and innovative contributions to society. In this regard the profession is a forward-looking one that is extending its domain of practice into areas other than the consulting room. And this is one of the functions of this book – to showcase the ways in which a mature use of the knowledge base and practice of counselling psychology is now firmly contributing to a range of therapeutic and social issues.

One perspective that was present at the birth of British counselling psychology and remains a core philosophical, academic, ethical and therapeutic priority for counselling psychology is the understanding of people as 'relational beings'. While collaborating with people and contexts that draw on a range of perspectives, including the traditional views of people as independent entities, counselling psychology has always recognised that relational perspectives have an enormous contribution to make to understanding people and working towards greater wellbeing. This focus is obvious in terms of relationships between therapist and client, within families and between intimate partners; but it is one that extends to understanding the relationships people have with themselves in terms of identity, self-esteem and the like, and in terms of our wider cultural and socio-political wellbeing.

The World in Which We Exist

Life has always been challenging and modern life is no different. It is complex, multi-factored and for some of the time, terribly stressful. Not only do we suffer from such existential constants of anxiety, isolation, death and meaninglessness, but we also feel cheated when the seductive promises of contemporary life fail to remove the hurdles we face and when our world is different from the way we hope, expect or want it to be.

People struggle in a variety of ways, sometimes with themselves, sometimes with families and friends and often with the world at large. The struggles that people experience are wide-ranging and manifest physically, socially and in more intimate ways. This is not to mention the damage that affects us when we are caught up in war, genocide or poverty. The fact that mild to moderate mental health problems are now termed 'common' is suggestive of significant difficulty and it is also interesting that, despite the fact that there has been measurable decrease in actual physical harm to children in Britain recently, our sense of concern has grown enormously in the last few years.

While these experiences might be seen as 'predictable difficulties' (Deurzen, 2009, p. 80) they are often painful and debilitating, affecting us mentally and emotionally, physically and interpersonally. There are times when the distress is considered excessive or the isolation too extreme and people turn to the range of professionals to help make sense of their panic, pain and confusion, which they hope these professionals can make it better. It is reassuring to know that psychological interventions *are* effective and helpful for people with a range of difficulties.

Engaging with the painful side of human experience is a part of the work of counselling psychologists, but of course, human experience is not always stressful and counselling psychology is not only about engaging with distress; we are also interested in human wellbeing. It's not only about exploring the experience of an individual; counselling psychologists also explore a much wider range of relevant human phenomena.

People's day-to-day interactions are intimately linked to the huge advances we have made in social, political and economic areas. These developments have advantages for our quality of life as we enjoy great health benefits, longer lifespans, medical assistance to cure and rehabilitate us after infections and illnesses. Physically our lives have become easier as we suffer fewer illnesses, recover more quickly when we do get ill and our everyday exertions are limited. Actually, it is getting to the point where our comfort may be what is bad for us, with few of us needing to walk great distances to secure food or water – if we don't just jump in the car to nip to the supermarket, we order online. Instead of walking great distances across the savannah as our bipedal species is designed to do, we now utilise the more comfortable technologies of the car, bus or train.

So counselling psychology, the scientific and applied field that it is, is interested in a holistic view of humanity's experience, what makes us tick, what hurts us and what is helpful. Of course, it is interested in psychological therapy, but its knowledge base is equally relevant to research, social policy and understanding the effects of oppression and exploitation. It is engaged with the personal and political, its knowledge and skills mean it has contributions to make at a therapeutic and policy level and with the overlap of the ethical and the scientific.

Therapy and Beyond

Change is happening at a furious rate in the field of public sector health care provision. The contributors and I recognise that today's professional reality may simply be stepping stones *en route* to a variety of other future identities and practices. Keeping this in mind, this book takes a moment to stop and consider the profession, its current body of knowledge and array of practices and to look at innovative and potential new developments.

The contributors and I hope that readers will find this book useful for a variety of reasons – it might be used to inform people about the profession, but it can also be used to facilitate critical thinking about wider issues and practices that counselling psychology is involved with alongside other applied psychologists, mental health professionals and government bodies.

As readers journey through the book, they are invited to reflect on – and debate – a number of therapeutic and social issues.

The book focuses on some of the main areas of psychotherapeutic and counselling psychology theory, practice and research and their application in a range of settings. Of course, there are inevitably domains that are not represented in this volume and while a complete encyclopaedia was not possible, we do regret the practical issues that mean we have had to limit the scope of this book . . . for now.

Section 1 provides the reader with an overview of the philosophical stances that underpin knowledge and practice and the ways in which counselling psychology engages with this rich spread of information. It addresses the ways in which this informs core aspects of the therapeutic professions, with attention to the therapeutic relationship, our understanding of human distress and consideration of what this means for the notion of ethical practice.

Section 2 looks at the contemporary use of traditional models of practice and the ways in which humanistic, psychodynamic, cognitive-behavioural and existential models are helpful in informative and innovative ways – not just as distinct ways of seeing the world or practicing therapy but also as perspectives to contribute to wider debates – therapeutic, social and political – as to what facilitates wellbeing and limits damage and distress.

Section 3 looks at new developments in the discipline and how counselling psychology is helping develop wider understandings of people and contributing to society in new and novel ways. It recognises that academic ghettos are limiting and draws on information and knowledge bases sometimes seen as the province of other sciences and other fields. In doing so, section three outlines the ways in which a counselling psychology perspective can assist individual and wider debates on such dimensions of human life as sport and spirituality, sexuality and the environment. In this way it is thought-provoking, provocative and highlights the importance of applying our knowledge base in creative ways.

Reference

Deurzen, E. van (2009). *Psychotherapy and the quest for happiness*. London, Sage.

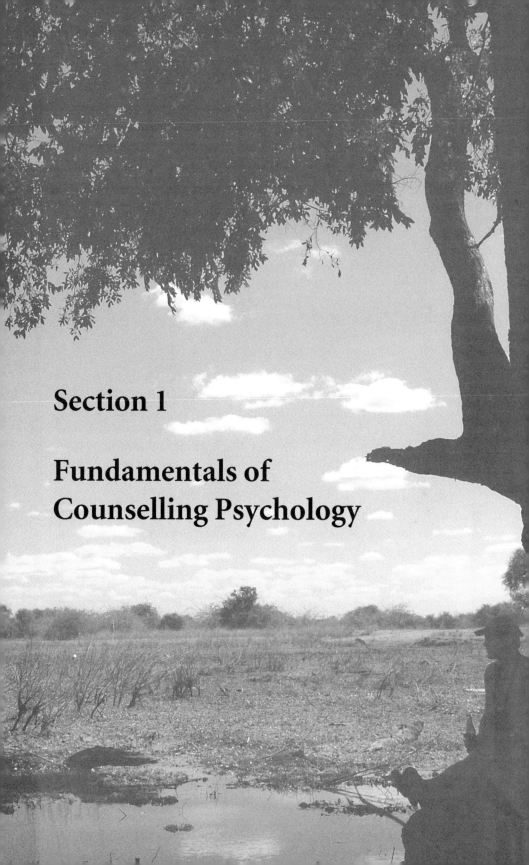

Section 1

Fundamentals of Counselling Psychology

Fundamentals of Counselling Psychology

Martin Milton

There are some aspects of counselling psychology which underpin *every* aspect of the profession and the tasks that counselling psychologists undertake. These aspects are fundamental in character and ever present whether they are overt or covert. While aspects of our practice change over time — sometimes in quite significant ways — in light of the therapeutic model embraced, the research method used or the contexts in which we work, these fundamentals remain central to the integrity of the profession. What are these fundamental characteristics, so crucial to the profession and the contribution counselling psychology makes to therapy and to the wider world? This section looks at just a few of them, including pluralism, relational ways of understanding the world, the understanding of distress, research and enquiry, ethics and the therapeutic relationship.

Such fundamental aspects are not easy, clear-cut phenomena and certainly not unidimensional in nature. Quite the contrary, these are sometimes rather ethereal, complex domains, requiring open, ongoing and curious engagement. In some contexts (e.g., in the debates about statutory regulation, the setting-up of professional bodies and the writing of therapeutic 'guidelines') the debates can be characterised by conflict, reliance on the exercise of power and the influence of status. This array of responses highlights the crucial nature of these fundamentals.

In light of this, it will come as no surprise to readers that the contributors to section 1 approach their topics — and, I suspect, the profession — from different positions. And in doing so, these six chapters draw readers' attention to the complexity of human experience and the ways in which counselling psychology knowledge and practice engage with this complexity so as to be of benefit to all involved.

In Chapter 1, Donal McAteer introduces the reader to the concept of *pluralism* and the epistemological tensions with which we live today and in which counselling psychologists function. Donal reminds us that counselling psychology eschews dogma and encourages an attitude of curiosity and continuous questioning of the assumptions we make in our daily lives both as counselling psychology practitioners and as human beings. As in the wider world, this presents a challenge to the profession and its practitioners as we attempt to negotiate with different theoretical and professional perspectives and as we wrestle with our own certainties or biases. This chapter also considers one of the core tensions experienced in the profession: 'directiveness and non-directiveness'. The chapter does not ask *whether* we influence people, but how we do, why we do, when we do, when we should, how we can communicate this, and what shapes the ways in which we influence.

This is followed by Elena Manafi's first chapter, which looks at counselling psychology's *relational framework*, well known when we think about therapy, but ever-present in all our professional activities and roles. The chapter outlines the different epistemological positions that counselling psychologists draw on and how these come together in a view of human experience as constructed and intersubjective. Counselling psychology shows just how crucial it is that we move beyond the traditional view of people as self-contained to understand them as intentional and relational in all aspects of our experience and behaviour. This has implications for understanding people, understanding 'pathology' and ways of preventing psychological distress.

In Chapter 3, Deborah Rafalin looks at one of our key activities – *research* – and the ways in which counselling psychology engages with the challenges and opportunities that psychological enquiry provides us. The discipline explicitly engages even-handedly with both quantitative and qualitative paradigms to answer its burning questions and to explore the nature of the questions being asked of it. This chapter explores how the counselling psychologist responds to the calls for 'scientific evidence' to support their clinical choices whilst valuing the subjective phenomenological experiences shared by their clients.

That emotional pain and distress are inescapable features of the human condition is not in doubt and when working with people experiencing this, the applied psychologies often have to engage with the notion of 'psychopathology'. There is a social and cultural acceptance of the logic of a medical model of distress and has seen a steady increase in the pathologisation of everyday life. In Chapter 4, Mark Craven, Adrian Coyle and I take a different stance and consider *human distress* through a postmodern lens, to highlight the benefits of relational frameworks when meeting clients in pain and to remind us of some of the damage that can be incurred when using outmoded, individualistic ways of understanding people. The chapter looks at 'psychopathology' *in relation* to the discipline of counselling psychology, which historically provides an alternative view of human functioning and dis-ease to that contained in the medical model.

As a profession, counselling psychology emerged from a desire to move towards a way of being with clients that would be non-directive, egalitarian and would take a holistic approach to understanding human wellbeing. So, in Chapter 5 Frances Gillies looks at one of counselling psychology's key foci – the *therapeutic relationship* – and suggests that this crucial aspect of practice benefits not only from being seen as a current relationship between the therapist and client in the consulting room, but also a relationship embedded in time. To this end, she shows how an evolutionary lens can usefully contribute to understanding the complexity of this key relationship.

The final chapter in this section is by Camilla Olsen, who considers *ethics* as a fundamental dimension of counselling psychology. In this chapter consideration is given to the ethical boundaries psychological therapy is governed by and the rationale for these boundaries. Attention is also given to how these same ethical boundaries can create difficulties between human beings, in particular where you as a person have contradictory ethical responsibilities. Many of us have experienced this in our workplace, and this can be particularly difficult when multidisciplinary input is required. It is also true for training institutions as well as for supervision.

These contributors show that whether thinking about epistemological positions, the ways individuals relate to self, others and the wider world, whether we explore a phenomenon in relation to the meaning it has for clients or the role it plays in the wider world, counselling psychologists draw on relational frameworks in an ever-changing landscape and this is done with an ethical mindset – how to do the best possible work so that people are helped and harm is avoided. The contributors also highlight the complexity in this endeavour and offer fruitful ways of orienting ourselves to this challenge.

Chapter 1

Philosophical Pluralism: Navigating the Sea of Diversity in Psychotherapeutic and Counselling Psychology Practice

Donal McAteer

'Ever not quite' has to be said of the best attempts made anywhere in the universe at attaining all-inclusiveness.

(James, 1909, p. 322)

This standpoint, articulated by the American philosopher William James in the first decade of the twentieth century, highlights a central tenet of the postmodern view: that there is no overarching truth to elucidate everything. Moreover, to aim for such certainty would inevitably leave some things unexplained, while excluding other legitimate explanations in the process. The concept of pluralism stems from such a view in that it puts forward a case for recognising the validity of multiple competing perspectives in answering the questions we are faced with in our personal and professional lives and in the wider world.

This chapter discusses how the notion of a pluralistic perspective applies to therapeutic practice and how it constitutes the very foundation of a counselling psychology approach to working with clients and to the realms beyond the consulting room, including such areas as research, service

Therapy and Beyond: Counselling Psychology Contributions to Therapeutic and Social Issues
Edited by Martin Milton
© 2010 John Wiley & Sons, Ltd.

development and how we relate to each other in our lives. It also incorporates the dialectical element of counselling psychology, referring to the negotiation of opposing and at times seemingly incommensurable viewpoints, and the promotion of active engagement with them. Through an emphasis on this dialectical stance, we shall see how the adoption of pluralism brings with it both great opportunities and significant challenges. This will include a discussion of one of the main challenges to pluralism in the profession – namely, *directiveness* and the degree to which we can, do or should influence clients in therapy or others around us.

Defining Pluralism

From Metanarratives to Pluralism

Given that the world in which we live consists of a multiplicity of people, of experiences, attitudes, beliefs and claims to the truth, counselling psychology, as a part of this world, adopts a pluralistic standpoint which recognises the variety within it. To foreground the notion of pluralism, it is necessary to give a brief account of the postmodern philosophy to which it is closely related.

As a philosophical movement, postmodernism arose in response to modernism and the Age of Enlightenment. The modern era had seen the rapid advancement of scientific enquiry and a search for universal laws to explain the world in which we live. It was felt that objective laws would be free from the myths, stories and beliefs that characterised premodern thinking to allow humankind to see the world as it 'really' is (Grenz, 1996). Postmodernism saw these laws and principles as essentially myths in themselves and as 'metanarratives' that serve to supersede all other claims to the 'truth'. Therefore, while science was concerned with the search for a theory of everything, postmodernism cautioned against this, challenging the notion that we can access the truth, and displaying what Lyotard (1984, p. xxiv) has referred to as 'incredulity toward metanarratives'. This position argues that instead of a single unifying answer to a given question or conundrum, we live in a complex world (or worlds) and there are multiple answers depending on a multitude of personal, political, cultural, linguistic and social factors.

In light of this postmodern counterargument to metanarratives or truths, pluralism emerged as a doctrine that valued the diversity of perspectives inherent in any conversation. Fundamentally, pluralism aims to avoid the dogmatic prescription of any particular epistemology in explaining our world or the people in it. This pluralistic epistemology is at the core of counselling psychology and represents its engagement with a wide variety of perspectives that clients bring to therapy, or that are evident when conducting research or when working with service and policy development. It could not be more clearly stated in the guidelines for practice in this profession, whereby models of therapy seek 'to elucidate, interpret and negotiate between perceptions and world views but not to assume the automatic superiority of any one way of experiencing, feeling, valuing and knowing' (Division of Counselling Psychology, 2008, pp. 1–2). Indeed, the definition of pluralism extended here is founded on this deliberate engagement and negotiation with diversity rather than simply a recognition that there are multiple viewpoints on offer. This engagement is not without its challenges though, whether that is in offering therapy or in navigating the vast array of perspectives we encounter in the world we inhabit. These challenges are explored in a later section, but first we must further elucidate the nature of pluralism as it applies to the field of therapy and to the particular discipline of counselling psychology.

Pluralism in Therapeutic Practice

There exist several hundred individually defined approaches to therapeutic practice (Cooper, C., 2003; Kazdin, 2000; Tillet, 1999). In fact, it is difficult to arrive at an exact number and no doubt it will have increased by the time you read this book. This makes it difficult to refer purely to 'therapeutic practice'. As Rowan (cited in House, 1997) argues, any attempt to represent the field of therapy as a single, cohesive profession fails to account for the fundamental differences in worldview that exist between these various schools and approaches. In light of this variety, the benefits of a pluralistic perspective in counselling psychology become apparent through an awareness of the different positions and an emphasis on their validity. Pluralism in this sense stems from a respect for the 'Other', and Cooper and McLeod discuss the importance of this stance in therapy:

> Pluralism, then, is not just an epistemological position, but an ethical and political commitment to respecting, valuing and being inclusive towards Otherness: other worldviews, other counsellors and psychotherapists and ... respectful to our clients.
>
> (2007, p. 136)

However, this valuing of otherness in a pluralistic approach does not always run smoothly. With such a variety of outlooks comes disagreement and, put simply, the therapeutic field is 'full of dispute' (Feltham, 1997, p. 119). For instance, major disputes have historically taken place between psychiatry and clinical psychology, between the various applied psychologies, and between particular approaches that endeavour to claim pre-eminence. It is with this dispute in mind that another element of the pluralistic focus of counselling psychology is utilised – this discipline not only acknowledges the variety, but enters into the arena of disagreement with a view to actively participating in it. Indeed, Samuels contends that 'the trademark of pluralism is competition and its way of life is bargaining' (1997, p. 201). This highlights the dialectical nature of pluralism. While it involves an attitude of recognition, respect and inclusivity towards different positions, it also promotes an engagement with this difference and the tension that it can bring. It is perhaps no wonder then that counselling psychologists can be found in the field of mediation and conflict resolution, given this emphasis within the discipline on dispute and negotiation (Spinelli, 2004; Strasser & Randolph, 2004).

It can be seen that *dialectical pluralism* is fundamental to counselling psychology. It is present in its engagement with different models in an informed approach to therapeutic practice (Clarkson, 1995). It is present in creating an atmosphere of openness and tolerance in which divergent research methodologies can be equally valid in exploring important questions both within and outside therapy (Barker & Pistrang, 2005). Naturally, those who adopt a position of active participation in the 'messiness' of difference are not always in comfortable territory. In negotiating the competing and contrasting theories on offer in therapy, a dialectical approach places importance on many features of engagement that we might prefer to avoid – disagreement, conflict, frustration, uncertainty – and argues that it is in the creative tension generated between therapeutic perspectives that the value of pluralism lies. More fundamentally, this negotiation begins with adopting a critical stance to our own assumptions and the fixed categories we create that obscure our view of the alternatives around us. Rowan (2001) states that such a stance quite simply entails a 'take nothing for granted' policy, which opens us to other perspectives and worldviews. The importance of this fundamental questioning is demonstrated for all of us in our relationships not just with others in therapy, but with other people in general – through accepting the potentially enriching influence of other faiths, cultures, races and genders without having to guard so heavily against them. These notions bring shades of grey, or preferably multicolour, to the proceedings in favour of a restrictive 'either/or' position, and include an element of paradox that once again takes it beyond clearly defined categories and sedimented knowledge. Through this attitude, counselling psychology becomes adaptable to the inevitable changes that a pluralistic world entails, and is able to grow continually within what is certainly a complex matrix of interactions and influences that are in a constant state of flux. As is perhaps becoming clearer at this stage, wrestling with the interplay of multiple perspectives can bring substantial challenges to those willing to wade into this sea of diversity.

The Challenge of Dialectical Pluralism

Roadblocks to Pluralism

Given this conflict, it comes as no surprise that adopting and maintaining such a stance can be difficult. This will immediately be apparent to therapists in the consulting room, and to those beyond the confines of this domain, who have grappled with the arguments posed by viewpoints different from that with which they are most comfortable. For the purpose of the point in question here, I shall focus on the challenges presented to therapists when working pluralistically in their practice. The following example should help to illustrate some of the complexity of pluralism in action:

> Consider a counselling psychologist working with a client who has come for help with his 'depression'. She works from, and allies herself predominantly with, a Rogerian, person-centred perspective; however, her training also included significant focus and exposure to other therapeutic theory and methods. She takes note of how the client seems to struggle with filling his day, due to the fact that he is not working and has little social activity. In attempting to adopt a pluralistic attitude, the therapist is faced with multiple questions. Will she continue with her chosen humanistic approach and empathise with the here-and-now difficulties her client experiences? Will she incorporate elements of a cognitive behavioural approach that might help him to specifically change the behaviour that is troubling him and the thinking that may be interfering with such a change? What impact will it have on her therapeutic relationship with this client? Moreover, what approach might the client find more appealing? What approach might be of more benefit to him, and what would this benefit look like? Should she rule out CBT, given her preference for the person-centred perspective, or does that mean she's being too dogmatic? Furthermore, what do other approaches have to say on this issue?

There are no easy answers here and this is but a sample of some of the questions – *pluralistic dilemmas* – which a dialectical stance raises. However, when engaging in a dialectical enterprise, 'answers' as such are not always being sought, nor are dilemmas always resolved, and the conclusion does not have to entail the agreement or synthesis between viewpoints (Downing, 2000). Rather than answers, this therapist's situation emphasises the conflict encountered when attempting to help others by moving around the therapeutic landscape with a dialectical compass. As Rowan puts it, '[t]he lessons of the dialectic are hard ones' (2001, p. 3). The values we maintain and the foundations on which we build our lives are open to question, and there can be a lot at stake when poking at the walls that hold our house up. This includes the theories we hold dear, whether therapeutic or philosophical, and these have already been arrived at through much deliberation and are inexorably connected to us as individual human beings. Samuels (1997) writes about the psychological difficulties of the very human endeavour of pluralism, namely that therapists or psychologists, being human, find it hard to maintain a consistent attitude of tolerance when engaging with those people or perspectives that oppose them. However, he once again underlines the value of this uncomfortable interaction and encourages that competition be brought into the open as a contribution to personal and professional growth. Furthermore, this growth will surely be to the benefit of the clients receiving support from those committing themselves to such personal exploration.

It is easy to see how, in this conflict-ridden paradoxical enterprise, there are not only intellectual dilemmas or roadblocks to pluralism in the form of understanding the complex landscape, there are also emotional roadblocks when entering this potentially threatening area of exploration. Downing (2000) discusses these emotional challenges as being associated with therapists' personalities, allegiances, personal worldviews and value systems or ethics. In specific reference to counselling psychology, Rizq (2006) argues that the profession's identification with a pluralistic and dialectical attitude places trainees particularly in emotional turmoil as they struggle to get to grips with multiple theories and the realisation that it is not possible for one single and clear set of rules to be given to navigate their way.

Beyond these personal struggles in embracing pluralism, there are the difficulties of balancing pluralism with the demands placed on us by the contexts in which we work. This exposes us to dilemmas of how to communicate our stance towards pluralism and highlights the relevance this has to all of us as people in a diverse, pluralistic world. Counselling psychology's commitment to evidence-based practice in therapy is also challenging as it requires the balancing of pluralism in producing and evaluating scientific evidence while respecting the phenomenological experience of individual clients or research participants.

Considering the difficulties in encountering the multicolour conflict that defines dialectical pluralism, the question arises: is it a case of 'many hands make light work' or 'too many cooks spoil the broth'? As is the dialectical prerogative, it's neither and it's both. Many hands or theories certainly don't make for light work when it comes to wrestling with these ideas, but nor do they spoil the broth. They *are* the broth. They are already in the mix, whether we like it or not, and the tension comes from communicating with opposing views we cannot ignore. However, we can, of course, *choose* to ignore or reject these other views (including the view of pluralism), and this point will be discussed towards the end of this chapter. Before that, there is a particular pluralistic dilemma in therapeutic practice that captures one of the major challenges in dialectical engagement and that helps to illuminate the issues under discussion here.

A Question of Direction

A significant barrier to pluralistic engagement with or between competing therapeutic approaches is the question of whether a practitioner sees the approaches as either 'directive' or 'non-directive' within therapy. This can be fundamental to the perception of a type of therapy and the therapists associated with it, and as such, it can have a bearing on which therapies practitioners choose to engage with if attempting to adopt a pluralistic attitude in their practice.

It can be unclear to what exactly the notion of directiveness refers. At first glance, the idea of being directive in therapy appears to relate to how a therapist guides the client and the process towards particular goals. Cooper, M. (2003) suggests that direction can involve the introduction by the therapist of their own topics and issues, and it is often associated with specific 'techniques' that the therapist employs or theories that are openly communicated to the client. Conversely, a stance of non-directiveness is one that communicates a fundamental respect for the client's autonomy by not imposing the therapist's views on where the process should be going or pointing the client in any particular direction (Levitt, 2005).

Research I have conducted in this area (McAteer, 2006) was concerned with the meaning of directiveness and what it might look like in practice. Specifically, it looked at cognitive behavioural therapy and existential therapy as these are traditionally seen as directive and non-directive respectively. The findings suggested that the concept of directiveness is not as straightforward as the terms above might imply. It does not seem to be a case of one therapist or type of therapy directing the client while the other does not, but more to do with direction and influence forming an integral and unavoidable part of the therapeutic process, regardless of the approach. The research also questions the notion of categorising therapies on the basis of a particular 'type'. Both approaches encompassed therapists who practised in a variety of ways and, consequently, had different effects on the direction of the therapeutic process. Therefore, it is concluded that the issue centres more on how we already influence our clients in our individual style of therapy and how we can remain aware of this, even if this relates to how we communicate our position in 'non-directiveness' that it would be more beneficial for them if we didn't explicitly direct the process. Deurzen (2009, p. 35) highlighted that this pertains to an approach that is 'neither directive nor non-directive, but directional, purposeful and searching instead', when attempting to assist clients in finding their own direction.

This idea of conveying our position or worldview to clients in therapy and the effect this can have has been underlined by Deurzen-Smith (1992), who argues that therapeutic dialogue can be a converting of the client to the therapist's political or ethical position, and 'by not intervening, one is still making an intervention and transmitting a certain view of the world' (1992, p. 18). In reference to Polanyi's (1967) work on the 'interiorisation' of theory in science, Downing considers what is required of clients in this respect when they enter therapy:

> In the complex exchange which follows, it is no doubt crucial that therapists teach clients to interiorise some implicit or explicit theoretical rationale and philosophical framework, just as they themselves have interiorised it.
>
> (2000, p. 250)

In light of these seemingly inevitable communications, it is important then that we remain aware of our influence and the fact that we play a part in co-directing the therapeutic process towards what we feel might best serve our clients. The following example may shed some light on maintaining a reflexive awareness of the influence we can have:

> As I have been writing this section, I have been conscious of overtly insisting that we should always remain aware of our directiveness, with the suggestion that this is the 'right' way to set about practising in an appropriately pluralistic fashion. I am wary of being too directive! But I am still trying to make a point, so perhaps I can be more explicit. My aim is to have an impact on you as the reader, otherwise I wouldn't have written this. However, my aim is also not to ultimately provide an 'answer' or to tell you what you should be doing in therapy or in your approach to life. Instead, I intend to open the doors to a conversation I feel is important and share my views on it. In resisting the prescription of a specific course of action, I am communicating the importance I place on the idea of you coming to your own conclusions based on our interaction through this text. Of course, this is because I feel your

viewpoint should be respected, just as other's should, without having to impose my worldview on you. Nonetheless (and perhaps you can see where I am going with this), I have just impressed on you the essence of my worldview and the pluralism at the foundation of this – namely, that I feel this is the way it should be and I have a preference for us to communicate in these terms.

What is being demonstrated here is the subtle, implicit nature of our influence and direction at times, but it is influence nonetheless. I am essentially asking you to buy into my worldview. But you can choose not to.

What if in the example above you demanded of me that I tell you the 'right' way to do things rather than leaving it up to you? I might insist that I am not in the position to determine what is right for you because I appreciate the fact that it would be my take on the issue, and I would not automatically assume the superiority of my view over yours. Thereby, my pluralism, and my direction towards that, is perhaps becoming a little more explicit through my active rejection of doing things differently from that which I value, and ultimately I *am* actually assuming the superiority of this view.

From McAteer (2006), it seems that the roadblocks we might face when attempting to engage with the range of therapies from our pluralistic stand-point can be challenged. In adopting a dialectical approach to the dilemma of whether to be directive or non-directive in therapy, we can see that this distinction is brought into question, as well as any definitive categorisation of therapies in practice. It therefore queries some of the bases on which different approaches to therapy may be thought to be incommensurable, although there will clearly be other hurdles to overcome. It causes us to look more closely at ourselves and the other, and in doing this, we can often find that our assumed differences are not as clear as we once thought and there is a blurring between the poles or supposed opposites. However, while applying these dialectical principles can help us tackle the roadblocks, it is unlikely to look the same across all situations and interactions within and outside of therapy. What if I encounter someone who insists on treating another with violence, oppression or discrimination on the basis of their difference from them? Would I implicitly suggest that my pluralistic or dialectical viewpoint be taken into account? Would I attempt to impose it? Would I shelve dialectics and pluralism and demand that they treat that person differently because what they are doing is wrong? It is clear that we are presented with many choices here and we can suddenly find that dialectical pluralism in action is once again a challenging endeavour.

Towards a Reflexive Pluralism

Choice within Pluralism

It appears that the initial pluralistic dilemma of 'to direct or not to direct' in the process of therapy in many ways represents the overall challenge we face when attempting to enact our pluralism in all areas of life. That is, given our respect for diversity, multiple perspectives and the individual's right to hold these, how do we decide how or when to intervene? The fear is that intervention may compromise the very respect that we set out to uphold in the first place. As we have seen, it is not possible for us to completely avoid directing, intervening or influencing. Therefore, we are confronted in pluralism with the element of *choice*, which is what our discussion has been leading to. Pluralism is not about a lack of action or deciding *whether* to have an influence on someone; rather, it is about acknowledging our inevitable influence, choosing *how* to act in light of this and justifying or assuming responsibility for the action we take and the views we communicate. In doing this, we challenge the fundamental roadblock and dialectic of directive versus non-directive in how we approach our therapy and the world beyond.

There is clearly room for the elevation of some views over others in a definition of pluralism that involves choice. It is not always a level playing field of neutrality in the sense of a relativistic 'anything goes'. It does not mean that counselling psychology only advocates the communicating of a pluralistic attitude without the expression of opinions or arguments, nor does it mean that we cannot be enthusiastic or persuasive in the views that we hold. Samuels argues: 'This is not a dry or woolly perspective; passion abides in dialogue and tolerance as much as it does in monologue and fanaticism' (1997, p. 209). Moreover, the professional guidelines in counselling psychology specifically require counselling psychologists to express their opinions and they highlight that we have obligations both to ourselves and to society:

> [Practitioners will] challenge the views of people who pathologise on the basis of such aspects as sexual orientation, disability, class origin or racial identity and religious and spiritual views.
>
> (Division of Counselling Psychology, 2008, p. 8)

It is clear that counselling psychology has an inherent responsibility to make a case for some views in preference to others and to challenge those that it disagrees with, and that this applies not only to therapy but to the discipline's contributions outside this arena.

Rescher's (1993) work on pluralism provides an insight into the justification of choices between perspectives and the advocating of some over others, within an attitude of fundamental respect for them. He cautions against what he refers to as 'relativistic indifferentism' (1993, p. 80), which is summed up by the stance that all views are equal and that there is no rational basis for choosing one above another. Instead, he argues that we can indeed be rational in our choices between standpoints without negating our appreciation of others in the process. Rescher (1993) therefore promotes the idea of *perspectival pluralism* based on the idea that, while a variety of perspectives are available, we do not automatically ascribe equal validity to all of them. We can put forward our own view and justify this through rational argument, while also remaining aware of and acknowledging that this view comes from our individual perspective, informed by factors such as our upbringing, culture, age, political affiliation, and so on. In turn, we appreciate that the basis on which these arguments or justifications are made might be different from another's perspective, be that an individual, group, organisation or school of therapy. This demonstrates that Rescher (1993) is proposing a compromise or negotiation between monism – that is, the promotion of one view as superior and 'true' – and the respect for the diversity of truths within pluralism (Seibt, 1994). There is again room for disagreement, taking us away from the horizontal plain of mutual appreciation and moving us towards growth.

Within the realm of therapeutic encounter, Downing concurs with the juggling of tension between conviction in our ideas and the uncertainty that causes us to examine our own position:

> Remaining cognizant of our dual nature – a strong need to believe and a complimentary need to question ourselves radically – may be our best hope for retaining our humanity and integrity as psychotherapists.
>
> (2000, p. 292)

We can see that he has extended this to the moral plane and the ethics of practice, and that it is necessary to maintain an awareness of the philosophical components informing the choices we make. Downing therefore discusses the different 'lived modes of knowing' (2000, p. 184), which point to how philosophical positions translate into our practice at different times, regardless of the approach to which we subscribe. Specifically, this refers to a spectrum ranging from realist through to representational, perspectival, dialogical, critical and nihilistic modes of knowing, which therapists will move between. Downing (2000) argues for an awareness of the movement within these different modes of knowing that highlights their dialectical nature and provides a set of 'checks and balances' for the therapist in an ethical, pluralistic approach to practice. This reiterates the challenge of the simple categorisation of therapies that was put forward earlier when discussing the notion of directiveness and calls for recognition of these different modes of knowing in counteracting any temptations to remain fixed within a chosen philosophical stance.

Maintaining Curiosity

A final note in this exploration of dialectical pluralism within counselling psychology is the move towards a reflexive approach in our efforts to engage with others. Due to the emphasis in the preceding discussion on the value of pluralism and the need to adopt a dialectical approach towards it, a potential contradiction presents itself here. If the message of this chapter can be interpreted as 'pluralism is right', then we are faced with the fact that this doesn't sound very pluralistic or acknowledging of other philosophical perspectives. It is actually beginning to sound as though pluralism is being proposed as an all-encompassing category that explains everything and that argues others should be subsumed under its influence. According to Wilkinson, we are on dangerous ground if pluralism becomes the dominant discourse:

> What are the totalitarian dangers of a unified world framework like this, as opposed to the unresolved conflict network of capital, science, religion, media, tribe and nationhood, the conflict we now have? Would it be an anti-fundamentalist fundamentalism? An intolerance of intolerance?
>
> (2002, p. 11)

Certainly, any attempt at a 'world synthesis' (Wilkinson, 2002, p. 11) such as this would denote pluralism as metanarrative and will have become the very force that it set out to counteract in the first place.

Therefore, in order to remain truly dialectical in our outlook, we are required to maintain a continuous attitude of curiosity towards our views and our arguments, including the pluralism on which these are founded. This curiosity is at the centre of counselling psychology and is a fundamental starting point for all its interactions. Foucault wrote about the importance of curiosity and captures the essence of this stance:

> It evokes 'care'; it evokes the care one takes of what exists and what might exist; a sharpened sense of reality, but one that is never immobilized before it; a readiness to find what surrounds us strange and odd; a certain determination to throw off familiar ways of thought and to look at the same things

in a different way; a passion for seizing what is happening now and what is disappearing; a lack of respect for the traditional hierarchies of what is important and fundamental.

(2000, p. 325)

In maintaining this curiosity towards our pluralism, we allow ourselves to be open to the challenging of others who may take a much more definitive stance on the absolute certainty of their own convictions. The concept of perspectival pluralism (Rescher, 1993) can also be useful in viewing the dialectical pluralism itself as one of many standpoints towards life and relationships – it can be rationally justified from our perspective, but we must appreciate that others will put forward different arguments from their perspective. In doing this, we challenge the monistic potential of our pluralism and maintain a reflexive and dialectical approach to both what we are encountering and to the ways in which we encounter.

Summary

By recognising our influence over others, the attitude of perspectival pluralism and an increasing awareness of the lived modes of knowing, we have seen in this chapter how counselling psychology can conceptualise itself both within therapy and in its reach beyond the consulting room. As such, while counselling psychology's foundation remains a pluralistic one, opinions are still held and arguments put forward, with an emphasis on the awareness of the processes within this. The move away from dogma towards curiosity highlights the importance that counselling psychology places on the reflective and respectful elements of our lives both as practitioners and as human beings in a diverse world. Some of the challenges in undertaking this task have been highlighted, but we have barely scratched the surface of the areas in which counselling psychology operates or the opportunities it brings. We shall see in the following chapters how the fundamental attitude of questioning has given pause for thought and shed new light on areas ranging from the environment and religion to issues such as race, sexuality and an innovative rethinking of theoretical perspectives in therapy. These discussions are told from multiple voices and styles representing the rich array of perspectives constituting the profession today. Through this plurality of expression and of relation in the way that it engages with different contexts, counselling psychology extends into arenas beyond therapy without undermining what it is or devaluing the principles at its core. Its dialectical nature means that it is not a static discipline with fixed and unchangeable features – it is evolving, organic and adaptable and it has much to say.

References

Barker, C. & Pistrang, N. (2005). Quality criteria under methodological pluralism: Implications for conducting and evaluating research. *American Journal of Community Psychology, 35*(3–4): 201–212.

Clarkson, P. (1995). *The therapeutic relationship: In psychoanalysis, counselling psychology and psychotherapy.* London: Taylor & Francis.

Cooper, C. (2003). Psychological counselling with young adults. In R. Woolfe, W. Dryden and S. Strawbridge (Eds.) *Handbook of counselling psychology* (2nd edn). London: Sage.

Cooper, M. (2003). *Existential therapies.* London: Sage.

Cooper, M. & McLeod, J. (2007). A pluralistic framework for counselling and psychotherapy: Implications for research. *Counselling and Psychotherapy Research, 7*(3): 135–143.

Deurzen, E. van (1992). Dialogue in therapy. *Journal of the Society for Existential Analysis, 3*: 15–23.

Deurzen, E. van (2009). *Psychotherapy and the quest for happiness.* London: Sage.

Division of Counselling Psychology (2008). *Professional practice guidelines.* Leicester: British Psychological Society.

Downing, J.N. (2000). *Between conviction and uncertainty: Philosophical guidelines for the practicing psychotherapist.* Albany, NY: SUNY Press.

Feltham, C. (1997). Challenging the core theoretical model. In R. House & N. Totton (Eds.) *Implausible professions: Arguments for pluralism and autonomy in psychotherapy and counselling.* Ross-on-Wye: PCCS Books.

Foucault, M. (2000). The masked philosopher. In P. Rabinow (Ed.) *The essential works of Foucault 1954–1984. Ethics* (R. Hurley, Trans.). London: Penguin Books. (First published 1984.)

Grenz, S.J. (1996). *A primer on postmodernism.* Cambridge: Eerdmans.

House, R. (1997). Therapy in new paradigm perspective: The phenomenon of Georg Groddeck. In R. House and N. Totton (Eds.) *Implausible professions: Arguments for pluralism and autonomy in psychotherapy and counselling.* Ross-on-Wye: PCCS Books.

James, W. (1909). *A pluralistic universe: Hibbert lectures at Manchester College on the present situation in philosophy.* London: Longmans, Green & Co.

Kazdin, A.E. (2000). *Psychotherapy for children and adolescents: Directions for research and practice.* New York: Oxford University Press.

Levitt, B.E. (Ed.) (2005). *Embracing non-directivity: Reassessing person-centred theory and practice in the 21st century.* Ross-on-Wye: PCCS Books.

Lyotard, J.-F. (1984). *The postmodern condition: A report on knowledge*. (G. Bennington and B. Massumi, Trans.). Minneapolis, MN: University of Minnesota Press.

McAteer, D. (2006). A portfolio of academic, therapeutic practice and research work, including an investigation of therapist directiveness in existential and cognitive-behavioural approaches to counselling psychology practice. Unpublished doctoral thesis, University of Surrey.

Polanyi, M. (1967). *The tacit dimension*. Garden City, NY: Anchor Books.

Rescher, N. (1993). *Pluralism: Against the demand for consensus*. Oxford: Oxford University Press.

Rizq, R. (2006). Training and disillusion in counselling psychology: A psychoanalytic perspective. *Psychology and Psychotherapy: Theory, Research and Practice*, *79*(4): 613–627.

Rowan, J. (2001). *Ordinary ecstasy: The dialectics of humanistic psychology*. London: Routledge.

Samuels, A. (1997). Pluralism and psychotherapy: What is a good training? In R. House and N. Totton (Eds.) *Implausible professions: Arguments for pluralism and autonomy in psychotherapy and counselling*. Ross-on-Wye: PCCS Books.

Seibt, J. (1994). A Janus view on Rescher's perspectival pluralism. *Philosophy and Phenomenological Research*, *54*(2): 433–439.

Spinelli, E. (2004). Hell is other people: Conflict resolution from a Sartrean perspective. *International Journal of Existential Psychology and Psychotherapy*, *1*(1): 56–65.

Strasser, F. & Randolph, P. (2004). *Mediation: A psychological insight into conflict resolution*. London: Continuum.

Tillet, R. (1999). Using psychotherapy effectively: Choosing an appropriate treatment. *Advances in Psychiatric Treatment*, *5*: 420–426.

Wilkinson, H. (2002). Editorial: The power and danger of pluralism in psychotherapy. *International Journal of Psychotherapy*, *7*(1): 5–12.

Chapter 2

Existential-phenomenological Contributions to Counselling Psychology's Relational Framework

Elena Manafi

No man is an island, entire of itself . . . because I am involved in mankind.

John Donne (1572–1631)

Conceptualising human beings in relational terms changes everything. We question the most basic assumptions regarding our nature and ethics, professional conduct and therapeutic practice. It is a similar stance to a dialogical process that takes the world and other people as a starting point and recognises consciousness as the centre of attention. Such a view criticises ontological and epistemological theories that are based upon essentialism[1], representationalism[2], and objectivism[3] – three epistemological stances that take as a starting point the division of the world into the mental and the physical. It therefore introduces a sense of ambiguity and fluidity that requires a terminology that challenges our understanding of ourselves, reality, and ways of perceiving and constructing meaning

One of the unique features of counselling psychology is its dialogue with other fields, such as psychotherapy, counselling and philosophy. It attempts to bridge the gap between research and practice and conceptualises human activity and meaning relationally. A crucial aspect of this is the place of consciousness, subjectivity and lived experience in our

Therapy and Beyond: Counselling Psychology Contributions to Therapeutic and Social Issues
Edited by Martin Milton
© 2010 John Wiley & Sons, Ltd.

inquiries. These issues have often been viewed with suspicion, especially by those who adhere to a positivist model of science and who are interested in the discovery of universal truths and objectivity. A review of mainstream psychological journals such as the *British Journals of Psychology*, *Clinical Psychology* and *Developmental Psychology* confirms the field's modernist, positivist/empiricist epistemological outlook and its influence on research, theory and practice. Consequently, questions such as the relation of human beings to the world and other people and of consciousness to the body have been ignored or considered inappropriate for scientific research. However, during the last decade the postmodernist turn has challenged traditional ways of knowing and restored the bridge that connects psychology to fields such as anthropology as well as cultural, gender and political studies that are equally concerned with humans' place in the world. Such a view argues that no subject matter can be studied in isolation; discourses about the world and human beings form a relational matrix and are dependent on societal structures, power, economy, technological developments and of course politics (Foucault, 1965, 2002; Fox *et al.*, 2009; Kvale, 1992).

Counselling psychologists are well versed in different theoretical paradigms and aware of the tension between human and natural sciences as well as differences between subjective and objective ways of seeing the world. Since our beginnings we have firmly grounded ourselves in a philosophy that promotes dialectic ways of practising and relational ways of doing research. This dialogical stance has coloured counselling psychologists' professional, personal and academic positions and has contributed to the formation of an identity that embraces difference and opens up to a pluralistic stance with regards to practice. As a result, traditional theories of mind based on a dualist epistemological framework have been challenged and previously silenced populations and issues around the construction of subjectivity and gender have been given voice and have become the centre of psychological research (see Bassaly & Macallan, 2006; Inayat, 2005; Toporek *et al.*, 2006). In recent decades counselling psychologists have been at the forefront of the development of cross-cultural (Clarkson, 1998), multicultural (Pope-Davies *et al.*, 2003; Vera & Speight, 2003), feminist (Kagan & Tindall, 2007) and lesbian and gay psychology (Hicks & Milton, 2010; Milton & Coyle, 2007).

Mainly due to the field's adherence to humanistic psychology and existential/phenomenological philosophy, counselling psychology embraces a view that springs from a holistic conceptualisation of human beings, that criticises dichotomies like self/other, mind/body, subjective/objective, inner/outer and is sceptical of the value of artificial binary oppositions such as normal/abnormal, reason/emotion and self/other (Woolfe *et al.*, 2007). Unlike mainstream approaches it focuses on wellbeing rather than psychopathology and promotes a *relational stance*, attempting to rephrase and reconstruct our understanding of human beings in terms that are dialogical in nature and respectful of and open to the otherness of the Other. Counselling psychologists are in a position to draw their expertise from different theoretical paradigms that are based on the humanistic, existential/phenomenological, psychoanalytic/psychodynamic, cognitive/behavioural, narrative, systemic and social constructionist traditions. They are committed to personal development and place the therapeutic relationship, and indeed the ability to form relationships with other people, at the forefront of their practice (Division of Counselling Psychology, 2004, 2005).

This chapter shows how counselling psychology's relational stance, which views humans as embedded, embodied, historical and political beings, creates an open forum where debates around research, politics and therapeutic practice thrive. It is theoretical in nature and should be read in conjuction with Chapter 11, where I explicate the therapeutic implications of such a relational framework. Both chapters argue that a relational stance strengthens the field's position in a world that is obsessed with marketing, predictability, calculability and control. It suggests a constructive dialogue in the recent debates with the Health Professions Council, where psychology is still defined as a 'health care' profession that imposes a medical stance to a field that is primarily social in nature.

In line with the field's ethos and philosophical underpinnings I sketch a view of existence that takes place in the 'interworld' – the space between human beings and the world. The twofold nature of human consciousness which oscillates between the personal dimension and the relational world, where dichotomies are dissolved, will be the centre of the discussion. Particular emphasis is placed on a critical analysis of current psychological knowledge around the concepts of 'Being' (capitalised to distinguish Being from beings) and ultimately of the 'self'. It is argued that contemporary psychology has retained a naturalist and dualist account of subjectivity undermining relational ways of being and assuming the existence of an inner self that is coherent, rational and autonomous. Such conceptualisation gives rise to models of psychopathology and has contributed to human beings' (self-)alienation from their natural habitat and other people. The chapter brings ontology and epistemology to the fore. Reference to the work of philosophers and theorists such as Nietzsche, Heidegger, Merleau-Ponty, Sartre, Foucault and Dreyfus illuminates the links between philosophy and counselling psychology and the ways in which the two disciplines co-construct a relational framework.

In the Shadow of Descartes

All movements are historical in nature and often spring from what preceded them; Enlightenment is no exception. Kant defined it as 'man's emergence from a self-imposed immaturity' (1784, p. 1) and tried to convey the importance of freedom and courage; the need for human beings to mobilise their own intellect and free themselves from dependence upon prescriptive ways of being handed down by religion.

It was in this spirit that René Descartes, the seventeenth-century French philosopher, set out to discover ultimate truths. By employing his method of doubt (*methodological scepticism*) he set out to discover *certainty* or a set of principles that cannot be doubted (Cottingham, 1993).

The only thing that survived this radical method was his existence as a *res cogito* – a *thinking being* – but what did Descartes mean by a 'thinking being' and why is it so closely related to philosophical dualism? The answers to these questions are linked to the method itself as the existence of this 'thinking being' is coextensive with its thoughts alone, not with its body or the world (Arlington, 2001; Descartes, 1960). Descartes made the mind/body dichotomy explicit:

> I know that I exist and at the same time I observe absolutely nothing else as belonging to my nature or essence except the mere fact that I am a conscious being; and just from this I can validly infer that my essence consists simply in the fact that I am a conscious being. It is indeed possible (or rather, as I shall say later on, it is certain) that I have a body closely bound up with myself; but at the same time I have, on the one hand, a clear and distinct idea of myself taken simply as a conscious, not an extended, being; and, on the other hand, a distinct idea of body, taken simply as an extended, not a conscious, being; so it is certain that I am really distinct from my body and could exist without it.
>
> (Descartes, 1641, cited in Rosenthal, 2001, p. 27)

It follows that the mind and body, as well as the mind, the world and other people are separate entities connected to one another only by means of mental representations. This is what we mean by 'Cartesian dualism' the result of which is the inference of the existence of a *solipsistic self* that is an autonomous, self-constituting, rational entity 'in a state of suspension of knowledge' (Dilman, 1993, p. 2).

The Cartesian framework has been the main tradition in modern Western thinking and has dominated psychology since its conception as a scientific discipline (Heath, 2002a, 2002b; Lagerspetz, 2002). Scientific psychology, like the natural sciences, set out to discover *objective facts* surrounding the nature of the world and human beings. Hence, 'traditional' psychological research treats the person in the way that the natural sciences treat the physical world; both are subjected to 'rational' and 'objective' scrutiny which can lead to the discovery of universal objective truths and laws (see Nagel, 1987, 1995; Papineau, 2002). Critical theorists (Durrheim, 1997; Harré & Gillett, 1994; Kvale, 1992) have argued that a framework can be traced back to basic empirical assumptions: one is that of a *knowable world*; another is the belief in the systematic application of reason and observation, free from any subjective interference.

Institutionalisation of Madness and the Rise of Mental Disorders

Regimes of truth govern what can be spoken about and they also define what will be seen as nonsense or madness

(Parker *et al*, 1995, p. 7)

Despite the pluralistic shift within our field, Descartes' ghost still haunts us; his unworldly philosophy continues to influence our conceptualisation of the human self and our practice. Human distress is still conceptualised in terms of (mental) disorders that begin and end in our minds, and the phantom of this 'perfect consciousness' that casts doubt on the existence of the world and other people is still very much alive in our intellectual pursuits.

Strawbridge (2001) critically reflected on the consequences of such a view for the theory and practice of counselling psychology, arguing that the medicalisation of psychological distress relocates human difficulties and problems in living from the personal and interpersonal fields to the arena of pathology where the concept of 'disorder' reigns. She argued that such movement undermines our field's philosophy and therapeutic aim, which ultimately seeks to restore the dialogue between the individual and the world and to empower our clients' sense of agency and responsibility for their own lives and ways of being.

The effect of the Cartesian framework on our understanding of psychopathology can hardly be overstated. Modern psychiatry and 'abnormal psychology' are the products of this very epistemology and its preoccupation with objectivity, reason and individualism. In the spirit of modernity, psychopathological discourses are firmly rooted in scientific networks that internalise psychological difficulties and construct mental disorders within binary oppositions. Mental illness is seen as the product of a disordered mind cut off from its historical, cultural and sociopolitical contexts. The Enlightenment's belief in progress and its confidence in the primacy of reason are also to be seen in the technological framework of psychopathology. Diagnostic statistical manuals and classificatory systems such as the *Diagnostic and Statistical Manual of Mental Disorders* (DSM-IV) (American Psychiatric Association, 1994) and the *International Classification of Diseases* (ICD-10) (World Health Organisation, 1992) are full of technical idioms constructing the ways we see 'madness' and human distress in general. As Foucault argued:

> The constitution of madness as a mental illness, at the end of the eighteenth century, affords the evidence of a broken dialogue ... The language of psychiatry, which is a monologue of reason about madness, has been established only on the basis of such a silence.
>
> (1965, pp. x–xi)

Counselling psychology, by promoting a framework that conceptualises human beings in relation to the world and other people, and understands subjective experience as inextricably linked to the social, political and historical dimensions of human living, has managed to break the silence and place madness back where it belongs – *in the realm of living.* Such a stance encompasses all modes of being that surpass the boundaries of human psyche and extend to the horizon of human existence. Human distress is understood against the background of our clients' entire life within the relational matrix that sustains it. In line with postmodern ideas (Fee, 2000; Parker *et al.*, 1995) counselling psychology criticises the medical model and the notion of psychopathology; distress is not seen as an illness, let alone a mental illness, but as 'difficulties in living' (Deurzen & Arnold-Baker, 2005) that no longer reside within the individual but in the space in-between, on the 'bridge' that connects the person to the world. What counselling psychology has to offer is an alternative, critical way of thinking that does not eradicate subjectivity but focuses instead on the clarification of human dynamics as they unfold in the four dimensions of existence (see Deurzen, 2002).

A Different Voice

> There are times in life when the question of knowing if one can think differently than one thinks and perceive differently than one sees, is absolutely necessary if one is to go on looking and reflecting at all.
>
> (Foucault, 1985, p. 8)

Philosophy is about adopting an inquisitive attitude, a refusal to take things at face value, and is a creative act with its roots in controversy and debate – an act that lies at the heart of counselling psychology, which, since it emerged, has embraced alterity and difference. Taking stock and questioning the relevance of existing theories and one's personal attitude can only bring us closer to understanding our clients' subjective experience and place in the world. Such a stance is both a professional responsibility and an ethical one since counselling psychology is not just an academic discipline but a therapeutic stance towards psychological difficulties.

In a pluralistic world and the flux in which we exist, all voices are of equal measure and one needs to learn to work with the tension without attempting to dominate or eliminate difference. Nietzsche noted, 'words are but symbols for the relations of things to one another and to us; nowhere do they touch upon absolute truth' (1962, p. 83), criticising objectivity and truth and promoting a view that became the centre of the postmodern movement. Nietzsche is talking about *perspectivism*, the idea that truth is relational and cannot be disconnected from the interests, intentions and desires of the speaker. It is an anti-representationalist and anti-essentialist stance which glorifies subjectivity without eradicating respect for the other and the relational systems that sustain us.

Counselling psychology has entered its second decade as a recognised profession with full divisional status within the British Psychological Society. Since its conception counselling psychologists have been driven by '"a desire to make a stand" – for subjectivity, for the inclusion of context in its research and practice' (Orlans & van Scoyoc, 2009, p. 18) and have contributed to a field that has become a 'tantalizing innovation' (Spinelli, 2001a, p. 1). The field continues to grow in relation to counselling and psychotherapy and to promote the relationship to the wider field of philosophy, especially existential and phenomenological philosophy. Such unique positioning creates a forum where practitioners exchange ideas on metaphysics (in our discussions of the nature of human beings and the world), epistemology (in relation to *how* we understand the world we live in) and, of course, ethics (with its central focus on professional conduct). It is an inherently relational stance towards research, supervision and practice. Through the use of systemic, narrative, social constructionist and existential/phenomenological paradigms that criticise Cartesian epistemology and bridge the artificial gap between *lived experience* and knowledge of the world, counselling psychologists contribute to the 'explosion of interest' in qualitative research (Smith, 2008, p. 1) and hold a strong position within the wider field of psychological theory and practice. This dialogical turn in knowledge acquisition is reflected in the promotion of interactive methodological frameworks which unify experiential and theoretical knowledge through merging 'the scientific demand for rigorous empirical inquiry with a firm value base grounded in the primacy of the counselling or psychotherapeutic relationship' (Division of Counselling Psychology, 2005, p. 1). As Corrie and Lane (2006) argue, the traditional notion of the *scientist-practitioner* with its original emphasis on 'pure knowledge' is being questioned. The notion of science as a value-free endeavour is being challenged and broadened to incorporate a wide range of methodologies that emphasise reflexivity and take into account the historical, political and social dimensions of research inquiry.

Counselling psychology's interdisciplinary, pluralistic stance goes beyond methodolatry and offers an alternative to the dominant model of science and its models of practice (Woolfe *et al.*, 2007). In line with postmodern thinking (Bayer & Shotter, 1998; Holzman, 1999) counselling psychologists recognise the transient nature of reality and its dependence on politics, power structures (Foucault, 2002) and 'language games' (Wittgenstein, 1965, 1980). The field is strongly attached to existential/phenomenological inquiry and emphasises a relational epistemology (Thayer-Bacon *et al.*, 2003) which views meaning as inextricably linked to experience and acknowledges the reciprocity between research and practice (Smith, 2008; Spinelli, 2001b). Moreover, it takes into account the 'contextual parameters' and the researcher's 'speaking position' (Lyons & Coyle, 2007) which influence one's understanding of phenomena and their subjective interpretations.

The Primacy of the Lifeworld

People's lived experience of their situation may be quite specific, but all life-worlds do have universal features such as temporality, spatiality, subjective embodiment, intersubjectivity, selfhood, personal project, moodedness and discursiveness.

(Smith, 2008, p. 12)

These fundamental characterstics of human nature lie at the heart of qualitative research and are the *sine qua non* of human existence. Counselling psychology's existential/phenomenological heritage offers a firm grounding in qualitative research methodologies and a clear conceptualisation of the epistemological foundations on which they rest. Phenomenology and existentialism both focus on the elucidation of the meaning of the phenomena as experienced in everyday life. Subjective experience, feelings and meanings are at the centre of qualitative research. Qualitative methodologies are closely linked to the philosophy of Edmund Husserl (1859–1938), who argued that scientific knowledge cannot be separated from our understanding of the lived world. It follows that any description and clarification of phenomena is dependent on the subject's *lived experience*. In other words, 'living precedes *knowing* ... we have experiential relationships with the world before we objectify our experience ... Consciousness is always of the world' (Deurzen & Kenward, 2005, p. 96; emphasis in the original) and as such it requires a relational understanding of human beings, cognitive processes and consequently construction of meaning.

Husserlian phenomenology had major implications for the practice of psychological research as its rigorous method offered an alternative to the natural scientific approach (McLeod, 2000, 2003; Smith, 2008; Willig, 2008). Specifically, Husserl (1970, 1977) introduced a 'first-person' perspective on the study of human experience. His philosophy, also known as transcendental or 'pure' phenomenology (Cooper, 1999), centres on the notion of *eidetic reduction* (commonly referred to as *epoché*).

According to this reduction, we need to 'bracket' or suspend our beliefs and assumptions about the world in order to reach the essence of the phenomenon we are studying. However, as argued by Merleau-Ponty, 'the most important lesson which the reduction teaches us is the impossibility of a complete reduction' (2000, p. xiv). This is the stance that existential epistemology (Dilman, 1993; Richardson, 1991) takes and gives rise to hermeneutics (i.e. description and interpretation). Both Heidegger (1962) and Merleau-Ponty (2000) criticised pure phenomenology as another form of Cartesianism, emphasised description and stressed the importance of language, history, culture and time, which they viewed as the basic structure of human understanding.

In relation to practice, Woolfe *et al.* (2007) stress the importance of the contextual, social, political and historical factors that are inseparable from one's sense of self, agency, wellbeing and ultimately psychological distress. The authors argue for a position that surpasses the artificial dichotomies imposed by the positivist/empiricist epistemological framework and unites the individual with the world and other people. Such fusion requires the therapist to be critically aware of her own experiences when attempting to reflect on the reality of another and to take into account the sociopolitical parameters of therapeutic work (see also Milton & Legg, 2000). Therefore, therapeutic practice is no longer confined within the boundaries of intrapsychic conflicts, but has broadened to include the relational field where people's everyday lives and difficulties take place. Moreover, the therapist as expert has been dethroned and now is located in the 'realm of living', where we all battle with life's adversities.

It is in this spirit that counselling psychology has created a legacy promoting the importance of personal and professional development through engagement with personal therapy and supervision across one's professional career (Division of Counselling Psychology, 2005). Both activities are seen as invaluable to the practitioner's growth and competence since (self-) knowledge and meaning-making are viewed as the products of an engagement with others, rather than an internal monologue detached from our social context and other people (Wosket, 1999). The dissolution of dichotomies which the relational stance demands situates practitioners and clients, as well as supervisors and supervisees, in the interworld where everyday activity and the construction of ways of being take place (Carroll & Tholstrup, 2001; Shillito-Clarke 2007).

This stance represents a major paradigm shift which constructs a different view of human nature. Understanding the subject as a relation requires us to 'zoom out' so that the wider context becomes more apparent. Human beings are to be understood in the context of a relational totality that connects them to other beings and to Being itself.

'Being-in-the-world-with': Restoring the Psychological Subject

Western tradition and ontological dualism have left us with a sense of 'broken totality' (Murdoch, 1953, p. 55) which has plagued our connection to the (natural) world, other people and ourselves. Our lives have become so entangled in artificial divisions that they separate us from each other, our bodies, subjective experiences and consequently our sense and understanding of wellbeing. It is no surprise that our technological success has coloured all aspects of our existence, including our lifestyles and the ways in which we understand ourselves and the world around us.

Ironically, it would not be necessary to discuss the possibility of the existence of an intersubjective way of being if it wasn't for Descartes' assumption that human consciousness is a self-contained, irreducible mental entity discrete from the body and the world. It could be argued that this estrangement from our everyday lives has come partly from the impetus for our interest in a radical paradigm shift within the academic and therapeutic fields. Indeed, recent developments within the psychodynamic and cognitive behavioural approaches as well as neuropsychology and neurophenomenology (Gerhardt, 2004; Harré, 2002; Harré & Langenhove, 1999; Varela, 1996; Varela *et al.*, 1991; Wheeler, 2005) have criticised Cartesian epistemology and have come to embrace a relational perspective that goes beyond the intrapsychic domain and the mainstream emphasis on disembodied cognitive processes.

Counselling psychology embraces the relational stance which springs from a philosophy that bridges the gap between body and mind, behaviour and experience and subjective/objective. It focuses on the space in between where life unfolds and offers an experiential account of human existence. Consequently, terms such as lived experience, life-world, temporality, embodiment and embeddedness replace the initial focus on the individual and emphasise the unitary phenomena of 'being-in-the-world' and 'being-in-the-world-with-other-people' – Heidegger's (1962) concepts of *Dasein* and *Mitsein*. The radical nature of this concept might initially escape the attention of the reader (Dreyfus, 1983); existential/phenomenological philosophy does not even speak of 'mind' but of the whole human being's relation to the world. 'Indeed, even "relation" is misleading, since it suggests the coming together of two separate entities – the human being and world' (Dreyfus, 1983, p. 2). Instead, *being-in-the-world-with-other-people* reflects the unity of the world, human consciousness and of course other people.

Being-in-the-space-in-between

Such a relational/intersubjective stance argues that nothing exists in isolation. From birth we are thrown into a world where we are expected to socialise according to the particular culture we belong to. This constant interaction with other people opens up possibilities and limitations as we soon realise our total dependence on others and our environment. We are relating to others even when we choose to withdraw and isolate ourselves – a need that would be rendered meaningless in the absence of our primordial state of connectedness.

It is a relational shift that is reflected in the theory and practice of recent developments in all paradigms that inform counselling psychology. Specifically, dynamic cognitive models (Gallagher, 2006; Harré & Gillett, 1994; Young *et al.*, 2006) conceptualise understanding and meaning-making as co-constructions between people. Consequently, psychological formulations are no longer the product of one individual (i.e. the therapist) but a collaborative achievement between therapist and client. Wheeler (2005) proposed a Heideggerian reconstruction of everyday cognition which articulates a genuinely non-Cartesian stance. Drawing on Heidegger's (1962) concepts of *Dasein* and *Mitsein*, as well as research in embedded/embodied cognitive science (Beer, 2000; Brooks, 1991; Clark, 1997; Collins, 2000; Gallagher, 1997; Rowlands, 1999), Wheeler promoted a cognitive science embracing a holistic account of human beings and placing cognition within the physical and interrelational domains. In the same vein Varela *et al.* (1991)

talk about mind's embodiment and embeddedness in sociocultural and historical contexts which place cognition in the space in between consciousness and the world.

Contemporary psychoanalysis, drawing on neuroscientific evidence, such as the discovery of *mirror neurons* (Gallese & Goldman, 1998; Gerhardt, 2004; Rizzolatti *et al.*, 2001), has proposed a relational account of the human self that bridges the gap between the subject and the world. Among others, Atwood and Stolorow (1984), Crossley (1996), Orange *et al.* (2001), Renik (1993) and Stern (2000, 2004), by focusing on the notion of intersubjectivity, provide coherent theoretical frameworks that illuminate the interaction between the self and the world, relocating meaning and psychopathology from the intrapsychic to the intersubjective realm of Being.

Equally, social constructionist, postmodern and critical approaches to psychological theories and practice (Burman, 1994; Fee, 2000; Henriques *et al.*, 1998; McNamee & Gergen, 1992; Parker, 1999) assume an historical and contextualised vantage point which views human beings as the product of an interaction with the world, thereby liberating human consciousness from postivist/mechanistic accounts, situating it in the world where individuals construct themselves in relation to one another through their choices, activities and projects.

A relational framework has major implications for our practice and understanding of human difficulties. The dissolution of binary oppositions renders the medical view of psychopathology meaningless. The individual's loss of a sense of wellbeing, manifested in anxiety, depression, (inter)personal difficulties (known as personality disorders) and issues relating to the body, is no longer seen as situated within the mental and intrapsychic domains. This does not imply that psychological difficulties are illusory; it does, however, criticise psychologism and reductionism and relocates human difficulties within the interpersonal domain. Psychopathology is reconceptualised in relational terms, and psychotherapeutic attempts to restore wellbeing go beyond self-analysis and attempt to capture, clarify and critically reflect on the tension that arises between the personal, social, physical and spiritual modes of human existence.

Being-in-our-bodies: The Philosophy of the Flesh

In the early hours of 11 February 1650, "René Descartes stopped thinking" (Gallagher and Zahavi 2008, p.137). His lifeless body no longer related to the world; temperature and gravity ceased to matter as his corpse was finally a mere object, the *res extensa*, he argued for in his living years.

Psychological theories have long perceived the body as an object of inquiry that can be studied in isolation and explained on a functional basis (Valle & Halling, 1989). Existential/phenomenological contributions to the mind/body dichotomy offer a radical solution that overcomes this dualism. *Contra* Descartes, human consciousness ceases to be a disembodied, mental entity and becomes an embodied/embedded *interplay* which needs the world and other people. As Cohn (1997) argued, being-in-the-world has two distinctive attributes that reflect the *situatedness* of human experience: the first is spatial/physical (i.e. the world) and the second, relational/involving (i.e. other people). So, human experience – from our modes of relating to the world and other people, to the ways we construct meaning and understand ourselves – is always contextual and heavily influenced by our embodiment.

The second edition of the *Handbook of Counselling Psychology* (Woolfe *et al.*, 2007) introduced a new chapter on the body (Wahl, 2007) which offers a concise history of recent developments in the psychological understanding of the concept and its application to therapeutic practice. The existentialist/phenomenologist Maurice Merleau-Ponty (1908–61) is the best known and most cited philosopher of embodiment. He broke with Western philosophical tradition and reconstructed human consciousness, perception and meaning-making in relational, embodied terms. Specifically, he argued:

> Perception is not a science of the world . . . it is the background from which all acts stand out and is presupposed by them. The world is not an object as such that I have in my possession the law of its making; it is the natural setting of and field for, all my thoughts and all my explicit perceptions. Truth does not 'inhabit' only 'the inner man', or more accurately there is no inner man, man is in the world and only in the world does he know himself.
>
> (2000, pp. x–xi)

For Merleau-Ponty (2000) life cannot be experienced in the absence of a body. Put simply, we are our bodies in the world and in this world we exist. Through our bodies we *shape* our experiences: we touch, smell, eat, shit, fuck and sleep. The relevance of embodiment to practice is obvious: when elated we relate to the world with excitement, when depressed we lose interest and living seems futile. How we feel in our bodies colours our perception of the world, and vice versa. In other words, 'the body is not a mere object in the world . . . it is also a principle of experience' (Gallagher & Zahavi, 2008, p. 134). Human beings can treat their bodies as objects, as means to an end (e.g. body-building, piercing), but such objectification presupposes a 'lived body' that has the capacity to reflect on their embodied being. This ambiguity allows our embodied nature to be twofold; it brings to the fore human capacity to alternate between pre-reflective and reflective ways of being (Merleau-Ponty, 2000; Sartre, 1998).

'Being-in-the-environment': One Step Closer to a Conclusion

One can see from space how the human race has changed the earth. Nearly all of the available land has been cleared for agriculture or urban development. The polar ice caps are shrinking and the desert areas are increasing. At night the earth is no longer dark, but lit up. All this is evidence that human exploitation of the planet is reaching a critical limit, but human demands and expectations are ever increasing.

(The 11th Hour, 2007)

In a special edition of *Counselling Psychology Review* (May 2008) some contributors expressed their views on human and professional relationship to the natural world. Reflecting on their lived experiences they stressed the importance of our link to the natural habitat and without exception voiced the pressing need to reconnect to our ecosystem. Reiterating Milton's (2008, p. 1) view, I find myself pondering the 'curious phenomenon' as he called it: psychology's disconnection from one of the most crucial debates of our time – humans' impact on the environment.

It seems that somewhere along the line we lost the plot and committed what the Ancient Greeks called hubris (ὕβρις); an act of arrogance and omnipotence against the very system that sustains us – namely, nature. Modern ontology, the primacy of reason and an emphasis on scientific and technological advancements have undoubtedly strengthened our omnipotence but at the cost of alienation from ourselves and the world we live in. Human beings can treat this planet as an object, as a means to an end, by exhausting its resources. But such short-sighted objectification lacks the ambiguity necessary for a dialogical relationship between the human being and the human being-in-her-environment.

On the other hand, I believe that our disconnection from the (natural) world has created sufficient distance for us to be able to appreciate its value and effect on ourselves and our everyday lives. As this book demonstrates, the current state of affairs calls for a different conceptualisation of the phenomenon at hand. Counselling psychology's conviction for a relational framework honours reflexive practice and takes us beyond the consulting room by appreciating and working with the multiplicity of 'being-in'.

Notes

1 The philosophical doctrine that defines human beings in terms of a number of (shared) essential properties.
2 The epistemological tradition that views knowledge as the product of mind's (accurate) representation/mirroring of the world. An assumption that is based on the mind/body and mind/world dichotomies.
3 A position which argues that the reality exists independent of consciousness and can be known through the process of concept formation. Epistemologically this view is based upon the subjective/objective dichotomy.

References

American Psychiatric Association (1994). *Diagnostic and statistical manual of mental disorders* (4th edn.). Washington, DC: American Psychiatric Association.
Arlington, R. L. (Ed.) (2001). *A Companion to the philosophers*. Oxford: Blackwell.
Atwood, G. & Stolorow, R. (1984). *Structures of subjectivity: Explorations in psychoanalytic phenomenology*. Hillsdale, NJ: Aronson.
Bassaly, A. & Macallan, H. (2006). Willingness to use psychological help among Polish immigrants in the UK. *Counselling Psychology Review*, 21(4): 19–27.
Bayer, B. M. & Shotter, J. (1998). *Reconstructing the psychological subject: Bodies, practices and technologies*. London: Sage.
Beer, R. D. (2000). Dynamical approaches to cognitive science. *Trends in Cognitive Sciences*, 4(3): 91–99.
Brooks, R. A. (1991). Intelligence without representation. *Artificial Intelligence, 47*: 139–159.
Burman, E. (1994). *Deconstructing developmental psychology*. London: Routledge.
Carroll, M. & Tholstrup, M. (2001). *Integrative approaches to supervision*. London: Jessica Kingsley.
Clark, A. (1997). *Being there: Putting brain, body and world together again*. Cambridge, MA: MIT Press.
Clarkson, P. (1998). *Counselling psychology. Integrating theory, research and supervised practice*. London: Routledge.
Cohn, H (1997). *Existential thought and therapeutic practice: An introduction to existential psychotherapy*. London: Sage.
Collins, H. M. (2000). Four kinds of knowledge, two (or maybe three) kinds of embodiment and the question of artificial intelligence In M. Wrathall & J. Malpas (Eds.) *Heidegger, coping and cognitive science: Essays in honour of Hubert, L. Dreyfus*. vol. 2, Cambridge, MA: MIT Press.
Cooper, E. D. (1999). *Existentialism*. London: Blackwell.
Corrie, S. & Lane, D. A. (2006). *The modern scientist-practitioner*. London: Routledge.

Cottingham, J. (1993). *A Descartes dictionary*. Oxford: Blackwell.

Crossley, N. (1996). *Intersubjectivity. The fabric of social becoming*. London: Sage.

Descartes, R. (1960). *Discourse on method and meditations (L. J. Lafleur, Trans.)*. New York: The Liberal Arts Press.

Deurzen, E. van (2002). *Existential counselling and psychotherapy in practice*. London: Sage.

Deurzen, E. van & Arnold-Baker, C. (2005). *Existential perspectives on human issues: A handbook for therapeutic practice*. Chichester: Palgrave Macmillan.

Deurzen, E. van & Kenward, R. (2005). *Dictionary of existential psychotherapy and counselling*. London: Sage.

Dilman, I. (1993). *Existentialist critiques of cartesianism*. Boston, MA: Barnes & Noble.

Division of Counselling Psychology (2004). *Competency statement*. Leicester: British Psychological Society.

Division of Counselling Psychology (2005). *Professional practice guidelines*. Leicester: British Psychological Society.

Dreyfus, H. L. (1983). *Alternative philosophical conceptualizations of psychopathology*. Berkeley, CA: University of California Press.

Durrheim, K. (1997). Social constructionism, discourse and psychology. *South African Journal of Psychology*, *27*(3): 175–189.

Fee, D. (2000). *Pathology and the postmodern: Mental illness as discourse and experience*. London: Sage.

Foucault, M. (1965). *Madness and civilisation*. London: Routledge.

Foucault, M. (1985). *The use of pleasure* (R. Hurley, Trans.). New York: Pantheon Books.

Foucault, M. (2002). *Power: Essential works of Michel Foucault 1954–1984*, vol. 3 *(Essential Works of Foucault 3)*. London: Penguin Books.

Fox, D. R., Prilleltensky, I. & Austin, S. (2009). *Critical psychology: An introduction* (2nd edn.). London: Sage.

Gallagher, S. (1997). Mutual enlightenment: Recent phenomenology and cognitive science. *Journal of Consciousness Studies*, *4*(3): 195–214.

Gallagher, S. (2006). *How the body shapes the mind*. Oxford: Clarendon Press.

Gallagher, S. & Zahavi, D. (2008). *The phenomenological mind: An introduction to philosophy of mind and cognitive science*. London: Routledge.

Gallese, V. L. & Goldman, A. (1998). Mirror neurons and the simulation theory of mind-reading. *Trends in Cognitive Science*, *2*: 493–501.

Gerhardt, S. (2004). *Why love matters: How affection shapes a baby's brain*. London: Routledge.

Harré, R. (2002). *Cognitive science. A philosophical introduction*. London: Sage.

Harré, R. & Gillett, G. (1994). *The discursive mind*. London: Sage.

Harré, R. & Langenhove, van L. (1999). *Positioning theory*. Oxford: Blackwell.

Heath, G. (2002a). Does a theory of mind matter? The myth of totalitarian scientism. *International Journal of Psychotherapy*, *7*(3): 185–220.

Heath, G. (2002b). Philosophy and psychotherapy: Conflict or co-operation? *International Journal of Psychotherapy*, *7*(1): 13–52.

Heidegger, M. (1962). *Being and time (J. Macquarrie and E. S. Robinson, Trans.)*. New York: Harper & Row. (First published 1927.).

Henriques, J., Hollway, W., Urwin, C., Venn, C. & Walkerdine, V. (1998). *Changing the subject: Psychology, social regulation and subjectivity*. London: Routledge.

Hicks, C. & Milton, M. (2010). Sexual identities: Meanings for counselling psychology practice. In R. Woolfe, W. Dryden & S. Strawbridge (Eds) *Handbook of counselling psychology* (3rd edn.). London: Sage.

Holzman, L. (1999). *Performing psychology. A postmodern culture of the mind*. London: Routledge.

Husserl, E. (1970). *The crisis of European sciences and transcendental phenomenology*. Evanston, IL: Northwestern University Press. (First published 1936.).

Husserl, E. (1977). *Phenomenological psychology*. The Hague: Martinus Nijhoff. (First published 1927.).

Inayat, Q. (2005). The Islamic concept of the self. *Counselling Psychology Review*, *20*(3): 2–10.

Kagan, C. & Tindall, C. (2007). Feminist approaches in counselling psychology. In R. Woolfe, W. Dryden & S. Strawbridge (Eds.) *Handbook of counselling psychology* (2nd edn.). London: Sage.

Kant, I. (1784). An answer to the question: What is enlightenment? In F. Gedike and E. Biester (Eds.) *Publication of the Berlin Monthly Magazine*.

Kvale, S. (1992). *Psychology and postmodernism*. London: Sage.

Lagerspetz, O. (2002). Experience and consciousness in the shadow of Descartes. *Philosophical Psychology*, *15*(1): 5–18.

Lyons, E. & Coyle, A. (2007). *Analysing qualitative data in psychology*. London: Sage.

McLeod, J. (2000). *Qualitative research in counselling and psychotherapy*. London: Sage.

McLeod, J. (2003). *Doing counselling research*. London: Sage.

McNamee, S. & Gergen, K. (1992). *Therapy as social construction*. London: Sage.

Merleau-Ponty, M. (2000). *Phenomenology of perception* (Colin Smith, Trans.). London: Routledge. (First published 1945.).

Milton, M. (2008). Guest editorial. *Counselling Psychology Review*, *23*(2): 1–3.

Milton, M. & Coyle, A. (2007). Sexual identity: Affirmative practice with lesbian and gay clients. In R. Woolfe, W. Dryden & S. Strawbridge (Eds.) *Handbook of counselling psychology* (2nd edn.). London: Sage.

Milton, M. & Legg, C. (2000). Politics in psychotherapy: Therapists' responses to political material. *Counselling Psychology Quarterly*, *13*(3): 279–291.

Murdoch, I. (1953). *Sartre: Romantic rationalist*. Cambridge: Bowes & Bowes.

Nagel, T. (1987). *What does it all mean?* Oxford: Oxford University Press.

Nagel, T. (1995). *Other minds: Critical essays*. Oxford: Oxford University Press.

Nietzsche, F. (1962). *Philosophy in the tragic age of the Greeks (Marianne Cowan, Trans.)*. Washington, DC: Regnery Publishing. (First published 1873.).

Orlans, V. & Scoyoc, S. van (2009). *A short introduction to counselling psychology*. London: Sage.

Orange, D. M., Atwood, G. E. & Stolorow, R. D. (2001). *Working intersubjectively. Contextualism in psychoanalytic practice.* Hillsdale, NJ: The Analytic Press.

Papineau, D. (2002). *Thinking about consciousness.* Oxford: Oxford University Press.

Parker, I. (1999). *Deconstructing psychotherapy.* London: Sage.

Parker, I., Georgaca, E., Harper, D., McLaughlin, T. & Stowell-Smith, M. (1995). *Deconstructing psychopathology.* London: Sage.

Pope-Davies, D. B., Coleman, H. L. K., Liu, W. M. & Toporek, R. L. (2003). *Handbook of multicultural competencies in counselling psychology.* London: Sage.

Renik, O. (1993). Analytic interaction: Conceptualizing technique in light of the analyst's irreducible subjectivity. *Psychoanalytic Quarterly, 62*: 553–571.

Richardson, J. (1991). *Existential epistemology: A Heideggerian critique of the cartesian project.* Oxford: Clarendon Press.

Rizzolatti, G., Fogassi, L. & Gallese, V. (2001). Cortical mechanisms subserving object grasping and action recognition: A new view on the cortical motor functions. In M. S. Gazzaniga,(Ed.) *The new cognitive neurosciences.* Cambridge, MA: MIT Press.

Rosenthal, M. D. (2001). *Materialism and the mind–body problem.* Cambridge: Hackett.

Rowlands, M. (1999). *The body in mind: Understanding cognitive processes.* Cambridge: Cambridge University Press.

Sartre, J.-P. (1998). *Being and nothingness: An essay on phenomenological ontology (H. Barnes, Trans.).* New York: Philosophical Library. (First published 1943.).

Shillito-Clarke, C. (2007). Ethical issues in counselling psychology. In R. Woolfe, W. Dryden & S. Strawbridge (Eds.) *Handbook of counselling psychology* (2nd edn.). London: Sage.

Smith, A. J. (2008). *Qualitative psychology. A practical guide to research methods.* London: Sage.

Spinelli, E. (2001a). Counselling psychology: A hesitant hybrid or a tantalising innovation? *Counselling Psychology Review, 16*(3): 3–12.

Spinelli, E. (2001b). *The mirror and the hammer: Challenges to therapeutic orthodoxy.* London: Continuum.

Stern, D. N. (2000). *The interpersonal world of the infant: A view from psychoanalysis and developmant psychology.* New York: Basic Books.

Stern, D. N. (2004). *The present moment in psychotherapy and everyday life.* London: W. W. Norton.

Strawbridge, S. (2001). Issues relating to the use of psychiatric diagnostic categories in counselling psychology, counselling and psychotherapy: What do you think? *Counselling Psychology Review, 16*(1): 4–6.

Thayer-Bacon, J. Kincheloe, J. L. & Steinberg, S. R. (2003). *Relational '(E)Pistemologies': Counterpoints: Studies in the postmodern theory of education.* New York: Peter Lang.

Toporek, R. L. Gerstein, L. H. *et al.* (2006). *Handbook for social justice in counselling psychology: Leadership, vision and action.* London: Sage.

Valle, S. R. & Halling, S. (1989). *Existential phenomenological perspectives in psychology: Exploring the breadth of human experience.* New York: Plenum Press.

Varela, F. J. (1996). Neurophenomenology: a methodological remedy to the hard problem. *Journal of Consciousness Studies, 3*: 330–350.

Varela, F. J. Thomson, E. & Rosch, E. (1991). *The embodied mind: Cognitive science and human experience.* Cambridge, MA: MIT Press.

Vera, E. M. & Speight, S. L. (2003). Multicultural competence, social justice and counselling psychology. *The Counseling Psychologist, 31*(3): 253–272.

Wahl, B. (2007). Counselling psychology and the body. In R. Woolfe, W. Dryden and S. Strawbridge (Eds.) *Handbook of counselling psychology* (2nd edn.). London: Sage.

Wheeler, M. (2005). *Reconstructing the cognitive world.* Cambridge, MA: MIT Press.

Willig, C. (2008). *Introducing qualitative research in psychology. Adventures in theory and method.* Buckingham: Open University Press.

Wittgenstein, L. (1965). *Philosophical investigations.* New York: Macmillan.

Wittgenstein, L. (1980). *Remarks on the philosophy of psychology*, vol. 1 (G. E. M. Anscombe, Trans.). Oxford: Blackwell.

Woolfe, R. Dryden, D. & Strawbridge, S. (2007). *Handbook of counselling psychology* (2nd edn.). London: Sage.

World Health Organisation (1992). *The international classification of mental and behavioural disorders* (10th edn.). Geneva: World Health Organisation.

Wosket, V. (1999). *The therapeutic use of self: Counselling practice, research and supervision.* London: Routledge.

Young, J. E. Klosko, J. S. & Weishaar, M. E. (2006). *Schema therapy. A practitioner's guide.* London: Guilford Press.

Chapter 3

Counselling Psychology and Research: Revisiting the Relationship in the Light of Our 'Mission'

Deborah Rafalin

The number of professional psychologists has risen significantly across the world since the latter part of the twentieth century. Facilitating this proliferation is the belief that there are many varying, yet valuable, ways of being a professional psychologist (Lane & Corrie, 2006). Such diversity can potentially be enormously enriching, however, it challenges each psychologist to define the way in which we practise and the professional identity we adopt. Understanding our relationship to research is a key part of self-definition.

Counselling psychology defines itself as being concerned with the individual's subjective experience, appreciating the complexity of difference and focusing on wellbeing rather than just cure. In homage to its humanistic roots, counselling psychology values a search for understanding, rather than demanding universal truths. Through this profession, psychology's historical fetish for insisting on answers has seen an evolution to a valuing of questions. This paradigm shift has underpinned the development of our profession and without doubt is critical when considering counselling psychology's relationship with research.

Therapy and Beyond: Counselling Psychology Contributions to Therapeutic and Social Issues
Edited by Martin Milton
© 2010 John Wiley & Sons, Ltd.

Our Commitment to Research

Counselling psychology's relationship with research is complex and multifaceted, with research avenues informing both theory and practice across many contexts. Although psychological therapy research is but one dimension of this relationship, the link between research and practice is undoubtedly pivotal when reflecting on counselling psychology's relationship with research.

As discussed in Chapter 1, a key defining and differentiating principle of counselling psychology practice is its driving concern to engage with people in ways that attend to each individual's unique experiences. It is this philosophy which endears counselling psychology to service providers, as is our commitment to research as a vehicle for change. We are clear in our commitment to research, but it is arguable that the nature of this relationship and how it fits within the broader domains of science and knowledge will benefit from further clarification.

Throughout history, it has been times of great societal challenge that have led to professional psychologists urgently re-examining their contributions to the knowledge-base of the changing social world. The period following the Second World War was such a time (Lane & Corrie, 2006; Murphy *et al.*, 1984) and in searching for increased usefulness of research findings, clearer expectations were laid down about the nature of the relationship of research to professional practice (John, 1998). This activity led to the official birth of the scientist-practitioner model at the now famous Boulder conference in Colorado, 1949 (see Raimy, 1950). Although there are varying interpretations as to what it entails in practice, the British Psychological Society (2005) identifies the scientist-practitioner model as central to the activity of professional psychology in the UK. Moreover, the scientist-practitioner model has been championed as a cornerstone of counselling psychology identity in the UK (Corrie & Callahan, 2000; Lane & Corrie, 2006; Woolfe, 1996) and provides the foundation for training in Australia, Canada and New Zealand (O'Gorman, 2001).

Counselling psychology's commitment to research as a route to transformative change is unequivocal. However, today yet again perhaps we are at another threshold of significant societal change where the nature of our discipline's relationship with research would merit further reflection.

Research in the Current Climate

Historically, applied psychologists have struggled to hold the multiple identities of both scientist and practitioner (Bernstein & Kerr, 1993; Fitzgerald &

Osipow, 1986; Heppner *et al.*, 1992; Stricker, 1997). Now more than ever, the professional contexts in which counselling psychologists practise demand that these challenges be overcome and that we integrate science and practice convincingly. Our employers in the non-profit, statutory and corporate arenas, driven by financial and political agendas, demand evidence for the effectiveness of psychological provision we provide. As a profession, we have always worked to understand and respond to these demands for evidence.

Evidence-based practice (EBP) involves a significant shift in the relationship between therapeutic practice and research. EBP in health care settings is described as involving information drawn from systematically collected data, clinical expertise and client preferences when considering service options for clients (APA Presidential Task Force on EBP, 2006) leading to the view that 'evidence-based practice is the integration of *best research evidence* with *clinical expertise* and *patient values*' (Institute of Medicine, 2001, p. 147). Decisions as to what counts as the best evidence are unlikely to be universal across all kinds of clinical knowledge or to be fixed (Mace & Moorey, 2001). EBP uses hierarchies based on methodology to discriminate between the quality of evidence for an intervention's effectiveness (e.g. Nathan & Gorman, 1998; Roth & Fonagy, 1996). The hierarchy of evidence is:

> Type I: at least a systematic review, with a randomised control trial.
> Type II: at least a randomised control trial.
> Type III: at least one well-designed intervention study without randomisation.
> Type IV: at least one well-designed observational study.
> Type V: expert opinion, including that of service users.
> (Department of Health, 1999, p. 6).

Wolf clearly articulates the power of the EBP movement:

> Evidence-based practice performs a kind of intellectual alchemy: The lead of research is reduced to systematic reviews and meta-analyses that are transformed into the gold standards of clinical practice guidelines.
> (2007, p. 233)

Clinical practice guidelines are frequently held up as proof that practice areas are 'scientific', with all the associations that this term holds for people, including the promise of improved client outcomes and effective spending of health care funds (see National Institute of Clinical Excellence (NICE) guidelines 2004a; 2004b; 2005 on the treatment of post-traumatic stress disorder, anxiety and depression). The 'Increasing Access to Psychological Therapies' (IAPT) initiative (DoH, 2008) clearly shows the scale of impact that EBP and resulting clinical practice guidelines can have on psychological therapy provision. In this way, it could be argued that research simply as a method of investigation is becoming less valued in certain contexts. Research could be said to be evolving into a method of regulation (see Corrie, 2003; Hart & Hogan, 2003; Monk, 2003; Walsh, 2003, for consideration of the challenges of EBP for counselling psychology).

Our professional lives are challenged by considerable social, political and professional tensions. We face societal challenges as our economic climate is changing, global relationships are redefined and ecological consciousness develops. Psychology itself faces the yet unknown challenge of statutory regulation. We are expected to navigate through a sea of socioeconomic tensions, facing the challenge of balancing individualistic, Western capitalist philosophies with an increased expectation of global responsibility and social awareness. Public sector service provision has seen a concomitant change with increased emphasis on clients' rights as consumers, changing funding mechanisms of services and clinical guidelines formalising 'what works for whom?' (Roth & Fonagy, 1996). These demands, alongside substantial technological advances, require that psychological practitioners continually re-examine who we are and what we do.

The provision of psychological therapy has become polarised between those researchers who insist that randomised controlled trials (RCTs) and systematic reviews of empirical literature are the only basis for prescribing the appropriate psychological intervention, and practitioners who insist that their clinical expertise as a result of extensive experience holds more value in defining and determining helpful practice (see Goodheart *et al.*, 2006; Norcross *et al.*, 2006). Psychological therapists and scientist practitioners must negotiate these challenges and find a way to embrace a more powerful relationship with research. It is our willingness to engage in a language of research that the gatekeepers can understand and our ability to overcome the 'method wars' that will ultimately free our practice. The need to grapple with the complexities of our relationship with research is greater now than ever for all psychological practitioners – including counselling psychologists.

Remembering Our Mission

In reflecting on the way forward, I am reminded of the 'Good Work Project' (Gardner *et al.*, 2001), which attempted to illuminate the supports and obstacles to producing 'good work' in an era of market forces and change. Good work is defined as work that is excellent in quality, carried out ethically and engaging to its practitioners. These principles resonate with counselling psychology, a discipline that sees a commitment to doing 'good work' at the heart of its philosophy, governed by a focus on ethics, context, reflexivity and professional development.

The researchers pose four questions that psychologists pursuing good work should ask of themselves. The first is 'What is the mission of my field?' (Verducci & Gardner, 2006). As counselling psychologists committed to doing 'good work', we need to return to considering the mission of our field in reflecting on the way forward with regard to our relationship with research.

Earlier in this chapter, I noted that a key defining and differentiating principle of counselling psychology is its concern to engage with people in ways that attend to each individual's unique experiences. Our mission is arguably to support people to work towards the change that they want, acknowledging and valuing individual differences and appreciating subjective and unique experiences. This explicit appreciation of diversity of experience and context marks us out as different from some other mental health professionals. The history of psychology has tended to be based on proclamations that a particular perspective, theoretical orientation or attention to a set of topics is the only way forward (Turiel, 2004). This has usually meant a commitment to defending the argument that a particular position is the 'truth'. The EBP movement and the resulting development of clinical practice guidelines can be seen in the same light, with guidelines claiming particular theoretical models as being the only way forward.

In contrast, continued engagement with conflicting viewpoints and worldviews is an important part of counselling psychology's mission of supporting transformative change for individuals and for wider society. We appreciate the importance of matching the most effective therapeutic approach to individual clients with particular difficulties in specific contexts, and we are continuously aware of the uniqueness of context, individual and circumstance. Our valuable holistic perspective gives us a unique contribution to make in challenging research that takes a reductionist, simplistic approach, ignoring multidimensional complexity and reducing answers to extremist positions.

Although we cannot deny the calls for accountability for the ways in which we deliver services, Mellor-Clarke *et al.* argue that 'we do have a choice about whether we allow ourselves to be simply flattened by the laden juggernaut of evidence, or whether we play a more proactive role by helping appropriately load and steer it' (2006, p. 84). So how do we load and steer the 'juggernaut of evidence'? Perhaps we can do this through a focus on, and appreciation of, *difference* as a pivotal value within counselling psychology research: taking a different methodological perspective, defining the parameters of our research gaze differently and appreciating different contributions to our research through true collaboration. As notions of difference permeate our mission, perhaps they can illuminate our research agenda too.

Appreciating Methodological Difference:
Methodological Pluralism

Although traditional scientific methods of inquiry have been elevated as transparent and value-free, contemporary philosophy of science has shown this to be untrue (see Polkinghorne, 1983; Roth, 1987; Slife & Gantt, 1999). Counselling psychology has recognised that positivist research methods may not place the participant in the line of enquiry and, as a result, quantitative methods seem to have largely lost their gloss for our discipline, seeming incongruent with its subjective interpretative base. Challenging the assumptions of traditional scientific methods has tended to result in a swing to qualitative research methods as more productive routes to eliciting meaningful findings and to opening up possibilities of transformative psychological research. The flurry of small-scale, interpretative qualitative research studies carried out by counselling psychologists in training illustrates this shift. A move to qualitative methods expounding the individual perspective and acknowledging the interaction of researcher and participant is exciting and, some argue, long overdue. Such counselling psychology research studies undoubtedly make a huge contribution to the field, illuminating diverse experiences of unique populations in particular contexts. However, qualitative research methods, like the 'scientific' method, rest on a set of assumptions about the world that restrict the questions that can be asked. Thus, avenues of potentially transformative psychological therapy research are closed down. Maybe the pendulum has swung a little too far, inadvertently limiting the potential of research and in doing so, has lost some of its ability to truly appreciate the value of methodological difference in research?

Pluralism can be defined as the 'doctrine that any substantial question admits of a variety of plausible but mutually conflicting responses' (Rescher, 1993, p. 79). It is a philosophical postmodern position which maintains that the search for consensus within scientific discourse is doomed to fail as human beings will inevitably have a range of unique experiences. Rescher fundamentally posits that this quest is ethically problematic in that knowledge is narrowed to exclude that which is different and diverse in others.

Chapter 1 notes the implications of this philosophical position, especially expounding the idea that different models of psychological distress and change may all hold validity, so that there is no need to try to reduce these to one 'unified' model of truth. Different explanations hold validity for different people at different times and therefore different therapeutic methods will be more helpful for different clients at different moments. As Lambert *et al.* state, there are 'many ways to health' (2004, p. 809).

Methodological pluralism advocates a new sophistication within psychological therapy research, which resonates with these core ideals of counselling psychology. The relational perspective of counselling psychology and methodological pluralism seem to dovetail. Instead of simply focusing on using a diversity of method designs or measures in scientific enquiry, a traditional multi-method approach, methodological pluralism also encompasses the diversity of methodological epistemologies and philosophies (Slife & Gantt, 1999). In response to the historical war between quantitative and qualitative research paradigms, methodological pluralism attempts to bring these divergent philosophies together within one philosophical framework. Slife and Gantt (1999) argue that although the differences between these paradigms can never be understated, their difference does not have to lead to incoherence. Counselling psychologists are uniquely placed to understand that the depth of that difference is what gives value to methodological pluralism. Using different methods and philosophies to understand a particular subject under consideration allows greater perspective. Slife and Gantt (1999) powerfully observe that objects of study are 'stubborn'; if we pay attention and look at them from different angles, they speak for themselves and illuminate whether or not or assumptions about them are correct. This idea resonates for me as a psychological therapist: the nature of my psychological therapy approach is dependent on each client and their difficulties in their unique context. This openness allows true detective work to take place, supporting me in finding the right path for them. If I listen attentively, my client tells me whether my assumptions about change will work for them. Likewise, unrestrained listening to the true questions underpinning research ideas will guide me to illuminating routes of discovery.

In this way, methodological pluralism asserts that complementary results are more illuminating than simplistic one-dimensional findings. If two divergent routes converge to illuminate our understanding, then we can have greater confidence in the justification and understanding of our enquiry. A real understanding of phenomena requires an understanding on both the quantitative and qualitative dimensions. Where political agendas are involved in discussions about knowledge and the provision of health care, methodological pluralism levels the playing field. Opposing research paradigms do not give all psychological therapy techniques, strategies or ideas an equal chance. As discussed earlier, a paradigm's unacknowledged underlying assumptions will favour certain constructs that share its assumptions. A pluralist approach to research can open psychological therapy to scientific advancement as areas of investigation, or ways of working, are not rejected as a result of the assumptions that underlie them. Methodological pluralism helps us engage with the complexity of the issues and contributes to exploring questions appropriately. It may even help us end the 'method wars'. As discussed earlier, the debates on the most valid or legitimate types of knowledge have become divisive. Psychological therapy will not be best served by a division between different theoretical approaches, research paradigms or scientists/researchers and practitioners. Good work (Gardner *et al.*, 2001) places our mission first. In doing so, we need to focus on the questions that matter and shift the focus from the philosophical route of enquiry to the object of enquiry. We need to be willing to engage with qualitative and quantitative paradigms as our object dictates. This will challenge the historical tendency to pit one therapy model against another, or argue either technique or relationship as the primary agent of change in a 'dogma-eat-dogma competition' (Beutler, 2004). These ideas are elaborated further in Chapter 7.

Methodological pluralism challenges exactly how one can achieve a complementary commitment to apparently divergent paradigms (Yardley & Bishop, 2008). It lacks the certainty of clear rules of engagement that other paradigms of research enquiry promise. It is this lack of rigidity and its focus on the object of enquiry rather than simply on the route to knowledge that gives it its value. Slife and Gantt assert that it can be viewed as more of an attitude than a procedure when they say, 'this attitude is, we believe, the core of the scientific spirit – that as much as possible everything is examined, including the examination process itself' (1999, p. 1463). As counselling psychologists we are well placed to negotiate the epistemological challenges of a methodological pluralist approach. As posited earlier, our fundamental commitment to appreciating that it is through difference that change can be achieved makes this way of conceptualising research entirely congruent and an attitude that we hold as familiar.

A Different Gaze: Community Psychology

Counselling psychology research has indisputably made a significant contribution to advancing our understanding of the experiences of 'hidden' individuals in often 'secret' contexts or communities. However, as discussed earlier, in line with the EBP agenda and the search for cost-effectiveness, accountability, consistency and evaluation-friendly practices, counselling psychology is increasingly being influenced by organisation-centred agendas as opposed to client-centred agendas. This presents an enormous challenge. Whilst we engage with the desired research questions of our gate-keepers, counselling psychology remains focused on our original mission, ensuring that our gaze is broad.

Hage *et al.* (2007) believe that psychology today needs to transform itself, remembering that it emerged as a profession from sociological roots. They remind us of the expression 'you can talk the talk, but can you walk the walk?' which asserts that real change takes place only when one not only states what one wants to change, but also matches words with actions. Like Brabeck and Ting (2000), they warn us that discourse without action can be dangerous. Perhaps we need to ask ourselves if we are really acting on what we profess to believe in?

James Kelly, in his 1969 address to the American Psychological Association, reflected on the need to redefine psychology, with broader definitions of therapeutic activities, expanded definitions of what it means to be a competent helper and the true participation of psychologists in their local communities. Thirty years on, Smail (1999) echoed this argument, asserting that psychology has still not broadened its ideas of how it should be 'helping' society in the UK today, and that loss of employment, lack of community and of power, deprivation, discrimination and oppression are not being appropriately tackled. The link between poor mental health and social disadvantage has been broadly documented (see Pilgrim, 1997) and Smail reminds us that 'useful therapeutic gains are made only by people who have the resources to make them' (1999, p. 188). Thatcher asserts that if we fail to take account of society's inherent power differentials and assume that 'by changing their minds people can change their lives' (2008, p. 8), we are in danger of becoming part of the oppressive regime that creates social injustice.

Counselling psychology has a pivotal contribution to make in facilitating social action and instigating transformative change through both practice and research. Counselling psychology places a commitment to understanding social context and socio-political processes at the heart of its mission, with the Division of Counselling Psychology's professional practice guidelines (2005) drawing attention to the need to focus on 'social contexts and discrimination' and to demonstrate 'high standards of anti-discriminatory practice'. By remembering this mission, counselling psychology, with its commitment to understanding individuals in their context and an appreciation of sociopolitical processes, is well placed to negotiate this challenge and support the repositioning of psychology within our society. Research is one obvious vehicle for us to engage with to facilitate professional change.

Like counselling psychology, community psychology is a critical, research-based practice which 'represents a different paradigm or world view of psychology' (Nelson & Prilleltensky, 2005, p. 4) and studies people in their context. It involves a more holistic, ecological analysis of people in the context of their multiple social systems, ranging from micro-systems (e.g. the family) to macro-sociopolitical structures. There is a strong belief that people and social processes cannot be understood apart from their context. Wanting to transform the world that we are a part of, we position ourselves as participants and have a naturalistic approach to our world and our communities. This requires an investment and involvement in our local communities and the increasingly global community in which we live. Such an ecological approach leads us to develop understandings of the multiple causes of social phenomena and social problems at different levels; to understand the roles of all stakeholders in our society, evaluating and analysing power dynamics.

Taking such an approach means we struggle with the uncomfortable position of claiming to be impartial, while condemning what is socially or morally corrupt in our society. It places a responsibility on us to work towards social change and transform the establishment where it contravenes our moral codes. Research provides us with the tools to engage with 'the social justice agenda' (Vera & Speight, 2003). Advocates ask that we switch our attention from the individual to society and commit to wrestling with the social processes and 'political and cultural discourses that influence our work' (Hart, 2003, p. 224). The changing societal challenges almost *insist* on a new research direction. Can we broaden our research gaze so that we better serve the representation of individuals' unique experiences by locating them securely within the sociopolitical context that shapes and colours them? By harnessing our willingness to engage further with the discourses of difference and power, we have the ability to challenge and present new perspectives on pervasive values and the status quo. Counselling psychology's affinity to qualitative methodologies and our substantive research skills make us ideally suited to attend critically to the moral, political and social processes that define our practice and professional identity.

Appreciating Difference: Collaboration

Taking an ecological, community-focused approach to research leads us to work in ways that involve other people as fully as possible, emphasising their strengths and their potential, and always with a focus on their lives. As researchers committed to innovation and to harnessing people's creativity, we are open to contributions that those outside of psychology can make and be keen to engage in collaborative cross-discipline and inter-professional work. Examples of this are elaborated in Section 3 of this volume.

Ecological community psychology values work at the 'edge'. Kagan (2007) use the metaphor of the edge of a forest or rocky seashore to explain this concept. These transitional spaces allow diverse resources from different biological communities to meet, often with greater biodiversity than in each of the contributing communities. As researchers, we can work at the ecological edges of our profession, where the rich interaction of communities enables greater potential for real impact and creates a unique environment for change. Just as the divergence of methodological pluralism allows a valuable perspective and a depth of understanding of the question under investigation, genuinely collaborative research enables a coherent, multidimensional understanding. Rich research collaborations at the intersection between psychology, other disciplines and the local community will enable psychology to become more visible and relevant to real-world issues – social exclusion, poverty, conflict, war and conflict resolution, the impact of global economic dominance and even climate change.

What would this research look like? It might be between-service projects, cross-industry collaborations, collaborations with the general public within our real community rather than in our consulting rooms, political dialogues with a social change agenda or engagement with the media. Taking such approaches would insist on our broadening our gaze and sincerely appreciating the value that different perspectives can bring. By truly valuing difference amongst researchers, as an important element of illuminating the questions of research, we could achieve transformative research with the potential for broad and powerful dissemination, significantly impacting on society.

Summary

Professional psychology is being challenged by changing social, political, global and professional tensions as evidence is demanded for the effectiveness of psychological provision. The need to grapple with the complexities of the relationship between research and practice is greater now than ever. Counselling psychology is well placed to negotiate this. In our quest to do 'good work', we need to remind ourselves of our professional mission and engage with actions that reflect our talk. It is time for us to redefine our relationship with research, ensuring that in doing so we remain congruent with our mission as counselling psychologists.

As scientist-practitioners, we have the opportunity to 'steer the juggernaut' (Mellor-Clarke *et al.*, 2006, p. 84) through our contributions as researchers as well as practitioners. We need to celebrate our research strengths and contributions, ensuring that we have pride in the manifestation of our own professional differences. However, we need to ensure that we do not get lost in awareness of our own difference to the point of marginalising ourselves from the changing world. I believe that continually revisiting our professional mission can reconnect us to the means to achieve this delicate balance. By placing our commitment to appreciating difference at the hub of all our work, we can find an illuminating way forward in our relationship with research.

This chapter has suggested three possible initial ways forward:

1. Methodological pluralism allows us to value and appreciate the varied research philosophies and methods of inquiry available to us as scientist-practitioners. By asking the question first, we can avoid shoe-horning the question into the method or epistemological position of choice. We need to reposition the object of inquiry as of primary importance, not how we gather data to explicate its understanding. By removing divisive philosophical divisions, we can contribute in the broadest and most valuable ways to expanding the knowledge of our field.
2. Engaging with a broader research gaze and exploring dynamics of difference and power within our changing society can enable us to develop a more powerful relationship with research. By appreciating the principles of community psychology and the intersection between its key values and our own professional mission, we can ensure that the research work we do can truly facilitate change on the personal, societal and global levels. Through attention to sociopolitical processes and embedding ourselves in society, our research can find a voice genuinely rooted in individual's experiences.
3. By expanding our appreciation of difference and seeking new perspectives to answer our pressing questions, we can enrich our research findings. Through appreciating the perspectives of others, valuing the richness of different contributions and by researching in a profoundly collaborative way, perhaps our research can be disseminated more widely, have even more convincing applied relevance and thus have a greater impact on our changing world.

References

APA Presidential Task Force on Evidence Based Practice (2006). Evidence-based practice in psychology. *American Psychologist*, 61(4): 271–285.
Bernstein, B. L. & Kerr, B. (1993). Counseling psychology and the scientist-practitioner model: Implementation and implications. *The Counseling Psychologist*, 21: 136–151.
Beutler, L. E. (2004). The empirically supported treatments movement: A scientist-practitioner's response [letter to the editor]. *Clinical Psychology: Science and Practice*, 11(3): 225–229.

Brabeck, M. M. & Ting, K. (2000). Feminist ethics: Lenses for examining ethical psychological practice. In M. M. Brabeck (Ed.) *Practising feminist ethics in psychology*. Washington, DC: American Psychological Association.

British Psychological Society (2005). *Subject benchmarks for applied psychology*. Leicester: British Psychological Society.

Corrie, S. (2003). Information, innovation and the quest for legitimate knowledge. *Counselling Psychology Review*, *18*(3): 5–13.

Corrie, S. & Callahan, M. M. (2000). A review of the scientist-practitioner model: Reflections on its potential contribution to counselling psychology within the context of current health care trends. *British Journal of Medical Psychology*, *73*: 413–427.

Department of Health (DoH) (1999). *National service framework for mental health*. London: Department of Health.

Department of Health (DoH) (2008). *Improving access to psychological therapies implementation plan: National guidelines for regional delivery*. London: Department of Health.

Division of Counselling Psychology (2005). *Professional practice guidelines*. Leicester: British Psychological Society.

Fitzgerald, L. F. & Osipow, S. H. (1986). An occupational analysis of counselling psychology: How special is the specialty? *American Psychologist*, *41*: 535–544.

Gardner, H., Csikszentmihalyi, M. & Damon, W. (2001). *Good work: When excellence and ethics meet*. New York: Basic Books.

Goodheart, C. D., Kazdin, A. E. & Sternberg, R. J. (2006). *Evidence-based psychotherapy: Where practice and research meet*. Washington, DC: American Psychological Association.

Hage, S. M., Roman, J. L. *et al.* (2007). Walking the talk: Implementing the prevention guidelines and transforming the profession of psychology. *The Counseling Psychologist*, *35*(4): 594–604.

Hart, N. & Hogan, K. (2003). Training counselling psychologists: What role for evidence-based practice? *Counselling Psychology Review*, *18*(3): 21–28.

Hart, N. (2003). The power of language in therapeutic relationships. In Y. Bates & R. House (Eds.) *Ethically challenged professions: Enabling innovation and diversity in psychotherapy and counselling*. Ross-on-Wye: PCCS Books.

Heppner, P. P., Carter, J. A. *et al.* (1992). A proposal to integrate science and practice in counselling psychology. *The Counseling Psychologist*, *20*: 107–122.

Institute of Medicine (2001). *Crossing the quality chasm: A new health system for the 21st century*. Washington, DC: National Academy Press.

John, I. D. (1998). The scientist-practitioner model: A critical examination. *Australian Psychologist*, *33*(1): 24–30.

Kagan, C. (2007). Working at the 'edge': Making use of psychological resources through collaboration. *The Psychologist*, *20*(4): 224–227.

Kelly, J. G. (1969). Antidotes for arrogance: Training for community psychology. Edited version of the Presidential address, Division of Community Psychology (Division 27), *77th Annual Convention of the American Psychological Association, Washington, DC, September*.

Lambert, M. J., Bergin, A. E. & Garfield, S. L. (2004). Overview, trends and future issues. In M. J. Lambert (Ed.) *Bergin and Garfield's handbook of psychotherapy and behaviour change* (5th edn.). Chicago: John Wiley & Sons.

Lane, D. A. & Corrie, S. (2006). What does it mean to be a scientist-practitioner? Working towards a new vision. In D. A. Lane & S. Corrie (Eds.) *The modern scientist-practitioner*. Hove: Routledge.

Mace, C. & Moorey, S. (2001). Evidence in psychotherapy: A delicate balance. In C. Mace, S. Moorey & B. Roberts (Eds.) *Evidence in the psychological therapies: A critical guide for practitioners*. London: Brunner-Routledge.

Mellor-Clarke, J., Barkham, M. *et al.* (2006). Reflections on benchmarking NHS primary care psychological therapies and counselling. *Counselling and Psychotherapy Research*, 6(1): 81–87.

Monk, P. (2003). Storm and stress: The experience of learning evidence-based practice. *Counselling Psychology Review*, 18(3): 14–20.

Murphy, J., John, M. & Brown, H. (1984). *Dialogues and debates in social psychology*. Hove: Lawrence Erlbaum Associates.

Nathan, P. E. & Gorman J.M. (Eds.) (1998). *A guide to treatments that work*. New York: Oxford University Press.

National Institute for Clinical Excellence (2004a). *Anxiety: Management of anxiety (panic disorder, with or without agoraphobia, and generalised anxiety disorder) in adults in primary, secondary and community care*. London: NICE.

National Institute for Clinical Excellence (2004b). *Depression: Management of depression in primary and secondary care*. London: NICE.

National Institute for Clinical Excellence (2005). *Post-traumatic stress disorder (PTSD): The management of PTSD in adults and children in primary and secondary care*. London: NICE.

Nelson, G. & Prilleltensky I. (Eds.) (2005). *Community psychology: In pursuit of liberation and well-being*. London: Palgrave Macmillan.

Norcross, J. C., Beutler, L. E. & Levant, R. F. (2006). *Evidence-based practices in mental health: Debate and dialogue on the fundamental questions*. Washington, DC: American Psychological Association.

O'Gorman, J. G. (2001). The scientist-practitioner model and its critics. *Australian Psychologist*, 36: 164–169.

Pilgrim, D. (1997). *Psychotherapy and society*. London: Sage.

Polkinghorne, D. E. (1983). *Methodology for the human sciences: Systems of inquiry*. Albany, NY: SUNY Press.

Raimy, V. C. (Ed.) (1950). *Training in clinical psychology* (Boulder conference) New York: Prentice-Hall.

Rescher, N. (1993). *Pluralism: Against the demand for consensus*. Oxford: Oxford University Press.

Roth, P. A. (1987). *Meaning and method in the social sciences: A case for methodological pluralism*. Ithaca, NY: Cornell University Press.

Roth, A. & Fonagy, P. (1996). *What works for whom? A critical review of psychotherapy research*. New York: Guilford Press.

Slife, B. D. & Gantt, E. E. (1999). Methodological pluralism: A framework for psychotherapy research. *Journal of Clinical Psychology, 55*(12): 1453–1465.

Smail, D. (1999). *The origins of unhappiness: A new understanding of personal distress.* London: Constable.

Stricker, G. (1997). Are science and practice commensurable? *American Psychologist, 52*(4): 442–448.

Thatcher, M. (2006). Are ethical codes ethical? *Counselling Psychology Review, 21*(3): 4–11.

Turiel, E. (2004). Historical lessons: The value of pluralism in psychological research. *Merrill-Palmer Quarterly, 50*(4): 535–545.

Vera, E. M. & Speight, S. L. (2003). Multicultural competence: Social justice and counseling psychology: Expanding our roles. *The Counseling Psychologist, 31*(3): 253–272.

Verducci, S. & Gardner, H. (2006). Good work: Its nature, its nurture. In F. Huppert (Ed.) *The science of happiness.* Oxford: Oxford University Press.

Walsh, Y. (2003). Testing the way the wind blows: Innovations and a sound theoretical basis. *Counselling Psychology Review, 18*(3): 29–33.

Wolf, A. W. (2007). Implementing the scientist-practitioner model in the hospital setting. *Journal of Contemporary Psychotherapy, 37* 229–234.

Woolfe, R. (1996). The nature of counselling psychology. In R. Woolfe & W. Dryden (Eds.) *Handbook of counselling psychology.* London: Sage.

Yardley, L. & Bishop, F. (2008). Mixing qualitative and quantitative methods: A pragmatic approach. In C. Willig & W. Stainton-Rogers (Eds.) *The SAGE handbook of qualitative research in psychology.* London: Sage.

Chapter 4

Understanding Human Distress: Moving beyond the Concept of 'Psychopathology'

Martin Milton, Mark Craven and Adrian Coyle

> One morning
> He could not find himself any more
> He had mislaid
> Or perhaps lost himself.
> (Cohn, 1999, p. 4)

Terms such as 'psychopathology', 'mental illness' and 'disorder' have become part of everyday discourse, marking people out as 'different', justifying the increase in the provision of mental health services and promoting the development of such professions as clinical and counselling psychology, counselling and psychotherapy. Reductionist explanations of psychopathology are dominant in both scientific and applied therapeutic worldviews and practices (Fee, 2000), stemming most recently from 'scientific' attempts to identify and classify 'objectively' the different types of disorders which fall under the rubric of 'abnormality'.

Counselling psychology faces a dilemma: on the one hand, there is an espoused utility of scientific psychology and, on the other, there is a recognition that understandings of 'psychopathology' are negotiated and constructed via sociocultural and historically-specific meanings

Therapy and Beyond: Counselling Psychology Contributions to Therapeutic and Social Issues
Edited by Martin Milton
© 2010 John Wiley & Sons, Ltd.

(Golsworthy, 2004; Parker *et al.*, 1995). With that in mind, the topic of distress and 'psychopathology' is a broad one which can be examined from a variety of perspectives. One approach we might have taken would be to explore phenomenological accounts of the experience of certain 'disorders' (e.g. Knudson & Coyle, 2002, on 'hearing voices'). Alternatively, we might have considered the organisational issues that affect the development of services for people with particular difficulties or, in a more traditional vein, we could have written an account of how to practise therapy for a specific disorder.

Instead, we have adopted a postmodern approach to highlight what has been taken for granted in the traditional literature concerning 'psychopathology'. We consider the interplay between theory and practice and the tension between psychological theory which is entrenched in modernity, and professional practice, which has to face human life in a postmodern age (Polkinghorne, 1992).

Psychological Distress across History: A Brief Sketch

While it is important to offer an historical overview of the field, it is equally important to point to the ways in which 'abnormal behaviours' and psychological distress have been conceptualised in different cultures over time. For practical reasons, our account has adopted a more linear and Western-centric account than is ideal and we refer readers to accounts that are broader-ranging, less linear and that take into account developing understandings of psychological distress in other parts of the world in light of cultural, religious and historical considerations (e.g. Al-Issa, 2000; Gielen *et al.*, 2004; Hook & Eagle, 2004; Horwitz, 2002; Laungani, 2004; Parker *et al.*, 1995).

A survey of core 'psychopathology' texts (Bootzin *et al.*, 1993; Davison & Neale, 1998; Halgin & Whitbourne, 1993; Holmes, 1998; Kendall & Hammen, 1998; Oltmans & Emery, 1998; Rosenham & Seligman, 1995; Sarason & Sarason, 1993) demonstrates the changing historical views of psychological abnormality. All of these texts note that a religious belief in possession by spirits, demons or witchcraft was once seen as the cause of psychological difficulties. Over time and in some settings, these views sat alongside and, in places, gave way to the mythological writings of the classical Greek era, and we see the evolution of a naturalistic approach with Hippocrates' suggestion that all illness, including mental disorder, should be explained on the basis of *natural causes*. During the classical Greek era curiosity developed about physical and psychological functioning, and the beginnings of the use of 'scientific method' to explore these issues can be discerned.

In the history of 'psychopathology', the next period is referred to as the Middle or 'Dark' Ages when few scientific or medical advances were deemed to have occurred beyond the important contributions made earlier by Hippocrates and Galen, some of which were clearly biological, with the emphasis being on Galen's humours, although Hippocrates seems to have espoused various psychotherapeutic approaches of a kind. This period is associated with the resurgence of beliefs regarding possession. Following the fall of the Roman Empire, people sought security, with a great number finding it in supernatural explanations of phenomena that were distressing or difficult to comprehend. Christianity grew from a persecuted minority cult to become the official religion of the Empire by the fourth century and contributed to a developing view of psychological difficulty, with 'mental illness' being conceptualised as the result of turning away from God and 'depression' as closely linked to sinfulness (but see Kroll & Bachrach, 1986, and note that these views were by no means inimical with conceptualisations of 'mental illness' as demonic possession).

The seventeenth and eighteenth centuries are often represented as the Age of Reason and the Enlightenment as reason/rationalism and scientific method again came to replace religious faith as ways to understand the natural world, though this was by no means universal. Two primary views were competing and these mirror current debates — that is, organic versus psychological explanations of psychopathology. Despite the tension between the two, some consensus was reached in the diminishing of supernatural forces within social representations of the causes of abnormal behaviour. Having said that, ideas of witchcraft and spirits remain a part of the view of the origins of psychological distress in diverse African contexts (e.g. Mulatu, 1999; Teuton *et al.*, 2007). By the end of the eighteenth century supernatural explanations had been formally replaced with a commitment to rationality and scientific observation. But of course, as today, people still attributed psychopathology to fate, punishment or an uneasy conscience.

The beginnings of modern thought and practice are attributed to, amongst others, the nineteenth-century physician William Griesinger (1817–68), who revived Hippocrates' theory of mental diseases by advocating that mental illness has a physical cause. Among his other contributions, in 1883 Emil Kraepelin (1856–1926) furnished a classification of mental diseases in terms of their organic bases. The enduring nature of Kraepelin's scheme is evident as it forms the basis of present-day classification schemes. The reviewed material comes up to date by acknowledging the continued dominance of the medical model into the twentieth century. Alongside these developments, Franz Mesmer (1733–1815), Jean-Martin Charcot

(1825–1893), Pierre-Marie Janet (1859–1947), Josef Breuer (1842–1925) and Sigmund Freud (1856–1939) have all contributed to an evolving understanding of and available responses to 'psychopathology'. The tension between organic and psychological explanations of psychopathology continues today. Whether useful or not, particular understandings of psychopathology cannot be taken at face value as 'objective' or 'true'. It is important to examine understandings and explanations of psychopathology alongside an examination of the parallel development of modern science.

Enlightenment thinkers engaged in critique of all forms of traditional and religious authority and in their place was substituted a belief in progress, reason and science and a vision of the world that valued material progress, prosperity, individual freedom and social justice founded on *rational* rather than religious or magical principles (Billington *et al.*, 1998). Of course, there is a tradition of rationalism in theology (see Thomas Aquinas co-opting Aristotelian ideas within his theology in the thirteenth century; see Owens, 1993) and a substantial literature that argues for the compatibility of reason/rationalism and religion (e.g. John Paul II, 1998; Polkinghorne, 2005; Swinburne, 1981; Ward, 2006). This process led to the prominence of rational thought over emotion and it was during the Enlightenment that 'madness' became a thing-in-itself, discoverable by dispassionate positivist inquiry (Foucault, 1965).

The Rise of Psychological Accounts of Distress: Psychology as a 'Child of Modernity'

Psychology has its beginnings in the second half of the nineteenth century when the principles of science were applied to the study of human beings (Giorgi, 1986). Science had effectively developed descriptions of the regularities that held in the natural realm and it was believed that application of naturalistic methods to the human realm would produce a body of knowledge that would make possible the prediction and control of human behaviour. Danziger (1979) notes modernism's emancipatory intentions, assuming that gathering such information would allow for the efficient education of children, the reform of prisoners and the *cure* of 'mental illness'.

Psychology adopted the modernist notion or belief in underlying fundamentals or *basic essences*. There are four overarching presumptions from modernism embedded in the discipline of psychology (Gergen, 1991). First, as we saw in Chapter 2, there is the belief in a knowable world and the premise that there is a basic subject matter to be elucidated. Secondly, by presuming a knowable subject, modern psychology is shaped by a belief in universal properties. Thirdly, psychology exemplifies these beliefs as it attempts to study psychopathology by *categorising* it, discovering laws and principles which can be generalised to other instances across time, situations and persons. Here we find the belief that, through the scientific method, obdurate truths can be discovered about what 'psychopathology' is and what causes it. This aim is still evident in such texts as *What Works for Whom?* (Roth & Fonagy, 2005), a particular take on 'evidence-based practice' (Corrie, 2003; Hart & Hogan, 2003; Milton, 2002; Monk, 2003), and in taxonomic systems such as the *Diagnostic and statistical manual of mental disorders* (DSM-IV) (American Psychiatric Association, 1994) and the *International classification of diseases* (ICD-10) (World Health Organisation, 1992). There is faith that such methods of classification are objective, prohibiting the entry of ideology and values when describing and explaining psychopathology. Finally, there is a belief in the progressive nature of the research enterprise leading to an illumination of the *fundamental* character of psychopathology (Gergen, 1991, 1992).

The scientific model has been of unprecedented value in helping us understand the nature of 'physical reality'. However, Newman (2000) highlights how the efforts of twentieth-century positivism have led to the 'scientising' of history and human understanding by attempting to make it fully explanatory. The explanatory and/or predictive mode of understanding is rooted in the capacity to deductively derive a definitive description of a specific phenomenon.

The rise of the scientific tradition led to the categorisation of mental illness, drawing on the medical model embodied in the DSM and ICD classification systems. One perspective on these systems is that they provide a convenient shorthand for describing issues faced by mental health professionals. From a modernist perspective, this approach to understanding, explaining and treating mental problems makes compelling sense (Schwartz & Wiggins, 1986) and is very influential in UK public sector health settings, government policy and legal proceedings. The assumption is that a diagnosis provides a reference point from which standardised modalities of 'treatment' begin. By extension, a diagnosis of psychological 'disturbance' should confer a similar sense of understanding and sense of deliverance from disease which occurs in medical diagnosis. However, unlike other biomedical classifications of pathology, psychiatric explanations of the aetiologies of 'psychopathology' have been a constant source of dispute (e.g. Grob, 1985; Klerman *et al.*, 1984) in academia, the consulting room and in dialogue between various mental health professions. Consequently, the DSM-IV has adopted a descriptive and apparently non-aetiologically-based approach to classifying psychopathology.

The case for the importance of classification makes sense when viewed from within the dominant framework. However, it is not unproblematic. At the base of this view is a 'knowable' world and the assumption that we can uncover the nature of the external world and the interior of individual people's minds. The classification systems assume that each disorder can be classified as a distinct entity, that psychopathology is a 'thing in itself'.

Querying the Categorisation of Distress

These realist assumptions are challenged by the alternative notion that our understandings of any mental illnesses are ideologically shaped and institutionally reinforced constructions rather than 'truths' (McNamee & Gergen, 1992). In order to make sense of notions of the 'abnormal', an account of what is 'normal' is required. Looking at the 'normal/abnormal' opposition in a wider historical framework, we find that this category simply reconstitutes the opposition between 'sane' and 'insane', 'healthy' and 'sick' (Parker *et al.*, 1995). The uses of the classification systems can be, and often are, used to define ideals of behaviour and to reflect and reinforce ideologies and cultural themes. The dominant meanings associated with what it is to be 'normal' or 'abnormal' not only constrain and influence people's behaviour, but also, as Hare-Mustin and Maracek (1990) note, serve to maintain the status quo and justify hierarchies of power. For example, until the revision of the classification system in 1980, homosexuality was included in the DSM as a category of mental disorder, which served to reaffirm the moral and cultural sanctions against non-heterosexual behaviour. Contrary to the predictions of the 'scientific project', Kutchins and Kirk (1997) argue that science, scientific fact and research findings were not the key factors in deciding whether or not to include or exclude this particular diagnosis in the DSM; it was a 20-year debate about beliefs and values. This adds weight to social constructionist claims that classification systems and their use to classify 'abnormal' functioning are products of their time and place.

Mental health practice utilises approaches underpinned by the belief that to address a complaint, you have to name it. The fact that the systems have utilised medical frameworks has played a significant role in shaping professional and lay conceptions of 'clinical reality' with respect to psychological difficulties.

Gergen warns of the danger of reifying a language of mental states:

> by constructing a reality of mental deficit the professions contribute to hierarchies of privilege, reducing natural interdependencies within the culture, and lend themselves to self-enfeeblement. This infirming of the culture is

progressive, such that when common actions are translated into a professionalised language of mental deficit, and this language is disseminated, the culture comes to construct itself in these terms.

(1990, p. 353)

Experience in the consulting room suggests that this is not just a theoretical risk: clients use psychiatric discourse and self-diagnoses when approaching practitioners. Repudiating the notion of correspondence between language and 'reality' renders problematic the discursive repertoire of 'objective' and decontextualised assessment, diagnosis and intervention, the use of classificatory systems and the status of theory informed by the metaphor of scientific discovery (Lowe, 1999). If we replace the representational-referential view of language associated with these systems with a perspective more akin to counselling psychology's values and understandings, that is, a relationally and rhetorically responsive view (e.g. Shotter, 1993), the realities created by diagnostic classifications are not seen as actual states of being but as historically situated ways of talking which have constitutive effects. This allows us to accept the lived reality while challenging the conceptualisation. This is important because these experiences have phenomenological 'reality'. The complexity of practice requires us to consider the implications of experiences as constructed by discourses, phenomenological experience *and* the ways in which these relate.

The Impact on Practice

Modernist models of practice are informed by assumptions of an underlying cause of pathology, the location of this cause within the individual, the diagnosability of the problem and its treatability via specific sets of techniques (Kaye, 1999). The individual is treated as the locus of pathology, thereby diverting attention from sociocultural factors in the genesis of psychological distress.

Implicit in these suppositions are the concepts of normality and abnormality, the normatively good or bad and the presumption of a 'true' cause, which can be objectively established, known and remediated. Thus, when practitioners are confronted with a client who is experiencing distress and they use diagnostic categories such as those found in the DSM-IV, they are entering a medical discourse. As Pilgrim (2000, p. 302) notes: 'Diagnosis is a medical task which creates a simple dichotomy between the sick and the well.'

From this viewpoint, therapy can be seen as an instrumental practice consisting of the treatment of what is *judged* to be psychopathology.

Practitioners working within these parameters attempt to bring about a restructuring or reprogramming of behaviour against some criterion of the 'normal'. Therefore, modernist therapy is concerned with altering behaviour patterns and belief systems with the establishment of alternative, more socially normative patterns. For example, the currently privileged evidence-based model of cognitive-behavioural therapy adopts a medicalised approach through its description of manualised, didactic forms of therapy for specific disorders. In this sense, it has 'created' discrete disorders for which it has conveniently developed therapeutic 'remedies'.

This conceptualisation perpetuates the concept of the therapist as having privileged knowledge, a socially accredited expert who provides a diagnosis (an authoritative and 'true' version of a problem) and acts according to a set of prescribed activities to correct it (Kaye, 1996). As such, the therapist enters the therapeutic arena with a well-developed narrative for which there is abundant support within the community of scientific peers. It is this background that establishes the therapist's stance towards the client's difficulties. A demarcation can be seen between the client's narrative, which is viewed as made up of the insubstantial stuff of daily life, replete with distorted memories and wishful thinking, and the scientific narrative, which has the seal of professional approval. In this meeting, the client's narrative is incorporated into or replaced by the professional account (Gergen & Kaye, 1992). This process of replacing the client's story with the therapist's metanarrative is in evidence in psychoanalysis, where the client's account is transformed by the therapist into a tale of family romance (i.e. the Freudian Oedipal story); in Rogerian therapy with the humanist odyssey of self-fulfilment, which encourages the client to accept their 'real self' and become more whole; and in cognitive-behavioural therapy where the story centres on reason and educates clients in more 'correct' or 'rational' ways of thinking and acting. Thus, the metanarratives provided by therapists can serve as organising frameworks, which simultaneously provide solutions to clients' problems (Omer & Strenger, 1992). However, as counselling psychologists are only too aware, such narratives suffer from a rigidity of formulation and are relatively closed to modification. By attempting to diagnose and categorise, modern narratives aspire towards universality and are left with very little to say about historical and cultural circumstances. We end up with similar formulations across clients because they suffer from the 'same' category of pathology. In this sense, they are insensitive and arguably fail to register the particularities of the client's life engagements.

Modernist approaches have major shortcomings: when people are approached as *objects* about which therapists know truths, their experience is often one of being dehumanised; it favours a form of personal blame and is often blind to the social conditions in which problems develop. Practitioners overlook their inevitably reflexive role in *creating* the version they think they perceive. At best, these versions fit the client, drawing distinctions which help them to generate new, less problematic possibilities for themselves; at worst, they represent a circular activity in which the therapist finds the 'disorder' that they hypothesise to be there and attempts to impose these on the client in a form of intellectual colonialism (Hoffman, 1993; McCarty and Byrne, 1988).

This chapter now ask: What is counselling psychology's relationship with 'psychopathology'? And is it able to offer more appropriate ways of viewing and working with the difficulties clients bring?

Living the Tension: Counselling Psychology in Action

Counselling psychology is concerned with the integration of psychological theory and research with therapeutic practice (Orlans & van Scoyoc, 2009). This is not a straightforward endeavour as many counselling psychologists work in public sector settings such as medical and prison contexts, which may take a particular view on the human condition, on truth and on outcome. Counselling psychologists have to attend to the tensions that exist between knowledge and values and the contexts in which they are used. The tension exists in light of the postmodern departure from the traditional view that it is possible for a self-contained expert to apply technique to a self-contained client suffering from an identifiable internal pathology. Counselling psychology's adherence to a phenomenological base and humanistic value system (which views human beings as free and autonomous yet inherently relational) is reflected in reactions against the medical model of professional–client relationships and a move towards focusing on facilitating wellbeing rather than on understanding psychological difficulties as sickness and pathology (Woolfe, 1996).

This tension may result in a view that postmodern perspectives (and counselling psychology with it) are opposed to 'prevalent discourses that shape the applied contexts in which counselling psychologists work' (Craven & Coyle, 2007, p. 246). Others recognise the opportunities that this engagement presents, namely opportunities to participate in and further develop our understandings of human experience and the ways in which we might intervene. In this regard, counselling psychology's critique of psychopathology and the use of classifications systems does not deny the 'reality' of the pain or suffering that clients present to mental health professionals, but it does allow questions to be raised as to how counselling psychologists engage with clients and the difficulties they bring, sometimes within that discourse and sometimes by subverting it.

"Little Narratives": Local Meanings and Understandings

Lyotard refers to overarching theories and belief systems as 'grand or meta-narratives' and describes the postmodern condition in terms of abandoning the search for these. Instead, he argues that in social science as well as every-day life, it is the small-scale theories and accounts that should claim our attention: 'the little narrative remains the quintessential form of imaginative invention' (1984, p. 60).

Counselling psychology seeks local understandings of people, informed by their subjective accounts of the world and experience (Woolfe, 1996). Rather than the pursuit of an 'objectively discoverable truth' (Strawbridge & Woolfe, 1996, p. 619), the discipline of counselling psychology gives primacy to exploring the ways in which individuals perceive and attribute meaning to their phenomenological realities (Deurzen-Smith, 1990). For example, counselling psychology's use of client and context-specific formulation minimises risk as it emphasises evaluating emotional and mental health with respect to a person's position in the lifecycle, along with their lifestyle and relationships (Woolfe, 1996). Rather than attempting to categorise clients and their distress, counselling psychology pays attention to the particular 'little narratives' which locate clients' behaviour and experience in a biographical and social context. The following anonymised vignette shows how counselling psychology goes beyond limited conceptualisations in an attempt to explore the difficulties in personal and meaningful ways.

Mary came to therapy with a diagnosis of depression and could name a number of the nine formal diagnostic criteria, including depressed mood, diminished interest in everyday activities, insomnia and feelings of worthlessness. Mary described a previous therapy where she "got bored with always focusing on my mother or on the symptoms" and found she could not do the between-session tasks.

Counselling psychology sees depression (and any other label) as both meaningful and relational. Reflection on what depression might mean in the context of Mary's life led us to consider her view of herself, her boss and the profession she worked in, as well as her familial experiences. These all seemed like much more interesting topics to Mary and offered a serious yet depathologising view of her experience. It was this that Mary felt allowed her to feel she could tackle her current difficulties, rather than just resign herself to them and leave therapy.

In this way the counselling psychologist tries to hear how depression is *experienced* rather than simply assuming our 'expert' knowledge is valid to the specific individual. This allows the relief that human relating can bring, as well as a greater possibility of understanding for the client.

From Within to Between

Counselling psychologists' use of formulation (rather than diagnosis and psychiatric categorisation) goes some way towards addressing and redistributing power within the therapeutic relationship. Rather than attempting to 'objectively' diagnose, the helping relationship is prioritised, characterised as it is by its system of cooperative inquiry which involves developing a shared understanding between client and therapist to address the client's concerns. This is characteristically postmodern in that it represents a move away from emphasising the psychology of the client – a one-person psychology (Kahn, 1996) – to a focus on what occurs *between* people – an intersubjective psychology where the therapist's perspective is acknowledged to impact on the client's experience of therapy (Strawbridge, 1992; Wilkinson *et al.*, 1997). Counselling psychologists' use of psychological formulation works *with* rather than *on* the client. It is more responsive to clients' own descriptions and understandings of their difficulties and is more sensitive to the psychosocial context of everyday behaviour, experience and language, thus avoiding technicalising and pathologising ordinary judgements.

Let's return to Mary:

Mary's depression was characterised by a sense of powerlessness – specifically in her work as a human rights lawyer but more broadly too. She struggled with personal effectiveness, her male manager, the lack of available support and the "pointlessness" of her work. Her previous therapy had explored a theorised identification with the passive mother. While this had some resonance, Mary felt that we "turned a corner" when we recognised that her powerlessness was also related to her boss's avoidance of difficulties and her profession's continuous witness of the onslaught of abuse, brutality and violence. Mary commented: "It's enough to make anyone want to hide away from the world, isn't it?" Mary was able to see the sense in her depression rather than to see it as a thing on its own.

Mary's therapy considered the importance of recognising one's disappointment in the family as well as the impact of living in a violent world. It allowed Mary to review her relationship with her mother (and to consider ways to accept her the way she is), as well as her relationship with her work, including a change of focus, systematic reflection at work and the need for more regular support.

Such context-specific formulations require what Kaye (1993) refers to as a receptive stance that sees the individual as an agent rather than an object. It implies curiosity about the client's experience, together with a search for meanings negotiated between the client, the therapist and their wider worlds. It rejects a reductive reframing of the presenting concerns in accordance with predetermined diagnostic categories: in Mary's case what the experience was *called* was less important than the fact that it became meaningful to her. Resting on a form of relational practice between therapist and client, counselling psychology seeks to reach a joint understanding (Shotter, 1993) wherein local meanings and understandings are collaboratively developed, not imposed. This helps ensure that distress is not unnecessarily translated into pathology akin to physical disease located within the person.

Summary

Whilst the aim of this chapter has not been to reach definitive answers — a modernist endeavour — it has attempted to contribute towards furthering constructive dialogue regarding the issue of understanding and working with psychological difference and distress. Strawbridge and Woolfe's contention that 'counselling psychology is not just a psychological activity but is also a cultural enterprise' (1996, p. 606), reflexively questioning its role in maintaining and/or challenging the existing social structure, marks it out as a critical form of psychology challenging the status quo in a constructive way, formulating new knowledge and improving practice. This is exemplified in counselling psychology's phenomenological and humanistic value base, its reaction against the rigid application of the medical model of professional–client relationships and its emphasis on wellbeing rather than pathology, even when working with clients experiencing extreme forms of distress in a range of settings. This has been illustrated by counselling psychology's use of psychological formulation, which brings into question the traditional use of diagnostic approaches and simultaneously forwards a non-pathology-oriented means of assessing and working with psychological difference. Most notably, it provides a mode of practice that collaboratively negotiates the *meaning* of psychological distress between therapist and client. Thus, contrary to traditional psychology, which tends to decontextualise clients' distress, viewing psychopathology as within the client, counselling psychologists encourage clients to distinguish between psychological and social aspects of the issues they are dealing with and find appropriate strategies for both. In this way, the client is not blamed but validated in their struggle and empowered to find social and personal solutions to their psychological distress. This can be done across the range of models used and the variety of contexts in which clients seek help.

Whilst having to address the fact that counselling psychology has its roots in modernist approaches and models that essentially began a century ago, it is evolving and modifying itself in light of the changing cultural context within which it is situated. It has developed models of practice and inquiry attentive to the problems inherent in the dominant view of science (Strawbridge & Woolfe, 1996). Its 'methodological pluralism' (Barkham, 1990) and pluralistic approach to practice seem open to diversity and generate understanding and acceptance among the innumerable 'local' meanings and interactions of human activity. Embracing a pluralistic outlook bodes well for its ongoing development as a discipline.

Perhaps the most revolutionary and exciting aspect of counselling psychology is that it replaces this binary 'either/or' logic with a 'both/and' position. Counselling psychology represents a critical recognition of the limits and excesses of modernism, yet a willingness continually to seek understanding without the certainties of modernist assumptions. As a corollary, the counselling psychologist is invited to conjoin the biological, personal, professional and the political. It is to be hoped that mental health professionals will be stimulated to enter the debate by considering their own responsibility to challenge and expose the shortcomings of traditional modernist forms of psychological inquiry and practice and their potentially normalising and pathologising influence, whilst continually developing more liberatory notions of psychological difference and emancipatory forms of applied practice.

References

Al-Issa, I. (Ed.) (2000). *Al-Junuun: Mental illness in the Islamic world*. Madison, CT: International Universities Press.

American Psychiatric Association (1994). *Diagnostic and statistical manual of mental disorders*. (4th edn.). Washington, DC: American Psychiatric Association.

Barkham, M. (1990). Counselling psychology: In search of an identity. *The Psychologist: Bulletin of the British Psychological Society*, *12*: 536–539.

Billington, R., Hockey, J. & Strawbridge, S. (1998). *Exploring self and society*. London: Macmillan.

Bootzin, R. R., Acocella, J. R. & Alby, B. (1993). *Abnormal psychology: Current perspectives*. (6th edn.). New York: McGraw-Hill.

Cohn, H. (1999). *With all five senses*. London: Meynard Press.

Corrie, S. (2003). Information, innovation and the quest for legitimate knowledge. *Counselling Psychology Review*, *18*(3): 5–13.

Craven, M. & Coyle, A. (2007). Counselling psychologists' talk about 'psychopathology' and diagnostic categories: A reflective account of a discourse analytic study. In E. Lyons & A. Coyle (Eds.) *Analysing qualitative data in psychology*. London: Sage.

Danziger, K. (1979). The social origins of modern psychology. In A. R. Buss (Ed.) *Psychology in social context*. Chicago: University of Chicago Press.

Davison, G. C., & Neale, J. M. (1998). *Abnormal psychology* (7th edn.). New York: Wiley.

Deurzen-Smith, E. van (1990). Philosophical underpinnings of counselling psychology. *Counselling Psychology Review*, 5: 8–12.

Fee, D. (Ed.) (2000). *The broken dialogue: Mental illness as discourse and experience*. In *Pathology and the postmodern: Mental illness as discourse and experience*. London: Sage.

Foucault, M. (1965). *Madness and civilization: A history of insanity in the age of reason*. New York: Vintage.

Gergen, K. J. (1990). Therapeutic professions and the diffusion of deficit. *The Journal of Mind and Behavior*, 11: 353–368.

Gergen, K. J. (1991). *The saturated self: Dilemmas of identity in modern life*. New York: Basic Books.

Gergen, K. J. (1992). Toward a postmodern psychology. In S. Kvale (Ed.) *Psychology and postmodernism*. London: Sage.

Gergen, K. J. & Kaye, J. (1992). Beyond narrative in the negotiation of therapeutic meaning. In S. McNamee & K.J. Gergen (Eds.) *Therapy as social construction*. London: Sage.

Gielen, U. P., Fish J.M. & Draguns, J. G. (Eds.) (2004). *Handbook of culture, therapy, and healing*. Mahwah, NJ: Erlbaum.

Giorgi, A. (1986). Status of qualitative research in the human sciences. *Methods*, 1: 29–62.

Golsworthy, R. (2004). Counselling psychology and psychiatric classification: Clash or co-existence? *Counselling Psychology Review*, 19(3): 23–29.

Grob, G. N. (1985). The origins of American psychiatric epidemiology. *American Journal of Public Health*, 28: 29–42.

Halgin, R. P. & Whitbourne, S. K. (1993). *Abnormal psychology* (international edn.). Orlando, FL: Harcourt Brace.

Hare-Mustin, R. T. & Maracek, J. (1990). *Making a difference: Psychology and the construction of gender*. New Haven, CT: Yale University Press.

Hart, N. & Hogan, K. (2003). Training counseling psychologists: What role for evidence-based practice? *Counselling Psychology Review*, 18(3): 21–28.

Hoffman, L. (1993). *Exchanging voices: A collaborative approach to family therapy*. London: Karnac Books.

Holmes, D. (1998). *The essence of abnormal psychology*. London: Prentice Hall.

Hook, D. & Eagle G. (Eds.) (2004). *Psychopathology and social prejudice*. Cape Town: Juta Press.

Horwitz, A. V. (2002). *Creating mental illness*. Chicago, IL: University of Chicago Press.

John Paul II (1998). *Faith and reason: Encyclical letter "Fides et ratio" of the Supreme Pontiff John Paul II to the bishops of the Catholic Church on the relationship between faith and reason.* London: Catholic Truth Society.

Kahn, E. (1996). The intersubjective perspective and the client-centred approach: Are they one at their core? *Psychotherapy, 33*: 30–42.

Kaye, J. D. (1993). On learning to see through the eyes of another. In I. Parker (Ed.) *Deconstructing psychotherapy.* London: Sage.

Kaye, J. D. (1996). Towards a discursive therapy. *Changes, 14*: 232–237.

Kaye, J. D. (1999). Toward a non-regulative praxis. In I. Parker (Ed.) *Deconstructing psychotherapy.* London: Sage.

Kendall, P. C. & Hammen, C. (1998). *Abnormal psychology.* Boston, MA: Houghton Mifflin.

Klerman, G. L., Valliant, G. E., Spitzer, R. L. & Michels, R. (1984). A debate on DSM-III. *American Journal of Psychiatry, 141*: 539–553.

Knudson, B. & Coyle, A. (2002). The experience of hearing voices. *Existential Analysis, 13*(1): 117–134.

Kroll, J. & Bachrach, B. (1986). Sin and the etiology of disease in pre-Crusade Europe. *Journal of the History of Medicine, 41*: 395–414.

Kutchins, H. & Kirk, S. A. (1997). *Making us crazy.* New York: Free Press.

Laungani, P. (2004). *Asian perspectives in counselling and psychotherapy.* London: Routledge.

Lowe, R. (1999). Between the 'no longer' and the 'not yet': Postmodernism as a context for critical therapeutic work. In I. Parker (Ed.) *Deconstructing psychotherapy.* London: Sage.

Lyotard, J.-F. (1984). The postmodern condition: A report on knowledge. *Theory and History of Literature.* vol. *10.* Manchester: Manchester University Press.

McCarty, I. C. & Byrne, N. O. R. (1988). Mis-taken love: Conversations on the problem of incest in an Irish context. *Family Process, 27*: 181–198.

McNamee, S. & Gergen, K. J. (1992). *Therapy as social construction.* London: Sage.

Milton, M. (2002). Evidence-based practice: Issues for psychotherapy. *Psychoanalytic Psychotherapy, 16*(2): 160–172.

Monk, P. (2003). Storm and stress: The experience of learning evidence-based practice. *Counselling Psychology Review, 18*(3): 14–20.

Mulatu, M. S. (1999). Perceptions of mental and physical illnesses in north western Ethiopia. *Journal of Health Psychology, 4*(4): 531–549.

Newman, F. (2000). Does a story need a theory? Understanding the methodology of narrative therapy. In D. Fee (Ed.) *Pathology and the postmodern: Mental illness as discourse and experience.* London: Sage.

Oltmans, T. F. & Emery, R. E. (1998). *Abnormal psychology.* (2nd edn). Upper Saddle River, NJ: Prentice-Hall.

Omer, H. & Strenger, C. (1992). The pluralist revolution: From the one true meaning to an infinity of constructed ones. *Psychotherapy, 29*: 253–261.

Orlans, V. & Scoyoc, S. van (2009). *A short introduction to counselling psychology.* London: Sage.

Owens, J. (1993). Aristotle and Aquinas. In N. Kretzmann & E. Stump (Eds.) *The Cambridge companion to Aquinas*. Cambridge: Cambridge University Press.

Parker, I., Georgaca, E. *et al.* (1995). *Deconstructing psychopathology*. London: Sage.

Pilgrim, D. (2000). Psychiatric diagnosis: more questions than answers. *The Psychologist, 13*: 302–305.

Polkinghorne, D. E. (1992). Postmodern epistemology of practice. In S. Kvale (Ed.) *Psychology and postmodernism*. London: Sage.

Polkinghorne, J. (2005). *Exploring reality: The intertwining of science and religion*. New Haven, CT: Yale University Press.

Rosenham, D. L. & Seligman, M. E. P. (1995). *Abnormal psychology*. (3rd edn). New York: W. W. Norton.

Roth, A. & Fonagy, P. (2005). *What works for whom? A critical review of psychotherapy research*. New York: Guilford Press.

Sarason, I. G. & Sarason, B. R. (1993). *Abnormal psychology* (6th edn). Upper Saddle River, NJ: Prentice-Hall.

Schwartz, M. A. & Wiggins, O. P. (1986). Logical empiricism and psychiatric classification. *Comprehensive Psychiatry, 27*: 101–114.

Shotter, J. (1993). *Conversational realities: Constructing life through language*. London: Sage.

Strawbridge, S. (1992). Counselling psychology and the model of science. *Counselling Psychology Review, 7*: 5–11.

Strawbridge, S. & Woolfe, R. (1996). Counselling psychology: A sociological perspective. In R. Woolfe & W. Dryden (Eds.) *Handbook of counselling psychology*. London: Sage.

Swinburne, R. (1981). *Faith and reason*. Oxford: Clarendon Press.

Teuton, J., Bentall, R. & Dowrick, C. (2007). Conceptualizing psychosis in Uganda: The perspective of indigenous and religious healers. *Transcultural Psychiatry, 44*(1): 79–114.

Ward, K. (2006). *Pascal's fire: Scientific faith and religious understanding*. Oxford: Oneworld.

Wilkinson, J. D., Campbell, E. A. *et al.* (1997). Trials, tribulations and tentative triumphs. *Counselling Psychology Review, 12*: 79–89.

Woolfe, R. (1996). The nature of counselling psychology. In R. Woolfe & W. Dryden (Ed.) *Handbook of Counselling Psychology*. London: Sage.

World Health Organisation (1992). *The international classification of mental and behavioural disorders*. (10th edn.). Geneva: World Health Organisation.

Chapter 5

Being with Humans:
An Evolutionary Framework for the
Therapeutic Relationship

Frances Gillies

The referral from community mental health services stated that Adele[1] was a 19-year-old woman, currently sleeping on friends' floors and working in casual jobs in the leisure industry. She was described as being 'anorexic with multiple-personality disorder'. It seemed that Adele was occasionally 'taken over' by one or more of these personalities and she would dissociate. At the referral meeting my colleague who had assessed Adele eagerly passed her care to me, saying that she had 'never met anyone as odd in presentation'. I nervously accepted the referral and rushed off to supervision.

I read Adele's referral to my colleagues in supervision and asked whether anyone had ever come across someone with 'multiple-personality disorder' and what I should do. Where do I find a manual for "treating" such a disorder? I was given some quizzical looks and then the suggestion that perhaps I could meet Adele, ask her about her experiences and sit with her while we made sense of them together. Ah yes, make a therapeutic relationship!

Therapy and Beyond: Counselling Psychology Contributions to Therapeutic and Social Issues
Edited by Martin Milton
© 2010 John Wiley & Sons, Ltd.

The restorative nature of a relationship between two (or more) people has been discussed for thousands of years by philosophers, medical
practitioners, spiritual healers and, more recently, by psychologists and psychotherapists (Clarkson, 1995; Gelso & Carter, 1985; Gilbert, 2007). Despite
there being some agreement that the nature of a relationship can be healing
in itself, there is debate about what it is within the relationship that effects
change. Counselling psychologists view the therapeutic relationship as central to the therapeutic endeavour and 'engage with' rather than 'do therapy
to' their clients. Whilst clinically and subjectively this approach feels helpful to clients, a variety of theories exist about why this type of relationship
might be therapeutic. Counselling psychologists recognise that compassion,
warmth, a non-judgemental approach, egalitarianism and 'realness' on the
part of the therapist promote good outcome in therapy. By using insights
from evolutionary psychology, this chapter outlines some of the reasons
why it is important.

Before we proceed it might be helpful to explain what is meant by the
therapeutic relationship. There are many relationships that are psychologically beneficial, such as the parent–child relationship, sexual relationships
or formal helping relationships, such as those between nurses and patients,
social workers and clients, spiritual leaders and their followers. Here, quite
simply, the focus is on the specific relationship between a therapist and client
engaged in psychotherapeutic work. The relationship stands apart from theories and therapeutic modalities and is known to effect change (potentially
both positively and negatively) for the client and for the therapist.

Differing Views on the Therapeutic Relationship

The various therapy models all have something to say about the therapeutic
relationship. Writers working within a specific therapeutic model will differ
in their recommendations as to the nature and form of the desired therapeutic relationship. A complete literature review of these differences and/or
similarities is beyond this chapter but in order to illustrate the complexity
of the issue it is useful to describe a few approaches.

Psychoanalysis traditionally saw the therapeutic relationship as a vehicle
for transference (Freud, 1914). The relationship would be one that fostered
the replication of characteristics found in other significant and developmental relationships. Analysts offer 'transference interpretations', with the
therapeutic aim being to create and dissolve transference neuroses. In the
service of allowing transference a platform, analysts have been described
as maintaining a 'blank slate' approach to the therapeutic relationship,

meaning that as little as possible of their own personality or countertransference 'muddied the waters'. More recently, psychoanalysis has broadened the remit of the relationship so that transference interpretation is one part of a greater whole. Non-specific factors such as support, affirmation, empathy, encouragement and elaboration are all seen as enabling a relationship in which deeper interpretations can be made (Holmes, 2001). Attachment theory (Bowlby, 1988) has many important things to say about the therapeutic relationship and will be discussed in greater depth later in this chapter.

Humanistic psychotherapies have traditionally understood the therapeutic relationship as central to the therapeutic endeavour. Rogers (1957) described relational attributes that, if present, enable a client to find their way towards inner change. The therapeutic relationship is characterised by, among other things, the conditions of unconditional positive regard, empathic understanding and congruence. These are understood to be conducive to growth and therapeutic change (Rogers, 1957). Empathic understanding refers to perceiving the world from the clients' perspective, which demonstrates acceptance and values the client and their worldview. Congruence alludes to authenticity and genuineness, meaning that the therapist is present and transparent and has no air of authority or hidden knowledge. These humanistic values are seen as *necessary* and *sufficient* for therapeutic change, and without the risk of rejection or condemnation the client experiences freedom to explore their thoughts and feelings.

Cognitive behavioural theory (CBT) has likewise developed its opinion of the therapeutic relationship. Beck *et al.* (1979) originally wrote that the therapeutic relationship was necessary *but not* sufficient for good outcome in therapy. Beck used the term 'working alliance' to suggest a relationship primarily characterised by collaboration: a clear, goal-oriented relationship where therapist and client were in agreement as to where the therapy was going. Whilst it is clear that warmth, empathy and encouragement enable a good working alliance, these aspects of therapy were not seen as therapeutic in themselves. The more recent wave of cognitive behavioural-based therapies such as dialectical-behavioural therapy and acceptance and commitment therapy all place greater emphasis on the therapeutic importance of the relationship (Gilbert, 2007).

Research on the Therapeutic Relationship

Despite the differences, it is clear that most models see the therapeutic relationship as one of the main tools for achieving client change (Luborsky, 1994). This view is supported by empirical work. Some researchers have attempted to quantify the outcome effects of the therapeutic relationship. Through meta-analysis of psychotherapeutic outcome literature, Lambert and Barley (2001) found that it is the non-specific aspects of the therapeutic relationship that account for change rather than the model of therapy. Similarly, Norcross's (2002) work suggests that 15% of outcome is due to expectancy effects, 15% to therapy techniques, 30% to common factors (such as empathy, warmth and the therapeutic relationship) and 40% to extra-therapeutic change.

The terms 'non-specific aspects' of therapy and 'common factors' are often used in the research literature and seem to map closely to the Rogerian principles of warmth, congruence and empathy. The research literature suggests that therapy without these factors is likely to be unproductive. It is unlikely that a good enough relationship will be made between client and therapist and no amount of brilliant technical model-based skill will produce a therapeutic outcome (Lambert & Barley, 2001).

Empirical work from a qualitative perspective also offers insight. It seems clear that clients want their therapist to be respectful, to listen to them, to be non-judgemental, to understand the importance of culture to individuals (Jim & Pistrang, 2007) and to have good interpersonal skills (Safran & Segal, 1990).

Counselling Psychology and the Therapeutic Relationship

Counselling psychologists traditionally see the therapeutic relationship as their most powerful therapeutic medium (du Plock, 2006). The discipline emerged from a desire to move towards a way of being with clients that would be non-directive, egalitarian and would take a holistic approach to understanding human wellbeing. The humanistic-phenomenological paradigm which underpins counselling psychology is seen as fundamental to this (Woolfe, 1990), as are the ethical values that run through counselling psychology. The moral principles of autonomy, beneficence, non-maleficence and fidelity (Shillito-Clark, 2001) are all experienced and embodied in relationships.

These values are guiding principles for the therapeutic relationship. Having training in at least two therapy models also allows counselling psychologists and their clients to find their way towards their own integrative model. Keeping all this – values, models and theoretical narratives – in mind is a complex and sometimes difficult task.

At this point it might be useful for us to peel away all the research, ideas and philosophies and take a look at what we are trying to do. The therapeutic endeavour involves two (sometimes more) people sitting – and being – together. We know that warmth, respect, genuineness and good interpersonal skills are necessary for a good therapy outcome; we have not yet looked at why. What is going on between two people that is therapeutic?

> I sat in my consulting room before Adele's first session trying to gather my thoughts and feelings about this referral. I was feeling nervous and on reflection thought that this might be connected to a sense of 'not knowing'. Adele was coming with a diagnosis that I was unfamiliar with and that I was in truth doubtful about. I had investigated the research literature and had been left more confused than before. I realised that I had been concentrating on the labels that were surrounding this referral and that I had yet to focus on the person. I readjusted my mind to a more curious, open-minded, flexible stance. I began to wonder about Adele herself and I set off down the corridor towards the waiting room to meet her.

The Evolved Mind and the Effects of Social Mentalities

Counselling psychology takes an integrative, holistic view of what it is to be human and so people are understood as embedded beings in their evolutionary histories as well as their present-day contexts (Milton & Gillies, 2007). It is not enough to try to understand a person's cognitions or emotions in the present in order to understand why relationships might be therapeutic. It is helpful to understand the evolutionary pressures that have moulded our minds and bodies so that we can understand why being with other humans can be both therapeutic and iatrogenic.

In his brief history of humanity, Dunbar (2004) outlines the view that the earliest primates lived 85 million years ago with the early ancestors of the hominids (the family of great ages and humans), migrating to Eurasia from Africa about 17 million years ago. The most recent species of humans, Homo sapiens, evolved between 400,000 and 250,000 years ago. Whilst there is much debate about the exact environmental pressures that guided modern human evolution, for the purposes of understanding the evolution of the mind it is useful to think about social pressures. An important factor is that humans evolved as social creatures. It is thought that early humans lived in groups of *up to* 150 members within which there were small sub-groupings (Dunbar, 2004). The biological driving forces for staying within the group include safety and genetic reproductive success. Those humans that evolved mental capacities that enabled them to be successful at staying in the group would have had a greater chance of passing on their genes.

Genetic reproductive success – your own and that of your kin – is known as an 'ultimate biological cause of behaviour'. Ultimate causes are based in unconscious, possibly hardwired psychological mechanisms which include care-giving and seeking, belonging to a group, mating and competing for resources within groups. Different organisms evolved different strategies for meeting these biological goals (Gilbert, 2005). Humans evolved into social beings and evolution provided a set of motivating and processing systems to meet these biosocial goals. Gilbert (2000) calls the mental competencies 'social mentalities'. These include attachment behaviours, social comparison, kin recognition, co-operation, competition and aggression towards others. Each social mentality contains a system whereby attention and motivation are elicited towards a biosocial goal.

Alternatively, 'proximate causes of behaviour' operate on the individual person over their lifespan. In other words, a person may be driven by their attachment system (ultimate cause) to look for affection, love, care-giving and care-seeking, but how they do this will be down to the proximate individual causes. For instance, a person might adapt to the social environment of their childhood in which love and care were restricted to times when the child succeeded by developing a narcissistic personality structure.

Evolved Social Mentalities and the Therapeutic Relationship

The client in your consulting room will bring ultimate and proximate biological causes of behaviour as do therapists, and so the therapeutic relationship is one that encompasses the layers of (conscious) day-to-day functioning as well as (unconscious) evolved social mentalities (Gilbert, 2000).

Attachment

Inspired by Charles Darwin, John Bowlby attempted to explain how our ancestors successfully overcame the first barrier to reproductive success – surviving the dangers of infancy (Holmes, 2001). He suggested that humans are hardwired to elicit care in others and to provide care for others. The important and useful point about attachment theory is the inclusion of the less than perfect environmental conditions (both physical and emotional) that influence different styles of being. In ideal conditions, a parent might be a secure base for the child, with the child and parent aligned in their care-eliciting and providing systems. When the child becomes scared the parent feels appropriate affect and responds well enough to the child for both of them to feel secure again. Both can then resume their work or play. In difficult (emotional or physical) environments the child, when scared, might attempt to elicit care, but the parent is not able to soothe the child appropriately. The child might then learn other methods of eliciting care, such as never letting the parent out of sight, or alternative methods of self-soothing (e.g. rocking, eating, etc.). In other words, the attachment system adapts to the circumstances it finds itself in.

This is an especially useful theory in the consulting room. By watching how our clients react to the therapeutic relationship through the lens of attachment theory, we are able to wonder about their attachment histories and their present relationships. Taking the idea that infants can only explore their environments freely when they feel they can return to a secure base, Holmes (2001) suggests that the therapeutic relationship needs to become a secure base from which clients can safely explore their inner worlds. If a client has a secure attachment history, this may be easy for the therapist to facilitate. By using the idea of a therapeutic frame (Milner, 1952), in which the therapist is on time for sessions, keeps to boundaries (both in session length and in sessions being held at the same time each week) and by sessions taking place in the same room, secure attachment is facilitated.

Fonagy (2002) has described a process of congruent, marked mirroring between a parent and infant whereby when a baby shows an affect, the care-giver responds by reflecting back to the baby that affect but in such a way that the baby knows that it is a reflection of its own affect. Unmarked mirroring by a care-giver happens when the care-giver responds to affect with their own affect. In other words, when a baby shows distress because of hunger a mother might respond with her own distress at the sound of the baby crying or she might walk away, showing disinterest or hostility. Neither is helpful. A therapist who is actively curious about and attending to the client in a calm manner, reflecting marked, congruent mirroring, will induce a sense of safety in a client.

However, a therapist needs to understand the nature of a client's attachment history as for some clients with a disorganised attachment history, activation of their attachment system can induce frightening affect. Allen *et al.* (2008) suggest that people with disturbed attachment histories become less able to think about their own and others' mental states (to mentalise) when they are faced with a raised attachment system. Unmarked or non-congruent mirroring can result in the baby forming a false sense of self, and hence the ability to think about one's own mental state and that of others becomes dysfunctional, especially when the attachment system is stimulated (Gergely, 2007). In mentalisation-based therapy (MBT), when the therapeutic relationship becomes activated, clients are helped to mentalise when their mentalising function is faltering. Allen *et al.* (2008) calls this 'mentalising in the trenches'. The therapeutic relationship in MBT is seen as a dance between activating the attachment system and pulling back so that mentalising can occur.

Staying in the Group

Literature from myriad disciplines suggests that social support is vital to physical, fiscal and mental wellbeing (Alloway & Bebbington, 1987). Being accepted by and kept within a group is a basic human need. This does not mean that people are all extraverts who want to be the life and soul of the party or that all people want to belong to the same group. We are drawn to different groups according to our backgrounds, our life experiences, our beliefs, and so on. The fundamental idea is that we are driven to belong to a group and that means that we are constantly comparing ourselves to others to find out if we belong or even if we might be related either biologically or psychologically. Bailey (1997) used Hamilton's theory of inclusive fitness and literature from social psychology research into in-/out-groups (Krebs & Denton, 1997) to develop a kinship theory of human nature. Bailey suggests that our psychological make-up includes mechanisms designed to promote social living (attachment behaviours, cooperation with neighbours) and to recognise the difference between those from your group and outsiders. Two mechanisms for successful group living are offered by the theory. The first is a mechanism for kin recognition. If a person is assessed as non-kin a cost–benefit assessment mechanism takes over. Bailey makes a distinction between psychological and biological kinship so that if a person is not kin, they can be recognised as a strong ally who is classed as psychological kin.

Kinship theory sees human distress as being caused by a mismatch between our modern way of living and the social aspect of the environment of evolutionary adaptedness (EEA) (Bailey, 1997). It would have been adaptive to have a strong response to strangers. In our modern world, we no longer live among our kin or even many psychological kin; instead, we are surrounded by strangers and it is suggested that reducing the anxiety and conflicts in relation to this mismatch is a major goal of evolutionary kinship therapy. This is played out in therapeutic relationships too. Although our modern mind accepts that the therapist is there to help us, our archaic mind still needs to assess our safety and potential for harm. Hence drop-out, resistance and non-engagement are always available evolutionary strategies.

The motivating feelings behind this social mentality may range from anxiety, fear, distrust and disgust to warmth, kin-like feelings and bonding behaviours, such as humour and agreements. Clients who have had negative experiences of being rejected by groups or being abused within groups may find the therapeutic relationship difficult to experience.

My first impression of Adele, sitting in the waiting room, was one of difference. She looked very young, seemed to be smouldering with anger, covered in facial piercings and very thin. As I called her name, she did not look at me but got up and followed me to the consulting room. As I walked in front of her, I found my mind wondering about how she was viewing me. I was making assumptions that she was probably thinking that I looked boring, middle-aged and similar to all the other mental health workers she had encountered so far. We reached the consulting room and sat down and I felt a million miles away from her. She looked, to me, angry, defensive and lonely.

Holding Mind in Mind

In the service of retaining group status, humans evolved social mentalities that have enabled us to understand that others have minds that are separate from our own, that others' minds might be different from our own and these social mentalities orient and motivate us to seek others' minds to receive us and hold us with good regard. In other words, we seek to be thought about, cared about, understood, wondered about and held in good esteem. At the same time, we are capable of understanding that we might be thought about with ill intent or that we might not be thought about at all. Although we may be born with the capacity for this theory of mind (Baron-Cohen, 1995), we need relationship for it to develop and function.

Most therapists will hold their client's mind in mind to some extent and this may well enable a sense of wellbeing in the client. However, in order to make this therapeutic, we need to foster a sense of caring for that mind, a sense that that mind matters to us, that we respect it and think well of it (this is not the same as colluding or blindly agreeing with the client). When counselling psychologists sit with clients using the values underpinning the philosophy of counselling psychology outlined above, they are essentially taking care of their client's mind in a manner that will engender a sense of wellbeing in the client. Research on mirror neurons (Brass & Heyes, 2005) has shown that emotional cues in one person can stimulate neurons in another's brain that activate the same emotion. This will work both ways in the therapeutic relationship as the client will be processing the therapist's emotional cues as well. This is resonant of the marked mirroring between infant and care-giver which engenders a healthy sense of self.

Of course, there are clients who have had negative experiences of being held in mind or for whom being held in mind is unfamiliar. For some clients, therefore, the experience of being held in mind by their therapist may induce distrust or, at worst, paranoia. Therapists need to be alert to how the relationship is affecting the client and withdraw as necessary. For example, if a client is showing signs of feeling uncomfortable in the therapy, a therapist might have to become a bit more distant (in a kind, not cold, manner) by looking away or allowing silence, or by talking about inconsequential issues. This might only have to be for a part of the session, just to allow the client to relax again.

Social Ranking Theory

Gilbert (1992, 2000) suggests that the human mind has evolved to be sensitive to attacks from other group members. Since human beings were evolving language and theory of mind, it became necessary for people to be able to wonder how other group members were perceiving them and whether or not they were acceptable to the group. If a person began to suspect that the group as a whole or some group members might expel them from the group, the person might use submission to avoid aggression or dismissal – a process apparent in the experience of depression (Gilbert, 1992). A person is safer being depressed on the margins of society than being cast out completely. Once a person feels included again, a useful member of a group, depression can lift. By using Rogerian values in the therapeutic relationship, therapists are enabling a depressed person to feel like a valued group member once again and they can then begin to shift from their depression.

Developing Ways of Being with Clients

Counselling psychology's relational and integrative stance allows for new, innovative and meaningful developments. For example, my colleague Hamilton Fairfax and I have integrated the above ideas and are developing and evaluating a group therapy, Adaptation-Based Process Therapy, for people who have had difficult attachment histories and have developed a negative self-relationship. The group is partly psycho-educational, where group members are given evolutionary explanations for their feelings and behaviours. They are encouraged to mentalise in the trenches when the affect of the group becomes raised and they are helped to develop a compassionate self-relationship. The group, meanwhile, acts as a secure base/in-group where the members can begin to explore issues of self-worth. The co-facilitators (two therapists) are encouraged to adopt an open, real, not-knowing stance to encourage the clients away from their possibly defensive positions towards more flexible and curious positions so that they then have more choice in how they feel, think and behave. The therapists hold in mind the idea that the group members have developed ways of dealing with less than ideal emotional environments. These coping mechanisms are validated as meaningful and understandable even though others may see them as problematic. The therapists reflect these back in a normalising way, using statements such as 'It's not surprising that you have had to feel like this . . .' and then use the group to come up with other possible ways of being. The therapists have an aim, through their stance and that of the other group members, of promoting each group member's social mentalities so that they can begin to function as if their emotional environment was a secure base.

Body Language

Given that so much of our social mental processing is unconscious it is likely that conscious, verbal language is but a small part of our communications with each other. When we sit with our clients our body language – most importantly our facial expressions – will affect the therapeutic relationships. When apes, and other animals, are observed it is possible to see how much they can communicate through body language. For instance, a horse will indicate its social ranking to other horses by putting its ears back and lengthening the neck, thereby initiating submissiveness behaviours, such as waiting in turn to get food. Apes spend much of their time grooming each other, which promotes group cohesion and security. However, it only takes a dominant male to stand up and stretch for the others to begin watching and possibly get ready to take action (Goodall, 1996).

In the consulting room, our facial expressions and body language will be communicating our inner world to some extent. Research has suggested that people with complicated attachment histories are more focused on picking up non-verbal cues. Whilst it is impossible to control some of our body language communication because it is non-conscious, we can also use this function to build the relationship. For instance, eye contact can be used to empower people who have adopted a depressive position as it might communicate an interest and respect. However, with other clients, it can be seen as a dominating, aggressive stance and hence some looking away in a submissive manner can de-escalate defensive stances. In general, taking a genuine, 'real' stance to the therapeutic relationship will mean that our verbal communication will match our non-verbal communication. In other words, if we feel confused, annoyed, irritated or ashamed, we might need to find a way of saying so – it is very possible that clients will sense it anyway. By being more open about what is in our minds, we can show the client that they are also in our minds and that minds can be influenced and changed.

Being with Humans and Their Evolved Minds

Researchers in social cognition have shown that attitudes, evaluations and impressions, emotions and social behaviour occur automatically and without awareness (Kihlstrom, 1996). It would seem that our ancient minds employ social mentalities to enable us to move effortlessly through the complexity of social living.

Evolutionary psychology literature suggests that in order to engender a sense of wellbeing in a client, we need to provide them with a secure base. By facilitating feelings of safety the client has a chance to explore; we need to show compassion so that the client can internalise self-compassion; feel empathy so that a client can learn about their own affect through mirroring processes and so that a client feels understood and thought about; hold the person in good regard to enable a person to feel like a valued, well-ranked member of a group; hold their mind in mind so that a client will feel thought of with good affect; be curious and flexible so that a client begins to understand that their mind can influence other minds; perhaps foster a kin-like relationship in order to promote beneficial physiological changes.

On paper, of course, this seems relatively straightforward. Before a session, a therapist can reflexively note their state of affect and engender, if necessary, a state of expectant warmth, respect and curiosity. However, in real life, a real person walks into the consulting room and the therapist is at once confronted with a stranger, who possibly activates various social mentalities in the therapist. According to their age, gender, ethnicity and sexuality clients will invoke meanings for each therapist, as will the therapist's 'badges of life' for the client. From the point of view of the therapist, the job is to notice their active social mentalities (in the consulting room or in supervision later) and move towards finding feelings of warmth and affect. By taking a stance of interest in the client, our partly unconscious defence processes can be addressed as the client moves from 'stranger' towards 'known' or even 'kin'.

Counselling psychology's pluralistic stance allows us to draw on an explanatory framework as to why and how the therapeutic relationship can be therapeutic in itself. By keeping social mentalities, ultimate and proximate mechanisms, the effects of body language, warmth, compassion and genuineness in mind, we can sit with our clients and be therapeutic.

The first few sessions with Adele were sometimes awkward as we both tried to understand this 'other' person. I found out that Adele had grown up in an extended family where she was one of eleven children who were either half- or step-siblings. Her history was so confusing that we decided to draw a genogram. This became so big that at one point we ended up with a poster-sized piece of paper on the floor side by side drawing out her 'who's who'. During this process, we discovered that we shared a sense of humour and this enabled us to begin to communicate. Once we had spent a few sessions lightly laughing, drawing on the floor, Adele began to feel secure enough to start exploring her inner world. However, throughout therapy, I had to tread a fine line between maintaining her trust and overwhelming her attachment system. I began to understand that when I started feeling deskilled she was probably feeling defensive and I needed to take a step back from the relationship.

During the therapy, Adele talked about other people that inhabited her. Using the principles of acceptance and non-judgement, I was able to be curious about what these personalities meant to Adele without having to make decisions or judgements about 'diagnosis'. Adele continued to talk about them but seemed less concerned by them and told me that she never wanted them to leave her as she would feel lonely. We began to make connections with her childhood and how she had felt lonely despite living with so many other children. It seemed that she was the only child that had no whole siblings and she had felt different from everyone else.

At the end of therapy, Adele said that other mental health practitioners had 'run screaming out of the room' (an exaggeration, I'm sure, but I understood her point) when she had walked in. She said that a turning point in our therapy had been when we had drawn her family tree together on the floor. She said that she had felt safe and she believed that I was interested in her and this had enabled her to continue returning to the therapy.

Note

[1] Adele is based on a true person. Her permission was sought to use this material and her name has been changed to ensure confidentiality.

References

Allen, J. G., Fonagy, P. & Bateman, A. W. (2008). *Mentalizing in clinical practice.* Arlington, VA: American Psychiatric Publishing.

Alloway, R. & Bebbington, P. (1987). The buffer theory of social support: A review of the literature. *Psychological Medicine, 17*(1): 91–108.

Bailey, K. G. (1997). Evolutionary kinship therapy: Merging integrative psychotherapy with the new kinship psychology. Paper presented at the annual meeting of the ASCAP Society, Tucson, AZ.

Baron-Cohen, S. (1995). *Mindblindness: An essay on autism and theory of mind.* Cambridge, MA: MIT Press.

Beck, A. T., Rush, J., Shaw, B. & Emery, G. (1979). *Cognitive therapy for depression.* New York: Guilford Press.

Bowlby, J. (1988). *A secure base.* New York: Basic Books.

Brass, M. & Heyes, C. (2005). Imitation: Is cognitive neuroscience solving the correspondence problem? *Trends in Cognitive Sciences, 9*: 489–495.

Clarkson, P. (1995). *The therapeutic relationship: In psychoanalysis, counselling psychology and psychotherapy.* London: Whurr.

du Plock, S. (2006). Just what is it that makes contemporary counselling psychology so different, so appealing? *Counselling Psychology Review, 21*: 22–32.

Dunbar, R. (2004). *The human story: A new history of man's evolution.* London: Faber and Faber.

Fonagy, P. (2002). Understanding of mental states, mother–infant interaction and the development of the self. In J. M. Maldonado-Duran (Ed.) *Infant and toddler mental health: Models of clinical intervention with infants and their families.* Washington, DC: American Psychiatric Publishing.

Freud, S. (1914). The history of the psychoanalytic movement (Trans. A. A. Brill). In *Nervous and mental disease monograph series* (No. 25). New York: Nervous and Mental Disease Pub. Co.

Gelso, C. J. & Carter, J. A. (1985). The relationship in counselling and psychotherapy: Components, consequences and theoretical antecedents. *The Counseling Psychologist, 13*(2): 155–243.

Gergely, G. (2007). The social construction of the subjective self: The role of affect mirroring, markedness and ostensive communication in self development. In L. C. Mayes, P. Fonagy & M. Target (Eds.) *Developmental science and psychoanalysis.* London: Karnac.

Gilbert, P. (1992). *Depression: The evolution of powerlessness.* Hove: Psychology Press.

Gilbert, P. (2000). Social mentalities. In P. Gilbert & K.G. Bailey (Eds.) *Genes on the couch: Explorations in evolutionary psychotherapy*. London: Routledge.

Gilbert, P. (2005). Compassion and cruelty: A biopsychosocial approach. In P. Gilbert (Ed.) *Compassion: Conceptualisations, research and use in psychotherapy*. Hove: Routledge.

Gilbert, P. (2007). Evolved minds and compassion in the therapeutic relationship. In P. Gilbert & R.L. Leahy (Eds.) *The therapeutic relationship in the cognitive behavioural psychotherapies*. Hove: Routledge.

Goodall, J. (1996). *In the shadow of man*. London: Phoenix Giants.

Holmes, J. (2001). *The search for the secure base: Attachment theory and psychotherapy*. Hove: Brunner-Routledge.

Jim, J. & Pistrang, N. (2007). Culture and the therapeutic relationship: Perspectives from Chinese clients. *Psychotherapy Research, 17*(4): 461–473.

Kihlstrom, J. F. (1996). Unconscious processes in social interaction. In S. R. Hameroff (Ed.) *Toward a science of consciousness: The first Tucson discussions and debates*. Cambridge, MA: MIT Press.

Krebs, D. L. & Denton, K. (1997). Social illusions and self-deception: The evolution of biases in person perception. In J. A. Simpson & D.T. Kenrick (Eds.) *Evolutionary social psychology*. Mahwah, NJ: Lawrence Erlbaum Associates.

Lambert, M. J. & Barley, D. E. (2001). Research summary on the therapeutic relationship and psychotherapy outcome. *Psychotherapy: Theory, Research, Practice, Training, 38*: 357–361.

Luborsky, L. B. (1994). Therapeutic alliances as predictors of psychotherapy outcomes. In O. A. Horvath & L.S. Greenberg (Eds.) *The working alliance: Theory, research and practice*. New York: Wiley.

Milner, M. (1952). Aspects of symbolism in comprehension of the not-self. *International Journal of Psycho-Analysis, 33*: 181–195.

Milton, M. & Gillies, F. (2007). From biology to *Being*: Evolutionary theory and existential practice. *Existential Analysis, 18*(2): 247–260.

Norcross, J. (2002). *Psychotherapy relationships that work: Therapist contributions and responsiveness to patients*. Oxford: Oxford University Press.

Rogers, C. R. (1957). The necessary and sufficient conditions of therapeutic personality change. *Journal of Consulting and Clinical Psychology, 21*: 95–103.

Safran, J. D. & Segal, Z. (1990). *Interpersonal processes in cognitive therapy*. New York: Basic Books.

Shillito-Clark, C. (2001). Ethical issues in counselling psychology. In R. Woolfe & Dryden (Eds.) *Handbook of counselling psychology*. London: Sage.

Woolfe, R. (1990). Counselling psychology in Britain: An idea whose time has come. *The Psychologist, 3*(12): 531–535.

Chapter 6

Ethics: *The* Fundamental Dimension of Counselling Psychology

Camilla Olsen

This chapter argues that ethics lies at the very heart of counselling psychology practice and is central to relational understandings. The importance of ethical thinking is apparent in therapeutic practice, supervisory work, research and activities that extend beyond the consulting room. But first, some definitions.

Ethics

Ethics has been defined as 'the science of morality or of duty' (Palmer Barnes & Murdin, 2001, p. 2). It is a complex domain, with understandings of ethics being influenced by concepts of morality as well as debates around the nature of human will. Western (capitalist) societies consider us as free human beings responsible for our own actions and, in light of this, we accept that we must take the consequences of these actions. Key ethical concepts include value judgements or morals, which are subjective stances taken in relation to someone or something. The role of values means that people view things as better or worse and we have responsibility and are accountable for that view (Palmer-Barnes & Murdin, 2001). Jordan and Meara (1990) make a useful differentiation between *virtue* and *principle*

Therapy and Beyond: Counselling Psychology Contributions to Therapeutic and Social Issues
Edited by Martin Milton
© 2010 John Wiley & Sons, Ltd.

ethics, describing virtue ethics as an underlying layer offering guidance on how to act as human beings generally, and principle ethics which are used to guide us as practitioners on specifics of therapeutic practice.

Key ethical principles include aiming to maximise benefit and minimise harm, respecting autonomy, achieving the greatest good and acting justly (Palmer-Barnes, 1998).

Morality

Moral principles are thought of as standards of intention and conduct created by and for individuals, or as obligations and duties that society demands (Ashley *et al.*, 2006; Boeree, 1999). Morality is complex, relating as it always does to actual people and real situations, with judgement being difficult from outside that situation. Truth is a matter of perspective with each individual constructing their own understanding of reality (Boeree, 1999).

Professional Complexity

In medicine, Percival wrote the first rudimentary guidelines to distinguish between good and poor medical practice (Leake, 1975), and professional bodies continue to recognise the obligation to set and uphold the highest standards of professionalism as well as the promotion of ethical behaviour on the part of practitioners.

When it comes to ethical decision-making, the guidance offered by professional bodies varies. The British Psychological Society Division of Counselling Psychology takes a broad stance in its guidelines in order to respect their application across varied contexts. Other bodies are more prescriptive (Bond, 2005). Either way, the objective has been to develop useful and practical concepts out of complex philosophical debates (Pope & Vasques, 1998). Ethical guidance is, of course, based on beliefs and values specific to the society in which the organisation operates (Cooper, 1992) and this has an impact on the structure and style of the guidance provided.

While professional bodies' codes of conduct rest on virtue ethics, guidelines for practice are considered as 'principle' codes as they focus on the way the therapeutic practitioner behaves in relation to the individual client, reminding therapists, for example, to value the dignity and worth of all persons, to attend to clients with sensitivity towards the dynamics of perceived authority or influence over clients; and also assist us in being mindful of a person's rights, including those of privacy and self-determination (British Psychological Society, 2004).

As well as providing guidance to their practitioners, Bond advocates that the professional body's role should also encompass the development of their members' ethical minds further, in order to enhance their ethical mindfulness (1999, 2005).

This chapter now offers insight into the range of contexts and tasks in which ethical thinking is both expected and useful.

Ethics in Therapy

Therapeutic work often takes place in private, with very little outside observation, relying instead on professional and ethical decision-making. Therapeutic work requires boundaries as it provides focus and facilitates a trusting working alliance – the key to effective therapeutic practice (Gelso & Carter, 1985).

Working with boundaries is helped by contracting with clients. Contracts are specific, depending on client, therapist and context, but usually incorporate confidentiality and the limits thereof, statements about where, how often and when the sessions take place, as well as clarifying other issues such as out-of-hours contact. Each of these components can be complex in itself.

We can take confidentiality as just one example. It is seldom absolute. In our culture a frequent limit to confidentiality are those circumstances where the client becomes a risk to self or others. Principle ethics reminds practitioners that we should consider the ways we can assist clients in engaging with relevant support systems in order to reflect on and manage any difficult periods they are facing, an aim that, at one level, seems quite straightforward. However, other factors affect our decision, some of which threaten the therapeutic relationship. Where a therapist thinks that other systems may be helpful the ethical therapist has to be mindful of *how* to obtain consent to contact others. Therapists have, after all, agreed to respect the client's confidentiality.

Often a discussion with a client leads to consent and participation. But there are some circumstances where consent is not granted and the practitioner may have to consider acting in a way that is contrary to the client's wishes. In these circumstances it is necessary to be clear about what the implications of breaching confidentiality are for the therapeutic relationship, the client's wellbeing and that of those around them.

The issue becomes more ethically complex when there is a need to inform a third party and also, in rare situations, where legal procedures require it, where practitioners might have to breach confidentiality *without* informing the client. This is a very rare occurrence, for example, in situations where illegal activity such as terrorism is present, and will follow legal advice. Alongside the care of the client the practitioner has to reflect on the risk to the wider population if the appropriate authority is not informed and whether any of the actions can be legally defended. In some cases, the breach of confidentiality may even have to be kept from the client in order not to obstruct any investigation. The concept of 'autonomy' can conflict with the requirement to act for the greater good.

While there are many other possible scenarios that could be provided, the point has been made: practice is ethically complex and, while closely related, 'legality' and 'ethical status' are discrete concepts.

Multidisciplinary working is another context where ethical practice is seen to be as a complex undertaking. One issue is perspective; another is power. It is not always obvious to different professionals when information should be shared; they may hold different worldviews in relation to human nature, therapy and the role of statutory services. It is important for teams to clarify what expectations there are for *all* the professionals involved with a client and what the confidentiality boundaries are and inform the client of where these boundaries lie. Having said this, the complexity means that it can be difficult to provide a clear-cut answer to this issue as it must always be focused on the current circumstances affecting the client, context, therapist and others.

Many multidisciplinary teams have a 'team confidentiality protocol', which allows all the practitioners involved with a client to discuss issues freely without seeking prior consent from the client. However, this does *not* mean that a practitioner has *carte blanche* to divulge what happens within the therapeutic relationship. Information would normally be shared on a 'need to know' basis, with the client's consent. Again, the reader will not be surprised that it can sometimes be difficult to ascertain when and what to share, as 'need to know' is a highly subjective concept. The practitioner's judgement may be called into question by different people. The only way to avoid unnecessary confusion is to create good communication channels based on good professional relationships among all parties involved.

Even the choice of therapeutic approach raises ethical questions for practitioners to consider. One ethical issue occurs when clients see the world differently from the therapist. Drawing on experience, latest research or NICE guidelines might lead a therapist to suggest a particular approach to specific difficulties. The model may have great value, but issues are raised when that approach makes no sense to the client. In those circumstances we have to ask 'Whose worldview has priority?' As well as notions of 'evidence', ethical thinking means we must reflect on power relationships in the outlining of approaches and agreeing ways forward. Power relationships are important to consider as they can be open to deliberate and/or inadvertent abuse by practitioners.

The development of competence in more than one therapeutic model is a key contribution of counselling psychology training as it supports a broader view on how to formulate psychological difficulties as well as ways of working with clients. A greater knowledge base enables the practitioner to take more angles into account when difficult ethical decisions need to be made. This is particularly relevant in a multicultural society, with different worldviews needing recognition, attention and consideration. (See Chapter 1 for an elaboration of the concept of pluralism.)

Ethics in Supervision

Supervision, another area of counselling psychology practice, is equally based on ethical principles, with much of the focus being on respect, competence, responsibility and integrity (Pope & Vasques, 2007). Research has shown that the best use of supervision happens when there has been good contracting between supervisor and supervisee (Morrissey, 2005). This is particularly important when supervisors are allocated rather than chosen. Contracting includes discussing and agreeing on at least the following: expectations, frequency, fee, confidentiality, roles, responsibilities and the purpose of meetings. Preferably, contracting occurs prior to initiating the supervisory relationship (Morrissey, 1998; Proctor, 1997). This may sound straightforward, but as in the therapeutic domain some of these issues are not clear-cut. For example, even though the supervisory relationship is *essentially* confidential, confidentiality is again not absolute since the supervisor may receive supervision on their supervision, or the supervisor may have to inform a training organisation or workplace as part of assessment or appraisal. Further, the role of the supervisor is primarily to encourage and support, challenge and evaluate the supervisee's clinical work so that harmful practice can be prevented. However, there may be times when it is necessary to breach the boundaries, for example, where the supervisee's fitness to practice is uncertain (Barden, 2005) or if there were ethical problems with the practitioner's conduct or work (Scaife, 2001). Due to this complexity it is important to be clear from the outset who is responsible for the supervisee's client work. In the UK it is normally the practitioner and not the supervisor (Bond, 2000), but there is much debate regarding the issue of clinical responsibility of the supervisor (Milton, 2009).

Supervisors are supported to a certain degree by codes of ethics; thorough discussions with colleagues and peers are also invaluable (Morrissey, 2005). Supervisory discussions enable practitioners to make ethical decisions by thinking the issues through, and being able to explain and justify any actions taken (Pope & Vasques, 2007). An illustration of mutual learning from my own supervision highlights the complexities of ethical decision-making.

> My colleague and I discussed the issue of dealing with visible, albeit undisclosed, domestic violence, and how hard it can be to contain and work with the 'unspoken' that the client brings. We attempted to think through the risk elements as well as other ethical dilemmas such as the right to autonomy and to therapeutic confidentiality. The most helpful aspect of the supervisory discussion was that we managed to highlight yet unseen therapeutic processes of communication of secrecy and fragility in order to elicit caring from others and by attending to them the index issue resolved itself and a therapeutic way forward was discovered.

Although ethical guidelines and various models of practice exist, practitioners need to use their professional judgement when weighing up multiple and often competing demands, needs and goals (Barnett *et al.*, 2007). While it is tempting to look for a code which answers all ethical dilemmas (West, 2002), Bond sees a number of challenges in trying to use just one code expecting it to fit all potential ethical problems. In a multicultural world, any such code would be so large as to be unwieldy. Therefore, Bond (1999, 2005) argues that a better answer is to be found in his notion of ethical mindfulness.

Ethics in the Research Process

Research has become an important part of evaluating the outcome of psychological therapy and it is important to be innovative and to develop theories and new practices for different forms of distress and life experiences. As noted in Chapter 3, counselling psychology, based as it is on the scientist-practitioner model, has long questioned the usefulness of quantitative (epidemiological) research as the *sole* focus in the quest for understanding the contributions the psychotherapies can make. Research based primarily on large-scale quantitative data can lead to ethical dilemmas. At the core of research ethics is the need to respect the needs of different constituents – individuals and populations – but large-scale quantitative research often cannot access the individual human experience. Therefore problems associated with the prioritising of large-scale trends must be considered. The advantage of using qualitative paradigms is becoming increasingly evident as they allow the perspective of individuals and their meaning-making to be heard (Willig, 2001). It is as useful to have multiple research models as it is to have multiple therapeutic models (Coyle & Olsen, 2005; Pope *et al.*, 2000).

The need to consider ethical issues at all levels begins at the very start of the research process. In universities and organisations such as the NHS, research proposals are usually scrutinised by ethical research committees. These committees play an important role in evaluating whether or not the proposed research will offer useful knowledge to a greater audience, the level of risk involved and the decision as to whether it is an acceptable risk. They will also be of assistance by helping consider the researcher's plan to disseminate the research findings as a way of influencing practice and policy (Cowie & Glachan, 2000). These committees ensure that researchers adhere to the key ethical principles (Emanuel *et al.*, 2000).

Informed consent is as important a concept in research as it is in psychological therapy. Ethically, all participants should be offered information of the research topic, an awareness of what participating will involve, the potential risks and benefits of the research, confidentiality and their right to withdraw at any time, as well as what happens to the data and how they can access the findings after the study's completion (see Coyle & Olsen, 2005). Attention also needs to be given to how participants who experience distress due to taking part will be dealt with immediately and how they will be followed up (Bowen & John, 2001; Roberts, 2002).

Ethics beyond the Consulting Room

When thinking mindfully about ethics, a challenge facing psychologists is to find a way to extend their understanding beyond their own area in order to relate to the widest range of people. Counselling psychology recognises that, as we live in a multicultural society, we influence, and are influenced by, our sociohistorical contexts. Therefore, ethical thinking is not just something to do with clients, but must be with us in our wider roles as well. For example, without thinking broadly, there is a danger that an exclusively Western approach loses sight of key norms and worldviews (Marsella and Pedersen (2004)). For example, leaving aside the complex issue of whether or not psychiatric diagnosis is ethical (Szasz, 1995), in the concept of post-traumatic stress disorder Marwaha and Livingston (2002) suggest that Western understandings of the disorder, with assumptions of individual trauma and individual pathways to recovery being seen as typical, mean that other understandings are considered atypical, or not considered at all. Although the value of individual experience is important, it is a Western idea that the individual is more important than the collective. In many cultures the collective experience is what people are aware of and it is this that supports the healing process (Satkunagaram, 2008).

Ethically, it is important to be aware of these insights so as to max-imise good and do no harm and to support communities where trauma has occurred. This may not sound particularly difficult. But as with other ethical dilemmas there are times when we need to understand experiences which could otherwise be judged meaningless or odd, or when the behaviours are judged to be negative or even unlawful. Pelling (2004) argues that coun-selling psychology is a leader in culture-centred practice in the USA, Canada and New Zealand due to the profession's valuing of a range of knowledge/s. He warns that the search for easy answers may lead us into a more prescrip-tive approach where we lose sight of individual meaning and our principle of respecting the subjective experience of individuals and communities.

Situations like this raise the question of whether or not codes of ethics can successfully cross international boundaries. If one accepts an abso-lutist approach, there is seen to be a universal standard of ethical conduct irrespective of cultural tradition. On the other hand, if ethics are relative, then culture and tradition negate any such universal standard. A compro-mise is that of 'soft universalism', which means that a universal standard is assumed, but which can be softened by individual cultures and traditions (Barnett *et al.*, 2007). Soft universalism, coupled with respectful dialogue, has been advocated as a very useful way to negotiate ethical differences where cultures (of countries or of individuals) do not correspond (Knapp & Van der Creek, 2007). The outcome should be to seek a solution that will satisfy professional values and the values of clients alike.

Suggestions

While all therapists aspire to ethical practice, there are questions as to how we *do* it. It is a complex task, crossing contexts and cultures. It may never be absolute, yet it is helpful when therapeutic practitioners feel they can at least clarify their ethical judgements to themselves as well as to lay people and other professionals. Haug (1999) argues that it is important before making any ethical judgement that practitioners ask themselves a range of questions, including:

'Will this be helpful to the client?'
'Will this cause harm to the client?'
'Is my action consistent with that of any of my colleagues'?'
'Have I allowed myself to become impartial or influenced so that my judge-ment will not be objective?'

In order to do this well, it is necessary to be familiar with one's core beliefs and value systems. This is important as we are likely to be faced with situations where it is necessary to suspend our own beliefs and values in order to reach ethical decisions. Therefore, it is imperative that we know what these values are.

It is also necessary to trust and respect dialogue. It is for this reason that counselling psychology values ongoing supervision and personal therapy. Another way counselling psychology has attempted to deal with flexible thinking about phenomena and human experience has been to embrace multiple theoretical and relational frameworks. Knowledge of several approaches to practice allows therapists flexibility and is important as it is unreasonable to expect all clients and supervisees to benefit from a single theoretical angle. Relational frameworks assist us in keeping the experiences of others in mind.

Conclusion

Although ethics can seem complex and frightening it adds a dimension to therapeutic work that enables the practitioner to remain focused on the quest for increased knowledge, greater attentiveness and more flexible practice. Only by thinking of standards of therapy and conduct can we question practice and be innovative and creative in the development of personal and professional methods that can aid people to become more content with their lives. The danger for practitioners is that if ethics is perceived as a threat to practice, then the only achievement will be a fear of change and stifling of knowledge; therefore, we are best served if we embrace the debates as a challenge to increase our understanding.

References

Ashley, B. M., DeBlois, J. & O'Rourke, K. D. (2006). *Health care ethics: A Catholic theological analysis*. (5th edn.). Washington, DC: Georgetown University.

Barden, N. (2005). The responsibility of the supervisor in the British Association for Counselling and Psychotherapy's code of ethics and practice. In S. Wheeler & D. King (Eds.) *Supervising counsellors: Issues of responsibilities*. London: Sage.

Barnett, J. E., Behinke, S. H., Rosenthal, S. L. & Koocher, G. P. (2007). In case of ethical dilemma. Break glass: Commentary on ethical decision making in practice. *Professional Psychology, Research and Practice*, 28(1): 7–12.

Boeree, G. (1999). *Ethics.* webspace.ship.edu/cgboer/ethics.html. Accessed 15 November 2008.

Bond, T. (1999). European developments. One size fits all? The quest for a European ethic for counselling and psychotherapy. *European Journal of Psychotherapy, Counselling and Health*, 2(3): 375–388.

Bond, T. (2000). *Standards and ethics for counselling in action.* (2nd edn.). London: Sage.

Bond, T. (2005). Developing and monitoring professional ethics and good practice guidelines. In R. Tribe & J. Morrissey (Eds.) *Handbook of professional and ethical practice for psychologists, counsellors and psychotherapists.* Hove: Brunner-Routledge.

Bowen, A. C. L. & John, M. H. (2001). Ethical issues encountered in qualitative research: Reflections on interviewing adolescent in-patients engaging in self-injurious behaviours. *Counselling Psychology Review*, 16(2): 19–23.

British Psychological Society (2004). *Code of conduct, ethical principles and guidelines.* Leicester: British Psychological Society.

Cooper, G. F. (1992). Ethical issues in counselling and psychotherapy. The background. *British Journal of Guidance and Counselling*, 20(1): 1–9.

Cowie, H. & Glachan, M. (2000). Designing and disseminating research in counselling psychology. *Counselling Psychology Review*, 15(3): 27–30.

Coyle, A. & Olsen, C. (2005). Research in therapeutic practice settings: Ethical considerations. In R. Tribe & J. Morrissey (Eds.) *Handbook of professional and ethical practice for psychologists, counsellors and psychotherapists.* Hove: Brunner-Routledge.

Emanuel, E. J., Wendler, D. & Grady, C. (2000). What makes clinical research ethical? *Journal of the American Medical Association*, 283: 2701–2711.

Gelso, C. J. & Carter, J. A. (1985). The relationship in counselling and psychotherapy: Components, consequences and theoretical antecedents. *The Counseling Psychologist*, 13(2): 155–243.

Haug, I. (1999). Boundaries and the use and misuse of power and authority: Ethical complexities for clergy psychotherapists. *Journal of Counseling and Development*, 77(4): 411–417.

Jordan, A. E. & Meara, N. M. (1990). Ethics and the professional practice of psychologists: The role of virtues and principles. *Professional Psychology: Research and Practice*, 21: 107–114.

Knapp, S. & Van der Creek, L. (2007). When values of different cultures conflict: Ethical decision making in a multicultural context. *Professional Psychology, Research and Practice*, 38(6): 660–668.

Leake, C. D. (1975). *Percival's medical ethics.* New York: Robert E. Krieger.

Marsella, A. J. & Pedersen, P. (2004). Internationalizing the counselling psychology curriculum: Toward new values, competencies and directions. *Counselling Psychology Quarterly*, 17(4): 413–423.

Marwaha, S. & Livingston, G. (2002). Stigma, racism or choice. Why do depressed ethnic elders avoid psychiatrists? *Journal of Affective Disorders*, 72(3): 257.

Milton, M. (2009). Supervision as we know it: An existential impossibility. In E. van Deurzen & S. Young (Eds.) *Existential perspectives on supervision in counselling and psychotherapy*. Basingstoke: Palgrave Macmillan.

Morrissey, J. (1998). Contracting and supervision. *Counselling Psychology Review*, *13*(1): 13–17.

Morrissey, J. (2005). Training supervision: Professional and ethical considerations. In R. Tribe & J. Morrissey (Eds.) *Handbook of professional and ethical practice for psychologists, counsellors and psychotherapists*. Hove: Brunner-Routledge.

Palmer-Barnes, F. (1998). *Complaints and grievances in psychotherapy: A handbook of ethical practice*. London: Routledge.

Palmer-Barnes, F. & Murdin, L. (2001). *Values and ethics in the practice of psychotherapy and counselling*. Buckingham: Open University Press.

Pelling, N. (2004). Counselling psychology: Diversity and commonalities across the western world. *Counselling Psychology Review*, *17*(3): 239–245.

Pope, C., Ziebland, S. & Mays, N. (2000). Qualitative research in health care: Analysing qualitative date. *British Medical Journal*, *320*: 114–116.

Pope, K. S. & Vasques, M. J. (2007). *Ethics in psychotherapy and counseling: A practical guide* (3rd edn.) (New York: Jossey-Bass.). (First published 1998.)

Proctor, B. (1997). Contracting in supervision. In C. Sills (Ed.) *Contracts in counselling*. London: Sage.

Roberts, L. W. (2002). Ethics and mental illness research. *Psychiatric Clinics of North America*, *25*: 525–545.

Satkunagaram, K. (2008). The realities of caring: A qualitative exploration of mental health professionals' experience of working with survivors of trauma in Sri Lanka. Unpublished doctoral thesis, University of East London.

Scaife, J. (2001). *Supervision in the mental health professions: A practitioner's guide*. Hove: Brunner-Routeledge.

Szasz, T. (1995). Taking dialogue as therapy seriously: 'Words are the essential tool of treatment'. *Existential challenges to psychotherapeutic theory and practice*. London: Society for Existential Analysis.

West, W. (2002). Some ethical dilemmas in counselling and counselling research. *British Journal of Guidance and Counselling*, *30*(3): 261–268.

Willig, C. (2001). *Introducing qualitative research in psychology: Adventures in theory and method*. Buckingham: Open University Press.

Section 2

Models of Practice

Models of Practice

Martin Milton

Section 1 has highlighted the importance of the key concepts and values that permeate counselling psychology. One well-known area of particular importance to counselling psychology is the psychotherapeutic approach taken in our practice with clients. This is the focus of Section 2.

In the past a great deal of energy was expended clarifying specific frameworks so that, for instance, psychoanalysis was viewed as something completely separate from cognitive-behavioural theory, which in turn was seen as having very little relationship to humanistic therapies. And in some respects this pressure continues today, with governmental and other pressures working to construct specific models of therapy as distinct from *all* others, so that, like branded sore throat remedies, they can compete with each other. This constructs the view that it is possible to assess *the* model that works for a specific person. This perspective is manifest in some versions of evidence-based practice, NICE guidelines for specific psychological disorders, National Occupational Standards, and the like.

Counselling psychologists recognise that people are seldom as uniform as this movement would have us believe. For many people, the issues that they struggle with are multi-dimensional. Presenting problems have a vast array of causes and experiences and it can be counterproductive to narrow down psychological knowledge and practice in a restrictive manner. Just as we know that climate change is not a one-factor phenomenon, but is affected by population growth, technological change, airplane exhausts, shipping and a range of other things, so counselling psychologists look at all the variables involved in what affects a specific client and what individual people will respond to. Therefore, in much psychological practice it is not a case of *either* CBT *or* psychodynamic therapy (certainly not prior to an in-depth understanding of the client), but rather how the therapist draws on all the appropriate and useful material available in the range of psychological approaches that are studied.

The preferred model has to be useful and adaptable to the range of people and contexts in which we as counselling psychologists work. Taking just one manual off the shelf limits us in meeting the real and varied needs of the range of people and complexity that we encounter. Flexibility and adaptability is a hallmark of counselling psychology practice and the contributors to this section outline their approaches in a number of ways.

In Chapter 7, Riccardo Draghi-Lorenz goes straight to the nub of the matter by outlining the impact that 'different theoretical differences and contextual influences' have on the form and function of different therapeutic approaches. This chapter proposes a model for theoretical integration which focuses on the role of social factors and considers the way in which the context influences our work and health care provision more generally. The chapter looks at some of the epistemological and practical challenges that exist in working in the various contexts and how these are managed. The chapter also illustrates the ways in which psychotherapeutic and counselling psychology practice can facilitate creative and sophisticated ways within these systems.

The authors of the next four chapters focus on particular therapeutic approaches. They resist the often encountered 'recipe book' approach and keep in mind the ways in which they work with this model *alongside* other information that their research and therapeutic work benefits from.

Heidi Ashley opens Chapter 8 with a brief discussion of the emergence of humanistic counselling in the 1950s and acknowledges the philosophical and epistemological debt owed by counselling psychology. The point is made, however, that counselling psychologists are not humanistic therapists but scientist-practitioners who navigate different models in a constant process of reflection. This chapter argues that an ethos of humanism is fundamental to this process.

Beginning with assessment and formulation, the chapter considers what humanistic contributions to pluralistic practice actually mean – for example, going beyond the mere taking of a history to elaborate personal meanings, extend awareness, 'depathologise' the client's narrative and offer a relationship. This is contrasted with the medicalised and pathologising language of psychiatric assessment and diagnosis. The chapter goes on to consider how a humanistic stance guides model selection and implementation by enabling practitioners to move between models whilst remaining grounded in relationship. The chapter also considers how a pluralistic approach based on humanistic principles provides a surer footing for evaluating therapies.

In Chapter 9, Debora Diamond gives us an insight into the ways in which psychodynamic theory and practice offer crucially important insights into people's experiences while still being drawn on in a flexible manner. This chapter explores the ways in which psychodynamic practice makes a contribution to counselling psychology practice by using examples from practice in in-patient settings. Thus it is not simply a chapter that describes 'psychodynamic' history, theory or practice, but one that addresses the ways in which it can be drawn on in new and creative ways, at times to challenge other forms of knowing but at times to facilitate a multiplicity of understandings that enhance our understandings of people, processes, people's talents and their struggles.

Chapter 10 sees Terry Boucher immerse himself in the different manifestations of CBT in an effort to demystify the myth of CBT that is growing (i.e. it is a thing to be applied through one specific manual). In doing so he highlights how CBT is not necessarily doomed to a mechanistic, manualised, diagnostic way of being. The chapter sheds light on the usefulness of the knowledge of CBT from a range of epistemological positions and ways of working. The chapter also shows the ways in which a relational counselling psychology perspective enriches this approach to therapy and contributes to work in community mental health and addictions services.

In Chapter 11, Elena Manafi provides a clear description of existential therapy before giving us a flavour of the experience through an extended reflection on therapeutic practice. The chapter demonstrates how the existential-phenomenological approach offers a meaningful and non-pathologising understanding of people, which enhances the ways in which therapeutic relationships can be offered to clients in a pluralistic world.

While the contributors to this section all reflect on the notion of practice in different ways, it is clear that they practise counselling psychology in a theoretically sound yet flexible manner. This section shows how, despite the forceful positivistic discourse that surrounds discussion of approaches to practice, the artistry (and humanity) of the therapist remains a crucial aspect of the work they do and of the benefit counselling psychologists offer people in distress.

Chapter 7

Different Theoretical Differences and Contextual Influences

Riccardo Draghi-Lorenz

Counselling psychology in the UK promotes openness to virtually any theoretical approach to psychotherapy, from those tied to experimental psychology, such as behavioural therapies, to those influenced by Eastern philosophies and religions, such as meditation practices. Such openness fosters variety, vitality, creativity, adaptability to context and the overall strength of the discipline. However, it also presents us with a challenge – how can we accommodate unlimited theoretical diversity yet avoid confusion or contradiction? Should we assume an eclectic stance and use different theories separately, each in its own right, or is such an open attitude non-scientific and should we instead reduce variation, for instance by way of theoretical integration? Or are there theoretical differences that call for integration, differences that require eclecticism and perhaps differences that demand yet other operations? Furthermore, how influential is our social, cultural and personal context on how we respond to theoretical differences?

The aim of this chapter is twofold. First, it identifies a set of 'different differences' among theories and the kind of operations that we can implement to reduce or contain them. Secondly, it draws examples from the history of psychotherapy to stress how our theoretical positioning has as much to do with the context as with the quest for truth and/or effective therapy. Albeit inherent, contextual influences are not always beneficial and it will be

Therapy and Beyond: Counselling Psychology Contributions to Therapeutic and Social Issues
Edited by Martin Milton
© 2010 John Wiley & Sons, Ltd.

argued that theoretical and epistemological openness is ultimately the best insurance against their negative effects. The overarching goal is to present a counselling psychology perspective on how to cope with the confusion and contradictions ensuing from this openness.

Differences between Theories

When comparing theories one can note several kinds of difference. Some may be formal and easy to discount, some appear more serious but can be still accommodated for, whilst others appear radical or even incommensurable. They can be grouped as differences of terminology, emphasis, content and epistemology. These differences are not categorical but as they cannot be stretched on a continuum either may be best considered separately.

Terminological Differences

Occasionally, new terms are coined to refer to phenomena or ideas that are not represented in existing theoretical terminologies. The term 'projective identification', for instance, was developed to indicate a specific unconscious interaction between two or more individuals for which no such succinct name was previously available (Klein, 1946; Segal, 1974). In similar cases new terms are clearly useful as they afford a shared means of reference. However, most often new terms are developed for referents that are already named and explained in other theories, leading to a mismatch between terminological differences and underlying theoretical similarities. This is an ever-recurrent phenomenon as the following brief history demonstrates.

In the late 1880s Pierre Janet argued that people can suffer from 'fixed ideas' or 'psychological systems' which act as subconscious organisers of behaviours, moods, affects and perceptions but are unrelated to present circumstances, derive from past traumatic events and are not subject to conscious will (Ellenberger, 1970). Later, Breuer and Freud (1957) offered a very similar definition of their term 'complex', which as summarised in Laplanche and Pontalis's dictionary of psychoanalysis reads:

> Organised group of ideas and memories of great affective force which are either partly or totally unconscious. Complexes are constituted on the basis of the interpersonal relationships of childhood history; they may serve to structure all levels of the psyche: emotions, attitudes, adapted behaviour.
>
> (1988, p. 72)

More than half a century later Rogers (1959) similarly described 'internal conditions of worth' as beliefs that are derived from interactions with significant others, which specify the conditions the individual must satisfy in order to be worthwhile and that, again, affect all psychological processes outside conscious awareness so that experiences or events inconsistent with them are denied or distorted. A decade later, Beck (1967) defined 'core beliefs' as rigid and emotionally charged learned assumptions about self and others, which affect thinking, perception, action and emotion below individual awareness. Around the same time Berne (1972) spoke of introjected parental 'injunctions' and 'counter-injunctions' which, once again, direct behaviour, feelings and cognition in the most important areas of life, limit awareness, spontaneity and autonomy and ultimately confirm maladaptive existential positions about self and others. Two decades later Young (1990) defined schemas as wide, pervasive themes regarding self and relationships with others, the foundations of which are developed in childhood and are dysfunctional to a notable extent. Furthermore, all these authors argue that whilst unhelpful and ultimately conducive to suffering, the ways of being resulting from these internal structures generate experiences and social responses that tend to reinforce them.

The conceptual similarities underlying these different terms are foundational as they describe the very genesis and maintenance of problematic psychological processes. To an extent this is reassuring as it suggests the existence of a shared reality to which these theorists refer. When Breuer and Freud introduced the terms 'psychoanalysis', 'complexes' and 'catharsis' Janet wrote:

> They called psychoanalysis what I called psychological analysis; they gave the name complex to what I named psychological system in order to designate the whole group of psychological phenomena and of movements, whether of the limbs or viscera, which remain associated together and thus constitute the traumatic memory; they christened 'catharsis' what I designated as a dissociation of fixed ideas or as a 'mental disinfection'! The names were different but all the essential conceptions . . . were accepted without modification.
>
> (in Berggren, 1975, p. 73)

Nevertheless, unnecessary confusion is also created by redundant terminological proliferation. Moreover, since new terms are often presented within new and yet undeveloped theories, their content is not only redundant but also reductive. For the sake of reference to recent developments of this kind consider the terms 'mindfulness', 'acceptance therapy' and 'compassion therapy' *vis-à-vis* those of the old terms 'meditation', aspects of 'existential therapy' and 'client-centred therapy', respectively. Whilst similar in gist,

these contents are clearly richer and better developed under the old terminologies. In brief, not only could many superficial differences between
theories be greatly reduced by noting the substantial similarities underlying different terminologies, but the richness of existing theoretical systems
would be also better preserved. *Why then does terminological proliferation
recur so frequently and systematically?*

Ignorance of existing theories and terminologies may play a part. In his
study of the roots of Freud's ideas Ellenberger (1970) makes a case for 'cryptomnesia', i.e. people's tendency to forget what they have learned and then
rediscover it as their own idea. However, there is so much terminological
proliferation around such basic ideas from so influential traditions that neither ignorance nor cryptomnesia is credible. It has been repeatedly noted,
for example, how some of Kohut's (1979) core ideas, including the importance of empathy in human development and therapy and the centrality of
clients' experiences, are similar to those earlier developed by Rogers (1951,
1959). Kohut never acknowledged this similarity to a significant degree yet
it is unlikely that he was unaware of Rogers' work (they even worked at the
same university). It is more likely that in such cases developing a different
language to describe the same idea can serve important social and personal
purposes which can override a fair recognition of one's sources.

Among these purposes some must be related to one's professional sense
of belonging and identity. Speaking of 'good and bad internal objects',
'positive or negative scripts', underlying 'core beliefs' or 'schemas' immediately identifies us as this or that kind of therapist, to ourselves as well as
others. It may not come naturally to established psychoanalysts, cognitive-
behavioural or humanistic therapists suddenly to start using terms from
other theories. Feelings that one is betraying one's community and/or fear
of rejection from that community may also arise. Bowlby was famously
ostracised by the psychoanalytic community for his explicit use of etho-
logical ideas and data to argue for the primacy of young infants' need for
attachment. Whether unconscious or intentional, the translation of ideas
from other theories can also satisfy one's own desire for personal recognition and success. Janet's work may be as foundational as Freud's and
yet, as a result of poor referencing, many today do not even know that it
was Janet who coined the term 'subconscious' (Ellenberger, 1970). Social
pressures of various sorts also contribute to the effect of these and other
personal motivations. In much of the Westernised world the constant quest
for novelty makes rebranding old ideas a powerful marketing strategy and
'new' therapies, up-to-date with the current jargon, are often automatically
considered better than available ones. In 1997 Salkovskis and Rachman
edited a book entitled *Frontiers of cognitive therapy* in which they described
some third-wave developments of cognitive-behavioural therapy (CBT) as

original even when their authors acknowledged their sources. The effect of this marketing or political aspect cannot be stressed enough. It is because they are represented as the latest CBT developments that mindfulness and acceptance therapy are currently promoted in public services much more than meditation and existential therapy ever were.

That said, many authors do carefully acknowledge their sources and even use this as their marketing strategy. Proper referencing and personal success are not mutually exclusive. Young (1990) presented schema-focused therapy as importing ideas from object relations theories and Gestalt, and Ryle (1982) introduced cognitive-analytic therapy (CAT) as a translation of analytic ideas into cognitive parlance. Similar cases clearly help to reduce the confusion generated by terminological proliferation. In their frequent and unwarranted absence, however, it falls on us to identify the common theoretical themes underlying different theoretical jargons.

Differences of Emphasis

Whilst much 'difference' between theories can be eliminated by seeing through unnecessary terminological variation, most theories also hold specific emphases, some of which could be easily lost in translation.

Whether termed complexes, conditions of worth or schemas, the internal structures referred to are invariably said to affect all psychological processes (behaviour, emotion, perception and cognition). What is said to be the relative contribution of the latter processes to the actual constitution of the former structures, however, differs widely. Authors of behavioural conviction stress the role of associations between external stimuli and behavioural responses (e.g. Eysenck & Martin, 1987). Cognitive theorists focus instead on the role of cognition (e.g. negative automatic thoughts, core beliefs) as a mediator between stimulus and response and the ultimate determinant of all other processes (e.g. Beck, 1967). Psychoanalysts tend to refer to internal structures that are affective and dynamic in nature, involving tensions and conflicts between different drives, external demands and the resulting defensive anxiety. A sense of the primacy of emotion over behaviour and cognition also permeates the thinking of 'third force' authors, see for instance Perls *et al.*'s (1951) description of the contact process, Rogers' (1959) stress on the importance of empathising with children's and clients' feelings, or Maslow's hierarchy of needs (1943).

Within an integrative mindset one could contend that differences in emphasis merely reflect choices to focus the therapeutic endeavour on different 'ports of entry' (Dryden, 1998), and that efforts to include differences in emphases within the same theory can be found in all main traditions.

Many psychoanalysts refer to cognitive representations in their descriptions of maladaptive internal structures (e.g. Mahler *et al.*, 1975; Stern, 1995); within 'third force' approaches Berne (1972) describes all basic psychological processes (emotion, cognition and behaviour) as equally causal and focuses on the thematic coherence across them; existential descriptions of being-in-the-world also refer to different psychological processes whilst concentrating on how they contribute to embed individuals in their context (Spinelli, 2003); and Young's (1990) schemas involve cognition, emotion and behaviours without apparent preference. However, it should be stressed that similar integrative efforts must either tolerate unresolved tensions or water down the original emphases. When explicit, this operation does not constitute a problem but a theoretical development which can be assessed, whether on the basis of logic, available evidence or clinical experience. However, when left implicit such developments may slowly influence mainstream thinking in subtle, unacknowledged ways, especially as generations of therapists succeed one another. For instance, there are many similarities between Young's schema theory and previous object relations and 'third force' ideas, yet terms such as 'schema' come with a rationalist slant that is at odds with the hermeneutic and phenomenological traditions to which those ideas belong. Unaware of such differences, one could be corralled into a specific perspective without being able to assess it against the alternatives.

Contextual factors play as important a role in shifts of emphasis as they do in terminological changes. Consider, for instance, the postwar re-evaluation of the role of 'real others' and de-evaluation of destructive drives in psychotherapy theories. It is easy to recognise in these changes the influence of North American environmentalist philosophy and optimism about human progress. The USA had just been on the winning side in the Second World War against a regime that abused nativist (i.e. non-environmentalist) ideas as grounds for its most repellent eugenic policies, and the majority of psychotherapy theorists were now from English-speaking countries or had recently moved there after persecution from that same regime. The 'love and peace' culture of the 1960s and 1970s, to which so many 'third force' approaches were closely tied, also was unsympathetic to the idea of natural destructiveness. The few theoretical exceptions to this trend seem to confirm the rule: Melanie Klein stressed the role of aggressive drives and her ideas were not well accepted in the USA until after the 1970s, while Perls (1969) focused on the positive role of aggression and was often criticised for being confrontational. To draw an example from the present context, the fact that the mainstream understanding of science is still tied to the rationalist tradition may well be responsible for the current success of the term 'schema' on the one hand, and the criticism of emotion-based terminologies as 'touchy feely' on the other.

It is important to note how contextual forces can easily override one's desire for theoretical consistency. Ryle's (1982) definition of 'emotional roles' as led by unconscious affect runs counter to the cognitive paradigm purportedly underlying CAT. The introduction of Buddhist ideas within a rationalist terminology such as the cognitive one is also theoretically problematic (the Zen master Nishijima (2008) refuses to use the term 'mindfulness' for this reason). Yet both developments occurred within and for public services, which are deeply rooted in CBT thinking, and their supporters may have felt the need to keep these and other inconsistencies quiet, possibly even to themselves.

In brief, when moving from one theoretical system to another and under the effects of the contextual forces, differences of theoretical emphasis may be easily missed, especially if they are not very evident or well understood. Yet their full recognition, whether made public or kept private, can only help us to gain a rounder view of phenomena, avoid theoretical trends we disagree with, or at least be aware of unresolved tensions.

Differences of Content

Differences of content can be identified whenever two or more theoretical propositions are incompatible. When sufficiently radicalised the differences of emphasis noted above can all fall into this group. According to radical behaviourists (Skinner, 1950; Watson, 1914) it really is behaviour that matters most; according to pure cognitivists it really is cognition; whereas for orthodox psychoanalysts it is affect. To introduce a new example, Lazarus (1991), and with him many authors of cognitive orientation, argues that it is cognitive processes that attribute meaning to events, which, in turn, evoke different emotional reactions. In other words, cognition is *necessary* for emotion to occur. Other authors argue instead that emotion *need not* be preceded by cognitive attribution and that, in fact, it often leads to such attributions (e.g. Zajonc, 1984). The contradiction here is stark and constitutes a classic case of thesis (emotion is necessary for cognition) versus antithesis (cognition is not necessary and in fact may be consequential to emotion).

More than differences of language or emphasis, differences of content require careful theoretical work. There are at least four ways to deal with them. One is to choose an eclectic stance and live with the ensuing contradictions whilst waiting for further evidence or ideas to resolve them. The main advantage or aim here is to retain the different explanatory powers of contradictory models. Eclecticism is different from a both are true stance, which constitutes a second possible solution. Although also viable, the latter usually requires some dilution of at least one of the original positions (more than is the case with differences of emphasis). Some psychoanalysts, for instance, see emotion and cognition as equally important (e.g. Fonagy *et al.*, 2002), yet in so doing they abandon one of the very ideas that distinguish the psychoanalytic from the cognitive tradition. The eclectic position, instead, uses contradictory ideas without changing them. A third way to resolve theoretical incompatibilities is, of course, the selection of one idea over others. This may be brought about by either theoretical problems or new decisive empirical evidence for or against given ideas. To continue with our example, strong evidence has emerged against the cognitivist stance as it is now clear that emotional reactions to stimuli are faster than their cognitive processing, i.e. that cognition cannot be necessary for emotion (for a review see Ellis, 2005). A fourth possible solution to incompatible propositions is their (Hegelian) synthesis. This deflates the original tension by constituting a radically new theoretical start. For instance, for many decades a debate flared between nativists and environmentalists. To an extent this tension still exists but most psychological processes and difficulties are now considered epigenetic in origin, that is, as determined by *inextricable* combinations of genetic and environmental information (the argument being that the informative powers of genes and contexts only exist in relation to one another). This kind of operation, where the original contradiction is transcended, can be regarded as *integration proper*.

Integration proper typically implies more theoretical changes than one may be immediately capable of. In principle the nature/nurture dichotomy is resolved, but in fact many old paradoxes arising from it still permeate mainstream explanations of development. Psychoanalysis, for instance, originally focused on the role of biological drives in the determination of experience over and above the influence of actual others, until the resolution of the Oedipal conflict at least. Yet how could this conflict emerge at all if the pre-oedipal infant could not perceive others as such? To avoid such logical paradoxes object relations theorists recognised infants' capacity to differentiate between self and others, and yet many still referred to the first weeks/months of infancy as 'symbiotic' or 'undifferentiated' (e.g. Mahler *et al.*, 1975). These positions are inherently contradictory, and the use of the term *object* relations to indicate relations with other *subjects* points to the same unresolved tension. Cognitive-behavioural theories fall into similar contradictions when arguing that social development is about *becoming* social by learning from others (e.g. Bandura, 1977), as if the latter did not presume the former. CAT uses Lev Vygotsky's concept of 'zone of proximal development', which contradictorily implies that social development is incipient and yet also dependent on social connection. Even phenomenological-existential theorists, who claim that intersubjectivity is a given, may fall prey to a similar problem if they concomitantly stress the loneliness of the human condition.

Among the contextual factors that influence how we cope with differences of content it is worth considering that there is only so much theoretical development a person can achieve in a lifetime. In addition, not only do radical theoretical changes require difficult adjustments in our personal worldview, but the worldview of our contemporaries must also be considered. Many of us have changed a client's theoretical formulation depending on our audience. Wanting to pass an essay or supervisor's report, having to justify one's course of action or present a case to colleagues, publish a paper or gain some research funding, all are common reasons for temporarily bracketing out our theoretical preferences. With sufficient repetition this bracketing may turn into oblivion of differences. Contextual pressures can override our desire for theoretical consistency in content just as easily as in emphasis and, again, in ways we may be unaware of. Involuntary eclecticism is endemic.

Epistemological Differences

Occasionally, however, the synthesis between thesis and antithesis leads to the revision of so many theoretical corollaries that the resulting change can be considered paradigmatic. A typical sign of paradigmatic change is that old debates become meaningless. Consider the question of neurological versus psychological explanations of human experiences such as depression. Is depression due to altered levels of serotonin or to psychological events such as unprocessed bereavement? If one sees human experiences, psychological and neurological processes as different in logical type, then this question becomes absurd. It is like asking if an army is made up of its divisions or its soldiers. The question is indeed based on what Ryle (1949) refers to as a category mistake, because it assumes that experiences and neurological processes belong to the same logical category, when they do not.

Paradigmatic differences can be regarded as epistemological (calling on different ways to know the world). There are several epistemological differences among psychotherapy theories, often based on their valuing different psychological processes. CBT's theoretical focus on cognition and behaviour is also evident in its epistemological stance; knowledge is considered valid when expressed rationally (e.g. a graph of the relation between core beliefs, resulting thought processes, emotion and behaviour) and evidenced quantitatively (e.g. a depression inventory). Instead, existential approaches often rely on a different, more philosophical, analysis of the human condition. Whilst still rational in itself, this also considers the epistemological value of non-rational processes, such as emotion, and is concerned with questions of meaning and value. Other approaches use analogies and metaphors, such as myths, poetry and stories, to represent the client's reality. This is particularly true within narrative approaches, the analysis of dreams and fantasies, the psychoanalytic use of Greek mythology, transactional analysis use of scripts and the systemic reference to family myths. Many psychodynamic and third force approaches also explicitly value intuitive processes, described as an immediate capacity for insight into the client's history and personality (Berne, 1972; Jung & Baynes, 1921). These approaches also analyse the therapist's countertransference, that is they consider therapist emotions as a valid and informative source of knowledge. For authors of phenomenological leaning, emotion is indeed a valid way of knowing in itself. Empathy is now considered the *sine qua non* in understanding clients' experiences by most, and many also stress the epistemological value of non-empathic emotions (e.g. amusement, irritation or boredom). Transpersonal approaches, finally, distinguish themselves for their reliance on the epistemological value of spiritual processes.

The tension between most rational and religious understandings of the human condition provides a good example of what Kuhn (1962) refers to as paradigmatic 'incommensurability'. All the factual evidence we have points towards the death of psychological processes in the absence of neurological activity, yet some religious systems ask us to believe in the immortality of the soul. Epistemologically, the two could not hold more different paradigms, since where science asks for proof, religions ask for faith. Such differences, if unrecognised and treated as of the same logical type (i.e. commensurable), may end up in serious conflict. More than once Western religion has fought science as it did witchery – on the pyre. Science, in turn, has long suffered a dictatorship of reason, so much so that the epistemological status of *all other* processes has been disregarded by the very practitioners who use them. Even Jung struggled with the epistemological status of non-rational processes:

> It is not only intelligible, but absolutely necessary, that all sciences have excluded both the standpoints of feeling and phantasy. They are sciences for that very reason. But how does it stand with psychology? If it is to be regarded as a science, it must do the same. But will it then do justice to its material? Every science ultimately seeks to express its material in abstractions; thus psychology could and indeed does, lay hold of the process of feeling, sensation, and phantasy in the form of intellectual abstractions. This treatment certainly establishes the right of the intellectual-abstract standpoint, but not the claims of other quite possible psychological points of view. These and other possible standpoints can only obtain a bare mention in a scientific psychology; they cannot emerge as independent principles of a science.
>
> (1923, p. 75)

Yet the incommensurability of paradigms does not imply their exclusivity. Like other parochialisms, paradigmatic exclusivity is promoted by contextual factors more than the quest for wider knowledge and understanding. The need to establish psychology as a discipline in its own right, independent of religious and moral authorities, played a major role here and we are still struggling with the consequences, just as Jung did. We now have strong evidence from the neurosciences that non-rational processes, emotive ones in particular, are both necessary for medium- to long-term adaptive and ethical decision-making, and faster than abstract reasoning (Damasio, 1994). This is not yet sufficiently acknowledged in official decision-making and there is room for cases of striking therapeutic short-sightedness. Ritalin is now prescribed for 1 in 23 children across England and in several deprived areas for more than 1 in 10 children (Gainsbury, 2008). From the standpoint of emotion, administering amphetamine-like substances to so many children, ultimately because they behave in ways we cannot cope with, *feels* wrong. It is a tragedy that we have to see the effects of this on their physical, affective and social development before over-prescription is stopped.

This is not to say that abstract reasoning is invalid and needs to be replaced with other sources of knowledge. Proper rational analyses of Ritalin use have come to the same conclusion (Breggin, 2002). However, knowledge can benefit from processes other than rationality and moving between paradigms can be an eye-opening experience. The exclusion of non-rational processes from the traditional standpoint of Western science is unfortunate.

Conclusion

The 'different differences' described here could be represented as organised along a spectrum, with discriminating bands of comparatively fast change. Figure 7.1 attempts to do so and summarises the characteristics of these difference, their functions, the operations that can help reduce or contain them, and the possible advantages and risks of these operations. The grey areas indicate the fuzzy nature of the boundaries between 'different differences'.

This socio-epistemological compendium should expose how tricky understanding the human condition can be and some of the reasons why counselling psychology does not *and should not* call for uniformity in psychotherapy theory. But there are other solid arguments against theoretical uniformity in science generally and human sciences in particular. Gödel (1931) famously provided mathematical evidence that theories can never justify themselves and that questions can be asked within their terms that necessitate the development of theories of a different logical order. Why this

	Differences of terminology	Differences of emphasis	Differences of content	Differences of epistemology
Characteristics	formal explicit redundant parochial pervasive	about focus, can be implicit & overlooked, widespread	about the gist, explicit, discriminatory, incompatible	foundational, underpinned by different psychological processes
Knowledge functions	identification of phenomena by naming	widening or complication of views on agreed phenomena	quest for a better/truer explanation of agreed phenomena	opening to radically different phenomena or 'realities'
Social functions	professional identification, personal gain, politics	implicit suggestion of theoretical fashion/trend	explicit suggestion of theoretical fashion/trend	definition of what is acceptable knowledge
Operations to reduce/hold the differences	recognition of similar underlying content	recognition + acceptance of varying perspectives	1. eclecticism 2. both are true 3. selection 4. synthesis	epistemological eclecticism
Advantage of operation	reduction of noise	'rounder' understanding	theoretical openness, progress in knowledge	opening of minds
Risk of operation	loss of different emphases	rising internal tension or incoherence	1. contradiction 2. dilution 3. mistakes 4. none	acceptance of unfounded worldviews

Degree of difference: Very low   Low   Medium   High   Very High   Incommensurable

Figure 7.1   Epistemological framework for theoretical integration and eclecticism

should be so is unclear, but reality is extremely complex and our brain capacity comparatively limited and focused. In addition, of the limited amount of information that we can process, only some is available to consciousness and even less to logical reasoning. Another insurmountable problem for psychology in particular is that here the human animal studies itself, with an identity existing between the system of reference of the 'knower' and the 'known'. This further reduces the scope for objective investigation as traditionally defined, and clarifies how any theoretical approach is looking at human reality from within it and necessarily assumes a specific perspective. In this situation of inherent, structural impossibility of consensus, general contextual factors such as culture, politics and economics, and more specific ones such personality and training, will all promote further theoretical variation.

One should also not confuse the theoretical story of an approach with the effectiveness and efficacy of its therapeutic practices. Exorcism can work, as can 'magic', although the stories behind them are doubtful. Franz Mesmer instead drew from the scientific concepts of gravity, electricity and magnetism to explain the effect of his (somewhat similar) therapeutic practice, yet his account is also unlikely to be correct (Ellenberger, 1970). Ultimately, logical theorising is only one way in which we can relate to and comprehend the human condition, albeit the most accredited in Western modern times. Sensory-motor, affective, intuitive and creative processes also deserve epistemological attention, as do literary stories, poetry, music and the visual arts. In a more daring vein than in the passage reported above Jung wrote:

> The intellect remains imprisoned within itself just so as long as it does not willingly sacrifice its supremacy through its recognition of the value of other aims. It recoils from the step which takes it out of itself, and which denies its universal validity; since from the standpoint of intellect everything else is nothing but phantasy. But what great thing came into existence that was not first phantasy? Just in so far as the intellect rigidly adheres to the absolute aim of science it is insulated from the spring of life. It interprets phantasy as nothing but a wish-dream, wherein it is expressed that depreciation of phantasy which for science is both welcome and necessary. It is inevitable that science should be regarded as an absolute aim as long as the development of science is the sole question at issue. But this at once becomes evil when it is a question of life itself demanding development.
>
> (1923, p. 77)

Indeed, from a counselling psychology perspective, the epistemology of psychotherapy theories should be explicitly redefined to include the systematic use of processes other than reason, such as perception, emotion, intuition, fantasy and even transpersonal processes. All these processes can lead us to false and unhelpful conclusions of course, *but so too has reason many a time*. All of them, like reason, are intentional in the philosophical sense (i.e. are 'about' the human phenomenological reality), but each in a different way or about a different aspect of this reality. Making space for them all is thus not only epistemologically justifiable but the only wise thing to do to limit the likelihood of abusive errors. If under certain circumstances this entails translating ideas from one approach to another, holding different emphases, contradictions and even epistemological paradigm together, so be it. The ethical integrity of the discipline can only benefit from this and so, ultimately, will its theoretical development and therapeutic effectiveness and efficacy. Theoretical and epistemological variety is ultimately inherent to the human condition and in the impossibility of total knowledge many partial perspectives are better than one only.

At the same time it should be clear that, from a counselling psychology perspective, *not just any understanding will do*, especially when its practical implications are noxious (as in the case of the organicist understanding of human distress behind most Ritalin prescriptions). Fortunately, human nature seems to dislike being boxed in at least as much as it can be reassured by the containment that comes with it. The human tendency towards variety can thus also act as an important antidote to the dangers of being corralled into unhelpful or dangerous perspectives. Promoting this tendency becomes paramount when strong contextual forces serve interests other than those of our clients. Consider, for instance, what is occurring to cognitive-behavioural approaches as they become central to most therapeutic services.

On the one hand, from a scientific perspective, this is an unwelcome development. Whilst there is more outcome research on CBT than any other therapy there is now enough evidence to conclude that even specific presenting problems such as phobias, anxiety or depression can be successfully addressed from other approaches (for a review, see Cooper, 2008). This evidence does not speak against CBT, but it does speak against it becoming the default approach. The data also suggest that what discriminates effective therapy are properties of the relationship (e.g. client's involvement, therapist's way of relating, awareness of transference, working alliance, empathy, etc.), something to which traditional CBT theory has paid comparatively little attention. (Still today many CBT courses do not require personal therapy and many CBT practitioners treat their clients with a series of technical operations carried out, in theory, with minimal personal involvement.) Furthermore, the basic theoretical paradigm of CBT, according to which individual cognition drives affect, perception and behaviour, has been seriously questioned by studies of the underlying neurological processes. In brief, not only is CBT just one of many effective therapies, but because its theoretical paradigm is flawed, its therapeutic effects must be due to processes other than those alleged and that are often secondary in its training and practice.

On the other hand, as more and more professionals are presenting themselves as CBT in orientation, this is becoming progressively enriched by the import of ideas about unconscious processes, transference, countertransference, projection and techniques such as the use of imagery, fantasies, the two-chair technique, transcendental meditation and existential acceptance of anxiety. These developments consist of recycling ideas and techniques from other approaches and the more recent, the more at variance with the original cognitive paradigm. Some of us may be irritated by the lack of proper referencing to the original sources but what really matters is the big picture, and this is looking good. Needless to say, there is still much ground to cover and there are contextual forces serving interests other than those of our clients that may come in the way. Many of us believe that in the UK the recent implementation of NICE (National Institute for Health and Clinical Excellence) guidelines through IAPT (Improved Access to Psychological Therapies) risks undermining the range and quality of psychotherapeutic services by imposing orthodox/manualised CBT as the main treatment for anxiety and depression (e.g. Gilbert, 2009). Once again, an important dynamic here is political, involving issues of money and power between government departments, different groups of health professionals and schools of psychotherapy. As is often the case, however, the scientific battle is between reductivists, who fail to understand how little we really comprehend, and those open to the ever-surprising complexity of the human condition. Theoretical and epistemological differences are to be carefully nurtured, for if science were to proceed by consensus, it would not proceed at all.

References

Bandura, A. (1977). *Social learning theory*. Englewood Cliffs, NJ: Prentice-Hall.

Beck, A. T. (1967). *Depression: Clinical, experimental and theoretical aspects*. New York: Hoeber.

Berggren, E. J. (1975). *The psychology of confession*. Leiden: Brill Archive.

Berne, E. (1972). *What do you say after you say hello?* New York: Grove Press.

Breggin, P. R. (2002). *The Ritalin fact book: What your doctor won't tell you*. Cambridge: Perseus Books.

Breuer, J. & Freud, S. (1957). *Studies in hysteria*. New York: Basic Books. (First published as *Studien über hysterie*. F. Deuticke, 1895.)

Cooper, M. (2008). *Essential research findings in counselling and psychotherapy*. London: Sage.

Damasio, A. (1994). *Descartes' error: Emotion, reason and the human brain*. New York: Putnam.

Dryden, W. (1998). The cognitive-behavioural paradigm. In R. Woolfe & W. Dryden (Eds.) *The handbook of counselling psychology*. London: Sage.

Ellenberger, H. E. (1970). *The discovery of the unconscious. The history and evolution of dynamic psychiatry*. New York: Basic Books.

Ellis, R. D. (2005). *Curious emotions: Roots of consciousness and personality in motivated action*. Amsterdam: John Benjamins.

Eysenck, H. J. & Martin, I. (1987). *Theoretical foundations of behavior therapy*. New York: Plenum Press.

Fonagy, P., Gergely, G., Jurist, E. L. & Target, M. (2002). *Affect regulation, mentalization and the development of the self*. New York: Other Press.

Gainsbury, S. (2008). Massive variation in Ritalin prescribing [electronic version]. *Health Service Journal*, 17 July. www.hsj.co.uk/massive-variation-in-ritalin-prescribing/1732568. Accessed 26 June 2009.

Gilbert, P. (2009). Moving beyond cognitive behaviour therapy. *The Psychologist*, *22*(5): 400–403.

Gödel, K. (1931). Über formal unentscheidbare Sätze der Principia Mathematica und verwandter Systeme, I. *Monatshefte für Mathematik und Physik*, *38*: 173–198.

Jung, C. G. (1923). *Psychological types*. London: Routledge & Kegan Paul.

Jung, C. G. & Baynes, H. G. (1921). *The psychology of individuation*. London: Kegan Paul Trench Trubner.

Klein, M. (1946). Notes on some schizoid mechanisms. *International Journal of Psychoanalysis*, *27*: 99–110.

Kohut, H. (1979). The two analyses of Mr Z. *International Journal of Psychoanalysis*, *60*: 3–27.

Kuhn, T. S. (1962). *The structure of scientific revolutions*. Chicago: University of Chicago Press.

Laplanche, J. & Pontalis, J. B. (1988). *The language of psychoanalysis*. London: Karnac Books.

Lazarus, R. (1991). *Emotion and adaptation*. New York: Oxford University Press.

Mahler, M. S., Pine, F. & Bergman, A. (1975). *The psychological birth of the human infant*. London: Hutchinson.

Maslow, A. H. (1943). A theory of human motivation. *Psychological Review*, *50*(4): 370–396.

Nishijima, G. W. (2008). *On mindfulness* 24 May. http://gudoblog-e.blogspot.com/ 2008_05_01_archive.html. Accessed 26 June 2009.

Perls, F. S. (1969). *Ego hunger and aggression: A revision of Freud's theory and method*. New York: Random House. (First published 1942.)

Perls, F., Hefferline, R. & Goodman, P. (1951). *Gestalt therapy: Excitement and growth in the human personality*. New York: Julian Press.

Rogers, C. (1951). *Client-centred therapy: Its current practice, implications and theory*. London: Constable.

Rogers, C. (1959). A theory of therapy, personality and interpersonal relationships as developed in the client-centered framework. In S. Koch (Ed.) *Psychology: A study of a science*. Vol. *3: Formulations of the person and the social context*. New York: McGraw-Hill.

Ryle, A. (1982). *Psychotherapy: A cognitive integration of theory and practice*. New York: Academic Press.

Ryle, G. (1949). *The concept of mind*. Chicago: University of Chicago Press.

Salkovskis, M. & Rachman, S. (1997). *Frontiers of cognitive therapy*. New York: Guilford Press.

Segal, H. (1974). *An introduction to the work of Melanie Klein*. New York: Basic Books.

Skinner, B. F. (1950). Are theories of learning necessary? *Psychological Review*, *57*: 193–216.

Spinelli, E. (2003). The existential-phenomenological paradigm. In R. Woolfe, W. Dryden & S. Strawbridge (Eds.) *The handbook of counselling psychology* (2nd edn.). London: Sage.

Stern, D. N. (1995). *The motherhood constellation*. New York: Basic Books.

Watson, J. B. (1914). *Behavior: An introduction to comparative psychology*. New York: Henry Holt.

Young, J. (1990). *Cognitive therapy for personality disorders: A schema-focused approach*. Sarasota, FL: Professional Resource Exchange.

Zajonc, R. B. (1984): On the primacy of affect. In K. R. Scherer & P. Ekman (Eds.) *Approaches to emotion*. Hillsdale, NJ: Lawrence Erlbaum Associates.

Chapter 8

Humanistic Contributions to Pluralistic Practice

Heidi Ashley

[I]n my early professional years I was asking the question, How can I treat, or cure, or change this person? Now I would phrase the question this way: How can I provide a relationship which this person may use for his own personal growth?

Carl Rogers (1999, p. 32)

This chapter begins with a discussion of the context for the emergence of humanistic therapy and then addresses the history of counselling psychology practice by acknowledging its philosophical and epistemological origins. The chapter then explores humanistic contributions to pluralistic practice, including assessment and formulation in ways that eschew medicalised and pathologising language or concepts and practice that offer assistance to people in overcoming their difficulties. The chapter considers how the humanistic underpinnings of counselling psychology offer useful and responsive contributions to research, practice and the understanding of social issues.

Therapy and Beyond: Counselling Psychology Contributions to Therapeutic and Social Issues
Edited by Martin Milton
© 2010 John Wiley & Sons, Ltd.

The Development of the Humanistic Approach

Person-centred therapy emerged in the 1950s within a psychological climate dominated by what some considered the mechanistic ethos of behaviourism and the authoritarianism of psychoanalysis. Rather than narrow the focus of therapy to internal dynamics or outward behaviours, Rogers encouraged a holistic approach to client work. Rogers (2000) noted that people became distressed because they had not felt loved and accepted, and encouraged therapists to offer a relationship which the client could use to develop a greater understanding of why he (the client – for the sake of convenience and clarity, the counselling psychologist is throughout assumed to be female and the client male) thought, felt and behaved as he did (Rogers, 1957). Rogers stressed the client's potential and own efforts to move on and suggested that therapists would do better to let go of the importance placed on theoretical knowledge and instead trust that the client already had everything he needed to recover (Rogers, 1995). Rogers thought that therapists should keep their directives and interpretations to themselves, believing that these were likely to get in the client's way, and instead closely follow and explore the client's moment-by-moment experience (Rogers, 1995). In 1957 he proposed the 'necessary and sufficient' conditions for psychological change, putting forward a valuing and respectful way of working with clients and their difficulties (for a fuller discussion, see Mearns & Thorne, 2007; Rogers, 1999, 2000). Mearns (1994, 2006) and Cooper (2007a; Mearns & Cooper, 2005) developed Rogers' theory by establishing the importance of the therapist's humanity and capacity to meet her client at the level of 'relational depth'.

But . . . First to Counselling Psychology

Counselling psychology is grounded in humanistic philosophy, which distinguishes it from other applied psychologies which have their roots in the experimental and behavioural sciences (Strawbridge & Woolfe, 2003). Counselling psychology offers an alternative to positivistic views of people and their difficulties, rejecting deficiency models and stressing growth and development. This branch of psychology also recognises that the therapeutic relationship is a significant component of therapy (Woolfe, 1996) and that people have a need to relate, suffering not just from their thoughts and feelings but also from the limits of their relationships. People are understood and restored in relationship. One of the first tasks for a counselling psychologist, therefore, is to establish a therapeutic relationship within which the client feels secure and which the psychologist can use to inform herself about the client's particular difficulties.

While owing an epistemological and philosophical debt to humanism, counselling psychologists are not humanistic practitioners for they navigate different models. Counselling psychologists recognise that psychological distress has many causes and maintaining factors and that it is impossible for any single model to capture all of these. A stance of *pluralism* acknowledges that no theoretical, methodological or epistemological approach is any 'truer' or more appropriate than another and that different people are likely to find different meanings or practices useful at different times (Cooper & McLeod, 2007). Whilst models overlap to some degree, each is unique and makes a specific contribution which can place it in marked disagreement with others. These differences are not always insignificant and at times the counselling psychologist must engage with a range of competing theoretical frameworks.

Rather than relying on one theory to guide their work, counselling psychologists make sense of distress by drawing on competing therapeutic models, each potentially with something important to contribute. A client's difficulty may be understood in terms of unconscious dynamics, self-critical thinking or the conditions and restrictions associated with their relationships. Having a preferred approach that 'fits best' enables the psychologist to release her self to follow her client, yet counselling psychologists are also receptive to other theories. Being aware of different models and of their strengths and limitations encourages an attitude of curiosity and a respect for difference that fits well with a humanistic ethos, encouraging counselling psychologists to develop responsive relationships and to tailor their approach to their client rather than expect the client to adapt to them (Cooper, 2007a; Cooper & McLeod, 2007).

Counselling psychologists move between the boundaries of schools, going 'beyond schoolism' (Clarkson, 2000). This does not mean that models are simply absorbed: psychologists work from a clear theoretical basis, evaluating models epistemologically, philosophically and in terms of their body of empirical evidence. Navigating opposing philosophies and methods whilst staying theoretically coherent *and* attuned to the client is demanding, and requires an ongoing process of reflection on practice in terms of 'an inevitable series of contesting possibilities' (Gillon, 2007, p. 3). However, humanism can provide a foundation from which counselling psychologists may approach pluralistic practice by remaining grounded in the therapeutic relationship, the 'here-and-now with my client'. Beginning with assessment and formulation, this chapter now considers what humanistic contributions to pluralistic practice actually are.

The Humanistic Dimension of Assessment
and Formulation

At assessment, the psychologist gathers enough information to begin to form an understanding of her client, guided by theoretical and contextual factors. It could be argued that assessment and formulation prioritise the psychologist's agenda and risk diminishing the client's own knowledge and understandings and therefore might be philosophically inconsistent with a humanistic ethos (Gillon, 2007). While this may be applicable to assessment in psychiatry, in which a history is taken so that self-reported symptoms can be matched against an existing syndrome (forming the basis of a treatment to manage or reduce symptoms), the approach to assessment and formulation in counselling psychology is very different. Assessment in counselling psychology is a process of negotiating understandings and establishing connections between elements of the client's experience, and is an invitation to enter into a purposeful relationship in which collaboration is emphasised from the outset.

At assessment, some areas that the counselling psychologist is likely to be interested in include the client's historical relationships and the sort of life that he leads now: these broad 'headings' form the psychologist's agenda and lend some structure to the assessment meetings. However, within these areas there is scope for exploration. The client is given space to direct the conversation and to talk about what is important to him, the psychologist following but mindful of where the client is taking her and of any areas that he seems to be overlooking or avoiding. Offering tentative reflective statements in order to convey understanding or picking up on underlying emotion allows the client to find his own direction and feel in control, and lets him know that the psychologist is 'with' him. By listening closely and allowing the client's response to guide her next intervention, the counselling psychologist stays close to her client's frame of reference rather than permitting her own assumptions to dominate the encounter. By allowing the discussion to unfold naturally within identified areas, before shifting the focus elsewhere, the counselling psychologist unobtrusively manages the assessment process and balances her need to gather information against her task of establishing a therapeutic relationship.

The assessment offers the client the chance to go beyond simply reporting information and begin to develop his story in relationship with the psychologist. Assessment meetings extend the client's awareness, beginning an exploration at a deeper level of emotion than before. A client on the 'edge of awareness' of a feeling or experience might be helped along with a reflective statement (Strawbridge & Woolfe, 2003). For instance, simply reflecting back how 'You've mentioned feeling "all at sea" with this a couple of times' may prompt the client to talk about feeling lost and overwhelmed. Although some clients need greater structure, for others expressions of empathic understanding are enough to encourage further exploration. The psychologist also encourages the client to reflect on experience, perhaps asking 'What was it about that relationship that was difficult?' or 'Have you given any thought to what your unease could be about?' These questions change the emotional tone of the encounter and open up new areas to explore together, introducing an emphasis on process and foreshadowing the therapy that may follow.

Assessment is a purposeful dialogue, leading to the development of a collaborative formulation. Exploring the client's experiences enables the client and psychologist to understand why certain beliefs have formed, and the client's difficulty becomes understandable in terms of a *meaningful* attempt to cope with adversity (Cooper, 2007a). For example, mistrust of others may make sense when reconceptualised as a strategy that emerged from necessity in early life. Formulation involves retelling the client's story in a more compassionate form, normalising difficulties even when these are longstanding and complex. Conceptualising the client's particular experiences and how he has engaged with them is an important beginning in counselling psychology. Different theories can guide this process; it is not necessary to obscure the client's subjectivity by forcing it into a particular theory. Indeed, to do so would, in some respects, be unethical. Likewise, the formulation should not become so set in stone that the counselling psychologist's assumptions begin to get in the way of her engagement with her client's immediate experience. Instead, a general initial formulation allows theory to be used to suggest possibilities and to develop ideas, getting the therapy started and so freeing up the psychologist to listen fully to and understand her client. The counselling psychologist is then able to stay alert to emerging patterns or themes without imposing them (Mearns & Jacobs, 2003).

During assessment there is no need to make firm plans for the sort of therapy that may follow. However, the first meetings set the tone, paving the way for a therapy that places the relationship at its core. Humanism emphasises the relationship within which interventions are offered and the client is supported to change, suggesting that it is more important to attend to the client's phenomenology than to abstract theoretical principles. These values can guide the selection and implementation of other models: a humanistic 'way of being' is easily incorporated into therapeutic practice independently of the model that suits the client best. Not all clients will find humanistic therapy the right 'fit'. Nonetheless, a humanistic attitude can be taken to all therapeutic encounters (Cooper, 2007a).

This chapter now moves on to consider how humanism can guide model selection and implementation. Examples from practice illustrate how humanistic values can enhance the use of ideas from other schools of therapy. But first, the chapter considers some of the advantages of 'straightforward' humanistic practice in offering assistance to people in overcoming difficulties.

Humanistic Practice in its Pure Form

Humanistic therapies stress the importance of the client's contributions in determining whether therapy has a successful outcome, a position that is well supported by research suggesting that client and relationship factors are the most important determinants of change (Cooper, 2007b, 2008). People have an inherent need to relate and develop within relationships, distress often being linked to an absence of intimacy or support or with difficulties relating (Mearns & Cooper, 2005). There would therefore seem to be a clear place for humanistic therapies, and counselling psychologists may turn to these models when clients seek opportunities to talk and think or when their difficulties seem related to problematic relationships (Cooper, 2007b). Humanistic therapies support clients to develop their understanding of their thoughts, feelings and behaviours. However, rather than label experiences for clients, or use theory as a basis from which to speculate or interpret, the counselling psychologist encourages a collaborative examination and description of experience. As therapy proceeds, habitual responses become more understandable, freeing up the client to consider other possibilities in terms of how he makes sense of and responds to events (Cooper, 2007a).

Humanism also stresses the importance of 'being with' the client, suggesting that therapy is likely to be helpful and meaningful only if psychologist and client are both engaged in an involved therapeutic relationship (Rogers, 1957). The offer of such a relationship can be extended to the client's whole self, including states of being associated with fear, vulnerability or shame (Mearns, 2006). Making contact at such a level of 'relational depth' (Mearns & Cooper, 2005) by establishing what experiences have meant to a client corresponds to working at the level of beliefs and assumptions about the self, others and the world. Effective therapy often involves movement between relational and task-focused aspects, and so clients can be offered such an in-depth relationship as a component of their therapy whilst they are also helped to work on specific goals or tasks, such as understanding how their patterns of thinking induce certain emotional states in them.

Humanistic Foundations of Pluralistic Practice

As well as humanistic therapy, counselling psychologists draw on a range of other models. I shall use an example from cognitive behavioural theory as this is what is being emphasised in the current climate. In its 'traditional' form, CBT assumes that a fully functioning person is like a scientist who accurately judges 'reality' (hence ideas of *hypothesis testing* and *collaborative empiricism*). The psychologist therefore introduces the client to an explanation of his difficulty in CBT terms and assumes that he is ready to start taking a more objective stance. The client's material is treated as 'data' which are appraised in terms of their functionality and soundness (Boucher, 2006). The psychologist might offer psycho-education, encourage the identification of thinking 'errors' or use questioning to guide the client towards alternative ways of thinking.

By bringing a humanistic ethos to the practice of CBT, the counselling psychologist is encouraged to accept the client's expertise in his *own* 'reality'. Rather than instruct, or impose meaning by fitting the client's experience into pre-existing categories, whose language – such as 'dysfunctional thinking', 'reasoning errors' or 'maladaptive behaviours' – is often subtly derogatory, the counselling psychologist can hold back and instead support the client to identify and interpret his *own* experience (Josefowitz & Myran, 2005; Safran & Segal, 1996). By retaining a humanistic stance, the counselling psychologist avoids assigning less validity or worth to certain experiences, freeing the client to talk, without feeling criticised or constrained. In this way, *all* experiences are valued and treated as potentially important.

Likewise, rather than move quickly into dispensing strategies to control depression, anxiety or anger, the counselling psychologist might first help the client to understand his experience by asking focused questions and providing reflective summaries. By encouraging the client to attend carefully to what he thinks, feels and does, the psychologist and client can establish a detailed picture of the client's process of responding in specific situations, encouraging self-awareness and helping the client to see that his responses are understandable (Cooper, 2007a).

By listening closely and with curiosity, the counselling psychologist also encourages her client to develop an interest in his thoughts and feelings. Thought records can help the client to stand back and reflect on his appraisal of events, enabling him to reach a point of noticing himself in the process of interpreting something negatively (Safran & Segal, 1996). The client can be encouraged to develop a phenomenological relationship with his own experience, noticing and accepting shifts in mood and associated thoughts without making distressing judgements or drawing conclusions ('catastrophising'). For example, the client might notice that 'I feel really anxious' and 'I am sweating' without interpreting this negatively ('I'm having a panic attack'; 'I can't cope'; 'I'll never get better'). Thoughts and feelings can therefore be acknowledged and valued whilst also reframed as transitory experiences (Bohart, 1982). Phenomenological methods also encourage the client to recognise that there are many ways to interpret events and that his usual responses are not immutable, but that he has some choice in how he construes a situation and then responds to it (Bohart, 1990; Cooper, 2007a; Corrie & Milton, 2000).

The counselling psychologist can help the client to develop self-awareness within a CBT framework by inviting him to try something new or do something differently to 'see what happens'. The humanistic underpinnings mean that rather than *direct* the client towards specific new ways of thinking, such experiments encourage new learning rooted in actual experience. These might be small, spontaneous experiments, such as seeing if the client feels any differently if he joins the therapist in a quick relaxation exercise, or larger and planned experiments, such as inviting the client to place himself in a situation which produces anxiety, such as going to the supermarket alone. The client is encouraged to pay close attention to the resulting thoughts, feelings and bodily sensations and to reflect on what actually happened: the insights gained from integrating a different experience of self are often more convincing than many sessions of psycho-education or debate and frequently lead clients into further action (Greenberg *et al.*, 1993).

By offering a respectful and valuing relationship, the counselling psychologist also intervenes at an experiential level, offering something more than 'collaborative empiricism' (Bohart, 1990; Safran & Segal, 1996). In CBT, the focus is traditionally on working with difficulties located 'out there', but the therapeutic relationship itself can offer a powerfully healing experience (Jacobson, 1989). Within this relationship, the client's interpersonal beliefs and strategies are evident and, by reflecting on the impact made by her client and her own congruent reactions, the psychologist becomes aware of the client's phenomenology and relational style (Safran & Segal, 1996). By offering the client specific feedback, the counselling psychologist brings herself fully into the relationship and encourages her client to become more aware of the messages that he conveys, using this to reflect on the sorts of difficulties that he experiences in other relationships. This may lead the client to look for further examples between sessions, or use the therapeutic relationship as a safe place to test beliefs about relationships and experiment with new ways of relating.

Mr Church[1] presented with a long history of depression and anxiety. He appeared fragile and I felt a strong 'pull' to be careful and gentle, as if challenge might somehow harm him. From a CBT perspective he held a number of core beliefs, seeing himself as incompetent and dependent, yet subtly manoeuvring others into taking care of him. Mr Church responded to CBT by resisting collaboration, saying that it was too difficult for him to carry out between-session assignments. I began to feel that I was being invited to take care of him, as if it was unreasonable to ask him to share responsibility for the therapy.

Rather than respond to the uncompleted 'homework' along traditional CBT lines – perhaps by problem-solving, or even concluding that Mr Church was not ready for therapy – I offered feedback about the strong 'pull' that I felt to respond as if he was a helpless child, encouraging him to think with me about this. Using a collaborative approach, we discovered that Mr Church typically approached others this way, inviting 'parental' responses that maintained his rather helpless stance. For example, he had been signed off work and spent his days in bed whilst family members cared for him. We considered how a fragile tone of voice and 'lost' look might convey a sense of helpless vulnerability and were then able to consider how our relationship could be different, encouraging Mr Church to experiment with asking for what he needed more directly and with taking responsibility for his own wellbeing. I pointed out what seemed to be happening when Mr Church attended with uncompleted 'homework' that he 'just couldn't manage', inviting his capable self back into the relationship when he appealed to be looked after and absolved of responsibility. We were then able to reintroduce CBT techniques, allowing these to emerge naturally from our relationship. These explorations offered Mr Church specific feedback as well as disconfirming his usual expectations of being in relationship.

If it attends to the lessons from humanistic theory and practice, CBT can be practised as a *relationship*-focused therapy, the client's approach to the therapeutic relationship providing information which can be explored together and perhaps applied to external relationships. An ethos of humanism allows the valuable elements of this model, such as offering the client a truly collaborative, transparent relationship alongside a purposeful and structured approach that actively supports his attempts to become more masterful, to be retained. The therapy can be humanised and enriched beyond the deployment of a series of technically skilful interventions. Indeed, CBT techniques are best offered within an empathic relationship and chosen because of their likely 'fit' with the client at that moment if they are not to be received as cold or mechanistic (Cooper, 2008). If chosen thoughtfully, the techniques and directives of CBT can be experienced by clients as containing and responsive.

Counselling psychologists also draw on psychodynamic therapies a great deal as these are useful in encouraging the client to understand the reasons behind his thoughts, feelings and actions and extending his repertoire of responses. Attention is paid to the client's phenomenology, but possible connections to developmental experiences are also considered, enabling the counselling psychologist to understand further dimensions of the therapeutic relationship. Both humanistic and psychodynamic therapists attend closely to their moment-by-moment experience of their client, using this to develop empathic understanding. However, humanistic therapists are more likely to consider self-disclosure if they judge this as likely to help the client. Freely revealing reactions to clients is unwise (Mearns & Thorne, 2007), but the *cautious* disclosure of an authentic response within the psychodynamic relationship can communicate transparency and involvement, encouraging a robust alliance in which feelings can be acknowledged and understood. This can be particularly helpful for clients who tend to evoke strongly negative feelings (Winnicott, 1984). Thoughtful self-disclosure from a robust position also offers 'a realness in the service of the client' (Cooper, 2007a, p. 14). Offering a genuine presence – not hiding behind an expert persona, or pretending – can be important when working with clients who are sensitive to falseness (Cooper, 2007a; Mearns & Cooper, 2005). A therapy grounded in a robust therapeutic relationship also allows difficulties and setbacks to be negotiated together.

The counselling psychologist can also draw on humanistic theory and practice to demystify the process of psychodynamic therapy for her client, keeping interpretations to a minimum and 'showing her working' by clearly explaining her perspective to the client (Mearns, 2006). 'Unconscious' processes are in fact often quite accessible to clients and so may be thought of as lying on the edge of awareness (O'Brien & Houston, 2000). Simply making an observation such as 'You seem to keep me at arm's length' may be enough to encourage reflection, without the need for direction or interpretation. Sharing such observations without linking them to the client's past has much in common with humanistic reflections (O'Brien & Houston, 2000) and offers the client an opportunity to make the connection for himself. If interpretations *are* made, the counselling psychologist can allow room for uncertainty, offering interpretations not as authoritative statements of fact but as straightforward thoughts or observations which the client is invited to 'try on' ('Something that's occurred to me is . . .'; 'Could it be possible that . . .'). If an interpretation is rejected, then rather than view this as *resistance* the counselling psychologist may view her intervention as not having fitted the client's experience at that moment.

Humanistic and psychodynamic models now focus less on the client's internal world and more on the immediate therapeutic relationship, in which difficult *processes* (Lambers, 1994; Warner, 2005), such as a client's need to try to control, may be evident. Like defences, these processes emerged from earlier adversity, but maintain the client's difficulties by distorting or limiting relationships with others. For example, the client may feel unable to show vulnerability and appear angry or controlling yet express puzzlement as to why his relationships do not work out (Mearns, 2006). Offering an empathic relationship to these clients, whose needs may be complex and intense, has much in common with self-psychology by enabling clients to process experiences with a soothing, regulating other who can help the client remain in contact with his emotion without becoming overwhelmed (Kahn, 2000; Warner, 2005). Respectfully negotiating the client's process allows the psychologist to make contact with the client at a deep level, 'right down to the very core understanding of who they are' (Cooper, 2007a, p. 15). Mearns (2006) discusses how the therapist can draw on different parts of her self to make contact at such a level of 'relational depth' – for example, using a lonely part of the self as a bridge to reach a client who feels intensely isolated, offering a depth of understanding and empathic identification. These 'existential touchstones' (Mearns & Cooper, 2005) are not unlike Winnicott's 'identifications belonging to the . . . analyst's personal experiences and development' (1984, p. 195), allowing the psychologist to attune in a personal and involved way which is very different from the traditional analytic presence.

Humanistic Perspective on Contextual Issues

The chapter now considers some of the excesses of the modern approach to psychological therapies. In this era of manualisation and problem specification, relationship-based therapies have a significant challenge on their hands as well as a substantial corrective to make.

Preoccupation with specifying and standardising 'treatments' is challenged by a body of research that suggests that effective helping depends on establishing a relationship of depth and quality as well as on the client's resources – their 'psychological-mindedness' and readiness to engage and try new things, for example (Cooper, 2004, 2008). These findings cast some doubt on the validity of trying to establish evidence bases for different 'disorders' (Cooper, 2004, 2008; Gillon, 2007). Attempting to demonstrate the supremacy of one model over others also limits the choice available to clients and the span of evidence-based practice (Cooper, 2007b; Cooper & McLeod, 2007). Finding creative ways to help is part of the challenge of practice, allowing counselling psychologists to go beyond the mechanistic application of theory and research to engage with complexity and uncertainty (Cooper, 2007a). By eschewing categorisation and focusing on clients' subjective experience, humanism encourages counselling psychologists to remain *person* -centred rather than disorder- or problem-centred and to stay open-minded, recognising that many difficulties are too personal to be easily categorised and addressed using standard interventions.

This is the case in research matters too. In primary and secondary care settings, humanistic therapies perform very favourably against CBT (King *et al.*, 2000; Stiles *et al.*, 2006). While building on these studies is important, there are also opportunities to develop an evidence base that otherwise seems over-reliant on positivist studies. Neither quantitative nor qualitative methodologies alone offer an adequate picture of the effectiveness of therapies, but a *pluralistic* epistemology in which 'opposing' methodologies may coexist can extend the evidence base and enable a more confident assessment of therapies (Cooper, 2008; Corrie & Callahan, 2000; Goss & Mearns, 1997). A pluralism of approach also fits well with the humanistic ethos of counselling psychology, which creatively interprets the scientist-practitioner model to include a variety of forms of knowledge and enquiry. In particular, qualitative methodologies are consistent with the phenomenological-experiential ethos of humanism and the values underpinning counselling psychology, and are evident throughout the research endeavour, for example in terms of the relationships developed with participants and the detailed descriptions of experiences obtained (Coyle, 1998; Coyle & Wright, 1996).

By foregrounding the importance of relationship – as a means both to enable effective helping and encourage wellbeing – humanism has a significant corrective to make in such a culture. By encouraging an understanding that effective therapy goes beyond simply reducing or managing symptoms, there is much to be gained from humanistic practitioners, alongside their existential and psychodynamic colleagues, presenting a united case for the importance of the therapeutic relationship (Mearns & Jacobs, 2003). Focusing on the healing potential of the therapeutic relationship and sheltering this from institutional forces offers the client an opportunity to experience a quality of relating that may be missing elsewhere. Within just a few meetings it may be possible to explore the client's difficulty, offer new perspectives and encourage insight. Engaging with the client as a whole person may also include consideration of his life in its social and cultural context. Attending to issues of race or sexuality, for example, or experiences of poverty can empower clients by highlighting possible connections between their distress and experiences of inequality or difference (Cooper, 2006; Peachey, 2006; Proctor, 2006).

Conclusion

Humanism helps counselling psychologists to focus on what is important in practice, namely attending to the healing potential of the therapeutic relationship and being prepared to be with the client in whatever way is needed whilst justifying this theoretically. Regardless of the therapeutic model used, the setting for the work or the nature or severity of the client's difficulty, offering a therapeutic relationship of genuine interest and concern is important and worth shielding from an excessive preoccupation with diagnosis, specific intervention techniques, the pressures of the waiting list or a need to portray oneself as the polished professional. A humanistic philosophy enriches many theoretical models, anchoring practice in the need to establish and respond to the specific needs of each client. When clients' difficulties seem connected to the limits and conditions of their relationships, or when their need to feel valued and understood in relationship has been neglected or ill-treated, offering a therapeutic relationship in which experiences are acknowledged and thought about is likely to be restorative, helping the client to begin to recognise and explore the choices he has made.

Note

[1] The client vignettes included in this text are based on material from several clients, plus additional fictional material. Any identifying information has been removed.

References

Bohart, A. C. (1982). Similarities between cognitive and humanistic approaches to psychotherapy. *Cognitive Therapy and Research*, 6: 245–250.
Bohart, A. C. (1990). Psychotherapy integration from a client-centred perspective. In G. Lietaer, J. Rombauts & R. Van Balen (Eds.) *Client-centered and experiential psychotherapy in the nineties*. Leuven: University of Leuven Press.

Boucher, T. (2006). In cognitive therapy, how would the therapist understand and work with difficulties that arise on the therapeutic relationship? *Counselling Psychology Review, 21*(3): 12–18.

Clarkson, P. (2000). Eclectic, integrative and integrating psychotherapy or beyond schoolism? In S. Palmer & R. Woolfe (Eds.) *Integrative and eclectic counselling and psychotherapy*. London: Sage.

Cooper, M. (2004). Towards a relationally-orientated approach to therapy: Empirical support and analysis. *British Journal of Guidance and Counselling, 32*(4): 451–460.

Cooper, M. (2006). Socialist humanism: A progressive politics for the twenty-first century. In G. Proctor, M. Cooper, P. Sanders & B. Malcolm (Eds.) *Politicizing the person-centred approach: An agenda for social change*. Ross-on-Wye: PCCS Books.

Cooper, M. (2007a). Humanizing psychotherapy. *Journal of Contemporary Psychotherapy, 37*: 11–16.

Cooper, M. (2007b). *Person-centred and relational approaches to psychological therapy: A review of the contemporary evidence*. Paper presented at the scientific meeting of the Division of Counselling Psychology (Scotland Branch), Glasgow, January.

Cooper, M. (2008). *Essential research findings in counselling and psychotherapy: The facts are friendly*. London: Sage.

Cooper, M. & McLeod, J. (2007). A pluralistic framework for counselling and psychotherapy: Implications for research. *Counselling and Psychotherapy Research, 7*(3): 135–143.

Corrie, S. & Callahan, M. M. (2000). A review of the scientist-practitioner model: Reflections on its potential contribution to counselling psychology within the context of current healthcare trends. *British Journal of Medical Psychology, 73*(3): 413–427.

Corrie, S. & Milton, M. (2000). The relationship between existential-phenomenological and cognitive-behavioural therapies. *European Journal of Psychotherapy, Counselling and Health, 3*(1): 7–24.

Coyle, A. (1998). Qualitative research in counselling psychology: Using the counselling interview as a research instrument. In P. Clarkson (Ed.) *Counselling psychology: Integrating theory, research and supervised practice*. London: Routledge.

Coyle, A. & Wright, C. (1996). Using the counselling interview to collect research data on sensitive topics. *Journal of Health Psychology, 1*: 431–440.

Gillon, E. (2007). *Person-centred counselling psychology: An introduction*. London: Sage.

Goss, S. & Mearns, D. (1997). A call for a pluralist epistemological understanding in the assessment and evaluation of counselling. *British Journal of Guidance and Counselling, 25*(2): 189–199.

Greenberg, L. S., Rice, L. N. & Elliott, R. (1993). *Facilitating emotional change: The moment-by-moment process*. New York: Guilford Press.

Jacobson, N. S. (1989). The therapist–client relationship in cognitive behavior therapy: Implications for treating depression. *Journal of Cognitive Psychotherapy, 3*: 85–96.

Josefowitz, N. & Myran, D. (2005). Towards a person-centred cognitive-behaviour therapy. *Counselling Psychology Quarterly, 18*(4): 329–336.

Kahn, M. (2000). *Between therapist and client: The new relationship* (revised edn.). New York: W. H. Freeman.

King, M., Sibbald, B. *et al.* (2000). Randomised control trial of non-directive counselling, cognitive behaviour therapy and usual general practitioner care in the management of depression as well as mixed anxiety and depression in primary care. *Health Technology Assessment, 4*(19): 1–83.

Lambers, E. (1994). Person-centered psychopathology. In D. Mearns (Ed.) *Developing person-centered counselling*. Sage: London.

Mearns, D. (1994). *Developing person-centred counselling*. London: Sage.

Mearns, D. (2006). The humanity of the counsellor. Paper presented for The Mary Kilborn Lecture, Glasgow, May.

Mearns, D. & Cooper, M. (2005). *Working at relational depth in counselling and psychotherapy*. London: Sage.

Mearns, D. & Jacobs, M. (2003). Colleagues or opponents? A dialogue between person-centred and psychodynamic therapy. Paper presented at CSCT Events Workshop, Regents College, London, March.

Mearns, D. & Thorne, B. (2007). *Person-centred counselling in action* (3rd edn.). London: Sage.

O'Brien, M. & Houston, G. (2000). *Integrative therapy: A practitioner's guide*. London: Sage.

Peachey, L. (2006). Personal reflections on training as a person-centred counsellor. In G. Proctor, M. Cooper, P. Sanders & B. Malcolm (Eds.) *Politicizing the person-centred approach: An agenda for social change*. Ross-on-Wye: PCCS Books.

Proctor, G. (2006). Therapy: Opium for the masses or helps those who least need it? In G. Proctor, M. Cooper, P. Sanders & B. Malcolm (Eds.) *Politicizing the person-centred approach: An agenda for social change*. Ross-on-Wye: PCCS Books.

Rogers, C. R. (1957). The necessary and sufficient conditions of therapeutic personality change. *Journal of Consulting Psychology, 21*(2): 95–103.

Rogers, C. R. (1995). *A way of being*. Boston, MA: Houghton Mifflin. (First published 1980.)

Rogers, C. R. (1999). *On becoming a person: A therapist's view of psychotherapy*. London: Constable. (First published 1961.)

Rogers, C. R. (2000). *Client-centred therapy: Its current practice, implications and theory*. London: Constable. (First published 1951.)

Safran, J. D. & Segal, Z. V. (1996). *Interpersonal process in cognitive therapy*. North Vale, NJ: Jason Aronson.

Strawbridge, S. & Woolfe, R. (2003). Counselling psychology in context. In R. Woolfe, W. Dryden & S. Strawbridge (Eds.) *Handbook of counselling psychology* (2nd edn.). London: Sage.

Stiles, W. B., Barkham, M. *et al.* (2006). Effectiveness of cognitive-behavioural, person-centred and psychodynamic therapies as practised in UK National Health Service settings. *Psychological Medicine, 36*: 555–566.

Warner, M. S. (2005). A person-centred view of human nature, wellness and psychopathology. In S. Joseph & R. Worsley (Eds.) *Person-centred psychopathology: A positive psychology of mental health*. Ross-on-Wye: PCCS Books.

Winnicott, D. (1984). Hate in the countertransference. In *Through paediatrics to psychoanalysis: The collected papers*. London: Karnac Books. (First published 1947.)

Woolfe, R. (1996). The nature of counselling psychology. In R. Woolfe & W. Dryden (Eds.) *Handbook of counselling psychology*. London: Sage.

Chapter 9

Psychodynamic Contributions to Pluralistic Practice

Debora Diamond

Therapy as an Art Form

If 'the relationship' lies at the heart of counselling psychology, then its soul must surely derive from within the traditions of psychoanalysis, for psychoanalysis has acted as a reference point for all contemporary therapies that emerged in its wake. As psychological therapies have developed over time, they have swung, like a pendulum, back and forth between action towards extending current practices and reaction against those same practices. Some of the therapies that have arisen post-psychoanalysis have been driven by a desire to achieve similar aims by offering the opposite in conditions, so that long-term therapies are replaced with brief treatments or free-floating conversations are replaced with manualised approaches.

This phenomenon of action–reaction is not specific to psychotherapy or psychology but is commonly acknowledged in every aspect of life, from the banal to the sublime – from something as unremarkable as the design of door furniture, through calculated methods used to wage war or elect politicians and beyond to the creative forces of music, literature and art. Sometimes the concepts of the past are later recognised as meritorious and earlier ideas are then incorporated into contemporary thought to achieve richer and more complex knowledge and meaning. Advances on what have gone

Therapy and Beyond: Counselling Psychology Contributions to Therapeutic and Social Issues
Edited by Martin Milton
© 2010 John Wiley & Sons, Ltd.

before mark out the difference between art and craft – to be good at what you do is craft, to add something new that makes sense across past and present spectrums constitutes the transformation into art. For instance, in the discipline of psychology, theory of mind (Baron-Cohen *et al.*, 1985) has helped to inform development of mentalisation-based approaches (Bateman & Fonagy, 2004) which are rooted in psychoanalytic tradition but which also speak fluently to cognitive behavioural and dialectic behaviour therapies.

The craft of therapy, irrespective of theoretical model, is to find new contexts and new understandings in which to place the lived experiences of those in distress, those desiring change and those whose needs may be unmet. As individuals we lead our lives in the present on the basis of what has happened in the past or on what has been inferred from the experience of the past. How fitting, then, that psychoanalytic theory invests much in the developmental histories of individual lives in order to contribute to the discovery of new experiences within relationships. It is also fitting that counselling psychology acknowledges the centrality of relationships across the whole of the spectrum of mental health presentations. Indeed, counselling psychology originates from an innovative movement intent on progressing professional understandings of the application of psychology from their clinical roots into the realm of the relational and the dynamic. In that sense, at its inception counselling psychology was an artistic departure from traditional clinical practice.

This chapter considers the contribution counselling psychology has made to individuals, their experiences of severe and enduring mental health problems and to those with complex trauma, often understood within medical perspectives as 'personality disordered'. It examines the ways in which counselling psychology has shaped experiences of mental health services and recovery from distress. Finally, the contribution counselling psychology has made to enhanced understandings of people and their processes, talents and struggles will be discussed. In exploring these issues, this chapter takes the contexts of acute and open inpatient care settings as its area of illustration. By examining the historical and contemporary interrelatedness of counselling psychology and psychodynamic practice, one aspect of acute treatment will be illustrated with an example from professional practice.

The Emergence of Counselling Psychology

In order to understand the distinctions between what psychoanalytic psychotherapy might undertake and the work of a counselling psychologist, it is useful to consider the historical developments of both disciplines.

Counselling psychology began when a groundswell of clinical practitioners, many of whom had undertaken postgraduate training in psychotherapy, sought to influence future mainstream training by enhancing the psychotherapeutic framework of the delivery of psychological therapy by moving away from medical models of treatment (see Van Scoyoc, 2005). At the time it was possible, and may still be, to train as a clinical psychologist without ever having engaged in meaningful, long-term psychotherapy as part of the training process. Many psychologists thus undertook postgraduate training from the vast stable of therapeutic models being developed in the 1960s and 1970s, including those emerging from a burgeoning culture of alternative practices. Amongst others, these included humanistic, existential-phenomenological, cognitive behavioural, feminist, constructivist, transactional and analytic approaches. As outlined in Chapter 7, Rogers' (1980) theoretical framework included what he termed the 'core conditions' necessary to the development of a positive therapeutic relationship. Perhaps the three best known of these – therapist acceptance, empathy and congruence – have had a lasting influence not only on the practice of therapy but also on the attitudes of practitioners towards their relationships with their clients. This fertile environment of client-centred approaches provided the backdrop against which the profession of counselling psychology was established within a structure of increasing scepticism and scrutiny concerning the delivery of psychological therapies. The prevailing scientist-practitioner model in which investigations of 'subjects' was the norm rather than the 'participants' of contemporary research was robustly challenged.

Increasingly, psychologists became interested in the phenomenological and ontological experiences of those to whom they offered their 'treatments' and, by 1982, the British Psychological Society had opened its membership to a Counselling Psychology Section. Ten years later the first professional trainings were offered and the graduates of these courses became the first Chartered Counselling Psychologists trained in the profession, following those first pioneering counselling psychologists who had 'grand-parented' into the profession.

The Psychoanalytic Tradition

The term 'psychoanalysis' originated back in 1896 with Sigmund Freud whose studies of the science of the human mind were popularised at around the turn of the twentieth century. Freud (1923) described the concepts of three states of mind or mental states – the preconscious, the conscious and the unconscious. His subsequent 'structural' model understood human processes in the context of three forces on the personality of the individual – the id, the ego and the superego (Freud, 1923). Freud described these structures as having their beginnings in infancy when personality first develops. Psychological disturbance occurs when aspects of the personality are unacceptable to the individual, who then employs what Freud's daughter, Anna, termed the 'mechanisms of defence' (Freud, A., 1958), which act as a way to protect the mind. Defence mechanisms allow us to avoid feared and unacceptable personal characteristics. These mechanisms are numerous and some quite complex, but all have the same outcome in that unconscious desires, usually sexual or aggressive, lie outside of conscious awareness (Freud, 1923).

Ultimately, Freud believed that an individual's need to employ defence mechanisms are largely due to innate, biological factors, with some people being better able to manage and accommodate their unacceptable thoughts, wishes and desires. However, he also postulated an interaction between environment and personality in which psychological disturbance could be alleviated by changes in circumstances that would allow the individual to sublimate their unconscious wishes. Freud also considered that psychological disturbance could be assuaged by making unconscious wishes known to the person in order for self-acceptance to occur and diminish fear and anxiety.

Psychoanalytic techniques were developed that encouraged facilitation of both of these processes of decreasing psychic disturbance and the subsequent symptomology that resulted from them (Smith, 1996). Despite coming from a tradition of scientific study, Freud (1904) disputed the Popperian stance that the exception is needed to prove the rule (see Popper, 1959), instead relying on the theory to substantiate itself. Therefore, at its inception psychoanalytic practice was committed to an ideology of scientist-practitioner although not supported by an empirical evidence base at this time. This legacy has been problematic for practitioners working in the political climate of the NHS, which functions from a particular perspective of 'evidence-based practice' (see Wilkes, 2008).

It is well known that a number of analytic schools have been the product of Freudian theory. These are known variously as the London, English, Viennese and American Schools due to the location of those subscribing to particular aspects of theory or to particular theoretical developments. Most notably from the 1920s onwards, Melanie Klein's theories predominated in what became known as the London School. Further to Freud's concepts, Klein (1946) argued that, from infancy, we learn to take in aspects of our environment and characteristics of those who people our environment intrapsychically – a process known as introjection. Klein also argued that we split off unacceptable or intolerable aspects of ourselves and project them onto the environment or onto others within the environment. This is known as projection. Although there is a departure of theoretical ideologies between Freud and Klein, classical Freudian analytic techniques are employed in order to facilitate a gradual acceptance that the person's past is connected to their present experiences. The work of psychoanalysis, and its offspring psychodynamic psychotherapy, lies in the negotiation of the minutiae within the relationship of the two people in the consulting room (Hinshelwood, 1994).

Even if this chapter offers only an incomplete view of the history of psychoanalysis, it enables appreciation of the relevance of three positions to the practices of both counselling psychology and psychodynamic psychotherapy. These are the centrality of the scientist-practitioner model within therapeutic practice; that of understanding the importance of lifespan development to psychological distress or disturbance; and the fundamental importance of the therapeutic relationship as the mutative agent of change. Some psychologists would go so far as to argue that the environment is all in the development of human personality.

> [E]very human being is a tabula rasa a white tablet, a clean slate. The circumstances of one's life are then written on the white surface. To this end the human being learns to live with their history and the alternating vicissitudes and pleasant episodes of life.
>
> (Cooper, 1996, p. 55)

That counselling psychology shares an emphasis on developmental history is shown by Woolfe and Dryden (1996, p. x), who suggest that 'life cycle and developmental issues are of central concern to counselling psychologists'. Increasingly throughout the twentieth century human beings have been understood as psychological beings. As Chapter 4 shows, people's difficulties have increasingly been seen as psychological rather than moral. The impetus for this change has comprised many elements, but psychoanalysis has figured prominently among them (Hinshelwood, 1994).

It is perhaps paradoxical that counselling psychology arose during a time of some discontent with psychoanalysis. The latter half of the twentieth century recognised that the relationship between analyst and client was undeniably a power-laden one in which the client develops a strong attachment and reliance on the analyst. In addition, concern has grown about the fact that most analyses are time-consuming and expensive, with 4–5 weekly consultations often continuing over a number of years. These criticisms of the model and its failure to offer robust evidence for its efficacy featured largely in the development of new approaches to psychotherapy. As moves towards evidence-based practice have become more commonplace, uncertainty regarding the efficacy of psychotherapeutic interventions has been voiced:

> I have grown very sceptical about much of Freudian theory. I have come to believe that the depth of our ignorance and the absence of objective means for investigating psychotherapeutic theories warrant a cautious and sceptical attitude towards all forms of psychotherapy.
>
> (Smith, 1996, p. 38)

Counselling Psychology as Transmodal Practice

Counselling psychology can be seen as a reaction to the somewhat mechanistic view of human beings inherent in more traditional psychological paradigms based on a conventional model of the nature of science and the technique of scientific investigation (Woolfe, 1996).

Until the early 1960s psychological thinking was dominated not only by psychoanalytic theory but also by the pioneers of behaviourism, B. F. Skinner and Ivan Pavlov. Bandura (1977) introduced the notion of the importance of cognitive processes to psychological functioning, thus challenging purely behavioural understandings of learned distress. Bandura and his colleagues argued for an approach that also took greater account of social factors in the development of individual psychology. Consequently, those concepts of behaviourism previously privileged within the clinical practice of psychology were being contested at about the same time as was the clinical practice of psychoanalysis.

In America, both Albert Ellis and Aaron Beck had similar concerns in the 1970s when they trained as analysts and became disillusioned with the lack of scientific rigour and demonstrable efficacy (Beck, 1976; Ellis, 1999). Beck went on to undertake a number of investigations of cognitive therapies beginning in 1976 when he compared cognitive therapy with pharmaceutical treatment of patients diagnosed with depression (Beck, 1976). It was this disillusionment with psychoanalysis that led to Beck's development of cognitive behavioural therapy (CBT) based on the understanding of distorted or maladaptive emotional states as arising from conditioned thinking patterns. Reacting against the theoretical principles of psychoanalytic perspectives, Beck and others turned instead to emerging understandings of information processing, based on developments within artificial intelligence, which were informed by innovations in early developments in computer sciences.

More recently, phenomenological and cognitive understandings of human distress have become part of dominant treatment approaches being developed internationally. Phenomenological perspectives have impacted on cognitive therapies such that we are now seeing what is termed, third wave CBT, which take a more holistic, formulation-based and client-centred approach than did early CBT therapies. In its early days CBT was criticised for its unrelenting focus on structure and adherence to a plan. In my own practice I saw a client who, disillusioned by his experience of CBT made the evaluation that 'the therapist had an agenda and I was incidental to it'. Delivery of CBT has since moved on so that in the area of CBT for psychosis, for instance, homework is often not considered appropriate and therapists no longer take the attitude that if the client is hard to engage, then they don't get the 'treatment'. Thus third wave CBT arose to some extent from concerns for the relational elements of therapy that distinguish first wave counselling psychology from clinical psychology.

The Multiple Domains of Counselling Psychology

As psychology has developed it has become, and is increasingly becoming, more pluralistic. In order to progress all types and models of practice clinicians are learning from each other – clinical psychology from counselling psychology, CBT from psychodynamic practice, and vice versa. Counselling psychologists have contributed much to the advancement of pluralistic practice in recent times and this marks the difference between the framework of counselling psychology and practitioners who inhabit a single therapeutic approach. Counselling psychologists train in a number of modalities and have a highly developed understanding of the advantages and disadvantages of the various approaches. They are thus well placed to understand and scrutinise the similarities and differences between the therapies they deliver.

In the public sector, counselling psychologists contribute to a range of primary, secondary and tertiary care settings. There is a growing recognition that severe and long-term mental health problems and complex traumas, labelled personality disorders, are helpfully approached from the perspective of the alleviation of distress. During the 1940s and through to the 1960s, psychoanalytic understandings of schizophrenia spectrum disorders, psychotic depression, bipolar disorder (then called manic depression) and other mental illnesses had been developed as primary interventions for treatment. Psychological treatments were seen as being vital to patient care rather than sole reliance being placed on medical interventions. All that changed in the 1980s when new anti-psychotic medications were introduced and it was believed they would alleviate symptomology so that sufferers would better adapt to functional community living because they would be symptom-free. Biological, medical approaches were once again at the forefront of care for those with acute mental health problems.

Fortunately, the nineteenth-century asylums were finally closed and psychiatric patients were housed within more residential, rehabilitation settings, with short-term acute care being provided within hospital settings. However, the new generation of anti-psychotic medications proved disappointing and did not provide the anticipated panacea for many of those receiving it. From the mid-1990s, the stress vulnerability approach (Zubin & Spring, 1977), with its broad spectrum across antecedents of biological, psychological and social factors to the development and maintenance of mental health problems, was again in favour.

Psychological therapies were, and remain, valued and recognised as important ingredients for the recovery of functional mental health. In the shift from rehabilitation to a focus on recovery which is currently transforming mental health practices, psychological practitioners are working in partnership with medical colleagues to deliver individual care packages to their clients which take account of all aspects of their lives. Crucially, developmental events, early relationships and processes experienced by service users are viewed as significant triggers for current mental health problems or for what is labelled as personality disorder.

Counselling psychologists are also trained in the audit of their own practices and those of the services they work in, and they have the capacity, training and skill to scrutinise and measure these using methodologies that range across quantitative and qualitative research perspectives and tools. Counselling psychologists also bring an evaluative scientist-practitioner position to their work. For this reason, counselling psychologists are well placed to provide psychological therapy to those who find themselves vulnerable to psychic distress, especially when they draw on their psychodynamic understandings of mental health. The counselling psychology perspective has the advantage of prioritising holistic perspectives of wellbeing and recovery.

Counselling Psychology's Contribution to Acute Care

In acute care, I worked with Jonathan Radcliffe (Radcliffe & Diamond, 2007) to create an inpatient environment that promoted the use of psychoanalytic principles within a bio-psycho-social model of treatment. We developed weekly, psychodynamically informed inpatient groups providing training to medical staff in order to advance psychological perspectives of acute mental illnesses. These were open groups, facilitated by both psychologists together with a ward nurse. Other staff members observed from behind one-way glass. We describe the aim of the group therapy as bringing the unconscious conflicts causing the psychiatric symptoms into conscious awareness. We argue that in order for this to happen, the therapists should not determine the content of discussion as in some other groups, but should allow patients to raise issues and concerns that come to their minds and to which other group members are invited to respond. This freedom for interactions to take place is the equivalent of the free association that is a hallmark of psychoanalytic psychotherapy. Spontaneously arising content and interactions reflect both conscious ideation as well as unconscious processes, which can be thought about in the group and interpreted by therapists and by other patients.

The notion of the unconscious has been robustly debated and is contentious for many outside psychoanalytic circles. However, in recent years some detractors have reconsidered their positions and Clark (1995), a staunch proponent of CBT, acknowledges the existence of the 'nonconscious' as an aspect of human experience. Perhaps because the unconscious is a poorly understood concept, the pendulum of psychotherapy has swung back and forth over its usage. As a direct translation of Freud's (1904) *Unbewußte*, the unconscious means: *that which we are not aware of.*

> Thus it need not be visualized as a dustbin for our more bestial desires but . . . can be understood as dispersed throughout the psyche-soma as long as the link of communication is broken. Thus the unconscious, although socially determined, is a burden borne by the individual as it is unshared knowledge.
>
> (Thornton, 1999, p. 23)

Individually, Radcliffe and I have continued to develop psychodynamically informed inpatients groups in Lewisham and Plymouth respectively. Not only do such groups provide their members with the opportunity to reflect on the issues that have led to their admission to hospital, but also to consider their experiences of mental health problems, the way in which a hospital admission affects their lives, families and friends, and the stigma they experience within a community, culture and society that often demonise sufferers. This provides patients with a space in which to ventilate their frustrations in a safe and contained environment and also to begin to tolerate the pain and distress that may be responsible for triggering an episode of psychological disturbance.

A Psychodynamically Informed Inpatient Group

What follows is an illustration of psychodynamically informed group therapy within an inpatient setting. It demonstrates how group dynamics are interpreted and acted on by the therapists and the beneficial effect that this can have on individual group members.

Helen and Martha

Helen[1] was a regular attendee at the ward group for the six weeks that she was an inpatient. When first attending, she found it difficult to sit down throughout the whole of the hour-long session, getting up from her chair and distracting herself with reading material that happened to be in the room and often changing the subject onto the work being carried out in the hospital garden. The garden was in a courtyard in the centre of the hospital buildings where the unit's psychiatric patients could go to socialise or for a cigarette, and which was contained by buildings or a high perimeter fence. Helen spoke of the garden as being a 'dump', with superficial attempts being made to dress it up but which wouldn't work because of the ugliness of the buildings and fences that surrounded it. She said that the work being undertaken was to make a pretence to patients that they were being cared for, but that these efforts were tokenistic and useless as the patients could see right through them.

In the group, Helen described her family background, saying that her father was a well-known comedian renowned for his many extramarital affairs with actresses. Helen's mother had left a promising business career to raise her family of four children. Helen was the eldest daughter. Helen described her mother's depression and fear that her husband would leave her for one of his girlfriends. This often left Helen in the position of comforting her vulnerable mother and taking care of her younger siblings while her father was away. As she grew up, Helen had some success as an actress and she described the ready availability of drugs in the acting profession, which she said were often taken to prevent weight gain. She gave up acting when she became pregnant with twins several years ago but she struggled to stay off drugs, continuing to feel concern for an increase in her weight. Eventually, Helen's children were taken into care and she became more entrenched in a drugs culture.

Over the weeks that Helen attended the therapy group, the psychologists suggested that perhaps she felt about herself in the same way that she was expressing about the garden. We wondered if Helen believed that she showed superficial, external care but underneath it all she thought there was only neglect and ugliness. At first Helen rejected this view, suggesting that we were defending mental health services despite their neglect of patients, but eventually Helen said that she had always provided care to everyone else but that she received nothing herself and that taking drugs had filled that void.

On one occasion a new patient, Martha, attended the group. Martha was tearful and distressed, saying that she had humiliated herself by her behaviour before coming into hospital. She described having a sudden understanding that she was the Virgin Mary and that all of those she came into contact with – family, friends, acquaintances and even strangers in the street – needed to accept this and pray to her. Martha recalled trying to convert her bewildered partner to this new way of thinking about her. As she started her story, Martha became increasingly distressed and this dialogue occurred between her and Helen:

M (weeping): I can't tell you how ridiculous I was, I'd be too embarrassed.
H (concerned): You can't be more ridiculous than me; you seem like a really nice person.
M (hesitating): I actually thought. . . .
H: Shall I get you a drink of water or a tissue?
M: I don't know.
H (rising from her chair and moving towards Martha): Don't worry Martha, we're all in the same boat here. We're all mad, aren't we?
M: I actually thought that I was the mother of Jesus Christ.
H (kneeling beside her): I thought I was chosen by the British government to bring about a Christian revolution and that I was going to fight terrorism.
M: I'm nothing . . . can't even keep my flat clean.
H: I could go and help you clean it up. Where do you live?

Rather than intervening in the conversation, the therapists let it carry on until another group member entered the dialogue. This allowed Helen to develop her interest in caring for Martha, which the therapists, together with the other group members, could then illustrate to her. Helen accepted that she had felt a need to take care of Martha and to make her feel better and that her own needs seemed to take second place. However, she argued that she couldn't take care of her own children, so she wasn't really the caring person she pretended to be. The therapists were able to suggest that perhaps Helen needed to have her own needs met first but that she was responding to her distress in a way that had become a habit over the years. Helen acknowledged that was the case and, on leaving the ward, she decided to put her own recovery at the top of the agenda. We arranged for long-term follow-up with residential psychotherapy in a therapeutic community. After several months Helen was reunited with one of her children and she is currently living in the community independently of mental health services and undertaking a university degree. Martha attended the group only once as she was discharged by the following week.

This example focuses on the dynamic interactions between two group members, whilst holding in mind the developmental histories reported by those attending. Psychoanalytic theory is used to perceive the ways that early experience might leave people open to later vulnerability to mental illness, expressed by both patients in this example in their descriptions of grandiose and psychotic thinking. Thus the task of the therapists is to make links between past experience and dynamic encounters in the present. Therefore, Helen's interaction with Martha in the group is understood as arising from early relational patterns within the family. Counselling psychology's emphasis on relationships sits comfortably with this perspective and can add a dimension by including a consideration of the cultural and social factors that might also contribute to patterns of behaviour and thinking.

Psychoanalytic Theory and Mentalisation

Psychodynamic inpatient groups mark a return to traditional principles that have been adapted to modern-day practices. However, there are also areas where the theoretical underpinnings of psychoanalysis have gestated into new conceptualisations of transmodal therapies to provide interventions that can be understood from a multiplicity of perspectives. Mentalisation-based therapy incorporates a synthesis of ideas that have emerged from psychoanalysis but are inclusive of a number of other therapeutic paradigms. Because counselling psychology is, at its heart, inherently transmodal, there is a potentially elegant meeting of the minds with mentalisation. Bateman and Fonagy (2004) describe mentalisation as the mental process by which an individual interprets the actions of himself and others, both implicitly and explicitly, as meaningful according to intentional mental states such as personal desires, needs, feelings, beliefs and reasons. Mentalisation is based on 'theory of mind', a concept researched by Premack and Woodruff's (1978) in their study of primates. It was developed by Baron-Cohen *et al.* (1985), who compared the cognitive development and functioning of those with and without autism. Baron-Cohen argues that having a theory of mind 'is to be able to reflect on the contents of one's own and other's minds' (2001, p. 174).

Because counselling psychology is essentially the practice of understanding human interaction and relationships, it is likely to incorporate aspects of mentalisation irrespective of the therapeutic model adopted. According to Holmes (2004), mentalising is a learned relational skill acquired in the course of psychological development. Irrespective of the techniques used in psychotherapy treatment, whether eye movement desensitisation readjustment (EMDR), graduated exposure or other forms of intervention, mentalising is central to the therapeutic process. The work of mentalisation-based therapy is to attempt to increase the client's mentalising function, especially within the dynamics of interpersonal relationships. Attachment processes provide the foundational base from which healthy mentalisation skills arise and as such can be understood within conceptualisations of psychoanalytic thought (Target *et al.*, 2003). Likewise, the sense of self arises in the context of other people and within attachment relationships. Mentalising is a natural function acquired in infancy and developed throughout life but which, if not properly nurtured or practised, can be lost. The facilitation of mentalisation is provided within safe and playful interactions with attachment figures but can fail to develop or be lost for biological reasons of genetic acquisition, or psychological and social reasons of insecure attachments, trauma or stress.

In order to assist the client's mentalisation in therapy, the therapist should accurately match the internal state of the client. Thus the therapist's stance is important, arising from a perspective of curiosity and not knowing and from an equal power base that generates multiple perspectives – the core values of counselling psychology. Because of its importance to any therapeutic endeavour, aspects of mentalisation can be practised by any psychological therapist or practitioner. Usefully, it employs language from psychodynamic and CBT therapies. In order to address deficiencies in mentalisation, the therapist needs to represent the clients' mind in reflections back to the client so that they develop their own sense of self. Because counselling psychologists attend to people's relationships, both past and present, and especially to the relationship as it unfolds in the therapy room, the use of mentalising interventions is inherent to the work. In order to provide containment, it is essential that interventions are supportive and empathic, providing clarification and elaboration of thoughts and feelings being experienced in the here and now. By providing a therapeutic model that accomplishes these goals, psychodynamic practices have addressed those criticisms levelled at traditional methods of practice. They also achieve a framework coherent with the practices of counselling psychology.

Conclusion

Counselling psychology has helped evolve practices across all therapeutic modalities by emphasising the importance of relationships. Many aspects of this are shared with conceptualisations of dynamic interaction within psychoanalytic practice. Some of the early criticisms levelled at traditional psychoanalytic treatments have been addressed by counselling psychology practitioners who have reinvigorated traditional psychoanalytic group therapy (e.g. Radcliffe & Diamond, 2007). Just as the influence of psychoanalysis resonates across all psychotherapeutic formulations of human mental well-being, so too is the shadow of counselling psychology cast across a landscape of emergent ideological perspectives. The focus of counselling psychology on relationship issues, irrespective of the therapeutic approach being practised, has helped to foster more holistic and humanistic psychology and psychotherapeutic practices and improve the experiences of those with whom we work.

Note

[1] The characters described in this vignette are a composite of inpatient groups and participants whose details have been anonymised to protect their confidentiality.

References

Bandura, A. (1977). *Social learning theory*. Englewood Cliffs, NJ: Prentice-Hall.

Baron-Cohen, S. (2001). Theory of mind in normal development and autism. *Prisme, 34*: 174–183.

Baron-Cohen, S., Leslie, A. M. & Frith, U. (1985). Does the autistic child have a 'theory of mind'? *Cognition, 21*: 37–46.

Bateman, A. & Fonagy, P. (2004). *Psychotherapy for borderline personality disorder: Mentalization-based treatment*. Oxford: Oxford University Press.

Beck, A. T. (1976). *Cognitive therapy and the emotional disorders*. New York: International Universities Press.

Clark, D. (1995). Perceived limitations of standard cognitive therapy: A consideration of efforts to revise Beck's theory and therapy. *Journal of Cognitve Psychotherapy: An International Quarterly, 9*(3): 153–169.

Cooper, C. (1996). Psychodynamic therapy: The Kleinian approach. In W. Dryden (Ed.) *Handbook of individual therapy* (rev. edn.). London: Sage.

Ellis, A. (1999). The main change agent in effective psychotherapy is specific technique and skill. In C. Feltham (Ed.) *Controversies in psychotherapy and counselling.* London: Sage.

Freud, A. (1958). Adolescence. *The Psychoanalytic Study of the Child, 13*: 255–278.

Freud, S. (1904). Freud's psycho-analytic procedure. In J. Strachey (Ed.) *The standard edition of the complete works of Sigmund Freud* vol. 7. London: Hogarth Press and the Institute for Psycho-Analysis.

Freud, S. (1923). The ego and the id and other works. In J. Strachey (Ed.) *The standard edition of the complete works of Sigmund Freud*, vol. XIX. London: Hogarth Press and the Institute for Psycho-Analysis.

Hinshelwood, R. D. (1994). *Clinical Klein.* London: Free Association Books.

Holmes, J. (2004). Mentalizing from a psychoanalytic perspective: What's new? In A. Bateman & P. Fonagy (Eds.) *Psychotherapy for borderline personality disorder: Mentalization-based treatment.* Oxford: Oxford University Press.

Klein, M. (1946). *The psychoanalysis of children.* London: Hogarth Press.

Popper, K. (1959). The propensity interpretation of probability. *The British Journal for the Philosophy of Science, X*(37): 25–42.

Premack, D. G. & Woodruff, G. (1978). Does the chimpanzee have a theory of mind? *Behavioural and Brain Science, 202*(4371): 991–994.

Radcliffe, J. & Diamond, D. (2007). Psychodynamically-informed discussion groups on acute inpatient wards. *Groupwork: An interdisciplinary journal for working with groups, 17*(1): 34–44.

Rogers, C. R. (1980). *A way of being.* Boston, MA.: Houghton Mifflin.

Smith, D. L. (1996). Psychodynamic therapy: The Freudian approach. In W. Dryden (Ed.) *Handbook of individual therapy* (rev. edn.). London: Sage.

Target, M., Fonagy, P. *et al.* (2003). The developmental roots of borderline personality disorder in early attachment relationships: A theory and some evidence. *Psychoanalytic Inquiry, 23*: 412–459.

Thornton, E. M. (1999). Does the unconscious mind really exist? In C. Feltham (Ed.) *Controversies in psychotherapy and counselling.* London: Sage.

Van Scoyoc, S. (2005). The future of our profession: Time to remember our history. *Counselling Psychology Review, 20*(2): 49–51.

Wilkes, R. (2008). A portfolio of academic, therapeutic practice and research work including a grounded theory investigation of therapists' experiences of evidence based practice. Unpublished PsychD portfolio: University of Surrey.

Woolfe, R. (1996). The nature of counselling psychology. In R. Woolfe & W. Dryden (Eds.) *Handbook of counselling psychology.* London: Sage.

Woolfe, R. & Dryden W. (Eds.) (1996). *Handbook of counselling psychology.* London: Sage.

Zubin, J. & Spring, B. (1977). Vulnerability: A new view of schizophrenia. *Journal of Abnormal Psychology, 86*(2): 103–124.

Chapter 10

Cognitive-behavioural Contributions to Pluralistic Practice: Reflections on an Issue of Some Contention

Terry Boucher

This chapter takes a reflective stance on the contribution of cognitive-behavioural therapy (CBT) to the concept of pluralistic practice in terms of its actual and potential contribution.

So What is CBT?

At first glance, this question seems a simple one to answer. We all know that CBT is a relatively modern therapeutic approach to the human condition, evolving from the work of Aaron Beck in the 1960s. The approach emphasises the role of our thoughts and beliefs (cognitions) in initiating and then maintaining our states of mind and mood (with the added complicity of our behaviours) (Beck *et al.*, 1979; Westbrook *et al.*, 2007).

However, when we scrape a little at the surface, things seem less clear-cut. Over the course of my training I read much CBT-oriented literature and in my final year produced a paper (Boucher, 2006) relating to CBT and the therapeutic relationship. This background, experience since qualification and a number of conversations with colleagues 'in the profession' have

Therapy and Beyond: Counselling Psychology Contributions to Therapeutic and Social Issues
Edited by Martin Milton
© 2010 John Wiley & Sons, Ltd.

drawn me to the conclusion that when we talk of CBT we may be coming from an array of quite different understandings. That said I feel it necessary to contrast two broad understandings of CBT, garnered from the literature and clinical experience, which I feel may illuminate this point further.

In the first, CBT is a theoretically heavy and technique-oriented approach to treating ailments with specific 'pathological' diagnostic criteria. The practitioner adopts a more prescriptive, manualised and directive stance with regard to a client's presenting issues. The emphasis of the therapy is on 'doing', as exemplified by out-of-session homework tasks and 'guided discovery' in session. The therapeutic relationship is a working alliance, one of collaboration and trust, and this is task-oriented which, while based on the client's goals, takes place in the context of a 'pathologising' diagnosis. Indeed, Beck saw therapy as 'a collaborative enterprise between the patient and the therapist to explore [the patient's] dysfunctional interpretations and try to modify them when the *therapist* finds them unrealistic or unreasonable' (Beck & Weishaar, 1989, p. 286; emphasis added). An example of how this approach might be presented is found in Adrian Wells' *Cognitive Therapy of Anxiety Disorders: A Practice Manual and Conceptual Guide* (1997) which offers robust theoretical modelling for differing 'anxiety disorders' and even sets out example treatment outlines a practitioner might find useful in guiding their own interventions.

In the second understanding, CBT is a far less technically-oriented approach where theory floats gently on the sea of core relational principles: warmth, respect, empathy, positive regard, congruence, autonomy. Indeed, Beck stressed the importance of rapport, which encapsulates many of these qualities, in the therapeutic relationship, stating:

> The term *rapport*, in general, refers to harmonious accord between people. In the therapeutic relationship, rapport consists of a combination of emotional and intellectual components. When this type of relationship is established, the patient perceives the therapist as someone (a) who is tuned in to his feelings and attitudes, (b) who is sympathetic, empathetic, and understanding, (c) who is accepting of him with all his 'faults', (d) with whom he can communicate without having to spell out his feelings and attitudes in detail or to qualify what he says. When rapport is optimal, the patient and therapist feel secure and reasonably comfortable with each other. Neither is defensive, overly cautious, tentative, or inhibited.
>
> (Beck *et al.*, 1979, p. 51)

In this second understanding, attention is paid to 'being with' an individual's experience rather than solely 'doing to' it, as in the more manualised application of method. The individual's experience is not fitted to the model; rather, a model is created around an individual to envelop the contours of their unique and valid experience. The therapist is not as focused on directing the therapy, but in following an unfolding cognitive narrative where the individual's unique ways of interpreting events and creating meanings is foregrounded (Beck & Weishaar, 1989). CBT in this context does not offer a rational guide to the discovery of reality and treatment of pathology, rather an opportunity to disrupt and manipulate meanings, interpretations and beliefs according to the client's subtexts, not the therapist's. Furthermore, in this understanding the interpersonal characteristics of the relationship are likely to receive much greater emphasis (Rudd & Joiner, 1997) as both a guide to, and an important source of information on, the client's cognitive and behavioural ways of being with another. An interesting developmental perspective relevant to such an understanding is presented by Hayes *et al.* (2006) in relation to the theoretical model and processes of acceptance and commitment therapy. Here Hayes describes a 'third wave' of behavioural and cognitive therapy which, he states, is:

> particularly sensitive to the context and functions of psychological phenomena, not just their form, and thus tends to emphasise contextual and experiential change strategies in addition to more direct and didactic ones. These treatments tend to seek the construction of broad, flexible and effective repertoires over an eliminative approach to narrowly defined problems.
>
> (Hayes, 2004, p. 658)

These two outlines exemplify how CBT can be understood in contrasting ways, more on a continuum of application than as one definite modality. To be more precise, while the theoretical base drawn on could be seen as largely the same in each understanding, its manner of reading or application is likely to be vastly different, something which is likely to depend on three particular variables – the practitioner's personal style, orientation and context. These three factors have largely acted as the forces in diversifying CBT's conceptualisation and practice over the years, leading to the continuum of understandings above.

The Therapist's Personal Style

A therapist's personal style, how they are with themselves in the world and how they are with another, is likely to impact on the way they employ CBT. When I first started applying CBT to my practice in the first year of my doctoral training, I did so in a manner that was more akin to the first description above. I was, at least initially, anxious with clients. I was unsure as to my abilities and competencies to be *with* clients *with* their difficulties. I found great comfort in more manualised applications of CBT models. This enabled me to subdue some of my anxieties and allowed me to build my skills and confidence in 'knowing' what I was 'doing' – CBT after all had been backed by the National Institute for Clinical Excellence (NICE). I would finish a session, go to a 'manual' (my then supervisor recommended Judith Beck's *Cognitive Therapy: Basics and Beyond* (1995)), and work out what the next session would cover. Sessions planned in this way would normally involve a mix of further questioning; psycho-education and socialisation to the CBT model for a certain 'condition'; and in session tasks to practise technique (particularly involving thought records) and setting 'homework'. Some clients engaged in this work with great fervour, taking on and running with the model to beneficial effect, others did not. With the latter I would 'fall back' on the Rogerian core principles of empathy, unconditional positive regard and congruence (Rogers, 1951, 1957), shelving the manuals, in line with my own all-or-nothing thinking!

The Therapist's Theoretical Orientation

As my training continued and my experience grew, I became less anxious and 'clumsy' in my style. My theoretical orientation changed, I moved from eclecticism to integration, and in this my appreciation of CBT's application broadened. I started using CBT techniques in more creative ways, adapting theoretical and relational values in line with a client's presentation and own style of being in the world. I found that more 'cognitively-oriented' clients seemed to hold true to Beck's assertion that the general therapeutic characteristics of warmth, accurate empathy and genuineness were *not* sufficient for 'optimal therapeutic effect' (Beck *et al.*, 1979, p. 45). These clients seemed to relish 'doing' therapy in a supportive working alliance, not wishing to get 'bogged down' in emotional aspects of their being, but taking great pride in the competence of their homework and comfort in their deepening cognitive self-understanding. However, I found that less 'cognitively-oriented' clients often seemed to respond better to the relational aspects of the therapy, as typified in the expression of Rogerian core principles (Rogers, 1951, 1957). They seemed to want to be listened to, valued and understood above all else. They found cognitive tasks a distraction, did not do their homework and often seemed to become frustrated with me bringing 'clever' conceptualisations to the room, and not just my-'*self*', with which they could be them-'*selves*'. I learnt different things worked for different clients.

Therapeutic Contexts

While my training, integrative as it was, and subsequent career have seen me diversify my theoretical orientation even further, I am now much truer to the second understanding of CBT, with a constructionist tilt. My therapeutic context is a major factor at play in the 'reality' of my therapeutic work. I currently work in a specialist alcohol service in the National Health Service (NHS), one of two psychologists in a multidisciplinary team of social workers, nurses, medical doctors and psychiatrists. The medical model is a rich seam running through our team meetings and I often have to remind myself to take a step back and not immerse myself in what can be quite an enticing way of seeing the human condition; after all when one pathologises another's experience one becomes more powerful. Indeed, it seems that power over what one does is *the* major professional dynamic in the NHS. In this context I find myself orienteering a diversity of expectations placed on my practice and me: service agreements around waiting times, caseloads and outcome measures; supervisory, line management and other team members' orientation and expectations of my therapy; organisational politics as to what is and what is not 'evidence-based' – all impact on my interventions. After all I have to 'justify' what I do and why I do it to those with more 'power' than I have – commissioners, managers, other therapists, clients (in that order it would seem).

While it is not my aim to politicise this chapter, it is important to recognise that while the above three influences – a therapist's style, orientation and context (in particular a therapist's training and exposure to different theoretical models) – are likely to have a major impact on how a practitioner comes to understand and then apply CBT. The weighting of power, influencing how their practice might be conducted in the consulting room, can often favour the demands of the therapeutic context, a point that is considered more fully later.

Pluralistic Practice, Counselling Psychology and CBT

The basic tenet of pluralism is very simple – there are many people and they are all unique – but on elaboration what this implies is quite staggering. There are many ways of thinking; there are numerous ways of behaving; there are multiple ways of feeling; there are different ways of relating to ourselves and to others in the world; there is a large variety of ways of understanding the world, each as rich and as *valid* as the others (I have stressed 'valid' as beliefs as to the 'truth' of this underlie epistemological difference between competing theoretical models). The therapeutic encounter is by necessity a place where this multiplicity of ways of being human is likely to play out with regard to how one individual might approach and help another individual with their difficulties. Drawing from this perspective Cooper and McLeod state of pluralistic therapeutic practice:

> A pluralistic standpoint holds that a multiplicity of different models of psychological distress and change may be 'true' and that there is no need to try and reduce these into one, unified model. . . . Different explanations will be true for different people at different points in time and therefore different therapeutic methods will be most helpful for different clients at different instances.
>
> (2007, p. 6)

In this, theoretical pluralism is embraced as a vital and necessary therapeutic stance, tailoring the therapeutic encounter to an individual's uniqueness, in the here and now, and thus making that encounter *therapeutic*.

Counselling psychology, with its inquisitive and open-minded attitude to how we come to 'know', enshrines many of the principles of such a pluralistic stance. Counselling psychology resists theoretical dogma, repeatedly questioning its own assumptions in an attempt to gain a richer perspective on what it is to be human. Counselling psychology encourages a diversity of research perspectives and evidence sources as it attempts to build a collage of understandings rather than a single definitive image of truth. It challenges 'pathologising' trends and traditional ways of seeing the 'individual' as self-contained entities, pointing to the relational ways of humans *being* with each other, in both their internal and external states. But most importantly, as outlined in Chapter 2, counselling psychology holds a relational therapeutic model, where being with another's 'otherness', in all its richness and diversity, is the apex of the therapeutic encounter from which a broad theoretical literature can be drawn on. Thus, a pluralistic approach allows for creativity in the therapeutic work that not only reflects an individual's uniqueness, but also responds to and is nurturing of it.

So now you have it: the building blocks of the contribution of CBT to pluralistic practice. CBT is one of many theoretical approaches that offer insight into how we might build an understanding of the human condition. My continuum perspective of CBT can be traced onto a continuum of epistemological perspectives. Here positivistic approaches, which might be sympathetic to my first outline of CBT, could be said to be at one end of the continuum, 'critical realist' approaches occupy the middle ground and social constructionist perspectives (which are likely to be more sympathetic to my second outline of CBT) rest at the other end. While I find my-*self* rests more easily at this latter end in my own practice, it is the dynamic of my profession which can operate across this diversity of epistemological contexts, whilst not aligning itself to a single one, and recognising that this is not always an easy and comfortable place to inhabit, that I find most exhilarating and freeing.

In this context CBT offers a rich perspective on how an individual might come to be experiencing phenomena at a certain time. In its focus on the interpretation of events rather than events themselves (clearly compatible with a pluralistic approach and a postmodern leaning), it allows a therapist a rich landscape to explore with a client, with the aim of mapping out significant features that might help the client navigate their future 'journey' outside of therapy. However, it must be said that CBT is not always credited with this flexibility. It is consequently to a discussion of the schism between CBT's existing and potential contribution to pluralistic practice that I now turn.

CBT and its Contribution to Pluralistic Practice: The Current State of Play

While one might accept that CBT can be understood in different ways on a continuum and that the therapeutic process will be influenced by the particular understanding taken, there is a certain naïve optimism to my discussion so far. It all sounds very nice, reflective and open-minded, but does it reflect the 'reality' in the consulting room? Possibly not. If one takes a more cynical stance to CBT's current application in health care settings (here I am largely talking about the NHS), one can see it in a very different light, as actually the *antithesis* of pluralistic practice. Here, one could argue, it is the narrower understanding of CBT (as presented above in its more prescriptive, manualised, directive format) that has been taken up by organisations such as NICE, an institution with a philosophy entrenched in a 'pathologising' medical model, and promoted as the psychological treatment of choice over all others. Here the evidence base for CBT is often referred to without question, ignoring concerns as to its validity (see Bolsover, 2007; James 2007), to close down discussion rather than engage in it, with possible reference to alternative evidence equally applicable to the therapeutic setting (Fairfax, 2008). This is nothing to do with cognitive-behavioural theory itself, but rather how it is portrayed and presented by individual and institutional 'proponents'. It is here that the *power* issue comes into play. While CBT offers a diverse and rich body of theory and model of practice which could be of great benefit in helping others in a pluralistic context, it has in many ways been a victim of the distortions and pressures of a modern, 'politicised' health service in which many self-interested factions, including psychology (this is far from being a unified profession, it has plenty of its own power struggles), vie for power over what one does, whether as an individual or as a profession.

I have attended training where CBT competency frameworks, which break down components of CBT practice into generic therapeutic competencies, basic, specific and problem-specific CBT competencies and meta-competencies (UCL, 2009) in support of NICE, are taught in strikingly rigid, unquestioning and self-assured ways, often showing no humility with regard to what they owe to other approaches as part of their evolution (see Chapter 7 for an elaboration of this phenomenon). I have worked in institutions (the NHS being the principal one) where practitioners are expected to apply CBT's 'cost-effective' approach as the primary course of therapy. In this a practitioner's judgement as to the therapeutic options for a client with whom they have met, discussed presenting issues and have started to form a relationship has to compete with what worked for someone else with 'similar' issues, as shown by a meta-analysis of randomised control trials. While I know I'm being a little unfair, as systematic reviews show what might have helped a number of people and are a great *guide* to treatment protocols, my point is that they should be used as guidance only, an aid to inform practice, not a rigid determinant of it. In fact, it is true that NICE produces such *guidelines*, but all too often, I hear about them being applied as if they are dogma, based on institutional demands rather than client need – certainly not the spirit in which Beck first conceived his ideas (Beck *et al.*, 1979), but quite the reverse in my reading of him. To illustrate my point I offer an example.

A little while ago whilst working with a psychiatrist colleague for whom I have great respect, I was asked for assistance with a client who presented with mild to moderate depression following the loss of a family member over a year earlier. My colleague reported they had introduced the cognitive model to the client and through discussion/exploration, identified a number of negative thoughts this client had about the future. The client was always on time for appointments but often had not completed thought diaries, seeming 'resistant' to changing their cognitions. My colleague felt they had a fairly good working alliance due to the timekeeping and the client's engagement in sessions, but was unsure how to continue with this client who continued to drink alcohol in a way that impacted negatively on relationships around them.

As always in such situations I offered a number of suggestions. In this instance these included exploring the meaning of the client's alcohol use, the attachment they might be replacing and the possibility of guilt in moving on from cognitions, as well as the possibility of being more present in the emotions of the client. My colleague asked how many sessions they should do this for before returning to the guidelines which suggest 6–8 sessions of CBT for mild/moderate depression. (NICE, 2007)

I present this illustration not to accentuate my own prowess or to denigrate my colleague's practice or profession. Indeed, knowing as I do the context, I can relate to similar questions I ask in my own practice – after all, I too have a caseload and waiting list to manage. Rather, the example illustrates how often the timeframe and the 'doing' aspects of CBT can be forgrounded over a client's unique constellation of presenting issues and the relational aspects of the encounter, relational aspects that facilitate that encounter to be *therapeutic*.

It is consequently felt that at present CBT's contribution to pluralistic practice is still being determined and is a contentious issue. Depending on your stance, CBT could be seen as offering great service to pluralism; after all it is pluralistic in conception (drawing as it does from both cognitive and behavioural theory), or part of pluralism's death knell.

CBT and its Contribution to Pluralistic Practice: The Future

So the battle-lines have been drawn, the challenge to my profession and applied psychology in general is set. Are we defenders of the 'faith' of pluralism, or do we sit tight in the 'security' of narrow conceptions of CBT, handed down to us by our powerful masters, entrenched in a medical model worldview?

Of course, I'm being a little dramatic when I write this, but the symbolism I use is often how I sense psychologist colleagues portray the modern dynamic in my profession. While this dynamic itself could be creative, where one's own assumptions and securities in 'knowledge' can be brought into question, I do fear that the scope for debate, the fuel for this 'dynamic', is somewhat being closed down (wittingly or unwittingly) by those serving the links between our academic institutions (which should always remain independent) and our public health care institutions, the latter seemingly coming with increasingly politicised agendas in line with government funding arrangements. Indeed, I have talked to a number of chartered psychologists who have informed me that their doctoral training only paid 'lip service' to theoretical/therapeutic models other than more manualised CBT.

So what hope for pluralism in the future?

There is a but, and it's a big but. All the chartered psychologists that I spoke to were in the process of seeking further training in other models of therapy, either through continuing professional development or additional formal training. As practitioners, then, it might be that we are drawn to expanding our theoretical knowledge base, possibly in recognition of our lived practice experience that it is not one but many things that produce therapeutic change.

In pondering this, could it be that as developing professionals we are engaged in a process of 'professional actualisation' as we move, with greater experience, toward a more pluralist outlook. That certainly seems to fit with my lived experience and mirrors that of other's with whom I have discussed this. It might consequently be that, professionally, the work lies not with advancing pluralism *per se*, but with dismantling the barriers to its natural course, the 'conditions of worth' if you like, of those outside or on the periphery of our profession!

Again and again the 'politics' of the issues seems to emerge in my text. On reflection this might simply be unavoidable – after all, the topic *is* a political one. The prescriptive application of CBT to professional practice is one of the most vibrant, lively and hotly debated issues in my profession and the government's goal of increasing access to psychological therapies is based on its expansion (see Nel, 2009). However, it must be noted that while there may be forces at work which seem to be promoting a narrow, unitary and dogmatic understanding of CBT and its application to practice, I also see other forces promoting CBT in a more open, pluralistic and flexible manner.

CBT practitioners over recent years have embraced developments in the field of mindfulness (Segal *et al.*, 2002), expanded traditional theory and pioneered new integrative therapies, such as schema therapy (Young *et al.*, 2003) and cognitive analytic therapy (Ryle, 1990), which have a growing application and evidence base. In fact, in my field – substance misuse and addiction – I regularly meet professionals who incorporate the concepts of motivational interviewing (Miller & Rollnick, 2002) into their practice and seek out new ways of working in their particular areas of interest. For me, then, pluralism is not dead in relation to the practice of CBT; it is happening, though we do not always admit it! Furthermore, I feel CBT's future contribution to pluralistic therapeutic practice is replete with opportunity. The question is, are we able, as a profession, to deliver it?

I would like to explore this question a little further, with regard to how I feel CBT is of direct value to the profession of counselling psychology using my own practice as an example, and also how counselling psychologists might act as a force in the further evolution of CBT's ideas and techniques, particularly with its attention to the process of therapy.

In my own practice I find the theoretical concepts and framework of CBT, with its emphasis on assessment and case formulation, very valuable. It sensitises my attention to the interplay between a client's early experiences, beliefs about themselves and the world, patterns and rules for living, critical life-events, coping strategies and current thoughts and presenting issues. In so doing it often but not always offers a skeleton or structure on which I can flesh out (build) the therapeutic approach taken, as the 'assessment' phase evolves into the 'treatment' phase (arbitrary and medicalised terms necessitated by my therapeutic context) of therapy, *with* a client's guidance. In this fleshing-out process I am particularly attuned to a client's *own* understandings of their issues, the context and systems in which they exist, as well as their own values, and the meanings they draw from their life thus far. Here theoretical models other than CBT, drawing from humanistic, psychodynamic and systemic traditions, are variously engaged with in my own internal narrative of formulation as they erupt through a client's discourse which I am active in exploring. I might be drawn to a transactional-analytic understanding (Harris, 1995), think that relational difficulties are circular (Vetere & Dallos, 2003) due to a *system* need around a client's 'basic fault' (Balint, 1968), or be struck by Winnicottian ideas about true/false self-formation (Winnicott, 1969). I simply do not know where my thinking will go, what will turn up in my 'free-floating *theoretical* attention'. I am with the client, with myself, and in this *with-ness* I manage my anxieties about what a particular model might tell me to *do* and draw from an acceptance that 'different [theoretical] explanations will be true for different people at different points in time' (Cooper & McLeod, 2007, p. 6). While this stance allows me an expansive array of ideas and concepts from which to draw, I find myself in my practice integrating what I take from different explanations, according to two considerations. First and foremost, a client's presentation, in the context of our relationship (i.e. what appears to resonate most with them during our explorative encounter) and in the context of how our encounter has impacted on me – I use my-*self*. Secondly, the cognitive-behavioural '*mainframe*' of my therapeutic context. While I find, with my less prescriptive take on CBT and my relative autonomy in my current service, that such considerations more often than not coalesce with general ease in helping clients, at times when they do not, I generally find support and understanding from my supervisor and colleagues when I explain, often *in the language of CBT* – the dominant language of my service – why an alternative approach to a 'straight' cognitive-behavioural one might be better taken. To illustrate:

> Some months ago, I was referred a client who reported suffering from bouts of depression and subsequent alcohol abuse since their childhood. They had

recently stopped drinking and their keyworker felt they would benefit from 'seeing' me. The multidisciplinary team, in one of its more prescriptive moods (teams certainly do have moods), asked me how long I might work with them, given they were not drinking, so they could move out of service – we had recently reconfigured the service and in our need to manage caseloads and waiting times there was much more emphasis on 'throughput'. This was the reality and I felt the team wanted me to say twelve sessions/three months of CBT, in line with an implicit service pressure.

I said I would have to assess this client, but we would probably be looking at twelve sessions/three months of CBT. The team satisfied and reassured, I went on to arrange the assessment.

In line with the client's presentation, I have brought this client back to the team on four occasions thus far. I have discussed issues of engagement, requiring a person-centred/CBT stance to build the therapeutic alliance. I have given the team a richer outline of this person's difficulties in terms of current thoughts and behaviours, core beliefs and early attachment disruption. I have emphasised that much of the work is focused at the level of schemas and that the therapy (by which I mean the relationship) is allowing the client to engage with past emotional experiences, feel validated and come to accept and move on from them. In this I have even mentioned the concepts of limited re-parenting as understood by schema therapy (see Young et al., 2003), the corrective emotional experience (Alexander & French, 1946) and mindfulness-based cognitive therapy (Segal et al., 2002).

The team can see in my language the cognitive-behavioural 'mainframe' of my practice. They have shown genuine interest in the broader theoretical concepts I have introduced and modelled in discussions of my work. I feel as a consequence of this that my reassuring cognitive language and my openness in discussing my thoughts – showing that I am not doing anything 'mystical' – the team have shown trust and faith in my professional judgement as to continuing this work far beyond the initial twelve session/three months proposal. My stance is further supported by the client's report to their keyworker of benefiting from the work, as well as some psychometric scores which also suggest this.

While in many ways the discussion and practice outline above could be taken as simply focusing on how I integrate CBT into my practice, in fact my aim is broader. What I am suggesting is that CBT, with its strengths and its limitations, can be used in the service of our therapeutic practice as a model in itself due to its strengths, and as a conduit to the introduction of *other* models due to its limitations. I feel that if we are open to and discursive about such issues, we could use CBT to broaden our professional practice, as well as that of other professionals, modelling pluralism and benefiting clients. To summarise my approach and thinking by metaphor: CBT is one arrow in my quiver, not my full crop (other theoretical models), and certainly not the bow (the therapeutic relationship). To extend the metaphor: I am the hand that holds and draws the bow, the client is the eye that guides the arrow and says when to release it. The relationship between us (both conscious and unconscious) determines the outcome. Sometimes we hit the target (unique to every client), sometimes we miss, we practise together, learning how we might work together and hone our skills. It is through *being in* this process that I believe the relationship becomes *therapeutic*. The more sensitive we are to this process the better the relationship, the better the relationship the better the outcome (Keijsers *et al.*, 2000; Krupnick *et al.*, 1996).

So this is what I believe CBT can bring to counselling psychology – an extremely useful set of conceptualisations, theoretical understandings and practical tools and techniques that are readily accessible in the service of the therapeutic work and ultimately the clients.

What counselling psychology can give CBT in return is a robust, thoughtful and considered appreciation of the *processes* of therapy. Counselling psychology pays great attention to the *process* in the therapeutic encounter as *other* meets *otherness* – a dynamic and ever-changing situation. When I read through the CBT manuals and theoretical outlines, rarely are issues of transference and countertransference mentioned, yet they were there in Beck *et al.*'s (1979) initial conceptions. Where have they gone? Descriptions of the therapeutic relationship are frequently discussed with an air of 'matter-of-fact', seeming technical and unidimensional (J. Beck, 1995), if they are mentioned at all. Considerations as to the mechanisms and value of using one's *self* in this person-to-person setting is practically non-existent. I could go on. This is where counselling psychology stands out, through its underlying reflexive and reflective client-centred tradition, as a profession well positioned to generate creative, new and open-minded ideas about how process issues might be recognised, valued more holistically and integrated into CBT practice (an already integrative model of cognitive *and* behavioural theory). In this, it would enable CBT to evolve further, expanding the breadth of its evidence base and consequently the robustness of its theory and practice (see Fairfax, 2008). While many of the process issues, which counselling psychology has a rich history of attending to, run through the pages of this book, some may be fearful of engaging with the *active* evolution of CBT (in case they are shot down as heretics). But in many ways this evolution is already underway. Looking at current discussions on the application of pluralism to therapeutic practice, it would appear that Hayes' (2004) third wave of broader behavioural and cognitive conceptualisations is already breaking on the shore, and many of the therapists with whom I have spoken while preparing this chapter, who purport to use CBT, would appear to be finding their practice drenched!

References

Alexander, F. & French, T. M. (1946). *Psychoanalytic therapy: Principles and application.* New York: Ronald Press.

Balint, M. (1968). *The basic fault: Therapeutic aspects of regression.* London: Tavistock Press.

Beck, A. T., Rush, A. J., Shaw, B. F. & Emery, G. (1979). *Cognitive therapy for depression.* New York: Guilford Press.

Beck, A. T. & Weishaar, M. E. (1989). Cognitive therapy. In R. J. Corsini & D. Wedding (Eds.) *Current psychotherapies* (4th edn.). Itasca, IL: Peacock Publishers.

Beck, J. (1995). *Cognitive therapy: Basics and beyond.* New York: Guilford Press.

Bolsover, N. (2007). Talking therapies and the NHS. *The Mental Health Review, 12*(1): 3–7.

Boucher, T. A. (2006). In cognitive therapy, how would the therapist understand and work with difficulties that arise in the therapeutic relationship? *Counselling Psychology Review, 21*(3): 12–18.

Cooper, M. & McLeod, J. (2007). A pluralistic framework for counselling and psychotherapy: implications for research. *Counselling and Psychotherapy Research, 7*(3): 135–143 (electronic version, pp. 1–19). eprints.cdlr.strath.ac.uk/5213. Accessed 5 March 2009.

Fairfax, H. (2008). 'CBT or not CBT', is that really the question? Re-considering the evidence base: The contribution of process research. *Counselling Psychology Review, 23*(4): 27–37.

Harris, T. A. (1995). *I'm OK – You're OK.* London: Arrow Books.

Hayes, S. C. (2004). Acceptance and commitment therapy, relational frame theory, and the third wave of behaviour therapy. *Behavior Therapy, 35*: 639–665.

Hayes, S. C., Luoma, J. B. *et al.* (2006). Acceptance and commitment therapy: Model, processes and outcomes. *Behaviour Research and Therapy, 44*: 1–25.

James, O. (2007). *Affluenza.* London: Vermillion.

Keijsers, G. P. J., Schaap, C. P. D. R. & Hoogduin, C. A. L. (2000). The impact of interpersonal patient and therapist behaviour on outcome in cognitive-behavioural therapy. *Behaviour Modification, 24*(2): 264–297.

Krupnick, J. L., Sotsky, S. M. *et al.* (1996). The role of the therapeutic alliance in psychotherapy and pharmacotherapy outcome: findings in the national institute of mental health treatment of depression collaborative research programme. *Focus, 4*: 764–777.

Miller, W. R. & Rollnick, S. (2002). *Motivational interviewing: Preparing people for change* (2nd edn.). London: Guilford Press.

Nel, P. W. (2009). 'Improving' access to psychological therapies: It's the end of the world as we know it (and I feel fine). *Clinical Psychology Forum, 194*: 7–11.

NICE (2007). *Depression (amended): Management of depression in primary and secondary care.* London: National Institute for Clinical Excellence.

Rogers, C. R. (1951). *Client-centred therapy.* Boston, MA: Houghton Mifflin.

Rogers, C. R. (1957). The necessary and sufficient conditions of therapeutic personality change. *Journal of Consulting and Clinical Psychology*, *21*: 95–103.

Rudd, M. D. & Joiner, T. (1997). Countertransference and the therapeutic relationship: A cognitive perspective. *Journal of Cognitive Psychotherapy: An International Quarterly*, *11*(4): 231–250.

Ryle, A. (1990). *Cognitive-analytic therapy: Active participation in change: A new integration in brief psychotherapy*. Chichester: Wiley.

Segal, Z. V., Williams, J. M. G. & Teasdale, J. D. (2002). *Mindfulness-based cognitive therapy for depression: A new approach to preventing relapse*. New York: Guilford Press.

UCL (2009). *The CBT competences framework for depression and anxiety disorders*. www.ucl.ac.uk/clinical-psychology/CORE/CBT_Competences/ CBT_Competences_Map.pdf. Accessed 24 February 2009.

Vetere, A. & Dallos, R. (2003). *Working systemically with families: Formulation, intervention and evaluation*. London: Karnac.

Wells, A. (1997). *Cognitive therapy of anxiety disorders: A practice manual and conceptual guide*. Chichester: Wiley.

Westbrook, D., Kennerley, H. & Kirk, J. (2007). *An introduction to cognitive behaviour therapy: Skills and applications*. London: Sage.

Winnicott, D. W. (1969). *The maturational process and the facilitating environment*. London: Hogath Press.

Young, J. E., Klosko, J. S. & Weishaar, M. E. (2003). *Schema therapy: A practitioner's guide*. London: Guilford Press.

Chapter 11

*Amor Fati**: Existential Contributions to Pluralistic Practice

Elena Manafi

I view psychological paradigms as attempts to describe and understand – but hopefully not explain, predict or control – the human condition. Over-reliance on these models distances us from our clients' subjective experience and narrows our understanding of human existence. In this chapter I portray my own conceptualisation and use of the existential approach which to me is more of an *attitude* than a unified theory. I argue that its philosophical heritage and commitment to a clarification of what it means to exist as a human being in the world informs practitioners' practice regardless of their theoretical orientation. All that is needed is a receptive attitude, free from dogma and open to the intricacies of living, an attitude which defines philosophy.

Counselling psychologists are concerned with their clients' wellbeing; therapeutic work goes beyond symptom reduction to encompass exploration and clarification of subjective experiences and meanings. Regardless of the nature and context of our practice, we are confronted with issues that reflect the struggles and tensions of everyday living. The existential approach highlights the personal and the collective and is concerned with Being (capitalised is to distinguish Being from beings), of the practitioner, the client and the space in-between.

---

* Trans. Love your fate. Nietzsche (1974).

Therapy and Beyond: Counselling Psychology Contributions to Therapeutic and Social Issues
Edited by Martin Milton
© 2010 John Wiley & Sons, Ltd.

It has been argued that existentialism (see Macquarrie, 1972; Warnock 1970) is more of a philosophical and literary phenomenon than a distinct tradition. Its application to clinical practice is equally not unified (Cooper, 2003), however, all authors who adhere to this movement acknowledge a number of existential themes that constitute the theoretical and clinical backbone of their practice. At the very centre of the approach lies a commitment to *lived experience* and the whole movement is the product of an involvement *with* life rather than a detached contemplation *about* life. Consequently, the epistemological and ontological assumptions that guide existential practice go beyond psychologism; they are rooted in philosophical concepts regarding life. Existential therapy approaches the client's experiences directly by reflecting on the immediacy of the encounter, rather than indirectly through the lens of pre-established theories.

The explication of existential themes and their relevance to everyday living can be invaluable to the practice of counselling psychology as they reflect everyday human concerns and aim at understanding the human predicament. They strengthen our field's philosophical and ethical stances which attempt to address psychological difficulties as relational rather than medical in nature. Existential practice intends 'to let philosophical reflection on the human condition throw light on the specific problems in living that arise in individual situations' (Deurzen, 1997, p. 132).

A description of the existential attitude inevitably involves the use of philosophical jargon which I keep to a bare minimum. I focus on an explication of a selection of philosophical premises that colour this attitude and its translation into practice. Through a discussion of my work with Ennio (who gave written consent to use the material presented in this chapter), I portray *a* way, but not *the* way, of incorporating existential principles to the practice of counselling psychology. One final note, the most important of all: existential therapy is all about felt experience and *being-with* another. Ultimately, what really matters is the relationship we create with our clients and for that relationship to be meaningful one needs to put theories aside and *be* – the kind of Being that communicates humanity with all its weaknesses and the strengths.

Pessimism or Paradox?

We must assume our existence as broadly as we in any way can; everything, even the unheard-of, must be possible in it. That is at bottom the only courage that is demanded of us: to have courage for the most strange, the most singular and the most inexplicable that we may encounter.

(Rilke, 2004, p. 51)

Søren Kierkegaard, Friedrich Nietzsche, Jean-Paul Sartre and Albert Camus have been cited as philosophers celebrating the malaise of the human condition which strives for survival in the midst of cosmic absurdity. Selected themes like Nietzsche's *death of God*, Kierkegaard's *dread*, Sartre's *nothingness* and Camus' notion of *the absurd* are often cited as portraying a sense of futility and gloom. As a pessimist myself I choose to celebrate human suffering or the meaninglessness of existence – I consider Arthur Schopenhauer's *Studies in Pessimism* (2004) as one of the greatest philosophical works ever written. I do disagree, however, with their diagnosis. In-depth reading of existential philosophy can only 'prove' the opposite; existentialism celebrates life and epitomises an attitude of passion, commitment, brevity and perseverance, positioning each one of us to take ourselves and everyday lives seriously.

Existential philosophers have turned nihilism on its head through a passionate engagement with life and emphasising meaning, human freedom, choice and responsibility. Nietzsche's *death of God* is an invitation to own one's life in the absence of a doctrine that prescribes a specific way of living. Kierkegaard's *intoxication of possibility* which requires a *leap of faith* is a necessary ingredient for an authentic life. Sartre's emphasis on *nothingness* and the *nausea* it evokes is the most important feature of consciousness without which human potential could never be reached. Camus' *absurd* and the recognition of our fundamental aloneness places suicide at the heart of philosophical inquiry, only to be rejected in favour of an exaltation of life and a desire for clarity and meaning. Camus' characters carry out their daily routines in the midst of life's adversities, contingency and their essential inability to control and predict their future. Ownership of their lives is achieved through a commitment to knowledge and awareness that spring from engagement with life rather than intellectual understanding. It is this involvement, full of desire and passion, that in the end liberates the characters and fashions their destiny. Camus' love for life and its vicissitudes is clear in the following passage:

> Everything that exalts life at the same time increases its absurdity . . . If there is a sin against life, it consists perhaps not so much in despairing of life as in hoping for another life and in eluding the implacable grandeur of this one.
>
> (2005, pp. 13–14)

By now the paradox of existence should be obvious: wellbeing is necessarily intertwined with despair. As Kierkegaard argued, *life is not a problem to be solved, but a reality to be experienced.* Human beings constantly strive for meaning but are confronted with absurd situations that defy logical argument. In the midst of life's inherent contradictions, we oscillate between polarities. 'There is no sun without shadow, and it is essential to know the night' (Camus, 2000, p. 110). It makes no sense to prioritise one polarity over another: happiness over sorrow, success over failure, reason over passion, life over death. There would be no civilisation or progress in the absence of necessity and no meaning, value and purpose in the absence of crises. Life's contradictions can generate intense emotions that become unbearable, but desensitising ourselves is not the solution; for feelings are our compass in life, steering our understanding of the world and of ourselves. As R. D. Laing argues, their eradication would lead to a disconnection from life itself. 'She lost her passion and her mission. She was cured. She was in despair. She felt dead. But she carried on normally as a perfect zombie' (cited in Deurzen, 1997, p. 131).

Our clients enter the consulting room in the midst of a crisis, over-whelmed by emotions that deprive them of any sense of control. Assisting them in regulating their feelings can indeed be a solution, albeit a temporary one. For wellbeing to be restored interventions need to embrace all dimen-sions of existence (the physical, personal, social and spiritual) so that clients can begin to understand their place in the world (Deurzen, 1997, 2002). From an existential vantage point symptoms are not pathological in nature, but phenomena that reflect our clients' ways of dealing with their difficulties in living, which stem from aspects of existence such as throwness, isolation, freedom, choice, responsibility, meaninglessness and ultimately death. As discussed in Chapter 2, the existential approach does not posit a psychic structure within the individual but views humans as beings-in-the-world. Symptoms are *relational* in nature, lying in the *area of interaction* with the world and other people (Cohn, 1997).

A time will come when we shall be confronted with 'unscheduled' crises. As beings embedded in time, our response to them partly defines the present, shapes the future and constructs the kind of persons we strive to become. The Chinese ideogram for crisis (危機) consists of 'danger' and 'opportunity'; a paradox matching the existential attitude to life. In this, our task is to achieve equilibrium through learning to live in the tension they create. Attempts to eliminate one of the two (usually the one that causes suffering) deprives us of the opportunity to confront our givens and extend ourselves to our principles, values and personal meanings. This is where existential therapy is most helpful; it goes a step further than psychological theories to embrace life's paradox and find value in suffering. As Deurzen argues, 'life is one long process of change and transformation . . . In times of crisis the attention is refocused on where priorities lie so that choices can be made with more understanding than previously' (2007, p. 204).

There is something heroic in this attitude which reflects our ability 'to go to meet simultaneously one's greatest sorrow and one's greatest hope'

(Nietzsche, cited in Hollingdale, 1977, p. 235). It is a daring act that reflects our clients' choice to enter a therapeutic relationship in the hope of facing and overcoming themselves and their difficulties – difficulties which manifest as loneliness, depression, anxiety, isolation, self-harm – which portray their ways of coping with life. Holding on to the difficult and clarifying its meaning can transform crisis into opportunity; it is a process through which we come closer to a clarification of our clients' personal meaning and to a way of being that surpasses adversity and allows them to (re)connect and live life to the full. Once again Nietzsche comes to mind: 'he who has a why to live for can bear almost any how' (cited in Frankl, 1963, p. 76).

Condemned to Living: An Existential 'Life Sentence'

> The gods had condemned Sisyphus to ceaselessly rolling a rock to the top of a mountain, whence the stone would fall back on its own weight. They had thought with some reason that there is no more dreadful punishment than futile and hopeless labour. The workman of today works every day in his life at the same tasks, and this fate is no less absurd.
>
> (Camus, 2000, p. 107)

The existential approach is philosophical in nature, concerned with living. A passionate engagement with life shows us there is no one 'truth'; our understandings depend on our value-laden engagement with the world. The scientific attitude strives for objectivity; rationalism condemns (extreme) emotions as pathological in nature. In contrast, the existential view is nothing but an exaltation of the passions that constitute one's subjective way of being in the world. Solomon argued that 'it is our passions, not our reason (and surely not "nature"), that constitute our world, our relationships with other people and, consequently, our *Selves*' (1983, p. 15; emphasis in the original). The passions 'are precisely those structures which commit and bind us' (1983, p. 19).

Counselling psychology's relational framework highlights the intersubjective nature of human existence. Emotions, no matter how extreme, reflect our clients' particular modes of being-in-the-world and ways of engaging with others. In therapy it is important to clarify meaning so that their often pre-reflective – and hence uncontained – nature can become reflective and open for contemplation (Strasser, 2005). It is through this process that clients can begin to realise themselves and their place in the world and consequently shift to a position that will enable them to embrace different possibilities. As Camus (2000) argued, passionate engagement with life is tragic in nature because the heroes – ourselves – are conscious! We are, to a greater or lesser extent, aware of our fate and 'it is senseless to think of complaining since nothing foreign has decided what we feel, what we live, or what we are' (Sartre, 1998, p. 554). Sartre echoes two themes that are present in all existential writings – freedom and responsibility. Facing both can bring us closer to a sense of empowerment, but this strength comes at a price: anxiety.

Nothingness and the Fragility of Being Human

Our imminent death, impermanent character of life and fragility of our sense of self evoke anxiety. It is a feeling that easily turns into dread and a sense of being swallowed by the void. The existential approach makes a distinction between fear and anxiety (i.e. anxiety's ontic and ontological nature). The former has an object and refers to our personal experiences in everyday life (e.g. fear of losing one's job), the latter is a given of human existence stemming from our fundamental insecurity, freedom, responsibility and ultimately awareness of our own mortality (Boss, 1979; Jaspers, 1950; Tillich, 2000).

It follows that anxiety inhabits Being; it can neither be divorced from living nor eliminated. Its inevitability and importance are such that anxiety is seen as the most fundamental human emotion that, if explored, can point us towards a more deliberate way of living. Kierkegaard (1980) saw an inherent conflict in anxiety which is manifested in one's struggle for survival against the threat of non-being. Contrary to common interpretations, he did not reduce anxiety to a fear of death, but saw it as the product of an individual's awareness of her possibilities and potential in life. He compared anxiety to the *dizziness of freedom* – the freedom to choose between alternative possibilities – and claimed that 'whoever has learned to be anxious in the right way has learned the ultimate' (1980, p. 153).

Similarly, Sartre 1998 views anxiety as an antidote to *bad faith*, or self-deception. For Sartre the deceiver is aware of his own deception: 'the one who practises bad faith is hiding a displeasing truth or presenting as truth a pleasing untruth' (1998, p. 49). Bad faith is therefore an active form of avoidance, of choice, responsibility and of the nothingness that we are. As argued in Chapter 2, consciousness is always in the world; it is relational in nature. There is no solid self; our illusory sense of concreteness is the product of conscious actions and interactions with the world and other people. For Sartre, 'consciousness is a being, the nature of which is to be conscious of the nothingness of its being' (1998, p. 47). We create ourselves out of nothing – hence anxiety's ontological status. It is a recognition that is emancipating *and* nauseating. Reflection on Sartrean themes of bad faith and nothingness can be liberating; strengthening our non-pathologising stance in relation to human issues; shedding light on our work with personality or relational difficulties. Cannon (1991) argues that in therapy we should aim at a deconstruction and simultaneous reconstruction of our clients' sense of self so that they can begin to embrace the fluidity of human existence. Holding rather than eliminating our clients' anxiety, which is intensified by the process of exploration, is necessary as it is through anxiety that one begins to taste the intoxication of freedom.

The Being that is Mine

Martin Heidegger saw anxiety as an emotion that individuates human existence: '[in] anxiety there lies the possibility of a disclosure which is quite distinctive; for anxiety individualises. This individualisation brings Dasein back from its falling, and makes manifest to it that authenticity and inauthenticity are possibilities of its Being' (1962, p. 235).

Falling refers to an unreflective mode of being which dominates most of our daily experience and which therefore can be seen as our default position (Deurzen, 1999). It follows that authenticity and inauthenticity are dimensions of being, and Cohn (2002) argues that both are equally valid ways of existing in the world. Choosing one over the other would introduce a 'normative assessment of reality', which goes against the essence of existential thought. Cohn asks: 'Is it the therapist's aim to lead the client from a state of "abnormality" to one that is considered closer to "normality"?' (2002, p. 90). The answer depends on one's vantage point. It would be arrogant to advocate any criteria that would distinguish between 'authentic' and 'inauthentic' modes of being. Given that both are part of the human condition, they should be explored rather than labelled. Once again the importance of polarities becomes relevant; our connectedness to the world highlights possibilities and limitations. The task of therapy is to explore the totality of our client's situation so that they can make informed decisions about their way of being.

Time is of the Essence

The existential view focuses on *lived time* which is *not* a linear concept.

> Past, future, and present we call dimensions of time ... all three dimensions are equally original, for there is none without the other two, and thus all three are equally open to us, though not uniformly so. At times, one dimension

dominates and becomes one that engages and perhaps imprisons us. But this does not mean that other dimensions have disappeared, the are only modified.

(Heidegger, cited in Cohn, 2002, p. 6)

Every moment contains the past and anticipates the future. This view has major implications for practice. Cohn (2002) argues that, unlike other approaches focusing on the 'here-and-now', the existential view acknowledges and seeks to explore the three-dimensionality of time. The exploration of each moment in therapy entails all dimensions of human existence, particularly that of time. This cyclical conceptualisation of temporality does not imply causality – who we are now is not determined by past events or future expectations. That would deny our transcendence, our capacity – on reflection – to rise above and transform our facticity through our actions and interpretations (always within contextual and existential limitations). The relevance to counselling psychology practice is evident: assisting clients to 'take stock of their lives' (Deurzen, 2002, p. 94), to make the implicit explicit through questioning, clarifying and exploring assumptions and values can only strengthen the ethos of our practice. Doing so prompts our clients to take an active stance, which allows them to become aware of their own experience and dynamics imposed by their facticity. It is this reflection on values, dilemmas and ways of being-in-the-world that instigates change.

'Life is for Living'

That's how Deurzen addressed the audience at the 20th anniversary conference of the Society for Existential Analysis. It should be clear that the existential attitude reflects a passionate engagement with life, stressing our connection to the world and other people, exploring the ways in which an individual's unique predicament relates to the universals of the human condition. Counselling psychologists could use this attitude and existential dimensions in living to broaden their explorations without undermining their preferred theoretical orientation. By affirming the ontological priority of human beings and stressing the *temporality*, *historicity* and *embodiment* of human existence, the existential approach attempts to restore one's sense of being-in-the-world by focusing on subjective experience and the clarification of the conflicts, dilemmas and tensions arising from life's paradoxes.

The goals of existential therapy can be incorporated within all therapeutic models as they reflect a way of being with our clients rather than a manual or guide that has its roots in a specific psychological theory. As argued by May *et al.*, '[existential psychology] does not purport to found a new school as over against other schools or to give a new technique of therapy as over against other techniques. It seeks, rather, to analyze the structure of human existence' (2004, p. 7).

The existential approach 'has the potential to augment and deepen narrower epistemological frameworks by providing a rich contextual base and soulfulness for understanding the overarching principles of what it is to be human' (Milton *et al.*, 2003, p. 115). The emphasis on ontology is evident; existential psychotherapy provides a foundation for all therapies because of its ontological status which seeks to describe rather than explain human existence. Counselling psychologists – through using the principles of the existential/phenomenological method (see Spinelli, 2005) and the approach's emphasis on an exploration of the four dimensions of existence (see Deurzen, 2002) – broaden their understanding of human issues without sacrificing preferred theoretical premises.

Deurzen (2002) summarises the aims of existential therapy: working existentially implies vigilance and openness to contradictions and paradoxes. The practitioner aims to assist her clients to reflect on their lives through a clarification of their values, beliefs, hopes and aspirations; to face life's paradoxes, conflicts, dilemmas and their ontic manifestations; to clarify the meaning of their difficulties and purpose in life; to widen their horizon, view of themselves and relations to other people; and finally, to enable them to become more grounded so that they can face and resolve life's crises.

And finally . . . *Memento Mori*

It would be hubris to ignore the only certainty in life which is *death*. We are being-with-death, it never leaves our side; the finitude of our individual existence is undeniable. Moreover, my death is *mine*, no one can take my place when the time comes. The importance of this moment in existential philosophy can hardly be over-emphasised; death is seen as one of the givens of existence, as our '*ownmost* possibility' (Heidegger, 1962, p. 307). (For implications for psychotherapeutic practice, see Boss, 1979; Deurzen, 1997, 1998, 2002, 2009; Yalom, 1980.)

The key to understanding the place of death in existential philosophy lies in Heidegger's use of the word 'possibility' (Smith, 1999). We cannot defy death but we can certainly face it with courage and dignity. So what is it that death makes possible? In two words: creativity and meaning. It is the inevitability of *my* death that *forces* me to take life seriously.

I hope I have shown in this chapter that the existential jargon goes beyond abstract theories and describes lived experience. Now it's time to move from theory to practice.

Ennio and I

My work with Ennio (pseudonym) begun with a paradox: it was his mother not he who contacted me. The following message was left on my answerphone:

> Hello, this is Mrs 'A'. I am calling you with regards to my son Ennio who I'm really worried about. I really want him to come and see you 'cause he has always found life difficult; even when he was little he wouldn't wanna play with the other children and would spend most of his time on his own burying himself in books. As a teenager he was not like his brother who was much more normal, you know, going to parties, bringing home girlfriends, you know what I mean! Instead he got depressed, only wore black and we had to hospitalise him. He got a bit better but he is now back to square one and refuses to sort himself out. We want you to see him and see whether he can get any better, if not he will have to go back into hospital. Can you please let me know if he makes any contact with you and let us have your payment details? Bye for now.

I listened to the message a couple of times feeling perplexed and slightly pressurised. I could hear the mother's concern for her son but I also noticed her urge to 'fix' him and the threat of imminent hospitalisation. I wondered about Ennio's age and how he felt about his mother taking charge of his life and state of being. I was faced with the paradox of existence and our inability to resolve it in rational terms. I stayed with my uncertainty as I was not able to figure out whether Ennio wanted to engage with me or not.

> On the day of our first meeting Ennio arrived 20 minutes late. He walked in without saying a word and without looking at me. He sat down in the armchair staring at the floor. I was reminded of the apprehension I felt during our phone conversation and I quietly sat down. I instantly realised how affected I was by his presence as usually, when I meet clients for the first time, I find myself being quite talkative – almost informal.

I looked at him, seeing a young, slender man, dressed in black, a colour that matched his hair and his almond-shaped black eyes, which I only saw much later in the session. I quietly said that I was glad to finally meet him. I got no reply other than a slight body movement.

Ennio's reluctance to engage with me filled me with an uncomfortable sense of power that is inevitably present in our profession. I was face to face with a common dilemma: staying with silence or interrupting it. I found myself stripped of all theories and psychological interventions, only facing the gap between the two of us. The only 'tool' I was left with was myself, counting on my intuition and ways of relating. I chose silence.

In the sessions that followed I oscillated between allowing for space while holding the tension/apprehension in the room and gently trying to make contact through various means. I used eye contact, body movements, direct questions and general statements. Ennio would remain guarded and paralysed. He would respond to direct questions with short, but clear answers, always giving me just sufficient information. All his answers felt automatic, he would never go beyond what I had asked him. He would not respond to eye contact or more general statements, but he would monitor my body movements closely. I felt blocked, unable to reach out to him.

Theories felt empty to me; connecting to him as a human being remained my priority. I found myself feeling unreal, like a piece of furniture in a room. I was lost for words when a passage from a Greek poem, which referred to the limitations of language, came to mind. Without hesitating or looking at him I translated it out loud. I was still staring out of the window when, to my surprise, I heard Ennio saying *poetry is the refuge of the lonely*. I looked at him and replied that I often feel like that.

We remained in this space for quite a few sessions; him avoiding engage-ment and me wanting to get to know him. Only after numerous attempts to directly state that it did not feel as if he wanted to be here, he started to overtly disclose his mistrust not only in me, but in all the helping professions, as well as his own family. His comments were hostile and attacking. I stayed with his anger, which to me was an indication that this man, who was 'sent' by his mother to sort himself out and who had been hospitalised against his will, was mirroring what he himself had experienced all his life: rejection and disapproval of his way of being. This is what he had learnt and this was the only way he was able to relate to the world around him, including me.

Although he was nearly attacking me, showing anger and disappointment, at least he gave me that much. At least he allowed me to understand his current thoughts and feelings, in particular about being in the room with me. I remained present, tolerating the negative emotions and his unwillingness to connect. This was a decisive moment as my reaction or non-reaction to his way of being would determine how therapy would be possible, if at all.

Accepting life's challenges as part of our lives without pathologising allowed me to stay with what Ennio was showing me in his behaviour. Initially, my openness and acceptance to his way of being, together with my willingness to hold what he was saying without fully attempting to understand or make it any different (let alone better), made him even more suspicious! It transpired that he thought I was adopting specific strategies to 'make' him trust me, which would then leave him vulnerable again. I accepted his interpretation but changed nothing. I persisted and remained open to whatever he was giving me – that was my main therapeutic intervention for a long time.

With hindsight, the first few sessions which were based on this open way of being with him were the most important part of the therapeutic process. It was my presence rather than technique that allowed Ennio, over time, to become less guarded.

Over time the full extent of his difficulties became clear. Ennio's parents were Italian; he was born in England, the second son of a family with strong gender-specific roles. His mother was the carer and his father the one who provided the income and made all major decisions. His older brother was a mirror image of the father and followed the father's footsteps to become a mechanic. The mother had always felt that Ennio was weird and different. Ennio described his father and brother as male chauvinists, even made references to the way they talked about and stereotyped women. Ennio, on the contrary, was interested in literature and arts. He talked about desperately wanting books and only receiving stereotypical toys for boys, such as cars and building blocks. He felt misunderstood and different from a very young age. Consequently, he was overprotected by his mother and pushed by his father to 'become' a man.

Freedom and limitations became the themes of our sessions. Ennio begun to think of his past, upbringing and position in the family. His inability to mirror himself in the gaze of the other and the subsequent feelings of loss and unreality became apparent. A reflection on his ways of surviving his experienced imprisonment and the emotional suffering that accompanied it shed light on his experience of himself in the present. Ennio was at the mercy of extreme anxiety, depression and feelings of unreality; his emotions had become him.

As a teenager he became a goth. The black clothes, black hair and the darkness of it all were exhibiting what he was feeling inside, alone and rejected. He also realised that he was attracted to men. This was a major problem, especially with regards to his father and brother. His feelings of nothingness and anxiety became unbearable. A short-lived sexual relationship with another boy at school at age 16 ended with Ennio being stalked to the extent that he feared for his life. Besides severe symptoms of depression he also developed symptoms of anxiety, specifically with regard to social situations. After leaving school he never started to work or engaged in any further relationships.

The fragility of his existence and lack of gravity in the world was overwhelming. Ennio and I continued to explore his being-in-the-world. Most of the time it would be the physical and social dimensions that dominated our discussions. Our work together enabled him gradually to manage his anxiety about leaving the house; however, his connection to the world and me came at a price – that of a recognition of his own lack and limitations. He would come to our sessions feeling furious with the world and the injustice he was experiencing. I could see the point in his rant about people having too much when he had nothing. I felt challenged and had to question my own values and ways of being. Over the next sessions his whole life-story unfolded.

Ennio was 28. He lived in the basement of his father's garage. He was tired, disillusioned, and described his life as a 'living death'. He did not want to live any longer. The only thing that kept him going between severely suicidal states was his writing. He was intelligent and eloquent and wrote poems and short stories. This was his world. However, he would neglect himself, he would not eat, wash, sleep, but exhaust himself in writing, at which point his family forced hospitalisation. His narrative around these events centred on the fact that he was not consulted, that he was not talked to, but that he was taken from his home without any notice. He could not live with the fact that his freedom had been taken away. He was in hospital for several months and had been given many diagnoses and medications. Ennio reported that he was told at some point that he suffered from psychosis. When he was eventually released from the hospital he was given the label 'treatment-resistant'.

On his return his family had renovated his room and in the process discarded huge amounts of paper from the basement, which was the last straw for him. His life's writings, the only thing that had some meaning for him, had been 'thrown away', rendered meaningless by his own family. This was about 12 months ago and since then, living had been unbearable. With no occupation, fear of leaving the house and lack of any meaning in his life, Ennio had felt that he had lost his battle with life.

His suicidal ideation made sense to me – why would he want to continue living in the absence of any meaningful connection to the world and other people? Indeed, for several sessions suicide remained an open possibility for Ennio. When we are confronted with clients who contemplate suicide, it is all too easy to fall back into assessing risks and reacting in order to ensure safety. However, what seems most important for the client is to know and feel that suicide can be talked about openly and its meaning explored, and for the therapist to remember that a chosen death is not necessarily a failure of the therapy/helping professions.

His account of life and experience of hospitalisation filled me with horror. Thinking of his narrative I could only just grasp his family's limited ways of showing care (i.e. by renovating his room), but all I was left with were feelings of intrusion, lack of understanding and emptiness. Ennio was surprised by my felt reaction, which I believe was another decisive moment in our work together, validating his experience and allowing him to relate to me in a non-combative way. From then on I had become a companion on his journey; we had made a connection. Ennio started looking forward to our sessions to which he would arrive on time. He begun to talk openly about his feelings and thoughts and he often posed questions about life that neither of us attempted to answer. Instead, we stayed with their relation to his own predicament and continued to unpack his worldviews and the unbearable emptiness he was experiencing. Our sessions turned into a philosophical discussion which was always grounded in his own lived experience. We revisited those places of isolation, loneliness and flirtation with death. We talked about his writings and pleasure in reading, which opened up a whole new dimension of Being that was for the first time accepted and valued.

We worked together for a year and a half; during these challenging months we came close to each other. Strangely, it was me who brought the reality of an ending to our sessions. It was a difficult period in my life during which I had gradually become disillusioned with everything. The day came when I told Ennio, not without nervousness, that I was planning to quit my job and leave the country to do conservation work in Central America. My fragility became evident to him, a fragility I didn't try to hide and that highlighted the fact that I, the other, the therapist, was grappling with similar issues. I had no idea what his reaction would be and I came close to tears when I encountered the peaceful smile on his face. My crisis in meaning worked as a catalyst. In the remaining five months, Ennio and I absorbed every single minute of our time together. I was asked many questions, which I answered truthfully. Chronos, the god of time, never left our room. His presence added further gravity to our sessions and Ennio begun to experience a sense of urgency, which forced him to prioritise his life.

We parted in deafening silence staring each other in the eyes. I closed the door, feeling the lump in my throat and holding the book of poems he had given me.

References

Boss, M. (1979). *Psychoanalysis and dasein analysis* (J. B. Lefebre, Trans). New York: Basic Books.

Camus, A. (2000). *The myth of Sisyphus*. London: Penguin Books. (First published 1942.)

Camus, A. (2005). *Summer in Algiers*. London: Penguin Books. (First published 1938.)

Cannon, B. (1991). *Sartre and psychoanalysis: An existentialist challenge to clinical metatheory*. Lawrence, KS: University Press of Kansas.

Cohn, H. (1997). *Existential thought and therapeutic practice. An introduction to existential psychotherapy*. London: Sage.

Cohn, H. (2002). *Heidegger and the roots of existential therapy*. London: Continuum.

Cooper, M. (2003). *Existential therapies*. London: Sage.

Deurzen, E. van (1998). *Paradox and passion in psychotherapy*. Chichester: Wiley & Sons.

Deurzen, E. van (1999). Heidegger's challenge of authenticity. *Journal of the Society for Existential Analysis, 10*(1): 115–125.

Deurzen, E. van (2002). *Existential counselling and psychotherapy in practice* (2nd edn.). London: Sage.

Deurzen, E. van (2007). Existential therapy. In W. Dryden (Ed.) *Dryden's handbook of individual therapy* (5th edn.). London: Sage.

Deurzen, E. van (2009). *Psychotherapy and the quest for happiness*. London: Sage.

Deurzen-Smith, E. van (1997). *Everyday mysteries: Existential dimensions of psychotherapy*. London: Routledge.

Frankl, V. (1963). *Man's search for meaning*. London: Hodder & Stoughton. (First published 1946.)

Heidegger, M. (1962). *Being and time* (J. Macquarrie and E. S. Robinson, Trans). New York: Harper & Row. (First published 1927.)

Hollingdale, R. J. (1977). *A Nietzsche reader*. London: Penguin Books.

Jaspers, K. (1950). *The way to wisdom*. (E. Paul and C. Paul, Trans). London: Routledge & Kegan Paul.

Kierkegaard, S. (1980). The concept of anxiety. In H. Hong & E. Hong (Eds.) *The essential Kierkegaard*. Princeton, NJ: Princeton University Press. (First published 1844.)

Macquarrie, J. (1972). *Existentialism: An introduction, guide and assessment*. Harmondsworth: Penguin Books.

May, R., Angel, E. & Ellenberger, H. F. (2004). *Existence* (2nd edn.). Lanham, MD: Rowman & Littlefield. (First published 1958.)

Milton, M., Charles, L. *et al.* (2003). The existential-phenomenological paradigm: The importance for psychotherapy integration. *Journal of the Society for Existential Analysis, 14*(1): 112–136.

Nietzsche, F. (1974). *The gay science* (W. Kaufmann, Trans). New York: Random House. (First published 1882.).

Rilke, R. M. (2004). *Letters to a young poet* (M. D. Norton, Trans). New York: W. W. Norton. (First published 1934.)

Sartre, J.-P. (1998). *Being and nothingness: An essay on phenomenological ontology* (H. Barnes, Trans). New York: Philosophical Library. (First published, 1943.).

Schopenhauer, A. (2004). *Studies in pessimism* (B. Saunders, Trans). Whitefish, MT: Kessinger Publishing.

Smith, R. (1999). Memento mori. *Journal of the Society for Existential Analysis, 10*(2): 63–82.

Solomon, R. C. (1983). *The passions. The myth and nature of human emotion*. Notre Dame, IN: University of Notre Dame Press.

Spinelli, E. (2005). *The interpreted world: An introduction to phenomenological psychology* (2nd edn.). London: Sage.

Strasser, F. (2005). *Emotions: Experiences in existential psychotherapy and life.* London: Duckworth.

Tillich, P. (2000). *The courage to be* (2nd edn.). New Haven, CT: Yale University Press. (First published 1952.).

Warnock, M. (1970). *Existentialism.* Oxford: Oxford University Press.

Yalom, I. (1980). *Existential psychotherapy.* New York: Basic Books.

Section 3

Counselling Psychology and the Wider World

Counselling Psychology and the Wider World

Martin Milton

'In an unwell person, it is most often not the body that is sick but the soul. Such a soul demands something from the soul of the community, and the treatment needs to be at the level of the relationship with others'
(Raymond Johnson, cited in Follmi & Follmi, 2005)

For many people within the mental health professions and beyond there is an assumption that, no matter how it is phrased, the role of the psychologist is one that is offered to individuals and it is usually in the consulting room. There is a view that, in a sense, the knowledge and practices described in Sections 1 and 2 are the only contributions that this book need highlight.

Yet our knowledge base and empirical evidence have shown us time and time again that people's distress is related to their place in the world. We know, for instance, that poverty can have an effect on the physical and psychological development of infants, children or adults; and we know that social and political oppression has an insidious effect on people's psychological wellbeing. Psychological information can be useful in a variety of ways, in enhancing our efforts with individuals, couples and families, but also by disseminating it. By 'giving psychology away' it may be possible to prevent some of the more destructive processes that do so much harm to people. Therefore, a counselling psychology perspective has to look beyond therapy. At times it need not only *look* beyond it, but *move* beyond it and participate in a range of different and innovative activities. In this section we have examples of how counselling psychologists are contributing to the physical, social, intimate and sociopolitical domains we exist in.

In Chapter 12 Natalie Hession looks at how counselling psychologists are contributing to the care of those experiencing chronic pain through an engagement with colleagues in medicine. This chapter offers an informative critique of the more established practices and argues that counselling psychologists' training in several therapeutic approaches allows therapeutic plans to be tailored to the needs and preferences of the client.

The area of pain is also instructive as it requires therapists to collaborate closely with other professions, often by joining multidisciplinary pain teams. This has been an opportunity for counselling psychologists, with their emphasis on the therapeutic alliance, meaning-making and competence in several therapeutic models, to work in an interdisciplinary style to alleviate and empower the client to manage their pain effectively.

These two foci – the body and interdisciplinary collaboration – are also addressed in Chapter 13, where Jill Owen explores the contribution that counselling psychology makes to the domain of sport and exercise. We are at a point when people seem more and more confused about their health, diet and the ways in which the mind and body are part of the same experience. This confusion manifests in increasing rates of overeating, obesity, diminished quality of life and all the psychological distress that accompanies these states. By focusing on the crucial role of sport and exercise, Jill Owen discusses the contexts in which counselling psychologists contribute to some of these areas, for example with teams or individuals of all levels wishing to improve performance and fitness, reduce anxiety or increase confidence and motivation in their chosen sport or exercise. In some ways practice in this domain takes us back to the core principles that lead to the establishment of the profession in the UK – interest in health promotion as much as recovery; wellbeing as much as distress; and a critical eye to the traditional structures of practice.

Counselling psychologists have long recognised the impact of such factors as race, gender and sexual identity on clients' experiences of themselves and on the possibilities that exist for them. Chapters 14 and 15 offer readers a chance to consider these pressures when Joanna Lofthouse explores the meanings of race and Colin Hicks looks at the meanings of different sexualities. These two chapters help us think about the ways in which our otherness can be overt or covert. The impact of race is an overt one in light of its visibility. The impact of sexuality has a number of different effects by virtue of the pressure, and ability, to hide that aspect of ourselves at times.

Chapter 14 explores how, within social and applied psychology, issues of 'race' and ethnicity are often treated as entities worthy of serious and sensitive discussion. However, one of the shortcomings is that psychologists may be left wondering how they can integrate their knowledge about 'race' into their therapeutic practice. A further shortcoming is that there is little scope for practitioners to explore their assumptions, opinions and prejudices about people from different racial groups, which should be an essential component of engaging in an open, honest discussion about 'race'. These factors sometimes result in avoidance of any racial issues for fear of 'getting it wrong', or in well-intentioned but naïve and clumsy attempts to address the 'race' of a client, regardless of the individual's needs.

In Chapter 15, Colin Hicks explores the fact that much traditional psychotherapeutic practice has viewed sexuality as set, formed or otherwise expected to follow specific structures and processes. The chapter questions the way in which psychotherapeutic practice has been hampered by limiting its view of healthy sexuality to monogamous heterosexuality. This chapter explores the contribution that counselling psychology makes to our understandings of sexuality and to non-oppressive therapy with clients of different sexual orientations, identities, practices and relationship structures. The chapter considers the reasons why clients may present to counselling psychologists. Attention is also paid to the particular psychological distress experienced by sexual minority clients in a society that values mainstream heterosexuality above other identities. Political and contextual issues that may impact on therapy are also considered.

In recent years, a substantial body of literature has developed which considers how various psychotherapeutic domains have approached, and ideally should approach, religion and spirituality in therapy. In Chapter 16, Adrian Coyle offers readers an overview of this literature and considers the value of engaging in a meaningful way with religious and spiritual issues where these are a salient dimension of a client's life-world. Attention is paid to the way in which some apparent 'challenges' and 'dilemmas' in engaging with religion and spirituality are not specific to these issues and can be usefully addressed through principles of good counselling psychology practice.

Increasingly, psychologists are being asked to contribute to public life by offering psychological insight through wider media – newspaper, radio, television and the internet. As a growing area of professional life there are useful things we can do to promote psychological health more broadly, but there are also significant shifts in practice we need to be aware of. In Chapter 17 Lucy Atcheson explores this and provides useful, firsthand experience of using a counselling psychology framework to contribute through those media, which are well beyond the consulting room.

While representatives of psychotherapy, counselling psychology and clinical psychology have often argued that the focus of our efforts should not be limited to the inner world or to the consulting room, there has long been a hesitance, perhaps born of confusion, as to how we attend to the wider sociopolitical domain, whether it be the political contexts our clients exist in or the physical domain. This is particularly true of such environmental issues as overpopulation, climate change, mass extinction of species and recycling. A respect for and of the planet and its inhabitants is a new area for counselling psychology practice. As well as learning from established practices that environmental psychologists, natural scientists and conservationists utilise, the final chapter argues that it is important and timely to review our paradigms. In Chapter 18 I argue that counselling psychologists are well placed to contribute to a shift from a relational psychology between people to one that attends to the relational implications of being part of the wider non-human world *as well*. This is important in understanding us as embodied beings, as well as understanding the impact we are having on the wider world. The chapter argues that this can be done and enhance the work we already do, as well as opening up possibilities for new and innovative ways of practice.

Reference

Follmi, D. & Follmi, O. (2005). *African wisdom: 365 days*. London: Thames & Hudson.

Chapter 12

The Counselling Psychologist Working in a Pain Context

Natalie Hession

Pain is the most common reason for individuals to enter health care settings and pain is the most common cause that prevents people working outside of the home (Breivik *et al.*, 2006). There has been a growing recognition that pain is a complex perceptual experience, influenced by a wide range of psychosocial factors, including emotions, the social and environmental context, sociocultural background, the meaning of pain to the person, beliefs, attitudes and expectations, as well as biological factors.

Pain is often classified as 'acute' or 'chronic'. Acute pain usually has a sudden onset and is associated with tissue damage or painful stimuli (e.g. skinned knee). Acute pain is often adaptive because it alerts us to the presence and location of tissue injury. Chronic pain, on the other hand, refers to the continuation of pain for an extended period despite medical treatment and coping efforts by the individual. In many cases, the cause of chronic pain cannot be identified. Chronic pain is not simply acute pain which has become unusually long-standing. Chronic pain is a complex phenomenon which, over time, impacts on a person's life, imposing widespread changes in relationships, goals and dreams, incorporating biological, psychological and social aspects.

In early theories of pain the importance of psychology in the expression, understanding and treatment was recognised. These theories were clinical

Therapy and Beyond: Counselling Psychology Contributions to Therapeutic and Social Issues
Edited by Martin Milton
© 2010 John Wiley & Sons, Ltd.

in nature as they arose from the growing issue of patients[1] suffering from chronic, unremitting pain and disability. Psychology also found its place in pain treatments after growing recognition that the extent of complaint and disability reported by many patients could not be explained by the extent of damage or disease (Gamsa, 1994). Medics looked to psychology to explain this discrepancy.

Psychologists and medics alike are aware of the complexity of difficulties that individuals experiencing persistent chronic pain present with. A large and growing number are highly distressed and present repeatedly for an array of medical interventions (Von Korff *et al.*, 1988). Patients experiencing chronic pain report associated problems, such as sleep difficulties and fatigue (Moldofsky & Lue, 1993) and disruptions to their sense of self (see Morley *et al.*, 2005; Osborn & Smith, 1998). The persistent attempts to react and adapt to pain and its widespread destructive consequences often result in a range of emotional difficulties, such as depression and pain-related fear, and negative effects on other aspects of cognition. Patients commonly complain of poor concentration and memory and increased failure to complete cognitive tasks (Schnurr & MacDonald, 1995). These emotional presentations are what counselling psychologists often deal with during their therapeutic work. While pain is not an area that counselling psychology has been traditionally involved in, medical staff and health care providers now recognise that counselling psychology has a contribution to make in pain teams. This has been an opportunity for counselling psychologists, with their emphasis on the therapeutic alliance, meaning-making and competence in several therapeutic models to work in an interdisciplinary fashion to alleviate and empower individuals in managing their difficulty.

The Development of Pain Perspectives

The Biomedical Model

The biomedical model proposes that injury activates specific pain receptors and fibres, which in turn project pain impulses through a spinal pain pathway to a pain centre in the brain. The psychological experience of pain, therefore, was virtually equated with peripheral injury or pathology. In the 1950s, the understanding of pain had no room for the psychological contributions to pain, such as attention, past experience and the meaning of the situation or one's experience. Patients who suffered from pain without presenting signs of organic disease were labelled as 'crocks' and referred to psychiatrists.

Gate Control Theory

In 1965, Melzack and Wall published the 'gate control theory' of pain, which argued that in human beings thoughts and emotions play an important role in determining whether pain impulses reach the brain and, if they do, how the brain interprets them. They hypothesised that certain higher-order functions, such as those relating to thoughts and emotions, could open or close a mechanism that operates like a gate in the nervous system. Powerful emotions, such as anger or anxiety, were thought to activate parts of the brain, which served to swing the gate fully open and allow pain signals to flow freely to the brain. Alternatively, more pleasant emotions or states of mind resulted in swinging the gate fully or partly closed. Psychological factors, which were previously dismissed as 'reactions to pain', were now seen to be an integral part of pain processing and new avenues for pain control were opened.

The Biopsychosocial Perspective

The biopsychosocial perspective (see Figure 12.1) views pain as a dynamic and reciprocal interaction between the purely mechanical and physiological processes and psychological and social-contextual variables that shape the person's response to pain.

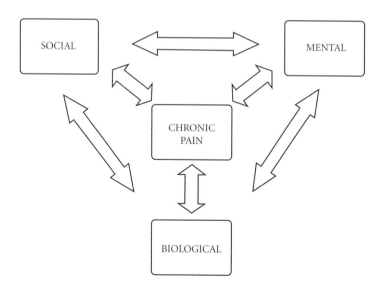

Figure 12.1   The biopsychosocial model of chronic pain.

A number of biopsychosocial models have been proposed to explain the individual's experience of chronic pain.

Psychodynamic Model of Chronic Pain

As a result of the recognition that a purely biomedical explanation of pain is limited, it seems only natural that psychoanalysis, which provided a model for explaining all of human behaviour, would address the difficulty of chronic pain. Freud proposed that his patients' pain symptoms were a result of the mechanism of conversion. In such circumstances the model asserts that unconscious, anxiety-riddled conflicts and needs are transformed into bodily pain as a means to restore psychic homeostasis. The symbolic theme of the precipitating unconscious motive is preserved in the form the pain adopts (e.g. sexual abuse manifesting as pelvic pain). Although the conversion model's empirical validity is in question (Turk & Flor, 1987), Freud is rightfully credited with drawing attention to the central contribution of psychological processes to somatic medicine.

Consistent with psychoanalytic ideology, chronic pain can be understood to result from developmental experiences that enhance the prominence of pain in childhood and give rise to the role of pain as a servant to adult defences. Engel's (1959) concept of the 'pain-prone personality' proposes that adverse events in childhood contribute strong and aberrant associations between pain and effect. For example, if parental relations include disproportionate themes of punishment and abuse, the child will associate pleasure with pain. As adults, these individuals will have a tendency to enter into masochistic relationships that re-enact these childhood dynamics. An adult defined as 'pain-prone' who has unbearable guilt, the urge to aggress or suffers interpersonal loss will be inclined to resurrect somatic pain as a saviour from intolerable psychic distress with pain serving as a psychological defence. The model of the pain-prone personality was widely accepted and may still have some impact, but the evidence for a specific relationship between developmental factors, personality traits and somatoform pain is sparse. There is a great deal of research which indicates an increased frequency of personality difficulties; however, there is no specific association between chronic pain and a personality profile (Gamsa & Vickis-Freibergs, 1991).

Several authors have proposed a model that views chronic pain as a variant of depression. Blumer and Heilbronn (1982) presented the most complete argument when they modernised Engel's thesis by incorporating evidence from neurophysiological studies of pain mechanisms. They hypothesised that a biological vulnerability to depression and personality characteristics that derive from psychodynamic conceptualisations of depression converge in the patient suffering from chronic pain. Blumer and Heilbronn's research was important in that it may correctly describe a subset of patients suffering with chronic pain; however, eventually it was challenged on the basis that the pain-as-depression model appears to be too restrictive as a general model of chronic pain as many of those suffering chronic pain are *not* depressed. The counselling psychologist working within a pain context should also be aware that if the patient's pain is misattributed to depression, they may become frustrated and defensive or feel betrayed by and alienated from the health care system.

More recently, a more relational emphasis has found increasing attention in the area of chronic pain (Basler *et al.*, 2002). The therapeutic application of the psychodynamic relational model to chronic pain is based on understanding the relational antecedents that can create vulnerability to developing chronic pain syndrome, as well as the psychosocial impact of chronic pain on the patient's life, especially with respect to relationships and relational roles. Relational antecedents may create a vulnerability to developing chronic pain and a propensity to experience suffering when it occurs. For some patients, a chronic pain syndrome and its associated relational roles – many of which are aspects of what has been termed the 'sick role' – are not the result of a breakdown in functioning or coping. It may reflect a conflict between two mutually exclusive relational roles – that is, genuinely wanting to get better and function autonomously versus a largely unconscious investment in the chronic pain relational configuration, especially being sick and nurtured. Consider the following case:

Anna [an amalgamation of past patients], aged 40, a clerical worker, had a long history of health issues from a very young age. She had been experiencing chronic lower back pain for 18 months and was unable to work or do many household chores. Anna wanted to get back to her 'normal' routine, but all efforts by the pain team and her husband to encourage this were met by fear and avoidance. At assessment it transpired that Anna had had a difficult relationship with her late parents. She described her father as 'a controlling alcoholic' and experienced her mother as emotionally unavailable due to severe depression throughout Anna's childhood. She recalled how her alcoholic father taunted her when she did well at school or when she expressed hopes and dreams for the future.

Anna's presenting (and previous) pain and disability prevented the symbolic surpassing of her father who threatened and responded with rejection when Anna, as a child, demonstrated competence and autonomy. Pain also maintained an internalised tie to her father who would not allow Anna to function autonomously because he could not relinquish the role of provider and controller. Anna reported feeling supported and cared for by her husband since having been unable to work, something she had always wanted and needed from her parents. Being sick was the only chance at getting attention. For Anna, to see herself as someone who could increase her physical functioning, although it may be consciously desired, would require the loss of the connection to her husband via the sick role, as well as the anxiety that would accompany a departure from a familiar relational position. At the same time it seemed important for her husband to nurture her as a parent would a helpless child. Having had parents who were not attuned to her needs, as an adult she had a chronic sense of deprivation, coupled with a largely unconscious belief that she did not deserve support unless she is visibly sick and distressed.

The psychodynamic model of pain helps us to understand the plight of the individual experiencing chronic pain. However, the contribution of the model has proved double-edged. It presumes psychological origin in cases in which pain does not ascribe to more biomedical views of pain mechanisms. Additionally, the psychodynamic model has failed to withstand the test of empirical scrutiny. With the ascendance of behavioural and cognitive-behavioural theories, the popularity of psychodynamic thinking within mainstream psychology has been waning, as is evidenced by the decline in published pain studies that consider a psychoanalytic perspective (Gamsa, 1994).

Behavioural Models of Pain

Behavioral Methods for Chronic Pain and Illness (Fordyce, 1976) remains one of the most influential texts on the relationship between pain and psychology. The behavioural model of pain centres on the operant conceptualisation of chronic pain (i.e. that rewards and environmental contingencies contribute to the maintenance of pain), but it also teaches us a great deal about the influence of psychological factors on pain in general. Fordyce's contribution lay in providing a framework that explains how the same learning processes governing the acquisition of other forms of behaviour could contribute to the profound levels of suffering observed in patients with pain. The behavioural model describes how social and environmental factors operate to exacerbate or alleviate problems of pain, illness and disability, and, equally important, how to harness those processes for effective therapeutic practice. Consider the following example:

Mark [an amalgamation of past patients] injured his lower back while lifting a heavy box at work. He went through the usual routine: multiple medical exams, X-rays, MRIs, physical therapy, time off work and, finally, surgery. His hopes for a full recovery were dashed many times, along with his spirits. He had worked hard in physical therapy and had followed his GP's advice: 'rest if in pain'. Almost a year after the accident, he was still off work, not doing household chores and spending most of his time watching television.

Within behavioural therapy we explored how following his GP's order to 'rest' too rigidly indirectly reinforced his pain behaviour. He avoided pain-eliciting situations such as light exercise, believing this avoidance to be analgesic when in fact it promoted further pain. He developed a symptom-contingent pattern of activity: doing more when he felt good and less when he was in more pain. Over time this led to a steady decline in his overall activity. In therapy, these patterns were replaced, encouraging Mark to behave time-contingently (as opposed to symptom-contingently) and to plan for achievable goals. Successes were reinforced. He was helped to problem-solve around some of the physical obstacles he faced, for example, how he could attend football matches without increasing his pain. This approach increased Mark's awareness of his pain situation. He realised that not doing household chores, which he formally despised, positively reinforced his pain behaviour, and subsequently he learned how to minimise their effects.

Mark revealed that he had avoided sexual intercourse for 18 months (six months before his injury) as he found great difficulty obtaining an erection. He described feeling ashamed and humiliated and was too embarrassed to speak with his wife about the situation. Although he wished he was pain-free, at the same time he reported that his pain allowed him to avoid any sexual encounters. Mark soon realised how this behaviour positively reinforced his pain and he developed skills to communicate his difficulty with his wife. Goal-setting helped Mark to work out a gradual and realistic return to work, which minimised the chances of re-injury and maximised his chances of success. He became adept at using relaxation to reduce muscle tension, thereby reducing his pain experience.

Behavioural programmes usually comprise of a variety of strategies, such as biofeedback and relaxation techniques, making the individual contribution of each intervention uncertain (Birket-Smith, 2001). Although operant factors undoubtedly play a role in the maintenance of pain and disability, the operant conditioning model has been criticised for its exclusive focus on motor pain behaviours, failure to consider the emotional and cognitive aspects of pain and failure to place importance on the subjective experience of pain (Turk & Flor, 1987). In many cases, a strict operant analysis or pain rehabilitation programme was insufficient to account for the totality of the patient's pain experience. In conclusion, the operant model of chronic pain has contributed significantly to our understanding and to therapeutic practice, but does not explain the development and persistence of pain in many individuals.

Cognitive-behavioural Model of Chronic Pain

In the years following the publication of Fordyce's book, cognitive-behavioural approaches began to gain widespread popularity in psychology. Although the philosophical roots of behaviour and cognitive theories may seem irreconcilable, they often complement each other in pain, in terms of assessment and therapy (Gamsa, 1994). The role of personal control, problem-solving, efficacy expectations, attributions and cognitive reframing within a cognitive-behavioural perspective of chronic pain is emphasised (Turk *et al.*, 1983). The cognitive-behavioural approach can be useful for patients experiencing pain and a large volume of research has now firmly established the importance of cognitive variables in psychological distress and physical disability of patients with chronic pain. The following example sheds light on how counselling psychologists can work using a cognitive behavioural approach with a patient experiencing pain.

Jill [an amalgamation of past patients] had suffered from osteoarthritis for several years. Jill was the 'carer' within the household, looking after her two children (now in their twenties), who had moved out in the past eight months, and her sick mother, who died 12 months ago from breast cancer. She reported her pain worsening following the death of her mother.

During assessment it became apparent that Jill was depressed, was exhibiting negative self-talk, lowered self-esteem, high pain ratings and greatly reduced physical activity. The first couple of sessions allowed Jill to put meaning on her experience and acknowledge the extent of the loss and distress she was experiencing since her mother's death, which appeared to have worsened when both her children left home. The CBT approach was explained to her, including the stress–pain–appraisal connection. She was able to recognise the link between periods of distress and pain as well as the meaning that pain held for her. Following this, relaxation training was introduced and she responded well, noticing that she experienced pain-free periods during relaxation. This helped to challenge her belief that she had no control over her pain.

Jill realised that she had reduced her physical activity as a result of her pain. The absence of her role to look after others meant that she was no longer involved in activities she found rewarding and that gave her a sense of pleasure. Subsequently, this had a negative impact on her mood. Jill was encouraged to develop insight into the automatic nature of her self-defeating and self-denigrating patterns of thinking which occurred when she experienced pain. Cognitive reframing allowed her to explore alternative ways of viewing her situation and she started seeing events in a more helpful manner. She was facilitated to problem-solve around some of the physical obstacles she faced, for example, she how could carry out household chores without increasing her pain greatly. This led to an engagement in activities she always hoped to do but could not find the time for while she was caring for her mother or raising her children.

Morley *et al.* (1999) conducted a systematic review and meta-analysis of all randomised controlled trials of cognitive behaviour therapy (CBT) for adults with chronic pain. Comparing a 'no treatment' control and another 'treatment', CBT produced significant effect sizes for the domains of pain, coping and pain behaviour. They concluded that 'published randomised controlled trials provide good evidence for the effectiveness of cognitive behaviour therapy for chronic pain in adults' (Morley *et al.*, 1999, p. 11). It is worth noting that these effect sizes are similar to those found in the psychotherapy research literature and are high when compared with non-psychological treatments for chronic pain. These results have largely been supported by more recent meta-analyses for specific pain conditions (Hoffman *et al.*, 2007).

The challenge to CBT for the management of chronic pain comes with the delivery of effective therapeutic programmes. There is little evidence for differential outcomes for different intervention methods. CBT is complex, lengthy and highly variable and is critically dependent on the quality and training of the health care professional and the appropriate content of therapy. Currently, there exists no national standard for treatment effectiveness and no requirement for audit and improvement. However, the effectiveness of appropriately designed and competently delivered CBT is well established and policies have strongly recommended its inclusion in routine pain clinic work (Clinical Standards Advisory Group, 2000). In addition, there is variation in the measures used to assess outcomes. This reflects the fact that the aim of psychological therapies is to change a person's experience of pain and their ability to cope despite the persistence of pain. There is still a substantial number of patients who do not appear to benefit from CBT interventions as well as there being relatively little known about the specific biobehavioural mechanisms that lead to chronic pain and pain disability (Vlaeyen & Morley, 2005).

The next generation of CBT for working therapeutically with those experiencing chronic pain will need to include a clear recognition that therapeutic intervention is designed for long-term changes and so will need to include methods of reducing relapse and attrition from therapy. Further therapeutic interventions will also need to address and quantify the effects of critical process variables, such as patient adherence to therapy and therapists' use of evidence-supported protocols. Perhaps the most significant challenges in the development of improved CBT are the ability to tailor interventions to individual needs and to develop programmes for specific groups, such as pain type (e.g. cancer pain) and client group (e.g. children) (Turk et al., 1993). Newer approaches, such as mindfulness, have been introduced in an attempt to remedy some of the limitations of CBT as a therapeutic approach for pain.

Mindfulness

Mindfulness-based stress reduction (MBSR) was adapted from the Buddhist practice of mindfulness meditation by Jon Kabat-Zinn (1982) to enable people to cope with illness, stress and pain. MBSR and its cousin, mindfulness-based cognitive therapy, propose a systematic programme for reduction of suffering associated with a wide range of medical conditions, including chronic pain. The potential benefit of using meditation for the self-regulation of chronic pain depends on the patient developing an ability to observe intense feeling in the body as bare sensation. By repeated practice the patient may learn to intentionally assume an attitude of detached observation towards a sensation when it becomes prominent in the field of awareness, and to observe with similar detachment the accompanying but independent cognitive processes, which lead to evaluation and labelling of the sensation of pain. Beyond the reduction in pain levels and pain-related behaviours, most patients evidenced attitudinal and behavioural changes, which can be attributed to the regular practice of mindfulness meditation, and cognitive changes which appear directly related to the experience of detachment and an increased awareness of oneself in relationship to others and to the world. The increased effectiveness of MBSR with regard to these outcomes may be related to the cultivation of a more accepting, observant attitude towards the whole range of one's inner experience, a view that is consistent with counselling psychology's focus on facilitating wellbeing rather than simply responding to pathology. Systematic research in MBSR is still in its infancy and its application to many pain types and therapeutic contexts is still unknown.

In many cases more than one model is therapeutically relevant. The distribution and frequency of psychodynamic, behavioural, cognitive-behavioural or any new and innovative models is unknown, and assessment instruments for determining which model is relevant in a therapeutic presentation are not available. Perhaps it is more helpful not to focus efforts on a characterisation of what the patient experiencing pain is or its exact cause. Understanding the complexity of each case may be more relevant than attempting to create a new category in which to fit this client group.

Challenges and Issues

Therapy for patients with chronic pain shares many issues with therapy for patients with other medical conditions and with mental health difficulties in general. However, this client group and the circumstances of their therapy can present with special challenges and complications that counselling psychologists are beginning to anticipate. One of these concerns fundamental differences health care professionals have in the conception of pain and thus the focus and course of therapy. The other areas are the context of the referral, confidentiality and related issues, autonomy and informed consent, and complications developing from medical treatment.

Differences in Conceptualising Pain

As previously outlined, there are different models to conceptualising pain. However, the biomedical model remains central to many medical practitioners, by patients as well as many third-party payers. This may result in a fundamental disagreement over the case conceptualsation between the counselling psychologist and other parties involved. Patients often expect health professionals to treat them actively by looking inside, poking, injecting, carrying out X-rays and medicating. This raises questions about how counselling psychology can effectively use their best model for working therapeutically with a pain condition and still present the patient with a rationale for therapy, justify the services to a third-party payer and collaborate closely with the medical staff. Some medics are resistant to psychological interpretations despite evidence that there is, at best, a modest relationship between objectively discernible physical impairments on the one hand, and pain reports and disability on the other (Turk & Monarch, 2002).

Faced with these differences in conceptualisation, the counselling psychologist often has to 'sell' the biopsychosocial model to colleagues. Feedback to referring professionals citing psychological contributory factors can aid this process. Providing these referring professionals with specific guidelines based on this perspective may help them see its heuristic value.

Therapeutic Context

Counselling psychologists are typically referred patients by medics or acquire the referrals as part of a pain management team in a clinic setting. The reason for referral, the medic's rationale to the patient and the circumstances of the referral (which is often made when the medic is frustrated or puzzled) begin the context of the therapy and can influence the patient's attitude. In some cases the patients may think the referral means they are fabricating their pain and will resist admitting to psychosocial influences even more strongly. In others, patients may have been ordered to seek psychological care under threat of dismissal from a clinic, in which case the patient may feel justified in resisting or engaging in therapy-interfering behaviours (Tumlin & Kvaal, 2004). The most frequent catalyst for a referral arises when medics themselves are uneasy with the presentation or behaviour of the patient and look to psychology to ease their perplexity. While there might be a sufficient and legitimate basis for the concern, it presents challenges to establishing rapport when patients may be unsettled by the involvement and request to see a psychologist. The challenge to the psychotherapeutic process of such misunderstandings is obvious. Taking on the role of the educator, the counselling psychologist can help prevent or reduce some of these relationship ruptures. In terms of the pain management team, counselling psychologists often develop, along with other pain team members, information booklets for patients which highlight the evidence-based, three-pronged approach to pain management (e.g. medicine, physiotherapy and psychology). This normalises referrals to psychology as a standard part of the programme. The meaning of the referral is best addressed with the patient as early as possible. Resistance should be confronted with a reminder that the patient is voluntarily seeking pain management services, and motivational interviewing (Miller & Rollnick, 2002) is one psychological approach that can be helpful at this time.

Confidentiality

Psychological societies' ethics standards are very clear on issues of confidentiality and privacy. These standards, although clear, are also fraught with difficulty in a pain management team or hospital setting as insurance companies often require patients to sign a consent form for the release of all information. Pain management team members often look to the psychologist for information that at times may be quite intimate and embarrassing to the patient. Counselling psychologists in pain management teams must develop understandings with medical collaborators regarding the limitations on what information is appropriate for sharing. It also is likely that the counselling psychologist will still face dilemmas in confidentiality, such as when a patient admits to misusing medication or in the case of psychological screening for surgical procedures. Framing the limitations of confidentiality clearly at the beginning of the therapeutic assessment, as well as being transparent about the dilemmas, is often the best approach. By the time patients are referred to a counselling psychologist they have experienced varying levels of transparency. As a result most patients value and respect the transparency offered in therapy, which often leads to a strengthening of the therapeutic relationship.

Autonomy and Informed Consent

Pain management teams are often structured around a team approach, where any number of health care providers (medics, psychologists, physiotherapists, nurses and occupational therapists) may be involved in the patient's care. Some programmes are 'packages' which include a clear understanding that, to be accepted into the programme, the patient must agree to participate in psychology and in all other aspects of the treatment protocol. Patients often find that they are required to see the psychologist for evaluation or psychological intervention before receiving invasive medical procedures or narcotic medications. It is in these situations that patient autonomy requires special consideration. Patients who would not autonomously participate in psychological assessment or therapy may feel subtle or overt threat from third-party payers or employers, including threatened loss of employment or compensation. Yet pain relief may be such an overriding goal that patients will agree, while feeling coerced into psychological therapy against their will.

Medical Complications

Many patients suffering with chronic pain use medications. Opioids and other pain medications (e.g. barbiturates, tranquillisers and antidepressants) can interfere with cognitive and emotional processes necessary for psychotherapy (Tumlin & Kvaal, 2004). Although patients can acclimatise, the blocking effects of these drugs can make the patient cut off and unable to express feelings, affect, thought processes and problem-solve and make for passivity (Hammersley, 1995). This is particularly prevalent in individuals experiencing chronic pain who have a limited capacity to use verbal communication (McDougall, 1989) and where the use of drugs may compound this. When working with patients who are taking strong pain medications it is important for the therapist to find what is effective at different stages. This may require that the therapist modify or expand his/her therapeutic approach, which is often an opportunity for counselling psychologists to make use of their skills and training in a number of psychological approaches. Counselling psychologists are particularly adept in using their own process and experience of a patient as part of the assessment and clinical judgement of the best psychological intervention. As medication is often necessary, the counselling psychologist needs to understand and accept the limitations that continued pain drug use (as well as psychiatric drug use) imposes. An understanding of the medications and how they are dosed is advised for counselling psychologists interested in this area (for a review, see Polatin & Gajraj, 2002).

Procedures and other aspects of biomedical pain treatment (not only prescribed medications) can create obstacles to psychotherapy. Patients who have agreed to nerve blocks or surgical procedures (with the expectation of a substantial reduction in pain) often struggle to tackle the psychosocial aspect, as it may involve accepting their condition as inevitably painful over the long term and require hard work in maximising coping and functioning despite their discomfort and limited resources. This runs counter to hope in the surgical procedures. The challenge is to enable patients to manage their pain as opposed to searching for the 'magic cure'. Otherwise, what often happens is that only after several years, when all of the possibilities and many resources are exhausted, is the patient prepared to accept their condition as being amenable to psychological therapy. Unfortunately that point is often characterised as one of despair and desperation.

Summary

The major tasks for psychologists are twofold: first, to further develop scientifically testable models that account for the variations in the experience of people with persistent, difficult to treat pain; and secondly, to devise therapeutic interventions that can sensitively address and ameliorate the range of suffering associated with pain. If pain cannot be eliminated, then a significant question remains and for each individual that question is: 'How can I lead a valued life in the presence of pain?'

Embarking on that ambition may involve reprioritising or even abandoning a significant goal that many patients experiencing chronic pain hold on to: the pursuit of a pain cure. Unsurprisingly, the process of addressing and coming to terms with this reality represents a significant challenge for many patients, their families and counselling psychologists alike. Given that experts in the field, from medics to physiotherapists, have highlighted that very little of the pain experience is accounted for by pain intensity and have emphasised the importance and value of psychological therapy in the treatment of chronic pain, therapeutic interventions have been placed centre-stage. Similarly, neuro-imaging has confirmed the impact and influence that psychological factors have on pain intensity and the experience of pain. Such evidence corroborates the value and role of psychology in addressing chronic pain. With great momentum in the field of pain research as a whole, this is an exciting juncture for the discipline of psychology, one that offers a timely opportunity for counselling psychologists to contribute by way of research and practice.

Note

[1] 'Patient' is derived from the Latin word *patiens*, meaning 'one who endures' or 'one who suffers'. Therefore, in terms of chronic pain, the use of the word seems fitting. As the majority of individuals referred to the counselling psychologist for pain-related issues are hospital patients, the term 'patient' will be used throughout. It is hoped that this does not detract from the aim for equality within the therapeutic alliance.

References

Basler, S. C., Roy, C., Grzesiak, R. C. & Dworkin, R. H. (2002). Integrating relational psychodynamic and action-oriented psychotherapies: Treating pain and suffering. In D. C. Turk & R.J. Gatchel (Eds.) *Psychological approaches to pain management: A practitioner's handbook.* New York: Guilford Press.

Birket-Smith, M. (2001). Somatization and chronic pain. *Acta Anaesthesiologica Scandinavica, 45*: 1114–1120.

Breivik, H., Collett, B., Ventafridda, V., Cohen, R. & Gallacher, D. (2006). Survey of chronic pain in Europe: Prevalence, impact on daily life and treatment. *European Journal of Pain, 10*: 287–333.

Blumer, D. & Heilbronn, M. (1982). Chronic pain as a variant of depressive disease: The pain-probe disorder. *Journal Nervous Mental Disorder, 170*: 381–406.

Clinical Standards Advisory Group (2000). *Services for patients with pain.* London.

Engel, G. L. (1959). 'Psychogenic' pain and the pain-prone patient. *American Journal of Medicine, 26*: 899–918.

Fordyce, W. E. (1976). *Behavioural methods for chronic pain and illness.* St Louis, MO: CV Mosby.

Gamsa, A. (1994). The role of psychological factors in chronic pain. 1. A half-century of study. *Pain, 57*: 5–15.

Gamsa, A. & Vickis-Freibergs, V. (1991). Psychological events are both risk factors in and consequences of chronic pain. *Pain, 44*: 271–277.

Hammersley, D. (1995). *Counselling people on prescribed drugs.* London: Sage.

Hoffman, B. M., Papas, R. K., Chatkoff, D. K. & Kerns, R. D. (2007). Meta-analysis of psychological interventions for chronic low back pain. *Health Psychology, 26*(1): 1–9.

Kabat-Zinn, J. (1982). An outpatient program in behavioral medicine for chronic pain patients based on the practice of mindfulness meditation: Theoretical considerations and preliminary results. *General Hospital Psychiatry, 4*: 33–47.

McDougall, J. (1989). *Theatres of the body: A psychoanalytical approach to psychosomatic illness.* London: Free Association Books.

Melzack, R. & Wall, P. D. (1965). Pain mechanisms: A new theory. *Science, 50*: 971–979.

Miller, W. R. & Rollnick, S. (2002). *Motivational interviewing: Preparing people to change.* New York: Guilford Press.

Moldofsky, H. & Lue, F. A. (1993). Disordered sleep, pain, fatigue, and gastrointestinal symptoms in fibromyalgia, chronic fatigue and irritable bowel syndromes. In E. A. Mayer & H.E. Raybould (Eds.) *Basic and clinical aspects of chronic abdominal pain.* New York: Elsevier Science.

Morley, S., Davies, C. & Barton, S. (2005). Possible selves in chronic pain: Self-pain enmeshment, adjustment acceptance. *Pain 115*(1–2): 4–7.

Morley, S., Eccleston, C. & Williams, A. (1999). Systematic review and meta-analysis of randomised controlled trials of cognitive behaviour therapy and behaviour therapy for chronic pain in adults, excluding headache. *Pain, 80*: 1–13.

Osborn, M. & Smith, J. A. (1998). The personal experience of chronic benign lower back pain: An interpretative phenomenological analysis. *British Journal Health Psychology, 3*: 65–83.

Polatin, P. B. & Gajraj, N. M. (2002). Integration of pharmacotherapy with psychological treatment of chronic pain. In D. C. Turk & R. J. Gatchel (Eds.) *Psychological approaches to pain management: A practitioner's handbook.* New York: Guilford Press.

Schnurr, R. F. & MacDonald, M. R. (1995). Memory complaints in chronic pain. *Clinical Journal of Pain, 11*: 103–111.

Tumlin, T. R. & Kvaal, S. (2004). Psychotherapeutic issues encountered in the psychotherapy of chronic pain patients. *Current Pain and Headache Reports, 8*: 125–129.

Turk, D. C. & Flor, H. (1987). Pain behaviours: The utility and limitations of the pain behavior construct. *Pain, 31*: 277–295.

Turk, D. C., Meichenbaum, D. & Genest, M. (1983). *Pain and behavioral medicine: A cognitive-behavioral perspective.* New York: Guilford Press.

Turk, D. C. & Monarch, E. S. (2002). Biopsychosocial perspectives on chronic pain. In D. C. Turk & R.J. Gatchel (Eds.) *Psychological approaches to pain management: A practitioner's handbook.* New York: Guilford Press.

Turk, D. C., Rudy, T. E. & Sorkin, B. A. (1993). Neglected topics in chronic pain treatment outcome studies: Determination of success. *Pain, 53*: 3–16.

Vlaeyen, J. & Morley, S. (2005). Cognitive-behavioral treatments for chronic pain: What works for whom? *Clinical Journal of Pain, 21*: 1–8.

Von Korff, M., Dworkin, S. F., Le Resche, L. & Kruger, A. (1988). An epidemiologic comparison of pain complaints. *Pain, 32*: 173–183.

Chapter 13

Working with Sport and Exercise Psychologists: A Winning Combination?

Jill Owen

The health benefits of physical activity are well recognised, as are the risks of an inactive sedentary lifestyle. The relationship a client has with sport and exercise is informative, helping us understand attitudes to health and the body, as well as the recreational and social aspects of their lives. Counselling psychology has a major contribution to make to the field of sport and exercise psychology through its philosophies, principles and models. This chapter focuses on a number of aspects of this, as well as addressing opportunities for learning from interdisciplinary collaboration. It concludes with a discussion of contributions to nationwide, multidisciplinary projects relating to physical activity.

Counselling Psychology and Physical Activity

In defining 'physical activity' and 'exercise', Caspersen *et al.* (1985) suggest that both involve movement of the body by the skeletal muscles and resultant energy expenditure which varies in intensity. According to the definitions, both are correlated with physical fitness, but with exercise it is very

Therapy and Beyond: Counselling Psychology Contributions to Therapeutic and Social Issues
Edited by Martin Milton
© 2010 John Wiley & Sons, Ltd.

positively correlated and it is maintaining or increasing this fitness that is an objective. The exercise definition contains the additional factor that the bodily movement is planned, structured and repetitive.

Some individuals choose planned and structured exercise (e.g. working out in a gym or attending exercise classes), whereas others are physically active to varying degrees as a result of their lifestyle, job, hobbies or sports. People differ in the extent to which they are content with their level of physical activity so exploration of the related motivational factors may be relevant in psychological intervention.

Counselling psychology philosophy encourages an open-mindedness to view exercise and physical activity from a broad perspective. Individuals vary in terms of their desire to engage in structured, planned exercise or sport, but almost all clients are engaged in some physical activity as most pursuits involve movement of the body. The problem in modern, industrialised societies is that many people's lives are too sedentary and include insufficient physical activity to maintain health.

The British Heart Foundation publishes statistics regarding obesity and physical inactivity levels (Allender *et al.*, 2008), and the contribution of these to diseases of the heart and circulatory system, which are significant causes of death in the UK. In 2004 the Chief Medical Officer highlighted the importance of physical activity in the prevention of heart disease, diabetes and obesity in his recommendation that adults should engage in at least 30 minutes of moderate-intensity activity at least five days a week (Department of Health, 2004).

As well as the benefits to physical health, a review of the research on the psychological effects (Biddle & Mutrie, 2008) suggests that exercise is associated with positive mood, improved psychological wellbeing, increased self-esteem and improved sleep patterns. The evidence also suggests there is a causal connection between exercise and the reduction of depression and non-clinical anxiety. Given that exercise improves general wellbeing and that insufficient physical activity impacts negatively on health, this is an important consideration for counselling psychologists. At a more global level, counselling psychologists can advise and contribute to government initiatives and projects to increase physical activity levels. In working with individuals, regardless of the setting, attention can be paid to attitudes towards the body, health and physical activity.

There is an overlap between the client populations seen by counselling psychologists and those with whom sport and exercise psychologists work. Sport and exercise psychology is regarded as being beneficial to amateur as well as professional athletes and for both groups the sport or exercise takes place within a context of other influential aspects of clients lives. Many clients seen by counselling psychologists engage in sport or exercise pursuits and the benefits of physical activity are relevant to all. Counselling psychology has a significant contribution to make to the domain of sport and exercise psychology, particularly as sport and exercise psychology evolves. This contribution is explored in more detail in the next section.

Historical Context

Athletes and coaches have traditionally placed emphasis on the physical aspects of training, but over time the tactical and psychological aspects have attracted greater focus (Dosil, 2006). Research suggesting the effectiveness of psychological intervention in sport is growing (e.g. Fournier *et al.*, 2005; Greenspan & Feltz, 1989; Weinberg & Comar, 1994). Increased public recognition of sport and exercise psychology and academic status led to the formation of the Division of Sport and Exercise Psychology within the British Psychological Society in 2004. Most psychologists in the field tend to focus on either sport or exercise.

> 'Practitioners in sport psychology offer services to athletes, teams and to others engaged in competitive sport, be it at recreational or elite level ... Practitioners in exercise psychology will typically work with individuals or organisations who wish to optimise the value of exercise as part of a healthy lifestyle'.
>
> (Division of Sport and Exercise Psychology, 2008, p. 8)

Although there is often a focus on the different aspects of sport and exercise, many individuals engage in both sport and exercise activities. Some may use structured exercise as a means to increase fitness to improve their sport performance, while others may aim to improve fitness through participation in active sport activities. Some of the suggestions in this chapter regarding the contribution of counselling psychology have more specific relevance to sport or to exercise, but many can be applied to both. Counselling psychology's recognition of the importance of the individual's wider context means sport or exercise behaviour will be regarded in the context of other activities in clients' lives.

Historically, the focus in sport psychology has been on psychological skills training (e.g. goal-setting, relaxation, imagery, refocusing and cognitive restructuring). Recent trends have seen a move towards a broader view of sport and exercise psychology that adds therapeutic interventions and philosophies, that values the individual's experience and that takes their overall context into account. The importance of the relationship between psychologist and athlete is gaining more recognition (e.g. Halliwell, 1990;

Petitpas *et al.*, 1999; Yambor & Connelly, 1991) as well as the need for reflection on the process of the work (e.g. Anderson *et al.*, 2004).

Research into the characteristics of effective sport psychology practitioners (e.g. Gould *et al.*, 1991; Partington & Orlick, 1987; Orlick & Partington, 1987) has emphasised accessibility, establishment of rapport, flexibility in meeting the needs of individual clients, trustworthiness and having something practical to offer. Features of ineffective practitioners included poor interpersonal skills, lack of sensitivity to the needs of individual athletes, adoption of a packaged approach when applying psychological skills and a lack of knowledge of psychology in relation to the specific sport setting.

Petitpas *et al.* (1999) suggest that training models often do not sufficiently support sport psychology trainees in developing the necessary humanistic skills to engage in athlete-centred practice. Some still retain a strong focus on techniques, paying insufficient attention to the processes involved in psychological intervention. Anderson *et al.* (2004) advocate an emphasis on reflective practice in professional sport psychology training and there is still a relative shortage in many programmes. This is an area to which counselling psychology can make a strong contribution.

Reflective practice in sport psychology allows practitioners to adopt an open, questioning approach (Anderson *et al.*, 2004), a philosophy shared with counselling psychology (Petitpas *et al.*, 1999). This openness helps avoid prescriptive use of skills packages, and practitioners are assisted in taking personal responsibility for monitoring their work while endeavouring to increase their effectiveness (Johns, 1995). Anderson *et al.* (2004) propose a 'knowledge-in-action' approach. This involves the application of professional knowledge within a framework of awareness of values, prejudices, experiences, aesthetic knowledge, ethical awareness, personal knowledge, social norms and empirical knowledge (Carper, 1978; Carr, 1989).

Interdisciplinary Collaboration

Sport and exercise work may run the risk of being seen as 'less psychological' and more superficial than areas of practice more typical to counselling psychology. Yet the idea that sport is 'only a game' and therefore does not involve significant issues is highly questionable. In many cases sport is a person's career, and even if recreational, may constitute an important part of their life or identity. It can be highly pressurised and emotive, as well as providing forums for intense self-evaluation and comparison with others. It is also the case that the difficulties or patterns a client manifests in sport or exercise may reflect longstanding patterns or more general issues in their lives. Their exercise behaviour may be indicative of their overall attitude to their health and wellbeing.

Until recently, sport was rarely associated with counselling psychology. As the areas of thinking within sport and exercise psychology expand, there is a much potential for interdisciplinary collaboration, which benefits both the sport and exercise psychologist and counselling psychologists. A special issue of *The Journal of Applied Psychology* was devoted to the application of sport psychology principles to other areas of life. In his contribution to this edition, Jones (2002) suggests that the principles of elite performance can be readily transferred to the business context, for example, in relation to organisational issues, team work, leadership, one-to-one coaching and coping with stress. Hays (2002) and Poczwardowski and Conroy (2002) explore the parallels in performing arts relating to performance, developmental issues, eating disorders, injury and retirement. Le Scanff and Taugis (2002) outline the benefits of implementing a psychological skills training programme for stress management in police officers. Learning more about psychological skills training may increase the resources of the counselling psychologist. The transferability of skills emphasises the usefulness of exploring the client's sport and exercise behaviours in relation to other areas of their lives. Identifying skills, resources and qualities that can be transferred to or from other arenas may add to the overall quality of the client's wellbeing.

There are many ways in which the models, principles and philosophies of counselling psychology contribute to the domain of sport and exercise psychology, particularly as the focus on reflective practice increases. Poczwardowski *et al.* (1998) suggested that counselling psychology is beneficial to the field of sport psychology with regards to supervision, theoretical frameworks, delivery models and service philosophy. Petitpas *et al.* (1999) later expanded the idea with regard to training and practice. Teaching on sport psychology programmes provided by counselling psychologists helps trainees by developing their awareness of the therapeutic process and their capacity for self-reflection, and focus on the psychologist–athlete relationship.

The Psychologist–Athlete Relationship

Petitpas *et al.* (1999) draw parallels between the psychologist–athlete relationship and the therapist–client relationship, while suggesting that this is an area from which sport psychology can particularly learn from the expertise of counselling psychology. There is empirical support for the importance of the relationship in the field of sport psychology (e.g. Gould *et al.*, 1991) and a counselling psychology perspective reminds us that a strong working alliance is necessary in order for progress to be made. Factors in the relationship may influence the choice of interventions and how the interventions are implemented may in turn affect the relationship.

Professional athletes often have numerous relationships within their team (coaches, managers, physiotherapists, doctors, fitness experts, nutritionists, teammates) and may vary in their expectations of what their relationship with their psychologist will entail.

This may be affected by the culture the client and psychologist exist within, with regard to sport and more generally. It may be that other professionals they deal with are didactic or prescriptive in style. Some athletes may consult a psychologist in the hope of having a more emotionally-based relationship in contrast to other situations in their domain where they feel they need to present a coping façade. Others may be comfortable learning skills or techniques but may not be at ease expressing personal or emotional information. When this occurs, the athlete may view the psychologist as an educator and minimise their own role in the process. If sufficient trust and communication are developed, the dynamics of the relationship may change significantly over time with the opportunity to integrate a greater range of intervention styles.

Amateur footballer Tim [names and all identifiable characteristics have been changes in all cases to protect confidentiality] tended to suffer from nerves before a game. He was initially reluctant to discuss the details of his experiences and requested skill-based strategies to combat the effects. Relaxation and refocusing exercises, together with some positive visualisation, initially appeared to provide him with some improvement and seemingly led to increased regard for sessions with the psychologist. Tim gradually appeared more relaxed and open in the sessions and one afternoon he arrived feeling very distressed about an argument he had just had with his father about his performance. It seemed that his trust in the therapeutic relationship had progressed to the degree that he was able to express his feelings about the situation and it was possible to make links with situations relating to his anxiety, such as his father's high expectations of him. In subsequent weeks he continued to make use of psychological skills, but also explored his own expectations of himself and realised they were very different from those his father held. He started to become more aware of his feelings, when they followed encounters with his parents and when they in fact did not reflect his own outlook. This awareness had a very positive impact on his nerves by his account and he became better able to focus on his game. He described benefits to the team performance as his passing became more accurate and he made fewer errors through depleted concentration.

Considerations of the countertransference and transference aspects of the relationship are relatively unusual in sport psychology (exceptions include Anderson, 2000; Strean & Strean, 1998) but may be very beneficial to practice in terms of providing information about patterns the client exhibits outside the consulting room. If, for example, a client consistently seems arrogant and dismissive in their sessions, it may be that they relate similarly to others in their sporting life, which may explain in part the client's complaints of harshness from teammates, opposition and coaches. As in therapy, if the psychologist experiences an emotion in the presence of the client, this can be informative of others people's possible responses. This can potentially lead to an exploration of the impact the client's behaviours may have on others and how their relationships may be affected.

At this point the chapter turns to the core models used in counselling psychology. This will highlight the way in which related frameworks enhance the contributions individual psychologists make to this area.

Therapeutic Models

Humanistic Approaches

The importance of the development of a strong working alliance has already been emphasised, reminding us that Rogers' core conditions are as important in work with athletes as in any other population. Adoption of a humanistic approach allows the practitioner to move between intervention styles and models while retaining the grounding of the relationship.

Humanistic philosophy places an emphasis on the individual's experience and the personal meanings relating to this experience (Hill, 2001). This means progress can be assessed in terms of the client's fulfilment, development and potential according to the factors that are of value to them rather than simply using scores and trophies as measures. Coaches sometimes suggest areas of work for clients, and if these offer little meaning to the individual, low levels of compliance may result. Although clients and therapists will need to take structures imposed by the sport or club into account, incorporating a focus on the aspects that are of most value to the client is important.

Psychodynamic Thinking

Although the psychodynamic model is rarely used as the sole model of practice with a client in a sport setting, there are many aspects that can inform practice or be integrated into the work. Countertransference and transference have already been mentioned.

The word 'defence' is used regularly in sport, but this usually refers to physical aspects of the game. The idea of psychological defences is considered less although all athletes have defences in place in order to perform. As a rugby player goes into a tackle, he needs to block out the physical risks associated with the move in order to avoid hesitation; boxers need to steel themselves for the impact of a punch and tennis players may need to defend against 'stage fright' or fear of losing.

Apitzsch and Berggren (1993) distinguish between adaptive and maladaptive uses of defence mechanisms, the former resulting in improved performance and the latter leading to decreased performance. A defence mechanism could be adaptive if a player continues to put considerable effort into trying to win even though the score line suggests this is unlikely. A maladaptive defence mechanism might lead an athlete to underestimate the demands of a race so that they prepare inadequately.

Importantly, the psychologist must take the athlete's defensive functioning into account. It may be that denying distress associated with a relationship breakdown may not be healthy for the client off the field, but it may be necessary while playing in order to retain focus. The timing in terms of training and matches needs to be taken into account, as well as the client's readiness to explore the usefulness of their defence mechanisms.

Cognitive-behavioural Approaches

The cognitive behavioural approach is frequently applied in sport psychology and a review by Dishman and Buckworth (1996) found cognitive behavioural interventions to be potentially effective at improving physical activity levels.

Cognitive behavioural therapy often forms the basis for psychology skills training. The use of deeper schema-focused models (e.g. Young, 1999) is less common but can help gather information about factors that could have contributed to some of the athlete's most influential core beliefs.

The core beliefs that influence a client's thinking on the field may have formed in relation to experiences that do not directly relate to sport or exercise. This emphasises the importance of openness to exploring a range of areas of a client's life.

Dan reported having been criticised by his parents for many years in relation to his schoolwork, with the repetitive theme that he did not apply enough effort. He felt he had always worked hard and expressed confusion as to the discrepancy between the perceptions of his effort level. Dan seemed to have developed the belief that he was inherently lazy and incapable of judging necessary effort requirements. In applying these beliefs in his sport he was demonstrating a tendency to over-train to the point of burnout and his self-evaluation was consistently critical.

Interventions that encourage challenging thoughts at the automatic level play an important role in managing emotions and it is beneficial for athletes to learn to do this early on so that they can optimise their mindset before performance and banish confidence-depleting thoughts when under pressure. Consideration of underlying core beliefs may inform the psychologist's work or may later be incorporated into the practice to produce longer-term understanding and change.

The factors that influence goals, models and interventions will be discussed in the following section with regard to wider counselling psychology considerations.

Factors Influencing Goals and Interventions

Factors Relating to the Practitioner

Arrival at an integrated model requires practitioners to have awareness and clarity regarding the approaches they adopt and how they incorporate them into the process of their work. This necessitates reflection on a number of factors, including those that relate to the practitioner, the client and the context. A counselling psychology perspective leads to reflection on the practitioner's own impact on the therapeutic processes in terms of values, biases, ideas, responses to the client, culture, personality, experiences of physical activity, qualifications, knowledge, skills and preferred theoretical models. Likewise, Poczwardowski *et al.* (2004) emphasise the role the practitioner's philosophy plays in sport-related practice.

Factors Relating to the Client

Clients may have sport-specific concerns (e.g. hesitation going into tackles in rugby or a fear of penalty taking in football) or there may be more general areas they believe would benefit from enhancement (e.g. concentration during play). In relation to exercise, a client might be struggling with a specific situation such as the boredom of a rehabilitation programme after injury or they may have more generalised motivational issues. It may be that the client has no specific goals in mind, particularly if it was not their decision to see the psychologist.

The athlete's goals and expectations of psychological intervention play an important role in informing choices as to the models and interventions that will be most appropriate. A client's expectations of how psychological intervention will progress will impact on the process, particularly with regard to the relationship with the psychologist. In addition, client expectations in the psychology setting may inform the practitioner about reactions they may have in a sport or exercise environment. If, for example, the client is unrealistically impatient in terms of their expectations of psychological intervention and shows signs of dropping out, it may be that they take a similar attitude to exercise if results are not achieved quickly. The decision to adopt an approach that allows exploration of this pattern could help the client avoid a barrier to maintaining their exercise programme.

The relational ethos of counselling psychology regards the person as a whole, considering all aspects of the individual's wider context and past rather than just the factors directly associated with sport and exercise. As Anderson and Van Raalte (2005) suggest, improvement in performance is unlikely if the athlete's life outside of sport is dysfunctional. In sports such as football and rugby, where domestic teams include players from various countries, there are additional pressures of living away from home, such as possible language barriers and adapting to the culture of an overseas club. The relational view and its requirement that we consider wider issues in a client's life influence the choice of therapeutic model applied and the levels of intervention within the model.

Contextual and Situational Factors

In some settings there may be expectations as to how the psychologist will work, for example, by implementing particular skills-based packages. The risk of such structures is that the meaning to the athlete will be ignored and levels of client commitment may be negatively affected. Additionally, the client's goals may be different from the coach's or management's and at times may be in conflict with them. Counselling psychologists can engage with such dilemmas through communication and by seeking to find a balance that makes the approach contextually appropriate while benefiting the client. Exploring the client's experiences of such dilemmas may be enlightening and a collaborative approach may lead to joint decisions as to how to manage the situation.

Further Ethical and Professional Considerations

In sport and exercise settings, decisions often need to be made regarding where the psychological work will take place (i.e. in the consulting room, during training or at the ground prior to a match). The freedom and potential implicit in this move beyond the consulting room may appeal to practitioners, but they will need to engage with the challenges involved in maintaining appropriate professional boundaries in situations where they are less clearly defined. Regardless of where the work is conducted, the setting must allow for the confidentiality agreement to be preserved. In situations where others are present, such as travel on the team bus, aspects of the 'real relationship' (Barr, 1987) may be more appropriate, but confidential subject matter will need to be avoided. Discussing such situations before they occur will optimise the potential for utilising all situations as effectively as possible.

In contexts where psychologists work with the whole club, it is important to take 'divided loyalties' into account. The psychologist may be expected to liaise with managers or coaches about the client and the confidentiality agreements may impact on the emotional levels at which the practitioner chooses to intervene with individuals. Maintaining transparency regarding confidentiality limitations and exploring ways of managing such issues with clients is essential.

Another important ethical question for psychologists concerns competence in working in the field of sport. Although interdisciplinary collaboration leads to shared learning that enhances both professions, counselling psychologists and sport psychologists retain types of issues and clients with whom they may be better suited to working. This highlights the importance of assessing clients' specific needs in terms of therapeutic planning and referral decisions.

The final section of this chapter looks at the ways in which counselling psychology can contribute to nationwide initiatives that address physical activity issues in a multifaceted way.

Physical Activity Intervention at a Global Level

In 2005 the government published *Choosing Activity: A Physical Activity Action Plan* in which they outlined their commitment to physical activity, and in January 2009 launched a major, multisectoral and interdisciplinary project to improve the lifestyle habits of the nation. The associated document *Be Active, be Healthy: A Plan for Getting the Nation Moving* (2009) outlines diverse and extensive plans for increasing the physical activity levels of individuals and communities. This involves the work of many government departments, policy-makers and a wide range of organisations. New ideas are set out for local authorities and primary care trusts to establish and respond to the needs of local populations. A number of national initiatives are in place, such as the government's *Free Swimming Programme*, *Walking for Health* and *Change4Life* which is accompanied by a high-profile informative media campaign.

The government plan could, of course, be subject to development and alteration in accordance with political changes, but there are many aspects of current thinking in keeping with the ethos of counselling psychology. Counselling psychologists have always been as interested in the promotion of health and wellbeing as in recovery. In addition to considering the direct impact of increased physical activity on individuals, the national project emphasises more global benefits. Limiting the number of car journeys taken by walking or cycling reduces traffic congestion, pollution and transport costs, which in turn feeds back into the health of communities. *Well@Work*, a joint programme led by the British Heart Foundation with funding from Active England and the Department of Health, piloted 'healthy interventions' in a range of workplace environments in order to achieve a greater understanding of how individuals can be healthier and in turn, companies can be more productive (see Bull *et al.*, 2008, 2008a). The British Heart Foundation's *Health at Work* programme continues to promote health and wellbeing in the workplace, for example, by encouraging more physical activity in work environments.

Also compatible with the principles of counselling psychology is the document's focus on individual differences and the awareness that people have different needs, preferences and perceived limitations in terms of the type of exercise they will be likely to continue with. Figures are presented relating to the physical activity levels of people from different age groups, locations, ethnic groups, cultures, income levels and physical ability. An emphasis on individual choice is clear in the plan, with a wide range of ideas for activity highlighted, including sports, gym-based exercise, active play, active travel (cycling/walking) dancing, gardening, DIY, housework and occupational activity (active/manual work).

There are many opportunities for counselling psychologists to contribute to these national projects. A key area for intervention is consultation with professionals and organisations involved in the national programme, such as GPs, health professionals, leisure centres, gyms, businesses, charities and government departments. Psychologists can inform organisations about individual differences and psychological factors that influence exercise behaviour by lecturing, running workshops and providing related literature. They can also deliver training that encourages professionals to listen to individuals, assess their requirements, preferences and concerns regarding exercise, as well as respond to the information elicited.

> Working with the fitness instructors in a gym and health club provides an example of psychological intervention of this type. The aim of the project was to address the problem of membership drop-out and look at how members' requirements could be elicited and better addressed. Workshops on the factors that may affect members' gym attendance highlighted issues relating to confidence associated with exercising in the gym, body image perceptions, types of thinking regarding comparison with others, enjoyment of different exercise types, perception of ability to use gym equipment or carry out moves, realism of expectations and excuses or justifications for not attending.
>
> Feedback from the instructors suggested the workshops led them to consider factors they had not thought about before and to take a much more open and enquiring approach to the needs of each individual client. Training in listening skills and collaborative goal-setting enabled the instructors to elicit these more effectively. The distribution of informative leaflets and posters about potential activities aimed to encourage members to make informed choices regarding their exercise. Feedback request forms provided more opportunity to assess and respond to their preferences.

Writing or contributing to media publications and broadcasts also provides an opportunity for counselling psychologists to inform a broad cross-section of people about the psychological aspects of exercise and the issues surrounding it. Knowledge relating to confidence, self-esteem, identity, motivation, perception and social factors enriches articles about physical activity and encourages people to become more self-aware as they make training choices and embark on their regime.

In working with individuals, counselling psychology intervention can parallel this global focus; for example, exploration with a client could look at areas in their life that may be underused in terms of possibilities for physical activity.

> Lucy (pseudonym) wanted to lose weight and had always expressed dissatisfaction that she did not have time to exercise due to the challenges of balancing work and family life. Exploring possible opportunities within the current structure of her life led to her becoming inventive in thinking

of ways she could be more active. Examples included replacing sedentary time with the children with trampolining or cycling, conducting
brainstorming meetings with colleagues while out for a walk rather than
in an office and skipping with a rope for 10 minutes several times a
week when she had a break. The confidence she reported from exercising
regularly, maintaining her progress and reaching her weight loss targets
led her to address other goals in her life. She had previously only seen
obstacles when she had considered options to progress her career. She
suggested that having overcome her perceived barriers to maintaining
exercise, she now believed she could tackle anything and could apply a
similar resourceful approach.

Research by McAuley *et al.* (1990) suggests that virtually all barriers to exercise are potentially within the control of the individual. The client who
engages in exercise can feel autonomous in their choice to do so. This
increases confidence that it is transferable to other aspects of their lives, as
in Lucy's case. This is in keeping with earlier discussions regarding counselling psychology philosophy in that neither the client nor their exercise
behaviour exists in isolation. This is also true of the disciplines of counselling psychology and sport and exercise psychology as there continues to
be great potential for interdisciplinary collaboration and learning. As counselling psychology expands its thinking out of the consulting room and as
sport and exercise psychology embraces new philosophies of working, the
possibilities for enhanced work continue to increase.

References

Allender, S., Peto, V. *et al.* (2008). *Coronary heart disease statistics.* London: British
    Heart Foundation.
Anderson, A. G., Knowles, Z. & Gilbourne, D. (2004). Reflective practice for sport
    psychologists: Concepts, models, practical implications and thoughts on dissem-
    ination. *The Sport Psychologist, 18*: 188–203.
Anderson, M. B. (2000). Beginnings: Intakes and the initiation of relationships. In
    M. B. Anderson (Eds.) *Doing sport psychology.* Champaign, IL: Human Kinetics,
    pp. 3–16.
Anderson, M. B. & Van Raalte, J. L. (2005). Over one's head: Referral processes.
    In M. B. Anderson (Eds.) *Sport psychology in practice.* Champaign, IL: Human
    Kinetics.
Apitzsch, E. & Berggren, B. (1993). *The personality of the elite soccer player.* Lund:
    Studentlitteratur.

Barr, J. (1987). Therapeutic relationship model. *Transactional Analysis Journal*, *17*(4): 141.

Biddle, J. H. & Mutrie, N. (2008). *Psychology of physical activity: Determinants, well-being and interventions.* (revised edn.). Oxford: Routledge.

Bull, F. C., Adams, E. J., Hooper, P. L. & Jones, C. A. (2008). *Well@Work: A summary report and calls to action.* London: British Heart Foundation.

Bull, F. C., Adams, E. J. & Hooper, P. L. (2008a). *Well@Work: Promoting activity and healthy workplaces final evaluation report.* Loughborough: School of Sport and Exercise Sciences, Loughborough University.

Carper, B. (1978). Fundamental patterns of knowing in nursing. *Advances in Nursing Science*, *1*: 13–23.

Carr, W. (1989). Introduction: Understanding quality in teaching. In W. Carr (Eds.) *Quality in teaching.* Lewes, UK: The Falmer Press.

Caspersen, C. J., Powell, K. E. & Christenson, G. M. (1985). Physical activity, exercise and physical fitness: Definitions and distinctions for health-related research. *Public Health Reports*, *100*: 126–131.

Department of Health (2004). *At least five a week: Evidence on the impact of physical activity and its relationship to health: A report from the Chief Medical Officer.* London: Department of Health.

Department of Health (2005). *Choosing activity: A physical activity action plan.* London: Department of Health.

Department of Health (2009). *Be active, be healthy – A plan for getting the nation moving.* London: Department of Health.

Dishman, R. K. & Buckworth, J. (1996). Increasing physical activity: A quantitative synthesis. *Medicine and Science in Sports and Exercise*, *28*: 706–719.

Division of Sport and Exercise Psychology (2008). *Qualification in sport and exercise psychology (Stage 2): Candidates' Handbook.* Leicester: BPS.

Dosil, J. (2006). Applied sport psychology: A new perspective. In J. Dosil (Eds.) *The sport psychologist's handbook: A guide for sport-specific performance enhancement.* Chichester: Wiley.

Fournier, J., Calmels, C., Durand-Bush, N. & Salmela, J. (2005). Effects of a season-long PST program on gymnastic performance and on psychological skill development. *International Journal of Sport and Exercise Psychology*, *3*: 59–78.

Gould, D., Tammen, V., Murphy, S. & May, J. (1991). An evaluation of U.S. Olympic sport psychology consultant effectiveness. *The Sport Psychologist*, *5*: 111–127.

Greenspan, M. J. & Feltz, D. L. (1989). Psychological interventions with athletes in competitive situations: A review. *The Sport Psychologist*, *3*: 219–236.

Halliwell, W. (1990). Providing sport psychology consultancy services in professional hockey. *The Sport Psychologist*, *4*: 369–377.

Hays, K. F. (2002). The enhancement of performance excellence among performing artists. *Journal of Applied Psychology*, *14*(4): 299–312.

Hill, K. L. (2001). *Frameworks for sport psychologists: Enhancing sport performance.* Champaign, IL: Human Kinetics.

Johns, C. (1995). The value of reflective practice for nursing. *Journal of Clinical Nursing*, *4*: 23–30.

Jones, G. (2002). Performance excellence: A personal perspective on the link between sport and business. *Journal of Applied Psychology*, *14*(4): 268–281.

Le Scanff, C. & Taugis, J. (2002). Stress management for police special forces. *Journal of Applied Sport Psychology*, *14*(4): 330–343.

McAuley, E., Poag, K. Gleason, A. & Wraith, S. (1990). Attrition from exercise programs: Attributional and affective perspectives. *Journal of Social Behaviour and Personality*, *5*: 591–602.

Orlick, T. & Partington, J. (1987). The sport psychology consultant: Analysis of critical components as viewed by Canadian Olympic athletes. *The Sports Psychologist*, *1*: 4–17.

Partington, J. & Orlick, T. (1987). The sport psychology consultant: Olympic coaches' views. *The Sport Psychologist*, *1*: 95–102.

Petitpas, A. J., Giges, B. & Danish, S. J. (1999). The sport psychologist–athlete relationship: Implications for training. *The Sport Psychologist*, *13*: 344–357.

Poczwardowski, A. & Conroy, D. E. (2002). Coping responses to failure and success among elite athletes and performing artists. *Journal of Applied Psychology*, *14*(4): 313–329.

Poczwardowski, A., Sherman, C. P. & Henschen, K. P. (1998). A sport psychology service delivery heuristic: Building on theory and practice. *The Sport Psychologist*, *12*: 191–207.

Poczwardowski, A., Sherman, C. P. & Ravizza, K. (2004). Professional philosophy in the sport psychology service delivery: Building on theory and practice. *The Sport Psychologist*, *18*: 445–463.

Strean, W. B. & Strean, H. S. (1998). Applying psychodynamic concepts to sport psychology practice. *The Sport Psychologist*, *12*: 208–222.

Weinberg, R. S. & Comar, W. (1994). The effectiveness of psychological interventions in competitive sport. *Sport Medicine*, *18*: 406–418.

Yambor, J. & Connelly, D. (1991). Issues confronting female sport psychology consultants working with male students-athletes. *The Sport Psychologist*, *5*: 304–312.

Young, J. E. (1999). *Cognitive therapy for personality disorders: A schema-focused approach.* (revised edn.). Sarasota, FL: Professional Resources Press.

Chapter 14

The 'R' Word

Joanna Lofthouse

In my experience a hush often descends when the topic of 'race' is raised in a professional psychology setting. After a brief gust of discomfort is felt by all, colleagues may begin to discuss the benefits of being aware of cultural differences and the virtues of cross-cultural therapy, whilst (possibly) reflecting on the challenges that such approaches may bring.

There may be nothing wrong with this *per se*, of course. This slightly hesitant response may be indicative of how issues of 'race' and ethnicity are often, understandably, treated as worthy of serious and sensitive discussion, not only within psychology, but in sectors beyond. Training on 'race' and ethnicity is often provided in specific cross-cultural therapy modules and enhanced by the use of well-regarded racialised identity models and guidelines on how to work with 'minority' groups (Helms, 1995; Sue & Sue, 1999). The emphasis is often on the impact of working with people whose culture differs from the perceived normative or dominant culture, as well as on developing awareness of how traditional models of therapy are inextricably linked to Western ideals and values. As counselling psychologists, we explore our own cultural assumptions, principles and expectations in order to help maintain a genuine, non-judgemental stance with our clients. All are undoubtedly important and necessary endeavours.

However, all too often 'race' gets subsumed by, or converted into, 'culture'. 'Race', and its impact, within the therapeutic relationship are rarely openly discussed as a discrete issue among therapeutic practitioners. 'Race', by

Therapy and Beyond: Counselling Psychology Contributions to Therapeutic and Social Issues
Edited by Martin Milton
© 2010 John Wiley & Sons, Ltd.

which I mean, quite simply, *skin colour*, seems to have become something that we tacitly know not to discuss. This is perhaps hardly surprising given the current social climate where it is apparently deemed rude and improper to refer directly to someone's skin colour (apart perhaps from commenting when the sun is shining that 'I wish I went a lovely colour like you . . .'). The simultaneous barrage and dearth of advice and guidelines about appropriate use of language, adequate knowledge of cultural idiosyncrasies and their accompanying litigious fog perhaps serve ultimately to silence a discussion that was already restricted, as it is widely acknowledged that one must avoid at all costs being perceived or described as 'racist'. Speaking of culture therefore often offers a safer territory within which to operate and provides an acceptable respite from and seemingly adequate response to the issue of 'race'. Obviously, though, this does not make the matter go away. 'Race' is something that affects us all and that we all have a personal and social response to, regardless of whether or not we choose to talk about it.

By focusing predominantly on 'race', it is not being suggested that culture is irrelevant or unimportant, or that a person's cultural frame of reference does not inevitably impact on the therapeutic (or any other) relationship. It is of course, at times, imperative that 'race' and culture be considered as interrelated in order to fully understand a client's presenting concerns. However, it is equally important for the effect of 'race' on the therapeutic relationship to be considered separately from culture, as clients from similarly different cultural backgrounds – e.g. a man from Lyon and a man from Paris – are likely to evoke different responses in the therapist – in this case when the Frenchman from Lyon is white and the Parisian is black.

This chapter considers some of the processes that need to be undertaken in order to enable therapeutic practitioners, other health care professionals and service providers to work with 'race' in a healthy and constructive way. The concept of 'race' will be explored, along with the rather unpalatable possibility that we all have the potential to, or may in fact be, fundamentally racist. I hope to go beyond the intellectual understanding of 'race' and engage with its complex and contradictory nature and its effect on the therapeutic relationship as a means to explore some of the subtleties that influence other, less defined relationships. As such this chapter offers a frank and unceremonious account of 'race' in a deliberate attempt to avoid intellectualising about or disengaging with an often emotionally charged subject matter. Some of the costs of being unable or unwilling to connect with this process will be outlined before recommendations for training, supervision and practice are made.

Counselling psychology's emphasis on the therapeutic relationship, on seeing people as inevitable products of their environment and experiences, as well as accepting that human wellbeing is a function of an engagement with oneself, others and the world, places it in a prime position to engage in a holistic, personal and professional discussion about 'race' that is useful in the consulting room and beyond. The application of counselling psychology's 'being with' rather than 'doing to' philosophy as a framework when considering the subject of 'race' removes some of the pressure of being an 'expert', which in turn facilitates a more confident and intuitive, less self-conscious discourse, and can also inform a wider debate among service providers in other professional sectors.

What is 'Race'?

The Compact Oxford English Dictionary of Current English (2005) defines 'race' as:

> **noun 1** each of the major divisions of humankind, having distinct physical characteristics. **2** racial origin or distinction: *rights based on race*. **3** a group of people sharing the same culture, language, etc.; an ethnic group. **4** a group of people or things with a common feature.

But this definition does not describe very much at all; indeed, it is quite vague. It simply suggests that 'race' refers to distinct groups of people, but makes no real reference to how these groups are categorised or created. Yes, it cites culture and language, but are these really the main features that people of different 'races' share? 'A group of people with a common feature' could refer to just about anything, but 'race' is rarely used beyond specific contexts. It is interesting that this dictionary definition is so empty, as it suggests that 'race' as a factual and truthful concept is hard to capture and may not even exist. Of course, when reading this definition the gaps are filled by our social, political and historical knowledge about 'race', so we all know exactly what is being referred to: skin colour.

I am aware that reducing 'race' to skin colour appears at best an oversimplification and at worst simplistic, but isn't that what we are talking about? Are we not talking essentially about black people and white people?

History

In the nineteenth century, scientists and anthropologists concluded not only that there were distinct differences between people of different backgrounds, but, by using methods such as measuring skull sizes, that white people were infinitely superior to black people in a variety of areas, among them intellectual ability and capacity for civilisation (Banton, 1988). With this level of understanding, 'race', which biologically refers to 'a distinct population within a species; a subspecies' (*Compact Oxford English Dictionary of Current English*, 2005), is an obvious choice of word to describe such differences between people.

However, by the mid-twentieth century any genetic or biological basis of 'race' was scientifically disavowed and it has been repeatedly shown that there are many more differences within the so-called 'races' than between them (Winston *et al.*, 2004). It is curious, therefore, that we continue to use a word whose coinage was based on a set of scientific facts that have long since been disproved. Perhaps it is unrealistic to expect such pervasive historical theories of 'race' (which were used as grounds for the oppression of millions of black and minority ethnic people via slavery and apartheid in various forms) not to be evoked when 'race' is referred to, even though in contemporary society 'racial' differences often seem accounted for in cultural and social rather than biological terms. Perhaps our collective willingness to continue using 'race' is indicative of our reluctance or inability to correct the inherent power imbalance that it denotes.

For the purposes of this chapter, 'race' will be used to refer to the socially constructed, superordinate category of which black and white are subordinate components. 'Black' will be used to refer to people who commonly fall into the category of 'Black and Minority Ethnic', or more simply, to use a term made popular in the USA, 'people of colour', whilst 'white' will denote people of Caucasian descent. The use of 'race' in dichotomous terms is intended to assist the discussion about the impact of colour within the therapeutic dyad rather than to generalise about the plethora of ethnic groups that each category includes. 'Race', therefore, will not be used interchangeably with either ethnicity, which has been described as the term given to cultural features such as language, religion, custom and traditions shared by people (Hall, 1992), or culture, which Laungani depicts as 'regulated social systems, communication networks, including regulatory norms of personal, familial and social conduct' (1999, p. 44).

'Race' and Power

'Race' has the potential to impact on most areas of life. Whether it is thought about frequently or rarely, everyone has a racialised identity which may become more or less salient according to the context. Racialised identity refers to those aspects of a person's identity that pertain to socially constructed ideas of 'race' and differs from other features of identity, such as gender or sexuality. Unlike gender or sexuality, which would perhaps be considered fairly pervasive features of identity by most of us, it is likely that many people would struggle to define how their racialised identity contributes to their worldview. Racialised identity is only likely to become pertinent if it is evoked in some way, and in contemporary British society overall it is more likely to be evoked in black than white people.

In the United Kingdom, 92.1% of the population are white (National Statistics, 2001). It therefore follows that white people could theoretically spend most of their lives having minimal or no contact with non-white people. White people are in the majority and therefore may feel they have no need or reason to explore or even contemplate their identity as a white person. Black people, by contrast, inhabit a different reality. Their racialised identity is likely to be significantly more salient throughout their lives as, even in areas that are densely populated by non-white people, black people will encounter white people in their daily endeavours as a matter of course and they will be aware, to a greater or lesser extent, of their minority status as a black person in a country that is predominantly white.

Racialised identity is not only more salient to black people owing to numbers however. They will have a greater sense of their 'blackness' owing to the racism that is 'embedded in western culture' (Mohamed, 2000, p. 64). Although racism towards black people is generally considered less overt than it was in the past, Mohamed (2000) suggests that racism is responsive to its historical context and adapts to accommodate the socioeconomic and political needs of the dominant society. There is considerable evidence available which suggests that this is the case. The Chair of the Commission for Racial Equality asserted that 'people are being put at an extreme disadvantage due to their ethnicity' and that 'is a triple whammy for ethnic minority people: they find it hard to get a job, they are likely to get paid less and they are still suffering from racial abuse in the work place' (Commission for Racial Equality, 2007).

It is important to acknowledge that racial inequality is not limited to faceless organisations, but also manifests itself within psychology and psychotherapy services. Access by black people to mainstream mental health services historically has been problematic and has been identified as still being of 'particular concern' (NHS, 2009). There is subsequently a disproportionate number of black people who only present to services at times of crisis (The Sainsbury Centre for Mental Health, 2006). Furthermore, it has been repeatedly suggested that even when minority ethnic groups present with psychological distress, talking therapies are generally not offered to them (Fernando, 2003; Littlewood, 2000; Tuckwell, 2003). According to Littlewood, this is owing to the widespread belief among therapists that 'therapy is not appropriate for minority groups because of their supposed lack of "verbal facility", or ability to understand and "work through" their problems' (2000, p. 6).

Who is Racist?

Despite all this well-documented disparity in treatment, I would suggest that one would be hard-pushed to find many people willing, openly or otherwise, to acknowledge that they are racist. Even British National Party leaders and members insist that they are not racist, but simply ensuring the rights of 'indigenous British people' (British National Party, 2007). Being described as a 'racist' has become the worst type of insult and something to be avoided, as it is synonymous with the archetypal skinhead, who is physically and verbally aggressive and not very bright. It would seem that again language is a problem as this image of a 'racist' inhibits any exploration of potential racist feelings that one might have.

Yet an honest exploration of the possibility that one may be harbouring racist feelings towards an individual or group is certainly what is needed if there is to be any hope of addressing racial inequality and apathy. As unpalatable as it may seem, surely it follows that, if racial discrimination is 'rife' in all sectors of society, many people are racist, whether they are aware of it (or admit it to themselves) or not. The vast majority of people will not be vindictive, disturbed or uneducated. Being racist and being a kind, caring and intelligent person are not mutually exclusive ways of being. Indeed, living in a society with visible (and invisible) racial imbalances undoubtedly encourages a culture of racial assumptions and prejudices, which are bolstered as we continue to overlook our own contribution to the process. It is therefore imperative to acknowledge, or at least consider, that everyone has the potential to or may even be a racist.

This is a society-wide issue, one that has the capacity to impact on everyday social as well as professional interactions. While one-to-one social dealings are significant, it is perhaps within organisations that the weight of latent racism is truly felt and where its power may be harmfully exerted. It would seem that counselling psychology's emphasis on the importance of engaging with our emotional and cognitive processes in relation to others or, indeed, in relation to our assumptions offers a valuable contribution to addressing this predicament.

The British Psychological Society states that psychologists should 'Respect individual, cultural and role differences, including ... race' and 'avoid all practices that are unfair and prejudiced' (2006, p. 10). This is not dissimilar to many other professions' codes of conduct and I am certainly not asserting that counselling psychologists, merely by virtue of their collective philosophy, are exempt from having racist feelings or from experiencing difficulties in addressing issues of 'race'. I recognise that the fear and discomfort surrounding 'race' is extensive and few of us are exempt. Despite the importance of ongoing personal development and self-awareness underpinning the ethos of the therapeutic professions, the potential for racism in practice appears to be rarely discussed or explored.

This suggests that there is a force at play more powerful than our collective professionalism. Perhaps our racial prejudices, cultivated via our parents, environment, upbringing, experiences and media, are too deep-rooted or beyond our consciousness. It is widely acknowledged within social psychology that we all hold prejudices and that these are an inevitable by-product of group membership (Brown, 1995), and by default racism is a prejudice that affects us all as we all belong to a so-called 'race'. Or perhaps we do not think it is relevant, or at least not relevant to us.

There will undoubtedly be cries of 'But I know I'm not racist!' on reading this. I would nevertheless suggest embarking (or continuing) on a journey of honest exploration . . . just in case.

Subtleties of Racism

One of the difficulties in accepting the possibility of a 'racist self' lies in the conflict between the intellectual and the emotional. If racism is the belief that members of minority groups are inferior in various ways (Baron & Byrne, 2000), it is hoped that most educated people would be able to state honestly that they do not hold this belief. We know, at an intellectual level, that specific qualities cannot be indiscriminately ascribed to a whole group of people. However, racism is rarely intellectual. It is intuitive and emotional. It concerns making (positive as well as negative) assumptions with or without awareness about a person's culture, background or religion, based on their 'race'. Macpherson emphasises this less clear-cut nature of racism in his definition: 'conduct or words or practices which disadvantage or advantage people because of their colour, culture, or ethnic origin' (1999, paragraph 6.4). This description perhaps renders it more difficult to detach oneself confidently, honestly and completely from the possibility of being racist, despite knowing rationally that racism is unacceptable. A white therapist may therefore, for example, experience tension between rational ideas about racial equality and uncomfortable emotional responses to a black client (Tuckwell, 2003). I would suggest, however, that the problem with this scenario has less to do with the fact that it has happened, but rather with the failure to acknowledge or process that it has happened, in order to reduce the likelihood of this negatively impacting on the therapeutic process, or worse, the client.

The tension between the intellectual and the emotional may contribute to the insubstantial consideration of racism among therapists as, intellectually, white therapists may acknowledge that they belong to a 'race' and that their 'whiteness' should be explored, but emotionally may feel it is not relevant or important to them. The prevalence of racial discrimination against black people and the attendant tension that the white therapist may feel if their own 'unmindful' contribution to its maintenance is acknowledged may well contribute to the reduced salience of a racialised identity for white people. 'Race' seems to have become synonymous with (the 'presence' of) colour in all of its meanings, and the problems thereof. Subsequently, as a concept, it is perceived to have little to do with white people, who perhaps embody an 'absence' of colour. An example can illustrate this:

> An acquaintance, whom I bumped into in a social situation asked me what I was writing this chapter about. I explained that I was writing about 'race' within the therapeutic relationship and how counselling psychology can contribute to this discussion. My acquaintance (also a therapist) nodded and said, 'Yes, as some of them can find it a problem, but there are some of them who don't'. I understood that she was referring to people of colour and so I said, 'I am actually exploring how we can all engage with "race", including white therapists and how we all can have prejudices that may affect the therapeutic relationship.' To which she replied, 'Yes, but even if I know I'm not prejudiced, I can't do anything about the client who is prejudiced towards me.'

There are many aspects of this brief exchange that are interesting. First, my colleague's casual reference to 'them' can be interpreted as either being rather disrespectful towards non-white people or (giving her the benefit of the doubt) indicative of a discomfort or confusion about how else to refer to 'them', for fear of 'getting it wrong'. That my colleague's immediate response was not even remotely to consider that she could be part of a discussion about 'race' and automatically to problematise 'them', or at least attribute any potential problems in the relationship to 'them', paves the way for at best a skewed perspective of a black client's presenting issues and at worst a deeply unsatisfactory experience of therapy for this hypothetical client. The stance adopted by my colleague would seem to be very defensive or at least uneasy. It was important for her to state that she is 'not prejudiced', which, in my experience, is a common response when discussions regarding 'race' ensue. As mentioned above, being regarded as 'racist' is considered abhorrent, so to state that one is not racist seems to be a regarded as a suitable and appropriate response to all matters of 'race'. It also acts as a (possibly desirable and therefore intentional) 'full-stop' to a discussion, as the person initiating the conversation about 'race' feels bad that they have made the other person (in this case my colleague) uncomfortable, or feels apologetic and embarrassed that they have possibly been perceived as suggesting that the person with whom they are talking is in some way racist. Thus the conversation quickly moves on to something altogether more comfortable, safe and uniting, such as (in our case) moving to another part of the room to meet other acquaintances.

Getting Stuck

I should point out that my colleague is white and, for the purposes of this chapter, I fall into the 'black' category as I am 'mixed-race' (black Jamaican mother, white English father). This dynamic undoubtedly exacerbated the uneasiness of this situation, which I felt too. By bringing up the subject of 'race', the usually unacknowledged racial differences between my colleague and me are difficult to ignore. Her use of 'them' whilst talking to me is particularly curious as I am of course one of 'them', but it would seem that part of our relationship relies on my being an 'exception', even an 'honorary white', that is, my colleague does not always 'see' me as black in the contexts within which we meet.

I acknowledge that I am also part of this relationship and that I am guilty of colluding in it. If I am honest, I admit I am often careful not to make reference to (my own or anyone else's) 'colour' in a professional context unless it is unavoidable (e.g. in relation to access or discrimination) and even then I will perhaps take a theoretical stance and play down its personal significance to me. I anticipate — maybe needlessly — that making reference to 'race' or indeed racism may result in some unease in the person or people with whom I am talking, and it is therefore usually my instinct to avoid such a situation, as I do not always want to feel responsible for making others uncomfortable. From an intellectual perspective, I recognise that I cannot be held responsible for others' discomfort about 'race', but nevertheless, on an emotional level, this is how it feels. Yet this is unsatisfactory as there are accompanying residual feelings of guilt and cowardice, as not only am I disallowing myself the right to express how I feel about a wider range of issues, I am also preventing my peers from responding and perhaps protecting myself (again perhaps unnecessarily) from their response.

The dynamic described is undoubtedly not unique to me and my colleague or uncommon within our profession and beyond. It merely illustrates that we are all part of a broader social system whose perceived codes we at times feel compelled to adhere to despite or in the absence of our better judgement. It is imperative, therefore, that ways are found to move beyond this falsely polite, potentially passive/aggressive and essentially 'stuck' position.

Working with 'Race'

It is pertinent that my colleague said that she would not be able to do 'anything about' a (black) client who came to her consulting room with racist feelings. The implication is that should this be the case, the therapeutic relationship would be doomed from the outset through no fault of hers. Yet, as an experienced and well-respected therapist, it is hard to imagine that she would proffer such a resigned attitude if faced with any other potential obstacle to engaging in and creating a sound working alliance with a client. Her detached position is possibly symptomatic of not knowing, or feeling unsure about, how to work with 'race'. She is unquestionably not alone.

There can be, of course, no rules about how to engage with 'race', not only in a therapeutic setting but also in other professional environments. Documents (e.g. the National Health Service's *Improving Access to Psychological Therapies: Black and Minority Ethnic (BME) Positive Practice Guide*, 2009) designed to help service providers in this endeavour have been compiled in order to address access issues and offer practical suggestions about how to 'engage with BME communities', such as linking with 'African-Caribbean community groups' in order to ask them what stops them from seeking help when they need it (p. 8) and providing a 'supportive environment' (p. 9). However, these suggestions lack depth and therapeutic meaning as at no point is the practitioner's self evoked. An environment will only feel supportive when genuine empathy and positive regard are felt by the therapist and communicated to the client and not simply because they are sitting opposite someone who is listening to what they are saying.

Counselling psychology strongly encourages attentiveness to the self in relation to others and the environment. I would suggest that for 'training' on 'race' to be effective within any professional sector it must, as a necessity, centre on personal exploration and development. It may need to be given specific consideration as it may not unfold naturally in conversation or even within reflective thought processes. In an attempt to offer some direction to those wanting to develop their engagement with 'race' and willing to contemplate their own relationship with this area, I have briefly suggested three broad areas for consideration as a starting point.

The Context

While I do not believe that it is necessary to research all there is to know about the plethora of cultures and subcultures that embody 'people of colour', it is important to have some awareness of the sociopolitical and racial climate of the country within which you are working, not least to prevent focusing solely on psychological processes (Tuckwell, 2003).

Some years ago, following a conversation where I offhandedly referred to there being few black people in society's top jobs, a colleague asked me, with absolute sincerity, 'Do you mean to say that racial discrimination exists in the UK?' His ignorance is extremely problematic and potentially dangerous as he could reach a psychological or pathological explanation for a black client referring to a fundamental and widely accepted reality. This level of unawareness also indicates (similar to the example outlined above) an absence of consideration of himself as a racialised being, where his own 'race' (he is a white middle-class man) is insignificant generally, but also specifically in relation to his hypothetical black client. Subsequently, any mention of 'race' or colour will inevitably be perceived as the client's issue or problem, which would be dismissive of the client's experience as well as unjust.

In order to engage properly with 'race', it is imperative that it is accepted that 'race' concerns all of us, impacts on social structures and consequently also on our own real or perceived social standing.

The Individual

The prevalence of information about the ways in which to work with black people and the emphasis on 'cultural competence' may result in practitioners rejecting their usually well-honed intuition and sensitive practice skills when working with black clients in favour of more 'textbook' practice, which can be fraught with pitfalls. An example illustrates this:

> When I was looking for a personal therapist at the beginning of my counselling psychology training, I scheduled initial appointments with three therapists in order to find a comfortable fit. About 10 minutes

into one of these sessions, the therapist (not meeting my eye) said, 'How would you feel working with me, with me being white and you being black?' This instantly felt distancing and hurtful. At the time I was aware that she had probably felt that she had had to ask me this question, yet I felt quite startled by the realisation that she saw me as a black client, rather than just a client. There was also the matter of answering her question. My instinct was to say, 'How am I supposed to answer that? It depends on what kind of white person you are and what kind of black person I am and neither of us knows any information about the other at this stage!' but instead I muttered, 'I'm sure it would be fine', and then counted down the minutes until I could leave.

In describing this incident, some of the many complexities of engaging with 'race' are highlighted. It would appear that the therapist felt under pressure to address the 'race' issue, possibly because that is what she had been advised was appropriate. However, in doing this she sacrificed 'being with' me, developing a sense of my needs as the client and responding to them accordingly. It also felt as though she had made a judgement about the salience of my colour to me, by assuming that the difference in our skin colour was a major consideration to me at that moment, when in fact I was far more concerned about her theoretical orientation and whether we 'clicked'. Salience of one's own 'race' will be different for every individual over time and according to context. There are no rules about when or whether to talk explicitly about 'race'.

Perhaps if I had continued working with this therapist, developed a sound therapeutic alliance and she never referred to my being a different colour from her, I might have experienced that as being problematic also. Essentially, as a client, I want to be able communicate to my therapist, 'Forget I'm black. And never forget I'm black', by which I mean that sometimes 'race' will be pertinent to the experience or feelings that I am describing, but at other times it could not be less relevant.

I appreciate that this sounds like a lot for the therapist to decipher and contain. However, the development of a good working relationship by showing empathy towards the client's experiences and being respectful of these should be a priority. I believe that it is essential that a therapist's intuition and awareness of the subtleties within the relationship are not disregarded in favour of the application of a 'textbook' response, and that by continually monitoring one's own processes, prejudices and needs, the likelihood of their needs being prioritised over the needs of the client will be significantly reduced.

The Self

Above all, the consideration of 'race' and its part in a therapeutic (or other) relationship necessitates taking a risk to engage with, at times, difficult material and accepting the possibility that we all may have racist feelings. No one, from whatever background, is exempt. As unpalatable as it is, if this reality remains hidden away or disguised by good intentions, harm may be unwittingly done to an individual or a group, but also a potentially rich composite part of one's sense of self will be left unexplored.

In order for there to be less trepidation about 'race', maybe we need to be brave enough to talk about it and include ourselves in that discussion. Although it would be unacceptable to be knowingly and openly racist in the name of honesty, it is important to allow ourselves to 'get things wrong' in the process of verbalising and acknowledging some of our fears, confusion and uncertainties. A starting point may be to explore the meaning of your racialised identity and how your perception of it shifts as different contexts are negotiated and new relationships are encountered, as well as how this changes again when faced with a group of people comprised of (perceived) similar or different racialised identities. A supportive and non-judgemental environment is essential to this endeavour.

I do not believe that there is a quick fix to addressing these issues. As I alluded to earlier, we are embedded within a social structure that pulls us towards normative functioning. A thorough discussion of 'race' necessitates contemplating numerous historical, cultural, social and emotional complexities – many more than this chapter has addressed. However, this should not deter us from engaging in such a conversation, as we all have the power to contribute to a gradual cultural shift by putting ourselves, rather than others, at the centre of this process. Maybe it is time to exercise this power.

References

Banton, M. (1988). *Racial theories*. Cambridge: Cambridge University Press.

Baron, R. & Byrne, D. (2000). *Social psychology* (9th edn.). Boston, MA: Allyn & Bacon.

British National Party (2007). *Is the BNP racist?* 23 December. www.bnp.org.uk/2007/12/is-the-bnp-racist. Accessed 5 August 2008.

British Psychological Society (2006). *Code of ethics and conduct*. Leicester: British Psychological Society.

Brown, R. (1995). *Prejudice: Its social psychology*. Oxford: Blackwell.

Commission for Racial Equality (2007). *Latest CRE statistics show racism is still rife in the workplace,* 17 May. 83.137.212.42/sitearchive/cre/default.aspx.locid-0hgnew0uv.Lang-EN.html. Accessed 18 July.

Compact Oxford English dictionary of current English (2005). Oxford. Oxford University Press:

Fernando, S. (2003). *Cultural diversity, mental health and psychiatry: The struggle against racism.* Hove: Brunner-Routledge.

Hall, S. (1992). The question of cultural identity. In S. Hall, D. Held, & T. McGrew (Eds.) *Modernity and its futures.* Cambridge: Polity Press.

Helms, J. E. (1995). An update on Helms's white and people of color racial identity models. In J. G. Ponterotto, J.M. Casas, L. A. Suzuki, & C.M. Alexander (Eds.) *Handbook of multicultural counseling.* Thousand Oaks, CA: Sage.

Laungani, P. (1999). Culture and identity: Implications for counselling. In S. Palmer & P. Laungani (Eds.) *Counselling in a multicultural society.* London: Sage.

Littlewood, R. (2000). Towards an intercultural therapy. In J. Kareem & R. Littlewood (Eds.) *Intercultural therapy.* Oxford: Blackwell.

Macpherson, W. (1999). *The Stephen Lawrence inquiry.* London: Home Department by Command of Her Majesty.

Mohamed, C. (2000). Race, culture and ethnicity. In C. Feltham & I. Horton (Eds.) *Handbook of counselling and psychotherapy.* London: Sage.

National Health Service (2009). *Improving access to psychological therapies: Black and minority ethnic (BME) positive practice guide.* London: Department of Health.

National Statistics (2001). *Ethnicity and identity.* www.statistics.gov.uk/cci/nugget.asp?id=455. Accessed 4 August 2008.

Sue, D. W. & Sue, D. (1999). *Counseling the culturally different* (3rd edn.). New York: Wiley & Sons.

The Sainsbury Centre for Mental Health (2006). *The costs of race inequality.* Policy paper 6. London: Sainsbury Centre for Mental Health.

Tuckwell, G. (2003). White therapists and racial awareness. *Counselling and Psychotherapy Journal, 14*(2): 12–16.

Winston, A. S., Butzer, B. & Ferris, M. D. (2004). Constructing difference: Heredity, intelligence and race in textbooks, 1930–1970. In A. Winston (Ed.) *Defining difference: Race and racism in the history of psychology.* Washington, DC: American Psychological Association.

Chapter 15

Counselling Psychology Contributions to Understanding Sexuality

Colin Hicks

Over recent decades Western society has started to recognise the rich variety of ways people can construct and experience their sexuality and integrate it with other aspects of their identity. Yet, much traditional psychotherapeutic practice has viewed sexuality as set, formed or otherwise expected to follow specific structures and processes. It has understood healthy sexuality as being monogamously heterosexual and has seen alternative experiences as pathological or at best suboptimal.

Having said that, the change in societal attitudes has to some extent been mirrored within the practice of psychotherapy, where we have seen rapid growth in the field of affirmative therapy with sexually minoritised clients (e.g. Ritter & Terndrup, 2002) and the development of professional guidelines on working with these clients (American Psychological Association Division 44/Committee on Lesbian, Gay, and Bisexual Concerns Joint Task Force on Guidelines for Psychotherapy with Lesbian, Gay and Bisexual Clients, 2000; Barker et al., forthcoming). However, the sex of one's partner is only one aspect of a person's sexuality. When explored further, sexuality is found to be a complex tapestry of identities, behaviours and attractions, all interwoven with other aspects of a person's identity to make up the totality of what they experience themselves to be.

This chapter explores counselling psychologists' contributions to non-pathological practice with a client's sexuality by focusing on three areas:

Therapy and Beyond: Counselling Psychology Contributions to Therapeutic and Social Issues
Edited by Martin Milton
© 2010 John Wiley & Sons, Ltd.

counselling psychologists' practice with clients engaged in non-traditional relationship structures; working with clients who engage in 'kink' or deviant sexual practices; and a consideration of double minority status (e.g. identifying as gay and being from an ethnic minority). The main themes are then drawn together and consideration given to the counselling psychologist's role in working with these clients and also, where appropriate, in tackling the sociocultural origins of these difficulties.

Contemporary Understanding of Sexuality

There is no single definition of what constitutes a person's sexuality, or whether sexual identity and sexual orientation refer to the same phenomenon, or whether these are essentialist or constructionist in nature. Understandings of sexuality are shaped by culture and change as the socio-historical context changes (see Ritter & Terndrup, 2002). Whilst we can see evidence of same-sex behaviours throughout history, it has only been relatively recently that the Western concept of sexual identities based on the biological sex of one's partners have become meaningful categories (Epting *et al.*, 1994; Herdt, 1997).

The concept of sexuality covers different dimensions, including attraction, behaviour, fantasy, identity, emotional, social and lifestyle preferences (Sell, 1997). Society generally holds a number of assumptions about one's sexuality: that the different aspects of one's sexuality will map onto each other, that these are relatively stable over time; and it is the biological sex of one's partner that is the primary marker in attraction. However, there is a significant minority for whom this understanding does not fit.

There is evidence that identity, orientation and behaviour are not always mutually congruent (Doll & Peterson, 1992) with both same-sex attraction and behaviour being more common than the adoption of a same-sex identity (Savin-Williams, 2001). There is also evidence that a person's sexuality is not inherently fixed across their life-course, that attractions, behaviours and identity are fluid and changeable (Diamond, 2000) and that biological sex is not always the variable that primarily determines attraction (Blumstein & Schwartz, 1990).

In summary, what is apparent is that sexuality is a complex phenomenon encompassing biological drives and social meanings. Counselling psychologists recognise and validate the full range of ways people can experience and understand their sexuality without pathologising those that do not conform to societal norms. Whilst it can often be easier to see diversity within the relationships of non-heterosexuals, counselling psychologists do not assume that heterosexually identified individuals automatically engender the norms of society either. The term 'non-heterosexual' is used to describe individuals of all sexual identities who do not subscribe to the cultural norm of heterosexuality. This includes people who may identify as heterosexual but whose attractions and experiences may be more nonconformist.

Working with Non-heterosexual Clients

Non-heterosexual clients may present in therapy with issues that are pertinent, or unrelated, to their sexuality. There is no one way of working with non-heterosexual clients just as there is no one way to work with clients in general. There is now an abundance of literature on working therapeutically with sexually minoritised clients and which has come to address the pathologising stance some of the mainstream psychotherapeutic literature historically has taken (e.g. Drescher, 2001).

Counselling psychologists have been at the forefront of movements working towards the recognition of non-pathologising ways of working with clients of all sexual identities. Our understanding of the pluralistic nature of society, as well as the consideration of humans as relational beings, means that we often find ourselves in challenging situations. These challenges extend not only to our engagement with the theoretical literature that informs practice, but also to relationships with colleagues who may hold different values about sexuality and in our private lives as well. Readers specifically interested in therapeutic practice with clients of different sexual identities are directed to Hicks and Milton (2010).

Different Relationship Structures

Most individuals grow up with heteronormative ideas as to how relationships should form and function – that coupling is best for happiness and long-term monogamous relationships are the ideal (Carl, 1990). By a monogamous coupling we refer to the notion of a relationship containing two participants (ideally one male and one female) who are sexually exclusive to each other. Yet monogamous relationships are not universal. Anthropological evidence suggests that many cultures exhibit different relationship structures (Herdt, 1997).

Society is often biased in its perception of non-monogamous relationships. Where they are present the dominant culture's language tends to invoke words such as infidelity and adultery to describe them, thereby presenting them as undesirable and destructive. However, what tends to be less visible or dismissed are open, non-monogamous relationships between consenting individuals for whom engagement in this 'deviant' practice is positive.

There is a great deal of diversity in the types of non-monogamous ('open') relationships or variations on monogamy that people of all sexual identities engage in (Rubin, 2001; Weinberg *et al.*, 1994). For example, the term polyamory is used to describe 'a relationship orientation that assumes that it is possible to love many people and to maintain multiple intimate and sexual relationships' (Sexualities, 2003, p. 126). Within polyamorous relationships the actual set-up can vary considerably (Barker, 2005). For example, set-ups may include having one or two primary partners, thereby living as a triad instead of a dyad, or involving secondary partners in the primary couple's sex life.

Individuals and couples engaged in, or considering, non-monogamous relationships may present to therapists for a variety of reasons. Whilst it should be acknowledged that in some cases non-monogamy may be symptomatic of problems within the primary relationship (Brown, 1995), it is a careless assumption that this is necessarily true. For some individuals therapy may prioritise helping to affirm the relationship as equal to a monogamous relationship, particularly in a society where prejudice is often directed at those that do not adhere to a perceived norm.

The difficulty for therapists is that the psychotherapeutic literature often reflects mainstream attitudes in its conceptualisation of non-monogamy. For example, some therapists argue that bringing a third person into the relationship is a way of avoiding intimacy (Shernoff, 1999). Therefore, an important role of the counselling psychologist is not to be a passive consumer of theory but to contribute actively to it in a way that offers more adequate understandings and an affirmative approach to clients of all sexual identities.

Azam (pseudonym) presented in therapy because of difficulties he had understanding his wife's desire to include another male partner in their relationship. Azam described how he had always assumed, unquestioningly, that people were meant to be in a couple and that his wife wanting another partner indicated a weakness in their relationship. He was worried that introducing someone else meant that she no longer loved him and that ultimately she would leave him. In therapy Azam was able first to explore the idea that there are many ways of creating relationships and that for some, loving more than one person is possible. He was then able to see it as a choice rather than indicative of a problem and consider it from a non-pathological perspective. With this insight he was able to discuss with his wife their relationship and ultimately decide together how they wanted their relationship to work.

As this case example illustrates, therapy can be used to help clients reconceptualise their understanding of a relationship. Inviting Azam to explore possible relationship alternatives in a non-judgemental, supportive environment allowed him to talk to his wife about their relationship and consider the differences they may have about it.

In summary, whilst monogamous heterosexuality remains the norm in our society, we must be aware of the diverse ways individuals organise their relationships as non-monogamous relationships may be constructed with different rules and codes of behaviour that are personally meaningful to the participants. As Shernoff suggests, for some gay men in open relationships, fidelity does not refer to sexual faithfulness but to the 'emotional primacy of the relationship between two men' (1999, p. 45).

'Kinky' Clients

We all encounter people whose sexual interests extend beyond the 'missionary position' into 'kink' practices incorporating BDSM (bondage and discipline, dominance and submission, sadism and masochism). Wiseman defined BDSM as: 'the use of psychological dominance and submission, and/or physical bondage, and/or pain, and/or related practices in safe, legal, consensual manner in order for the participants to experience erotic arousal and/or personal growth' (1996, p. 40).

We meet participants in BDSM practices not just as clients but also as friends, colleagues and family members and may ourselves recognise or repress interests in this area. BDSM or kink practices (for simplicity I assume these terms can be used interchangeably) occur in individuals of both sexes and individuals of different sexual orientations (Sandnabba *et al.*, 2002) and refer to engaging in certain sexual behaviours or to the adoption of a particular lifestyle (Williams, 2006). Lawrence and Love-Crowell (2008) suggest that the prevalence of BDSM practices in adults may be similar to that of same-sex sexual activity. Evidence of alternative sexual practices can also be seen throughout history, dating back to ancient Egypt (Bloch, 1935; Ellis, 1936) and can be seen in different cultures (Vatsyayana, 1964; Wedeck, 1962). However, it was not until the late nineteenth century that the diagnostic categories of sadism and masochism were constructed as sexual pathologies and psychological theories developed to explain their occurrence. Yet the categorisation as to what constitutes normal and deviant sexual practices is not clear-cut. Kinsey *et al.* (1953) noted that both scratching and biting are often found in pre-coital play in what would be regarded as conventional sex. Furthermore, research suggests that participants in BDSM practices are often psychosocially well adjusted (Alison *et al.*, 2001; Sandnabba *et al.*, 2002) and experience similar attachment patterns to the general population (Santilla *et al.*, 2000).

Whilst a client's engagement in kink practices *may* prompt their coming to therapy, Lawrence and Love-Crowell (2008) report that BDSM is more typically a background issue for clients. Where it did present as a problem they identified that shame and guilt were frequent issues. One explanation for this is that people with kink interests will have grown up in a society which invalidates and is prejudiced against people who engage in such practices. Participants will often have internalised views of BDSM as being 'weird', 'abnormal' or as symptomatic of a deeper underlying psychological problem (Nichols, 2006). The problem may be further compounded by the relative invisibility of positive role models and access to others who share similar interests.

Counselling psychologists recognise the importance of providing a safe environment in which issues of sexual practice can be disclosed and discussed in a non-judgemental way. For us to be able to do this we must first charge ourselves with the exploration and understanding of our own responses to such practices. Nichols argues that practitioners 'must discard most pathology-oriented paradigms of sexuality; adopt new models that allow for neutrality and, at times, celebratory attitudes towards diverse sexuality' (2006, p. 299).

Paul (pseudonym) was referred by his GP in light of his depression and anxiety. His GP felt it noteworthy to say that Paul presented with some mild abrasions on his wrists (presumably from handcuffs) which Paul had explained came from taking a submissive sexual role whilst attending a 'kink' group. In the team's discussion it became apparent that several colleagues felt that kink behaviours were a target for 'treatment' and hypothesised that they were symptoms of his depression. This perspective was very much informed by their theoretical model and the classification of masochism (which this was argued to be) in the DSM-IV. It was also apparent that some colleagues found his lifestyle uncomfortable to discuss and made pejorative comments about what 'type' of person Paul might be. As a counselling psychologist I was able to challenge some of these assumptions coming from a position of valuing the diverse ways people choose to organise their life and help orientate the team towards taking a more affirming approach in their work with Paul.

This case example illustrates the important role of the counselling psychologist beyond the consulting room in questioning and challenging a team's attitude to working with a client, particularly where the assumptions held by team members may serve to reinforce the pathologising view of society – something that may have caused the individual to seek help in the first place.

In working with kink clients it is important to bracket the assumption that their reason for coming to therapy is related to their sexual interests (Kleinplatz & Moser, 2004). Within medical discourse, the question as to whether or not kink practices represent a specific pathology and therefore warrant a psychiatric diagnosis and treatment is still being debated (Karasic & Drescher, 2005; Moser & Kleinplatz, 2006). However, counselling psychologists do not automatically align themselves with the medical discourse. We recognise that clients' distress may not necessarily be evidence *per se* that these practices are pathological and recognise that it is often the meaning our culture gives to 'deviance' that causes psychological distress rather than the 'deviance' itself.

Double Minority and Identity Confusion

Whilst there has been a growth of research into sexuality, ethnicity, religion and culture, a limitation of this expansion has been its often unidimensional format (Coyle & Rafalin, 2000; Greene, 1994a; Morales, 1990). Until more recently the 'double minority' status that some individuals face has remained unconsidered. The term 'double minority' has been coined to describe individuals who have to face discrimination based on membership in two minority groups (e.g. race and sexual orientation; Jones & Hill, 1996). 'Triple jeopardy' has been used to signify when gender comes into the equation as well (Bridges *et al.*, 2003; Greene, 1994b).

There are well-documented, negative mental health effects of living with racism (Williams & Williams-Morris, 2000), sexism (Swim *et al.*, 2002) and homophobia (Meyer, 2003). It is probable that membership in a double minority will present individuals with unique challenges and may increase their vulnerability to psychological distress. I shall endeavour to attend briefly to three different double minorities: non-heterosexuality and ethnicity; non-heterosexuality and religion; and non-heterosexuality and disability.

Non-heterosexual Sexuality and Ethnicity

Our culture and sexual orientation are often two important dimensions around which we develop our concept of self (Greene, 1997). For most heterosexual people these dimensions can be neatly interwoven. However, for many non-heterosexual individuals this may not be the case.

As we saw in Chapter 14, in the UK being a member of an ethnic minority group alone can pose difficulties in a society that values 'whiteness' and in which racism, ignorance and prejudice are still present. However, ethnic minority individuals are often part of a visible minority, an identity they share with their family. This provides individuals with strong familial ties and a culture that can afford them some protection against the dominant culture's prejudice and serves as an important resource as they develop their own ethnic/cultural identity.

Yet many ethnic minority groups have very traditional views of sexuality and view the adoption of different sexual identities as a challenge to gender roles (Bridges *et al.*, 2003), a threat to the continuation of the family line or as a rejection of one's role within society (Chan, 1992; Garnets & Kimmel, 1991). Ethnic minority non-heterosexual individuals are socialised within their culture long before they come to consider their sexuality and through this may have come to internalise their own culture's prejudices about non-heterosexuality. This poses a conflict, as to adopt a non-heterosexual identity may result not just in rejection by their family and community but also an inner turmoil as they wrestle with their own internalised homophobia. These individuals are therefore left with the challenge of trying to reconcile the apparent mutual exclusivity of these two aspects of self. As Greene (1994) notes, this is often experienced as a felt pressure to decide between these communities as to which they primarily fit. If they 'choose' to adopt a non-heterosexual identity, they risk losing their family and friends. However, if they do not, it may mean repressing their desires and attractions. Furthermore, racism and discrimination are problems within the lesbian, gay and bisexual (LGB) community itself which individuals may also have to face (Greene, 1997), potentially without the support and resources their family may afford them.

Counselling psychologists working with non-heterosexual ethnic minority individuals are acutely aware of the different values individuals may hold regarding the importance of family, community and cultural heritage. Counselling psychologists seek to understand the cultural significance of engaging in non-heterosexual sexual behaviours or even the viability of adopting a sexual identity recognising that cultural norms do not automatically apply to all members of the group.

When drawing on psychological models of therapy and development we need not just be vigilant in challenging the heterosexual bias of dominant models of therapy but also their implicit cultural and racial prejudices as well. Furthermore, if we draw on affirmative models of sexual minority identity development, we need to use these in a sensitive manner as traditional models of identity development and the 'coming-out' process have not always considered cultural issues (Bridges *et al.*, 2003; Parks *et al.*, 2004). In fact, while there has been a wealth of research conducted into same-sex sexuality, little exploration of the interaction between ethnicity and sexuality has been done (Greene, 1997). This has started to change and there is now a small body of literature that considers the ways in which sexual identity interacts with an individual's cultural identity (Chan, 1995; Coyle & Rafalin, 2000; Greene, 1994a).

Non-heterosexual Sexuality and Religion

Different religions have had a history of condemning same-sex sexualities, with Christianity, Judaism and Islam being particularly condemnatory, viewing anything other than heterosexuality as immoral and unnatural (Davidson, 2000; Halderman, 1996). These views are powerful forces within our society shaping people's attitudes and influencing social policy and the legal framework (Walton, 2006). For religious clients, questioning their sexuality can lead to a conflict between the conservative values of their religion and their emerging sexuality where the adoption of a non-heterosexual identity may lead to rejection by their religious community.

For individuals who begin to explore their religiosity having developed a non-heterosexual sexual identity, the homophobic teachings of mainstream religion may lead them to feel alienated and estranged from religion, reaffirming the belief that it is not possible to reconcile their religiosity with their sexuality. Halderman (2002) notes that anti-religious feelings often exist in LGB communities, causing individuals to find it harder to come out as spiritual or religious in that community than to come out as LGB in their spiritual or religious community. For some, this engenders a split, an identity crisis, where they must determine which aspect of self will dominate in a mindset which will not allow the integration of the two.

This does not necessarily have to be the case and individuals can be creative in the ways they integrate these two aspects of self (Schuck & Liddle, 2001). Walton (2006) conducted a qualitative study looking at how eight men who identified themselves as both gay and evangelical Christians integrated these different aspects of their identities. Walton found that participants adopted a variety of strategies as a means to integrate their identities, for example engaging in a more critical than literal understanding of biblical texts that concern sexuality. Importantly, it was not about fitting their gay identity into their Christian identity or vice versa, but rather about considering how they impact on each other in a dynamic, reciprocal way.

There are a number of challenges that therapists face when working with clients who are struggling to integrate their religious identity with their sexual identity. First, as many sexually minoritised individuals are not members of organised religious faiths and often are hostile to them, therapists can be misled into thinking that faith/spirituality/religion is unimportant to them (Ritter & Terndrup, 2002).

Secondly, therapy becomes more complex when we are called on to respect two opposing forms of diversity (Yarhouse & Burkett, 2002). In doing this, we need to be acutely aware of our own views of religion and sexuality and the relative value we place on each. For example, for a secular or atheist gay male therapist it may be easier to validate and affirm clients' non-heterosexuality than their religious views. To illustrate this tension consider how you might consider working therapeutically with Marie in the following case example and what issues it may bring up for you.

Marie (pseudonym) self-refers to your private practice describing issues of inner turmoil and angst which she is unable to resolve. Marie describes feeling she has always been attracted to women and had her first same-sex relationship when she was 17. After this ended she began questioning the exclusivity of adopting a lesbian identity and whether instead she might be bisexual. Marie describes herself as always having had spiritual views but it was only after her mother's death (when Marie was 30) that she started to consider her religiosity. Marie had a strong drawing to Catholicism but understood Catholicism to view her sexuality as a sin and as her religious identity was more important to her than her sexual identity at the time she came to therapy, she considers the possibility of stopping her attraction to women and entering into a relationship with a man.

Whilst we consider the difficulty a non-heterosexual person may have integrating their sexuality with their spiritual or religious beliefs we must also consider the role of society in this. What if one's religious beliefs are also discriminated against in society? We are not just talking about Christian gay men and lesbians; what about Jewish gay men, Muslim lesbians or bisexual Jehovah's Witnesses? Marginalisation, as with ethnicity, may occur based not just on one's sexuality but also on having non-mainstream or diverse religious beliefs (e.g. Dworkin, 1997).

Non-heterosexual Sexuality and Disability

There is a shameful absence of literature that considers the double minority of disabled and non-heterosexual individuals. What little literature there is has tended to focus on disabled individual's heterosexuality (e.g. Brown *et al.*, 2000). One might conclude from this that the disability is often seen as the individual's primary identity and his/her sexuality as a secondary aspect or one that is dismissed altogether (Thompson *et al.*, 2001). For disabled individuals questioning their sexuality this leaves them in the position of potentially not just having to assert their sexuality, but having to assert their non-heterosexual sexual identity as well.

Like other double minority individuals, young men with learning disabilities have reported ostracism from their own community when they revealed their sexual identity and may experience rejection from the gay community for being different (Davidson-Paine & Corbett, 1995; Thompson, 1994), one possible reason being the value placed on particular styles and ascetics within the gay community which men with intellectual disabilities are often unable to conform to (Bennett & Coyle, 2007).

To compound this problem, the dependence that disabled individuals may have on other people can act as a barrier to the exploration of their sexuality. Dependency may prevent them being able to access information about ways of constructing their sexuality other than as heterosexuals. Equally, making contact with other non-heterosexual individuals may be difficult for disabled non-heterosexuals because of the possible reliance they have on family members for support and travel (Greene, 2003). Therefore, decisions about 'coming out' need to be more considered where someone's very means of support may be in jeopardy. Scheer (1994) comments that disabled and sexually minoritised individuals have the experience of not automatically sharing their minority status with their family and that they learn about this through contact outside the confines of the family. If this contact is limited or controlled, then the opportunity to develop a healthy, integrated sexual identity may be compromised (Bennett & Coyle, 2007).

Counselling psychologists working with disabled clients questioning their sexuality recognise that the therapeutic space may be the only avenue open to them to consider their sexuality. However, working therapeutically with disabled and sexually minoritised clients can feel like working in the dark. There is no body of literature readily available to inform practice even if we take into account the fact that counselling psychologists draw on a range of related bodies of literature.

Reflections

Fundamental to this chapter has been the idea that we reside in a social context that gives meaning to experience and prioritises and privileges some over others. The psychological theories and the concepts of pathology we use to inform our practice are arguably no different. Diagnostic manuals are not immune to the prevailing social attitudes of the time and our concept of what constitutes mental ill-health changes over time.

Counselling psychology practice does not limit itself to the diagnostic and treatment model that seems to dominate much therapeutic discourse and health provision. Our knowledge base and codes of ethics mean that we are responsible for the way we construct meaning with clients. Counselling psychologists develop flexible views of sexual identity as it varies across individuals and social groups, recognising that it is not possible to separate ourselves from the society in which we live. We are not just therapists and observers of human behaviour, but our very being in society means that we help to shape, reinforce and challenge social stereotypes and assumptions. It is important that when we step out of our consulting room we do not forget the role we have as a member of society.

As counselling psychologists we embody the role of scientist-practitioner, we are not just avid consumers of research but are influential in its development. With our knowledge of qualitative and quantitative research and emphasis in our training on cultural diversity we are in prime position to contribute to the challenge of exploring these important issues and advancing the debates. Counselling psychology values and models of practice offer significant contributions to all those we work with. Consideration of context, culture and diversity, along with our psychological theories, are helpful to clients; among multidisciplinary teams our training means that we can attend to the diversity of the clients we see and not just to standard diagnostic categories; and when consulting on government proposals we offer a relational and phenomenological dimension that is crucial for those we see in the consulting room and those that make their way without availing themselves of the use of therapy.

References

Alison, L., Santilla, P., Sandnabba, N. K. & Nordling, N. (2001). Sadomasochistically oriented behaviour: Diversity in practice and meaning. *Archives of Sexual Behavior, 30*: 1–12.

American Psychological Association Division 44/Committee on Lesbian, Gay, Bisexual Concerns Joint Task Force on Guidelines for Psychotherapy withLesbian, Gay, Bisexual Clients (2000). Guidelines for psychotherapy with lesbian, gay, and bisexual clients. *American Psychologist, 55*: 1440–51.

Barker, M. (2005). This is my partner, and this is my . . . partner's partner: Constructing a polyamorous identity in a monogamous world. *Journal of Constructivist Psychology, 18*: 75–88.

Barker, M., Butler, C. *et al.* (forthcoming) *Guidelines for psychologists working therapeutically with sexual minority clients.* Leicester: British Psychological Society.

Bennett, C. & Coyle, A. (2007). A minority within a minority: Experiences of gay men with intellectual disabilities. In V. Clarke & E. Peel (Eds.) *Out in psychology: Lesbian, gay, bisexual, trans and queer perspectives.* Chichester: Wiley.

Bloch, I. (1935). *Strangest sex acts.* vol. 1. New York: Falstaff Press.

Blumstein, P.& Schwartz, P. (1990). Intimate relationships and the creation of sexuality. In D. P. McWhirter, S.A. Sanders& J. M. Reinisch (Eds.) *Homosexuality/heterosexuality: Concepts of sexual orientation.* New York: Oxford University Press.

Bridges, S. K., Selvidge, M. M. D. & Matthews, C. R. (2003). Lesbian women of color: Therapeutic issues and challenges. *Journal of Multicultural Counseling and Development, 31*: 113–130.

Brown, H., Croft-White, C., Wilson, C. & Stein, J. (2000). *Taking the initiative: Supporting the sexual rights of disabled people.* Brighton: Pavilion.

Brown, L. (1995). Therapy with same-sex couples: An introduction. In N. S. Jacobson & A.S. Gurman (Eds.) *Clinical handbook of couple therapy.* New York: Harrington Park Press.

Carl, D. (1990). *Counselling same-sex couples.* London: W.W. Norton.

Chan, C. S. (1992). Cultural considerations in counselling Asian American lesbians and gay men. In S. H. Dworkin & F.J. Gutierrez (Eds.) *Counseling gay men and lesbians: Journey to the end of the rainbow.* Alexandria, VA: American Association for Counseling and Development.

Chan, C. S. (1995). Issues of sexual identity in an ethnic minority: The case of Chinese American lesbians, gay men, and bisexual people. In A. R. D'Augelli &

C.J. Patterson (Eds.) *Lesbian, gay and bisexual identities over the lifespan: Psychological perspectives*. New York: Oxford University Press.

Coyle, A. & Rafalin, D. (2000). Jewish gay men's accounts of negotiating cultural, religious and sexual identity: A qualitative study. *Journal of Psychology and Human Sexuality, 13*: 21–48.

Davidson, M. G. (2000). Religion and spirituality. In R. M. Perez, K.A. DeBord & K. J. Bieschke (Eds.) *Handbook of counseling and psychotherapy with lesbian, gay and bisexual clients*. Washington, DC: American Psychological Association.

Davidson-Paine, C. & Corbett, J. (1995). A double coming out: Gay men with learning disabilities. *British Journal of Learning Disabilities, 23*: 147–151.

Diamond, L. M. (2000). Sexual identity, attractions and behaviour among young sexual-minority women over a 2-year period. *Developmental Psychology, 36*: 241–250.

Doll, L. S. & Peterson, L. R. (1992). Homosexually and non-homosexually identified men who have sex with men: A behavioural comparison. *Journal of Sex Research, 29*: 1–24.

Drescher, J. (2001). *Psychoanalytic therapy and the gay man*. London: Routledge.

Dworkin, S. H. (1997). Female, lesbian, and Jewish. In Greene, B. (Ed.) *Ethnic and cultural diversity among lesbians and gay men*. Thousand Oaks, CA: Sage.

Ellis, H. (1936). *Studies in psychology of sex*. vol. *1*. New York: Random House.

Epting, F. R., Raskin, J. D. & Burke, T. B. (1994). What is a homosexual? A critique of the heterosexual–homosexual dimension. *Humanistic Psychology, 22*: 353–370.

Garnets, L. D. & Kimmel, D. C. (1991). Lesbian and gay male dimensions in the psychological study of human diversity. In J. Goodchilds (Ed.) *Psychological perspectives on human diversity in America*. Washington, DC: American Psychological Association Press.

Greene, B. (1994a). Ethnic-minority lesbians and gay men: Mental health and treatment issues. *Journal of Consulting and Clinical Psychology, 62*: 243–251.

Greene, B. (1994b). Lesbian women of color: Triple jeopardy In L. Comas-Diaz & B Greene (Eds.) *Woman of color*. New York: Guilford Press.

Greene, B. (1997). Ethnic minority lesbians and gay men: Mental health and treatment issues. In B. Greene (Ed.) *Ethnic and cultural diversity among lesbians and gay men*. Thousand Oaks, CA: Sage.

Greene, B. (2003). Beyond heterosexism and across the cultural divide: Developing an inclusive lesbian, gay and bisexual psychology: A look to the future. In L. D. Garnets & D.C. Kimmel (Eds.) *Psychological perspectives on lesbian, gay and bisexual experiences*. New York: Columbia University Press.

Halderman, D. C. (1996). Spirituality and religion in the lives of lesbians and gay men. In R. Cabaj & T. Steins (Eds.) *Textbook of homosexuality and mental health*. Washington, DC: American Psychiatric Press.

Halderman, D. C. (2002). Gay rights, patient rights: The implications of sexual orientation conversion therapy. *Professional Psychology, Research and Practice, 33*(3): 260–264.

Herdt, G. (1997). *Same sex, different cultures*. Oxford: Westview Press.

Hicks, C. & Milton, M. (2010). Sexual identities: Meanings for counselling psychology practice. In R. Woolfe, W. Dryden, S. Strawbridge & B. Douglas (Eds.) *Handbook of counselling psychology*. (3rd edn.). London: Sage.

Jones, B. & Hill, M. (1996). African American lesbians, gay men, and bisexuals. In R. Cabaj & T. Stein (Eds.) *Textbook of homosexuality and mental health*. Washington, DC: American Psychiatric Press.

Karasic, D. & Drescher, J. (2005). Sexual and gender diagnoses of the diagnostic and statistical manual (DSM): A re-evaluation. *Journal of Psychology and Human Sexuality*, *17*(3/4): 1–5.

Kinsey, A. C., Pomeroy, W. B., Martin, C. E. & Gebhard, P. H. (1953). *Sexual behaviour in the human female*. London: W. B. Saunders.

Kleinplatz, P. & Moser, C. (2004). Towards clinical guidelines for working with BDSM clients. *Contemporary Sexuality*, *38*: 6, 1 and 4.

Lawrence, A. A. & Love-Crowell, J. (2008). Psychotherapists' experience with clients who engage in consensual sadomasochism: A qualitative study. *Journal of Sex and Marital Therapy*, *34*: 67–85.

Meyer, I. H. (2003). Prejudice, social stress, and mental health in lesbian, gay, and bisexual populations: Conceptual issues and research evidence. *Psychological Bulletin*, *129*(5): 674–697.

Morales, E. (1990). Ethnic minority families and minority gays and lesbians. In F. W. Bozett & M.B. Sussman (Eds.) *Homosexuality and family relations*. New York: Harrington Park Press.

Moser, C. & Kleinplatz, P. J. (2006). DSM-IV-TR and the paraphilias: An argument for removal. *Journal of Psychology and Human Sexuality*, *17*: 91–109.

Nichols, M. (2006). Psychotherapy issues with 'kinky' clients: Clinical problems, yours and theirs. *Journal of Homosexuality*, *50*: 281–300.

Parks, C. A., Hughes, T. L. & Matthews, A. K. (2004). Race/ethnicity and sexual orientation: Intersecting identities. *Cultural Diversity and Ethnic Minority Psychology*, *10*(3): 241–254.

Ritter, K. Y. & Terndrup, A. I. (2002). *Handbook of affirmative psychotherapy with lesbians and gay men*. New York: Guilford Press.

Rubin, R. H. (2001). Alternative lifestyles revisited: Or whatever happened to swingers, group marriages and communes? *Journal of Family Issues*, *22*: 711–726.

Sandnabba, N. K., Santilla, P., Alison, L. & Nordling, N. (2002). Demographics, sexual behaviour, family background and abuse experiences of practitioners of sadomasochistic sex: A review of recent research. *Sexual and Relationship Therapy*, *17*(1): 39–55.

Santilla, P., Sandnabba, N. K. & Nordling, N. (2000). Retrospective perceptions of family interaction in childhood as correlates of current sexual adaptation among sadomasochistic males. *Journal of Psychology and Human Sexuality*, *12*: 69–87.

Savin-Williams, R. C. (2001). *'Mom, dad, I'm gay': How families negotiate coming out*. London: American Psychological Association.

Scheer, J. (1994). Culture and disability: An anthropological viewpoint. In E. J. Trickett, R.J. Watts, & D. Birman (Eds.) *Human diversity: Perspectives on people in context*. San Francisco: Jossey-Bass.

Schuck, K. D. & Liddle, B. J. (2001). Religious conflicts experienced by lesbian, gay and bisexual individuals. *Journal of Gay and Lesbian Psychotherapy*, 5: 63–82.

Sell, R. L. (1997). Defining and measuring sexual orientation: A review. *Archives of Sexual Behaviour*, 26: 643–658.

Sexualities (2003). Special issue on polyamory: Call for contribution. *Sexualities* 6(1): 126.

Shernoff, M. (1999). Monogamy and gay men: When are open relationships a therapeutic option? *Family Therapy Networker*. www.gaypsychotherapy.com/ MONOGAMY_CASE.htm. Accessed 10 October 2004.

Swim, J. K., Hyers, L. L., Cohen, L. L. & Ferguson, M. J. (2002). Everyday sexism: Evidence for its incidence, nature and impact from three daily diary studies. *Journal of Social Issues*, 57(1): 31–53.

Thompson, D. (1994). Sexual experience and sexual identity for men with learning disabilities who have sex with men. *Changes: An International Journal of Psychology and Psychotherapy*, 12: 254–263.

Thompson, S. A., Bryson, B. & De Castell, S. (2001). Prospects for identity formation for lesbian, gay or bisexual persons with developmental disabilities. *International Journal of Disability Development and Education*, 48: 53–65.

Vatsyayana (1964). *Kama Sutra*. New York: Lancer Books. (First published *c*. AD 450.).

Walton, G. (2006). 'Fag church': Men who integrate gay and Christian identities. *Journal of Homosexuality*, 51(2): 1–17.

Wedeck, H. (1962). *Dictionary of aphrodisiacs*. London: Peter Owen.

Weinberg, M. S., Williams, C. J. & Pryor, D. W. (1994). *Dual attractions: Understanding bisexuality*. New York: Oxford University Press.

Williams, D. J. (2006). Different (painful!) strokes for different folks: A general overview of sexual sadomasochism (SM) and its diversity. *Sexual Addiction and Compulsivity*, 13: 333–346.

Williams, D. R. & Williams-Morris, R. (2000). Racism and mental health: The African American experience. *Ethnicity and Health*, 5(3): 243–269.

Wiseman, J. (1996). *SM101: A realistic introduction*. San Francisco: Greenery Press.

Yarhouse, M. A. & Burkett, L. A. (2002). An inclusive response to LGB and conservative religious persons: The case of same-sex attraction and behavior. *Professional Psychology: Research and Practice*, 33(3): 235–241.

Chapter 16

Counselling Psychology Contributions to Religion and Spirituality

Adrian Coyle

In recent years, a body of literature has developed which examines how various psychotherapeutic domains have approached religion and spirituality. It considers how therapists can respond constructively to religious and spiritual issues in ways that advance therapeutic processes. In some respects, this might seem to be a rather surprising development. After all, current Western concerns about the sociopolitical implications of 'fundamentalist Islam' have seen a range of questions debated regarding the social risk and value of religion in general and its role in the public domain in particular. These debates have become polarised, with definitive anti-religious positions attracting considerable attention, most notably in the form of Richard Dawkins' (2006) best-selling book, *The God Delusion*. This book, and others embodying a similar outlook, represent belief in God as irrational, constructing religion as having a corrupting influence on values and ethics and as having lain at the heart of a variety of social evils throughout history. Some psychologists have shared this representation of religion as an irrational defence and have tended to regard clients' religious beliefs and practices as part of pathology or as lying outside the remit of psychotherapy. These outlooks, allied with possibly low levels of religiosity and possible hostility towards it among therapists (see Bergin & Jensen, 1990), have meant that clients' religious and spiritual material has not been routinely engaged

Therapy and Beyond: Counselling Psychology Contributions to Therapeutic and Social Issues
Edited by Martin Milton
© 2010 John Wiley & Sons, Ltd.

with in useful or even respectful ways. Sometimes it has not been engaged with at all in the sense of either being actively ignored or else not being considered important to a contextualised understanding of the client's world (King-Spooner, 2001).

Does this really matter, given the charges that can be laid at the door of religion and given its associations, within social discourse, with conflict, control, judgmentalism and anti-intellectualism? Why should we be concerned with bringing religion and spirituality into the therapeutic context in a constructive way? After all, in Chapter 1, it was noted that counselling psychology eschews dogma and encourages continuous questioning of the assumptions we make in our daily lives. Given that religion has been represented as responsible for all sorts of conflict and oppression, why should therapists not aim to assist clients in deconstructing their religious (or spiritual) commitments, revealing the oppressive discourses that they tend to sustain and perhaps directing them to the latest tomes from Dawkins and his disciples as bibliotherapy?

The answer is that to do so would contradict some of the defining features of counselling psychology. The domain's commitments to holism and egalitarianism require the practitioner to engage actively and openly with clients' meaning-making systems and life worlds. This commitment is discernible in the way practitioners are advised to consider the effects that a client's gender, ethnicity, culture and sexuality, for example, may have on how they understand and respond to their presenting problems. Taking proper, respectful account of the role of clients' religion and spirituality in their meaning-making is part of this commitment to contextualised understandings. The potential adverse implications of the absence of this approach are noted by Bergin and Payne (1991, p. 201) who observed that, 'Ignorance of spiritual constructs and experience predispose a therapist to misjudge, misinterpret, misunderstand, mismanage, or neglect important segments of a client's life which may impact significantly on adjustment or growth'. To move automatically to a challenging approach towards a client's religion and spirituality would represent a failure of understanding and empathy on the part of the practitioner – a failure to embody the sort of 'being with' the client that defines counselling psychology. This would also limit the populations with which psychologists might work. For example, reflecting on the role of the transcendent as a standard and often central feature of African world views, Clarkson (2002, p. 17) warned, 'If there isn't place for God in our psychotherapeutic psychology, there isn't place for the African experience in it either'.

Of course, it may be valuable to facilitate a client's critical reflections upon their religion or spirituality during therapy but the practitioner's task is not to ride roughshod over what may be an integral part of a client's world view. The task is to enter into that world view in a profound way in order to understand the client's meaning-making from their perspective. This represents a principle of good practice found in most therapeutic approaches. When working with a client for whom religious or spiritual issues are central, it requires a willingness to attend to that dimension in meaningful ways.

There may also be an empirical rationale for engaging with clients' religious and spiritual material, founded upon the far-from-consensual research literature on religion, spirituality and health/well-being. On the one hand, religion and spirituality have been positively associated with a more secure sense of self, optimism about the future, existential certainty and more satisfying relationships, and negatively related to suicide, substance abuse, stress and depression (for example, see Joseph, 1998; Seybold & Hill, 2001). On the other hand, associations have been reported with guilt, shame, anxiety, obsessiveness, authoritarianism, rigidity and dependency (see Gartner, 1996; Mental Health Foundation, 2006). This diverse research picture tends to be attributed to methodological shortcomings (see Miller & Thoresen, 2003), which may reflect complex relationships between religion, spirituality and mental and physical well-being that pose challenges for research. Whatever the exact nature of the relationships between these dimensions, the literature suggests that any assessment of clients' well-being would benefit from the routine consideration of the potential relevance of the clients' religious and spiritual beliefs and commitments and the development of hypotheses about their possible implications for well-being.

This chapter considers how some psychotherapeutic schools have conceptualised and responded to religion and spirituality. Consideration is given to how counselling psychology's principles might shape practitioners' engagement with clients' religious and spiritual material. Consideration is also given to some ways in which counselling psychologists might usefully look beyond therapy in this endeavour and, more generally, to the possibility of counselling psychology contributing constructively to the domain of religion and spirituality. First it is necessary to review definitions of key terms in order to develop an understanding of the dimensions with which relevant literature has been concerned.

Defining Terms: 'Religion' and 'Spirituality'

Defining 'religion' and 'spirituality' is no simple task. Even 'religion', which might appear to be the more concrete term, has evaded attempts to define it in a way that achieves scholarly consensus. One useful response is that of Loewenthal (1995) who offered a definition through describing several beliefs shared by the major religious traditions, namely a belief in the existence of a non-material (spiritual) reality; a belief that the purpose of life is to increase harmony in the world by doing good and avoiding evil; and, in monotheistic religions, a belief that the source of existence (God) is also the source of moral directives. Furthermore, all religions involve and depend on social and institutional organisation for communicating these ideas.

Recent decades have seen a shift away from religion and towards spirituality in the Western cultural world, something that has been termed a spiritual or spirituality 'revolution' (Tacey, 2004; Woodhead & Heels, 2004). This has been linked to religion's negative associations but has also been regarded as a manifestation of a broader cultural 'subjective turn' away from external/'objective' roles, duties and obligations and towards subjective experiences as prime factors in shaping lives. This general claim relates primarily to Western Christianity and exceptions can readily be found. However, what it posits is that, as institutional, organised religion loses its appeal, there has been a development of less formal, more personal, fragmented spiritualities and spiritually-based practices, often drawing upon or connected to Eastern, mystical, esoteric and pagan traditions. This process has not seen the latter simply occupy the same space as the former. Rather, until recently, commentators observed this shift occurring within the context of a more general cultural indifference to religion and, to a lesser extent, spirituality in the West. Within recent years, this has given way to a cultural fear and panic about one particular religion: Islam. Nonetheless, the observation about a Western shift away from religion and towards spirituality remains pertinent.

It is possible to identify (at least) nine dimensions in the definitions of 'spirituality' offered by various writers (see Elkins *et al.*, 1988; Emmons, 1999; Gorsuch & Miller, 1999; Zinnbauer *et al.*, 1997). These relate to meaning and purpose in life; a sense of mission or calling in life; a transcendent dimension, involving external and internal factors such as deities, spirits, inner guides or higher selves; a belief in the sacredness of life; an emphasis on wholeness and connectedness; the notion of an essential and perhaps eternal soul; the idea of a spiritual journey or path; a belief that pain and suffering are an inescapable part of life and may be meaningful; and a belief in personal transformation. The breadth of meaning attached to spirituality may owe a lot to the concern with differentiating it from (institutional) religion, avoiding the latter's negative connotations whilst retaining some of its core 'holy', 'numinous', 'divine' and 'sacred' qualities, however those terms might be understood.

A related concept is 'the transpersonal', a dimension said to lie beyond our usual, individual, rational ways of relating to the world. Rowan (2003) differentiates the transpersonal from spirituality on the grounds that the transcendent is not the *sine qua non* of spirituality in the same way that it is for the transpersonal. This depends on a particular understanding of 'the transcendent'; furthermore it does not deny that spirituality and also religion can be transpersonal.

The challenge in defining spirituality may be due partly to the difficulty of capturing spirituality in language without lapsing into clumsiness and banality and failing to convey its potentially numinous, sublime qualities. Instead spirituality may be something that needs to be experienced rather than spoken, written or read about. O'Donohue (1997) suggested that attempts to define and discuss spirituality within the standard discourses of psychology and psychotherapy are doomed to failure: he contended that these discourses are modernist, 'scientific' and inappropriate for something that can only be expressed in poetic, symbolic, metaphorical and/or mystical language.

Psychotherapeutic Psychologies, Religion and Spirituality

As counselling psychologists locate their practice within various theoretical models, their responses to clients' religious and spiritual material may be shaped by the outlooks of these models as well as by the commitments that characterise counselling psychology. It is therefore worth considering how some psychotherapeutic psychologies have responded to religion and spirituality. Some have done so in complex and nuanced ways, so the accounts that follow should be regarded as merely indicating some core features of their responses.

Freud and Jung

At the start of this chapter, it was noted that there has been a history of silence, resistance and indeed pathologisation of religion and spirituality within some domains of psychotherapy. This has been especially so within psychoanalysis where religion and spirituality have been regarded as neurotic, regressive and comforting illusions that people use to defend themselves against the reality of human vulnerability, limitations and hopelessness (see Freud, 1989). More specifically, Freud regarded religious piety as being grounded in infantile helplessness and in a consequent wish for an all-powerful protective father and he saw ritualistic religious practice as a defence against various sexual and egoistic impulses.

The fundamental problem with Freud's theorising about religion is that he took particular aspects (such as the concept of a Father-God and ritualistic behaviours) and treated them as characterising all religion: to any religious person, Freud's version of religion would appear simplistic and impoverished. Yet it is important not to dismiss psychodynamic theory as having nothing to say about religion and spirituality outside a framework of pathology. As Wulff observed, 'The outcome of applying psychoanalytic theory to religious phenomena is dependent above all on the interpreter's fundamental attitude toward religion' (1997, p. 276). Hence, if an interpreter begins from the assumption that religion may point to some sort of transcendent reality, they may be able to use psychoanalytic theory to gain useful insight into religious beliefs and behaviours. There are examples of scholars and practitioners who have applied psychodynamic ideas to religion and spirituality in constructive and insightful ways (see Rizzuto, 1979), with some holding out hope of meaningful integration between these domains (Strawn, 2007).

In contrast to Freud, the work of Jung is often represented as according a central role to religion and spirituality. Jung was a leading figure within the emerging psychoanalytic movement but, following disagreements with Freud over the nature of the unconscious, the libido and religion, he developed what became known as analytical psychology, which can be represented as an integration of ancient religious and modern psychological wisdom. Others subsequently took Jung's insight that spirituality and religion could form an integral and valuable part of psychotherapeutic practice and made use of it in different ways. For example, the mid-1960s saw the development of psychosynthesis, an approach to psychotherapy that sought explicitly to foreground the transpersonal (Assagioli, 1965); the broader transpersonal perspective emerged in the late 1960s (Rowan, 2003). For various political reasons, these approaches have not generally been taken up as part of public sector psychotherapeutic service provision. However, a version of the most commonly-encountered theoretical model in the public sector that has been described as embodying an openness to the spiritual has become popular in recent years: mindfulness-based cognitive therapy (Segal *et al.*, 2002).

Mindfulness-based Cognitive Therapy (MBCT)

This was developed with the aim of reducing relapse among clients who are vulnerable to depression. As well as exercises from cognitive therapy, MBCT utilises simple breathing, meditation and yoga. This approach has been criticised on the grounds that mindfulness and cognitive (behavioural) therapy are based on quite different approaches, with the former promoting non-attachment to and letting go of cognitions and the latter being concerned with identifying and evaluating them (Solly, 2005). More generally, on issues such as human freedom and human limitations, therapeutic and spiritual viewpoints may diverge significantly and so therapists may adhere to their professional discourse rather than trying to reconcile understandings that may seem irreconcilable.

Moreover, one might query the validity of representing MBCT as incorporating a spiritual dimension. Mindfulness meditation involves cultivating awareness, insight, wisdom and compassion (Kabat-Zinn, 1994). This could be said to overlap with some aspects of spirituality as noted earlier, although it does not explicitly involve a concern with the transcendent. More importantly, its employment within MBCT tends to be as a technique oriented towards therapeutic outcomes rather than as a spiritual practice or as a means of orienting to clients' spiritual concerns. MBCT could thus be represented as psychotherapeutic colonisation and over-writing of a spiritual practice, stripping it of its spiritual context and orientation. This is far from inevitable: counselling psychologists may employ mindfulness techniques within a context of respectful openness to and curiosity about clients' spirituality without locating their practice within the spiritual framework of mindfulness meditation.

Working with Religious and Spiritual Issues in Counselling Psychology

We now consider how counselling psychology's commitments might usefully shape practitioners' engagement with clients' religious and spiritual material. The problem is, however, that, in common with other mental health professionals (see Crossley & Salter, 2005), relatively few counselling psychologists have been equipped by their training to address religion and spirituality constructively in anything more than a tokenistic manner and so may feel that they lack clear guidance for this. Providing clear guidance is not easy due to the diverse meanings attributed to religion and spirituality, the diverse roles these dimensions may play in clients' lives and the theoretical diversity that characterises counselling psychology. However, some recurrent themes and issues can be discerned in the growing literature on religion, spirituality and psychotherapy. Some of these will be examined in this section. For a more detailed consideration of other issues, readers are referred to specialist texts such as those of King-Spooner and Newnes (2001) and Pargament (2007).

Some of the principles involved in working with religious and spiritual material can be understood as reflecting general good practice in counselling psychology. For example, some writers have considered how best to create a therapeutic space in which practitioners and clients can feel comfortable in raising and exploring religious and spiritual issues and in being open to a spiritual quality of human relatedness and possibly to the transcendent (Clarkson, 2002; King-Spooner, 2001; Purton, 1998). These therapeutic relationships have been described in terms that strongly echo the qualities of any good therapeutic relationship. This should not be seen as merely stating the obvious: practitioners who lack training in engaging with spiritual and religious issues may feel deskilled in this domain (especially if they position themselves as 'outsiders' to religion and spirituality). Hence it is worth offering reminders that the building blocks for effective work here are found in the fundamentals of good counselling psychology practice: working with clients' religious and spiritual material does not require an entirely new set of competencies. This maxim informs much of what follows.

Assessment of Clients' Religious and Spiritual Beliefs and Experiences

Central to the provision of good quality therapeutic input is the undertaking, where possible, of a thorough, contextualised assessment of a client's functioning and presenting problems. Such assessment is usually seen as preceding any intervention, although its conclusions are subject to revision in light of material that emerges during interventions. Exploring a client's religious and spiritual beliefs and/or experiences at the pre-intervention assessment phase can usefully convey to the client that it is permissible to discuss these aspects of their life world in therapy (although it might equally be interpreted by some clients as suggesting that their religion and spirituality are being somehow connected to their presenting problem).

Pargament (2007) recommends using a few basic questions at the assessment stage to address the salience of spirituality and religious affiliation for the client (for example, 'Do you see yourself as a religious or spiritual person? If so, in what way?') and the salience of spirituality for the problem and potentially for any resolution (for example, 'Has your problem affected you religiously or spiritually? If so, in what way?'). However, one of the challenges in assessing client spirituality or religion pre-intervention is that clients may be unwilling to disclose and discuss such potentially intimate material at an early stage, especially if they fear that such disclosure might be evaluated negatively; there is evidence that clients with strong religious beliefs may be wary of seeking therapy in non-religious settings due to such fears (see Mayers *et al.*, 2007). Even clients who are willing to discuss their religious and spiritual beliefs may have difficulty in doing so in clear and articulate ways due to a general difficulty in adequately capturing these dimensions in language, as noted earlier. Thus practitioners might draw premature conclusions about a client's religious and spiritual outlook on the basis of an impoverished picture. Furthermore, some clients may not make a connection between their presenting problems and spirituality until some way into the therapeutic process.

For these reasons, an assessment of a client's religious and spiritual beliefs and experiences may need to unfold progressively within the context of a secure therapeutic relationship. This unfolding assessment may cover a client's religious or spiritual background, family beliefs, important spiritual events, current religious and spiritual beliefs and practices, involvement in religious and spiritual communities, how they make sense of the issues that have brought them to seek therapeutic services, images of and perceived relationship to higher powers, and ideas about the meaning of their life. Some of these areas will be relevant to all clients and others will be more salient for clients with expressed religious or spiritual commitments (Gorsuch & Miller, 1999). This information may often be most appropriately obtained through a mixture of open-ended and closed questions, although questionnaires designed to assess spirituality might also provide useful data (see Pargament, 2007, pp. 234–236). Sometimes it may be valuable to elicit a client's 'spiritual story', that is, their 'search for the sacred', especially if their past or present religious or spiritual path is deemed relevant for their presenting problems or as a source of potential resources for resolving difficulties. Pargament (2007) suggests a loose four-part framework for this, which involves developing open-ended questions on the client's spiritual/religious history, 'sacred destinations' (where or what the client sees their search for the sacred as orienting towards), 'sacred pathways' (spiritual practices and resources) and 'spiritual efficacy' (perceived implications of their spirituality in their lives).

Given the potential difficulties that both clients and practitioners may experience in conveying religious and spiritual concepts clearly in words, it may be worth considering whether non-linguistic media might be fruitfully used in assessing and exploring some religious and spiritual issues. For example, a counselling psychologist might invite a client to try to convey some particularly elusive materials through drawing or painting, perhaps following this with an invitation to discuss the foci of the artwork. Although this could create anxiety for some clients, for others it could offer a means of giving preliminary form to material that is otherwise difficult to communicate. A participant in Suarez's (2005) study of client experiences of spiritually integrated psychotherapy reflected on how such an approach had been used in her therapy:

> We did a lot of art work and clay work and this kind of thing and one of the things . . . was actually a drawing of what my soul looked like . . . I had never been asked [to do] that before and had no idea but I drew something the way you do with these things and it completely mirrored what was . . . happening for me on the inside.

During the process of developing a sense of a client's religious and/or spiritual outlook, the practitioner may find that their background knowledge is limited and, in the case of less mainstream religious and spiritual beliefs, it may be difficult to obtain useful information to help them understand a client's position. The client may thus become the prime informant about their religious or spiritual tradition. Of course, this simply represents another instance of general good practice: no matter how much background reading a practitioner may do about a client's context, it is the client's understanding of, reactions to and experiences within that context that are most important. Even when the psychologist has substantial background knowledge about a client's religious or spiritual tradition, it is still necessary to explore the client's interpretations of that tradition.

Disclosure of Practitioners' Religious and Spiritual Outlooks

Questions about the advisability of the practitioner disclosing to the client information about their own religious or spiritual outlook do not lend themselves to a generic response (although some theoretical models will adopt a clear view on this in principle). Where a model permits it, disclosure depends upon the needs of the client and on what might be gained in the therapeutic process (Farber, 2006). Some clients with strong religious beliefs in a study by Mayer *et al.* (2007) reported that having their therapist disclose their religious background facilitated the discussion of religious issues and contributed to a trusting relationship. Yet, therapists have reported unease at such self-disclosure, fearing that they could risk imposing their own spiritual beliefs on clients (Baker & Wang, 2004).

The question of the therapist's disclosure of their *professional* perspective on religion and spirituality is much less contentious. If it appears at the outset that religious or spiritual issues might be a salient factor in a client's presenting problems (as a contributory factor or as a potential resource for coping), the practitioner may reveal their professional perspective so that the client can reach an informed decision about how safe it might be to proceed with this practitioner. In a counselling psychology context, this is seldom an either/or, 'take it or leave it' conversation but an exploration and negotiation of the possibility of common ground for future work. If salient religious or spiritual issues emerge in the midst of the therapy rather than at the outset, such exploration may be more risky for the client as they will have already invested in the therapeutic process. Alternatively, it could possibly be easier as the counselling psychologist and client may be able to build upon an established process of open dialogue as part of their working relationship.

Responding to Problematic Religious and Spiritual Material

Thus far, the emphasis has been on an open and respectful engagement with clients' religious and spiritual material. Yet, it is important to remember that some clients' difficulties may be related to their religion or spirituality. For example, these difficulties may be associated with spiritual development. The accounts offered by noted spiritual writers of their spiritual trajectories are often characterised by moments of spiritual awakening and insight, preceded by periods of desolation, emptiness and despair (see Coe's, 2000, reflections on the 'dark night of the soul' experienced by St John of the Cross). Equally, client difficulties may arise from spiritual or religious material that is unequivocally problematic. The question then arises of how to challenge such material. This may be seen as an ethical question involving a clash between two principles of ethical practice, namely autonomy (in this case involving the client's right to choose and hold their own spiritual beliefs) and beneficence (involving the practitioner's responsibility to bring about the greatest psychological 'good' for the client).

In Crossley and Salter's (2005) study, clinical psychologists reported responding to such situations in various ways. One unsatisfactory response was to withdraw from an examination of this client material. An alternative response was to refer the client to a relevant religious or spiritual leader. Depending upon the response the client receives however, this could lead to increased distress. It might be more appropriate for the practitioner to liaise with the religious/spiritual official in order to ascertain their perspective before referring the client and to ensure that the practitioner and the clergy member are engaged in a collaborative endeavour, each knowing their role and how that contributes to the care of the client. This requires the development of trusting relationships between practitioners and clergy. Indeed, a lack of trust has been identified as undermining the possibility of fruitful collaboration (McMinn *et al.*, 1998).

A more complex response reported in Crossley and Salter's (2005) study was to explore the scope for clients to reinterpret problematic spiritual or religious material in ways that were consistent with their beliefs. One participant spoke of how a Muslim client had estimated the likelihood of a traumatic event recurring as unknowable because the matter was entirely in the hands of Allah, whose actions could not be predicted. By exploring conceptualisations of divine action, the client developed an understanding of Allah interacting consistently with the world, which permitted him to see the likelihood of recurrence as very low, which reduced his distress. This response may require the counselling psychologist to have considerable knowledge of the client's religious or spiritual tradition in order for lines of exploration to be seen as credible and useful on an ongoing basis outside therapy. Yet this is not necessarily so: if a trusting therapeutic relationship has been established, the client may feel empowered to take the lead in and take responsibility for this interpretative exploration themselves under the facilitation of the counselling psychologist.

Turning to what might be considered more obviously problematic material, the nature and location of the border between some accounts of religious and spiritual experience and psychotic experiences are open to debate, although some writers have tried to offer clarification (see Clarke, 2001). The need to explore the meaningfulness of what may seem to be unusual religious or spiritual beliefs and experiences is especially pertinent in light of the turn towards diverse forms of spirituality noted earlier and the accessibility of diverse spiritual ideas and resources through the internet. Thus clients may report beliefs and experiences that lie outside many orthodox religious frameworks but these should not automatically be considered as implying psychopathology without exploring their role within the client's personal and/or cultural meaning-making system.

From within to beyond the Therapy: Counselling Psychology and Religious/Spiritual Development

So far, attention has been focused largely within the consulting room. This risks positioning counselling psychology as needing to respond to and perhaps integrate material from religion and spirituality in a unidirectional way. Yet this can be a mutual relationship: counselling psychology can make important contributions to religion and spirituality.

Some of these contributions arise from work conducted with individual clients within the consulting room that extends beyond this context, whereas other contributions are not tied to work with specific clients (such as the use of psychotherapeutic theories and concepts to provide new insights into sacred texts: see Leslie's (2007) interpretation of Jesus as logotherapist in the Biblical story of his interaction with 'the Gerasene demoniac'). The most obvious example of the former relates to individuals being facilitated to realise more fully their religious and/or spiritual potential. Models of religious and/or spiritual development tend to include phases of profound reflection upon one's past in general terms or upon particular life traumas, with these reflections potentially leading to new insights and facilitating development. Fowler's (1981) well-known seven-stage model of faith development includes a penultimate stage of 'paradoxical-consolidative' faith. The person in this stage is said to engage in profound reflection upon their past, developing a capacity for a multi-perspectival stance on situations and an understanding of the complexity of reality, whilst retaining a wish to prioritise the needs of the self, family and affiliative groups. This is held to foster a capacity to live with contradictions in their own self-system, together with an openness to amending favoured outlooks (including religious and spiritual outlooks).

The processes and outcomes associated with this stage overlap with some general aims that counselling psychologists may have for a range of clients, especially if their work is located within or informed by existential, Jungian or (to some degree) person-centred approaches. An openness to change, a capacity to tolerate contradictions within the self and an ability to engage constructively with the perspectives of others without consistently sacrificing the perspectives and needs of the self are all qualities that represent components of psychological and social well-being within various theoretical models. Hence, regardless of whether or not sessions are focused upon religion or spirituality, the pursuit of such therapeutic aims may foster spiritual development, especially where this is already a salient life domain. Similarly, therapeutic work with clients who have experienced traumatic events may facilitate religious or spiritual development. Bereavement is one type of trauma that may be particularly associated with religious or spiritual questioning. For example, Batten and Oltjenbruns (1999) have reviewed how the death of a sibling may spark a quest for new meaning among adolescents and may act as a catalyst for spiritual development, resulting in new perspectives on self, on life and death and on the notion of a 'higher power'.

Religious or spiritual development is more usually a specific and explicit aim within spiritual direction and pastoral counselling. These domains and counselling psychology differ in their aims and in their expectations of practitioners and 'clients' (see Tisdale *et al.*, 2003). Counselling psychologists might usefully form part of supervisory teams for pastoral counsellors and spiritual directors to consider the parameters of those domains (in general terms and in relation to the profile of expertise of pastoral counsellors and spiritual directors working with specific 'clients') and might also provide referral possibilities for clients with complex needs that may lie beyond the expertise of pastoral counsellors or spiritual directors. These professional relationships might usefully involve two-way consultations, with pastoral counsellors and spiritual directors offering advice to counselling psychologists on understanding and responding to clients' religious and spiritual material and also providing referral options.

Conclusion

This chapter has provided a rationale for counselling psychologists to include religious and spiritual issues as a routine aspect of an ongoing client assessment process. Where these issues are salient concerns, counselling psychologists are well placed to engage with them respectfully and effectively through the lens of their profession's commitment to a therapeutic relationship characterised by contextualised understanding and mutuality, whilst retaining the possibility of facilitating a reworking of religious and spiritual beliefs and commitments that contribute to client distress. Of course, this assumes that counselling psychologists are allowed the scope for implementing their profession's values within the settings in which they work.

Inevitably when examining an emerging practice concern, commentators call for increased attention to be paid to the issue in the training of practitioners – and the area of spirituality, religion and counselling psychology is no different. The materials from which training could be crafted are readily available in the psychotherapeutic literature on religion and spirituality. Subject-specific expertise among training teams in counselling psychology is increasingly available, although it remains important to locate training on this issue within basic principles of good counselling psychology practice. There is no reason why a consideration of how practitioners might respond respectfully and effectively to clients' religious and spiritual material should not take its place alongside considerations of counselling psychology responses to other aspects of clients' life worlds, such as sexuality, gender, culture and ethnicity, in an integrated way. Counselling psychology's commitments render it ideally placed to provide a model of open, respectful, contextualised engagement with clients' religious and spiritual issues in ways that enrich the therapeutic process and foster positive therapeutic outcomes. The challenge now is to ensure that this potential is progressively realised for the benefit of clients.

References

Assagioli, R. (1965). *Psychosynthesis: A manual of principles and techniques.* New York: Hobbs, Dorman & Company.

Baker, M. & Wang, M. (2004). Examining connections between values and practice in religiously committed UK clinical psychologists. *Journal of Psychology and Theology, 32*: 126–136.

Batten, M. & Oltjenbruns, K. A. (1999). Adolescent sibling bereavement as a catalyst for spiritual development: A model for understanding. *Death Studies, 23*: 529–546.

Bergin, A. E. & Jensen, J. P. (1990). Religiosity of psychotherapists: A national survey. *Psychotherapy, 27*: 3–7.

Bergin, A. E. & Payne, I. R. (1991). Proposed agenda for a spiritual strategy in personality and psychotherapy. *Journal of Psychology and Christianity, 10*: 197–210.

Clarke, I. (2001). Psychosis and spirituality: The discontinuity model. In I. Clarke (Ed.) *Psychosis and spirituality: Exploring the new frontier.* London: Whurr.

Clarkson, P. (2002). *The transpersonal relationship in psychotherapy.* London: Whurr.

Coe, J. H. (2000). Musing on the dark night of the soul: Insights from St John of the Cross on developmental spirituality. *Journal of Psychology and Theology, 28*: 293–307.

Crossley, J. P. & Salter, D. P. (2005). A question of finding harmony: A grounded theory study of clinical psychologists' experience of addressing spiritual beliefs in therapy. *Psychology and Psychotherapy: Theory, Research and Practice, 78*: 295–313.

Dawkins, R. (2006). *The God delusion.* London: Bantam Press.

Elkins, D. N., Hedstorm, L. J. *et al.* (1988). Towards a humanistic-phenomenological spirituality. *Journal of Humanistic Psychology, 28*(4): 5–18.

Emmons, R. A. (1999). *The psychology of ultimate concerns: Motivation and spirituality in personality.* New York: Guilford Press.

Farber, B. A. (2006). *Self-disclosure in psychotherapy.* New York: Guilford Press.

Fowler, J. (1981). *Stages of faith: The psychology of human development and the quest for meaning.* San Francisco, CA: Harper & Row.

Freud, S. (1989). *The future of an illusion.* New York: W. W. Norton. (First published 1927.)

Gartner, J. D. (1996). Religious commitment, mental health, and prosocial behavior: A review of the empirical literature. In E. P. Shafranske (Ed.) *Religion and the clinical practice of psychology.* Washington, DC: American Psychological Association.

Gorsuch, R. L. & Miller, W. R. (1999). Assessing spirituality. In W. R. Miller (Ed.) *Integrating spirituality into treatment: Resources for practitioners.* Washington, DC: American Psychological Association.

Joseph, M. (1998). The effect of strong religious beliefs on coping with stress. *Stress Medicine, 14*: 219–224.

Kabat-Zinn, J. (1994). *Wherever you go, there you are: Mindfulness meditation in everyday life.* New York: Hyperion.

King-Spooner, S. (2001). The place of spirituality in psychotherapy. In S. King-Spooner & C. Newnes (Eds.) *Spirituality and psychotherapy*. Ross-on-Wye: PCCS Books.

King-Spooner, S. & Newnes, C.(Eds.) (2001). *Spirituality and psychotherapy*. Ross-on-Wye: PCCS Books.

Leslie, R. (2007). The Gerasene demoniac. In W. G. Rollins & D. A. Kille (Eds.) *Psychological insight into the Bible: Texts and readings*. Grand Rapids, MI: Eerdmans.

Loewenthal, K. M. (1995). *Religion and mental health*. London: Chapman & Hall.

Mayers, C., Leavey, G., Vallianatou, C. & Barker, C. (2007). How clients with religious or spiritual beliefs experience psychological help-seeking and therapy: A qualitative study. *Clinical Psychology and Psychotherapy, 14*: 317–327.

McMinn, M. R., Chaddock, T. P. *et al.* (1998). Psychologists collaborating with clergy. *Professional Psychology: Research and Practice, 29*: 564–570.

Mental Health Foundation (2006). *The impact of spirituality on mental health: A review of the literature*. London: The Mental Health Foundation.

Miller, W. R. & Thoresen, C. E.(Eds.) (2003). Spirituality, religion, and health: An emerging research field. A special section of the *American Psychologist, 58*: 24–35.

O'Donohue, J. (1997). *Anam cara: Spiritual wisdom from the Celtic world*. London: Bantam Press.

Pargament, K. I. (2007). *Spiritually integrated psychotherapy: Understanding and addressing the sacred*. New York: Guilford Press.

Purton, C. (1998). Unconditional positive regard and its spiritual implications. In B. Thorne & E. Lambers (Eds.) *Person-centred therapy: A European perspective*. London: Sage.

Rizzuto, A-M. (1979). *The birth of the living God: A psychoanalytic study*. Chicago, IL: University of Chicago Press.

Rowan, J. (2003). Counselling psychology practice: A transpersonal perspective. In R. Woolfe, W. Dryden & S. Strawbridge (Eds.) *Handbook of counselling psychology* (2nd edn.). London: Sage.

Segal, Z. V., Williams, J. M. G. & Teasdale, J. D. (2002). *Mindfulness-based cognitive therapy for depression: A new approach to preventing relapse*. New York: Guilford Press.

Seybold, K. S. & Hill, P. C. (2001). The role of religion and spirituality in mental and physical health. *Current Directions in Psychological Science, 10*: 21–24.

Solly, A. (2005). Mindfulness and cognitive therapy. *Clinical Psychology, 45*: 10–11.

Strawn, B. D. (2007). Slouching toward integration: Psychoanalysis and religion in dialogue. *Journal of Psychology and Theology, 35*: 3–13.

Suarez, V. (2005). A portfolio of academic, therapeutic practice and research work including an investigation of psychotherapists' and clients' accounts of the integration of spirituality into psychotherapeutic practice. Unpublished practitioner doctorate (Psychotherapeutic and Counselling Psychology) portfolio, University of Surrey.

Tacey, D. (2004). *The spirituality revolution: The emergence of contemporary spirituality*. Hove: Brunner-Routledge.

Tisdale, T. C., Doehring, C. E. & Lorraine-Poirier, V. (2003). Three voices, one song: A psychologist, spiritual director and pastoral counselor share perspectives on providing care. *Journal of Psychology and Theology*, *31*: 52–68.

Woodhead, L. & Heels, P. (2004). *The spiritual revolution: Why religion is giving way to spirituality*. Oxford: Blackwell.

Wulff, D. H. (1997). *Psychology of religion: Classic and contemporary views* (2nd edn.). New York: John Wiley.

Zinnbauer, B. J., Pargament, K. I. *et al.* (1997). Religion and spirituality: Unfuzzying the fuzzy. *Journal for the Scientific Study of Religion*, *36*: 549–564.

Chapter 17

Counselling Psychology and the Media: The Highs and Lows

Lucy Atcheson

One of the core foci of counselling psychology is the therapeutic relationship and its impact on people's difficulties. Within therapy we look at the dynamics of relationships and try to facilitate clients making positive changes in their lives. But counselling psychology isn't only useful in the consulting room; it has a role in providing psychological input beyond therapy, to society in general. The media acts as a context for delivering this input, so, when involved in the wellbeing of wider society, counselling psychologists find themselves in a relationship with the media. When facing the complexity of the process of taking counselling psychology beyond the consulting room via the media, counselling psychologists foreground the ethical dimension in order to help navigate the complexities of the topic by expanding the context and frame of the therapeutic relationship.

This chapter provides an overview of the ways psychologists can engage with the media. It considers the issues involved in taking psychology out of the consulting room, and also discusses the advantages and disadvantages of this process. This is important as different parts of the media offer diverse opportunities and challenges.

Therapy and Beyond: Counselling Psychology Contributions to Therapeutic and Social Issues
Edited by Martin Milton
© 2010 John Wiley & Sons, Ltd.

The Importance of a Working Relationship between Psychology and the Media

A well-established relationship between psychology and the media exists in the British Psychological Society Press Committee, which has, as its primary role, promoting psychology in society through the media. In order to engage with the media effectively, it is important to consider the ways in which practitioners are able to integrate psychological theory and practice into this context. In some ways this is a very similar reflection process to that of integrating different psychological approaches into the therapeutic relationship. Norcross and Grencavage state that integration is 'a theoretical process combining many different approaches to create a new therapeutic approach, which is more than the sum of its parts' (1990, p. 3). Counselling psychology's contribution comes by way of its relational framework, which allows the therapeutic relationship to remain central to decision-making about client welfare. This is important at all times when trying to work with clients in the broader context of the media.

This chapter now turns to the worlds of publishing, news, television and radio, from the ephemera of articles and comments to the more substantial input of television programmes, series and books.

The Printed Media

Writing and Publishing Self-help Books

Academic writing is a way of ensuring that new insights are brought to the attention of those in the profession and is therefore vital to the continual development of psychology as a science and practice. Within the scientist-practitioner paradigm, writing as a scientist includes a formal style in reporting research and the development of new theories or the continued development of existing ones. Writing as a practitioner, however, it is perhaps necessary to meet the needs of wider society and this may entail writing for readers as if they are clients outside of the consulting room. Thus, thinking about and at times meeting readers' needs ethically is the main aim. This medium may include self-help in the form of books or articles written by psychologists as well as comments to journalists for their articles.

Writing a book or article for the public involves overcoming many obstacles.

First, there is the relationship to the material: is the writer appropriately informed? Is it sufficiently interesting and helpful?

Secondly, there is the relationship between the material and the reader: Who is the target? Whom will it help? Is it written in an accessible style?

Thirdly, there is the relationship between writer and publisher. How will the material be made accessible? How much compromise is required to make it an interesting enough project for the publisher? Can the psychologist limit the sensationalism sometimes required to sell the book?

Relationship with the Publisher

Once a psychologist feels that they have enough specialised and evidenced material to merit writing a book or article, and that it may be helpful to members of the public, they then have to nurture their passion for the material and the project while they find a way of communicating their message. It is important to recognise that if a publisher buys the publishing rights, a compromise may be required.

The compromise comes about because of the different requirements of each of the parties. In order to write psychology effectively (i.e. in a way that the reader can understand and will find useful), it has to be written in a way that results in the reader trusting the material. In order to nurture trust psychologists must only make realistic claims and therefore often needs to be tentative or conjectural. Yet, in an age of preferred certainty, this can take a lot of discipline and effort as it risks the material sounding weak or uncertain. And this is the focus of the publisher, who is well aware that tentative claims rarely sell and so may want to encourage authors to describe their material as 'ground-breaking', 'perfect' or some type of miracle cure in order to enhance its sales appeal. This requires attention as there is a risk that it may not feel ethical or comfortable. So the tricky negotiation begins between the psychologist's original vision and that of the marketing professionals.

Another area of negotiation is related to the style of writing. This changes when moving from formal academic writing to something intended for a wider, less specialised audience. The style has to be more accessible and one often has to fight to keep references within the text, for the Harvard-style referencing system, central to academic psychology, has long been abandoned as too cumbersome and a deterrent to the reader. At best it can be very disconcerting for writers schooled in an academic style to start writing in the first person and 'talking' directly to the reader. Further, abandoning traditional referencing systems can look like plagiarism, which no ethical author wants to commit.

Sometimes this negotiation will be unsuccessful and the material may be rejected if the writer is unwilling to compromise and replace their evidence-based data with more speculative material. However justified one feels, it is still disappointing to receive the communication that articles or projects are to be dropped (the media term is 'killed' and you receive a 'kill fee' for your work). To be told that your work is to be killed can have a very powerful and negative effect from which it is hard to re-group and have continued belief in your 'expertise' and work. This interaction can be likened to experiencing negative transference from a client, and has to be contextualised and internalised with an awareness of its origins. It is helpful to understand it in a non-defensive yet protective manner.

The Relationship with the Agent

The relationship between the psychologist and their agent is also fraught with difficulty. A literary agent acts as an intermediary negotiating between the psychologist and publishing houses. They can be vital as psychologists do not often have sufficient understanding of the culture of publishing to represent themselves and am agent can nurture you through an unfamiliar process. However, this is not their only role; although they act as your support, they are also there to sell the material. Therefore, they have a financial interest in making your material saleable. This can result in a powerful pull to make sensationalist claims and endorsements of your work, and perhaps to make your findings or opinions and suggestions more forceful than you might be comfortable with.

These pressures can be conscious and deliberate but often are more systemic in nature. They can be both personally and professionally uncomfortable as no one wants to claim something that they cannot deliver and, of course, all psychologists have an ethical obligation not to work, write or claim something beyond their professional competence. Therefore, the deliberations require the psychologist to think on their feet about the content being discussed and the process that is occurring. It is important to work with agents and publishers to develop appropriate resolutions to the tensions and issues of each project. To suggest one clear answer to these dilemmas would be sensationalist as each situation and relationship needs to be considered individually. All anyone can do is be aware of these potentially problematic dynamics and ensure that we do not collude with them and lose our integrity or ownership of material.

The Relationship with the Readers

Clearly, the writer of a self-help book cannot write with *each* of their readers in mind, as readers may have a variety of responses to your work. But what writers *can* do is keep in mind the emotions involved with their topics. People struggle with issues that cause them to turn to self-help and they need to be reassured by the material, not alienated or misunderstood. The style needs to be accessible, with a content that appeals to people struggling with particular issues. The material needs to encompass sufficient issues to appeal to all. Case studies should be composite rather than specific; they should never be identifiable. Ethically, there is debate on whether case studies should be used at all. Certainly, they should not be included as light entertainment or reassurance that there are others who are even worse off than the reader. Case studies need a clinically sound rationale for their inclusion. One useful strategy for self-help is to seek the views of those suffering from the main issue before finishing the final draft.

Writing for wider society can be very rewarding. Self-help has an ever-increasing place in the delivery of psychological therapies, especially as the waiting lists for psychological input in the NHS continue to grow. Self-help can provide a useful stopgap until face-to-face therapy can be provided. Further, for those who want some informed help but do not feel ready to seek individual or group therapy, it can start to break down the mystery surrounding therapy and help demystify psychology and make it a little more familiar and accessible.

Comments for Journalists

When commenting on topics for journalists to use as 'expert opinion' there are other issues to consider and negotiate. Again, the relationship between psychologist and material is paramount. The psychologist can be portrayed by the journalist as an expert in the field, someone the reader can trust.

In light of the aura of 'expertise', psychologists need to ensure that they comment *only* on topics about which they do feel that they have sufficient specialist knowledge and evidence. As the journalist will have succinct word counts to adhere to, there is little room for tentative comments and quotes must be unequivocal and definite. Therefore, the psychologist must ensure they avoid sensationalist and clinically inaccurate statements for the sake of article length.

This may seem obvious, but how does a psychologist ensure accuracy when they have no say over the final edit? How can someone ensure they are not misquoted by editing? Further, the interviews are rarely scheduled weeks in advance but are far more likely to be carried out within hours or minutes of the original contact, leaving little or no time for reflective preparation. Again, there is no easy solution, so perhaps the only thing to do is to undertake some media training to develop the art of thinking fast in a way that does not leave room for misquotation, so messages are delivered succinctly and at the same time are clinically appropriate. Of course, while this is a distinct experience in relation to the media, counselling psychologists are frequently asked to think on their feet by clients in the consulting room, by students on training courses or when commenting on public consultations. Thinking is key as tabloid style journalism by definition sensationalises and often reconstructs situations to make them more shocking. This has already happened to certain areas of psychology with, for example, Freud seldom being mentioned other than as a caricature whose sole contribution to psychology was to state that everyone wants to have sexual relations with the parent of the opposite gender. Very little of the rest of his work is communicated – explicitly – to a wider audience. Psychological involvement with the media and popular psychology needs to be considered carefully to prevent such inaccuracy and sensationalist misrepresentation.

The Media of the Spoken Word

Guest Professionals on Interview Shows

In the same way that psychologists can be called on to provide written quotation for articles, psychologists can be asked to provide expert opinion in the form of sound-bites for television. This often takes the form of 'guest expert' on interview shows. Perhaps the most difficult aspect of this is time constraints. Often topics are discussed in minutes, when they are so complex they could easily fill hours. The psychologist has to be concise and to the point without compromising on accuracy. If it is not possible to say something with certainty, then some equivocation is required. This is why so many psychologists start with 'In most cases . . .' or 'It may be that . . .'. There is a pull to be definite, but it needs to be explained that a more definite (yet inaccurate) response would diminish rather than enhance credibility.

These shows are often broadcast live, so words cannot be edited; therefore the psychologist has no control over how they come across to the audience. Due to the dynamic nature of these shows and the ensuing pressure, media training before undertaking such projects is a useful and supportive process. When appearing on such shows, the psychologist has to be aware that they are not only talking to the presenter, more importantly they are communicating with the audience at home. How do you deliver your message in a way that their audience can relate to? Just as in written media the reader becomes the client, in interviews or the spoken word the listeners are the counselling psychologists' clients. Therefore, their welfare is central in the decision-making processes regarding what to say and how to say it. It would be easy to alienate and cause stress to those with either very different or very similar experiences to those being discussed on the show. This may sound obvious, but when under pressure it an be harder to remember than one might imagine. Most psychological topics are emotive for different population groups, and when these are discussed in a television interview they need to be treated with sensitivity and awareness of the distress they may cause even though it is not possible to be aware of all of the individual experiences of the audience. It is perhaps best to be aware of those most likely to be affected by the topic being discussed, so that when they resonate with the content this will help them feel supported rather than misunderstood or, worse, being treated as amusement for others in a 'problem page style'.

Problem pages are sometimes read by those who take reassurance from the fact that there are others worse off than they are, or those who want to laugh at what may be perceived as the hilarity of other people's suffering. Media presenters may perhaps not do so willingly, but unintentionally they could hold up some people's suffering and difficulties for ridicule. For example, when discussing phobias it might seem reasonable for some people to ask: 'What is the strangest phobia you have ever encountered?' If the psychologist were to answer this, they would be colluding with the notion that some phobias are strange, in fact so strange that they should be amusing for everyone else. Therefore, the answer needs to start with 'No phobia is strange' and continued with something like: 'Almost anything can be the cause of phobias due to the nature and development of these fears.' Basically, careful yet speedy consideration is required of both the overall message and the words used to communicate it. In situations like this it is always better to make one strong point carefully and accurately than many different points.

Involvement with Television Series

Along with other applied psychologists, counselling psychologists are involved with television programmes. I will draw on my own experience to highlight the range and nature of such work.

One area where psychologists are involved is the debate on the physical disciplining of children – clearly a complex topic that requires thought. Dr Tanya Byron has promoted nurturing and effective ways of modifying children's behaviour on her TV show *House of Tiny Tearaways*. My contribution was a programme I presented in 2006 called *I Smack and I am Proud*. In this show parents who felt justified in smacking their children were helped to consider the destructiveness of their behaviour and how they risked sabotaging their child's attachment to them. My role included helping parents to become more discerning observers of their child's behaviour and only discipline them when it was absolutely necessary, such as when they put themselves in harm's way. Furthermore, as in therapy, the parents and I tried to construct disciplinary techniques such as 'time out', which allowed non-physical discipline.

On a different project, *Panic Room*, with a colleague, Felix Eckonamis, I was involved in trying to bring psychological knowledge to the public. In this show we looked at the reality of phobias. Phobias are much maligned and ridiculed in society. People find the object of phobias amusing and baffling and therefore those suffering with a phobia often feel humiliated and isolated. In the series we tried to raise awareness that phobias have very real causes and do not merit amusement but support. Again, psychological input is necessary to raise understanding of fear and other psychological issues.

The relationship with the television media is a complex one, and the counselling psychologist working in television series must attend to many different relationships, often with contrasting needs. Unfamiliar juggling of priorities may be required.

First, before any work can be agreed, there is the developmental phase, which may proceed something like this. A media agency decides to develop a show that a channel might buy, so they try to make their idea into a tempting and attractive format. Often it is at this point that they begin to approach the professionals they want for this show, who will be billed as experts. When the professional is approached with the idea the first relationship they have to be aware of and realistic about is the relationship they have with themselves and their specialist knowledge.

There is also the relationship between the psychologist and the development executive to consider. In just the same way as assessments are done within therapy to decide whether the client feels comfortable with the psychologist and the psychologist feels capable of working with that client in a clinically effective way, an assessment is needed. Does the media agency believe that the psychologist will come across well on television and does the psychologist feel they can work with the subject matter in a clinically effective way? Is the subject within their areas of expertise? Currently, there seems to be a trend for voyeuristic or sensationalist television shows. These do not help anyone and are clearly only made for entertainment purposes, often at someone else's expense. Counselling psychologists tend to avoid this type of show and this would seem appropriate as counselling psychology wants to take psychology beyond the consulting room to inform and help wider society, not destroy people or the reputation of counselling psychologists and the discipline as a whole.

If both psychologist and development executive feel comfortable, the development progresses to the next phase. The agency will approach the television channels with the idea and several things may follow. The channel may pick up the idea or they may not. By this point the psychologist will have put a lot of work into the development of the show as their professional opinions and strategies to effect changes will have been sought. However, the psychologist will not usually be involved in the presentations and will not be aware of their outcomes. This can prove frustrating, especially since the lapse of time might be the only indicator that the idea has not been taken up.

Where projects are not commissioned, the counselling psychologist will need to reflect on a relationship with wider society via the media without being disappointed about the unsatisfactory ending of their relationship with a particular TV proposal. The same way that counselling psychology recognises the need for appropriate endings in therapy even if the work was not entirely positive, as with written projects the lack of any formal ending or closure can be difficult. But if psychologists are to have a voice in society via the media, they must be able to cope with the obstacles that exist within the media culture.

But let's be optimistic: what if the idea is taken up? More complexity exists when the idea is bought by a channel and developed into a show. Most television shows requiring professional input are classified as 'factual entertainment'. The relationships at this stage become even more dynamic as the psychologist has a relationship with:

- their own knowledge and how they feel sensitive topics should be managed, which requires a relationship with the channel producing the show and their directors and producers;
- the contributors, who are effectively their clients;
- their audience.

The Relationship between the Psychologist and the Programme Makers

As the media tend to present professional contributors as experts, the expert needs to feel sufficiently comfortable with their specialist knowledge to justify such an attribution. Both theoretical and practical specialist knowledge is required. Most factual entertainment involving a psychologist is based on the therapy of one or more contributors. Therefore, as in work within the consulting room, the psychologist needs to plan and provide clinically appropriate therapy. The psychologist needs to feel comfortable with the subject matter of the show. The guiding principle should be that the show will in some way be helpful to the contributors and the audience, and not detrimental or ridiculing. Psychologists have a moral obligation not to take part in shows that take advantage of people, mislead people, are potentially exploitative or lead to emotional distress. This is particularly important as psychological involvement could add an air of respectability to shows that are blatantly exploitative.

The relationship with the channel requires trust about how the expert and their material will be presented; in some ways it might be seen as a need for a strong working alliance. The expert must trust that they will not be presented in a problematic fashion and that the material will not be cut to portray them in an unprofessional, uninformed or insensitive light. Trust is important as psychologists (or indeed any contributors) are unlikely to have any say over the final cut. Most contracts preclude this, and it would be a very favourable contract that granted an 'expert contributor' an input into the edit.

The absence of any editing voice need not stop someone from engaging with a series about which they feel passionately. It is just that the contributor should be alert for warning signs that a trusting and collaborative relationship with the producers is unlikely. Trust can often be developed though as the media usually want to present their 'experts' as such, and collaborative and positive relationships can be formed and are perhaps the normal way of working within the media. In order to facilitate a strong working alliance, early discussions and shared understandings about the aims and objectives of the series are very useful as well as prudent and reassuring.

The psychologist needs to facilitate a sound working alliance with the channel in order to provide a strong therapeutic alliance with the client (Clarkson, 1995; Gelso & Carter, 1985). Rogers (1951) theorised that the therapeutic elements of empathy, unconditional positive regard and congruence were vital to establish a secure and effective therapeutic relationship. These factors remain vital in therapeutic relationships – even in the context of the media.

The Relationship between Psychologists and Their Clients

Just as psychological therapy requires an assessment, so does client work in the context of a television show. The clients' fitness to take part needs to be very carefully considered. In some cases the channels prefer a different psychologist to undertake the assessments. Their reasoning is often about 'televisual' factors, such as authenticity when they film the original meeting between client and psychologist. In these cases it is advisable for the assessing and contributing psychologists to discuss the client assessments prior to the start of filming. The psychologist also needs to ensure that the contributor has realistic outcome expectations and an awareness of any possible disadvantages resulting from their participation in the series, so that the contributor can make a fully informed decision about their participation. Sometimes the opportunity of having '15 minutes of fame' can blind people to the negative consequences of such a venture.

The emotional wellbeing of clients must be carefully monitored throughout the filming process. Perhaps the best way of doing this is a discussion off-camera at the end of each session. The psychologist also needs to implement models of best practice for both their interventions and the channel's overall treatment of the clients throughout the filming, and so effective collaboration between psychologist and channel is again paramount.

When working on *Panic Room* we needed 12 people suffering with phobias to contribute to the show. They were assessed and chosen by another psychologist as the producers wanted the clients and psychologists to meet for the first time in front of the camera. This was obviously problematic, as my colleague and I had no chance to assess the clients prior to filming. However, we were able to trust that our colleague's assessments were appropriate. Moreover, we secured agreement with the producers that we would debrief with the contributor after the first filming session and we could comment on fitness and motivation to contribute after that meeting. We were fortunate that everyone was clearly, carefully and appropriately selected, but this could have been an example of the uneasy alliance of psychology and television making.

The client needs to feel that they have a collaborative and secure working alliance with the psychologist in much the same way they do within the context of a brief therapeutic relationship. The psychologist needs to attend to this secure working alliance in the same way they would within therapy. This might be more easily said than done as there are significant differences between the two contexts. The obvious difference is confidentiality. Because the interventions are to be screened on television they *cannot* be confidential. However, the psychologist can and should discuss the implications of this fully with all the clients. Further, provision needs to be made for off-camera, fully confidential discussions, so that the client can discuss anything they do not want to be televised but that may affect their feelings or the effectiveness of psychological interventions and outcomes. It is best to formalise the working alliance within this context by having an individually tailored therapeutic agreement between the psychologist and client. This might work in the same way as making a therapeutic contract with clients in the different settings psychologists normally work in. This can facilitate and ensure that all the necessary discussions take place effectively and supportively, and that there is a sound shared understanding of the psychological processes surrounding the desired change and therapy within the context of making the television series.

In order to help the psychologist implement best practice models throughout the filming process, a clause can be added to their contract with the channel that states that they should not be asked to undertake any action that contravenes the British Psychological Society's codes of professional conduct. As the context of programme-making can be unpredictable, it is best to expect the unexpected and have formal agreement about the ways of working and the therapeutic process before filming begins so boundaries, client welfare and models of best practice can be protected.

Brief strategic therapy is a useful model in this context as work on a television series is likely to have stringent time constraints for practical reasons. In this domain psychological interventions are likely to be extremely time-limited. Therefore, brief therapy practice models are of particular relevance and the psychologist not only has to have a thorough understanding of the theoretical content, but also a sound knowledge of working within these paradigms.

Within the context of time-limited programme-making, counselling psychologists are likely to face challenges when providing therapeutic interventions. There is not enough calm or quiet reflection in the moment when delivering interventions to allow unconscious communication to be prioritised. Therefore, logical challenges and prescriptive therapy may be much more effective than the more psychodynamic way of working. The therapeutic communications of CBT are less likely to be lost or destroyed by the 'noise' and invasions of filming than other ways of working. This is not to say the unconscious communications should be ignored; the psychologist should still try to be aware of them, their content and their impact. A strong working alliance with unconditional positive regard, empathy and congruence will also make the client feel secure enough to benefit from the CBT. As the psychologist is billed as an expert, there is inevitably going to be the perception of them as educator rather than skilled helper, so it is perhaps more clinically effective to work within a therapeutic approach that embraces this perception rather than one that would be hindered by it.

The counselling psychologist needs to take some responsibility for the way in which their clients portray themselves to the audience, and psychologists working in the media need to recognise their influence on the way their clients portray themselves to the wider audience. No one wants to finish a television series only to find themselves ridiculed or criticised by the viewers and the press. Therefore, the psychologist needs to remind the client that they are on television and that they need to consider what they want to divulge on camera. Confidential off-camera discussions with the psychologist limit the client needing to say something on camera that they later regret. Any television series that actively aims to set up their contributors to become figures of hate or ridicule should be avoided as psychologists will not be able to ensure that their clients are portrayed in a sufficiently positive light.

The Relationship between the Counselling Psychologist and the Television Show's Audience

As well as needing to deliver sound therapeutic intervention to their clients, psychologists also have a responsibility to portray their profession and therapeutic models effectively to the programme's audience. If the media bill the psychologist as an expert, the audience will perceive them as such. By taking part in a television programme the psychologist is taking psychology out of the consulting room and into the homes of thousands of people. This is done with a mind to enhance the profession's and the psychologist's profile and therefore continue the promotion of the profession within society, as well as, most importantly, be of some use to the client and the audience in much the same way as a self-help book aims to help its readers. The programme may be the audience's first encounter with psychology or they may be struggling with the same issues as the clients on television. It is important that the psychologist portrays useful and effective therapy, delivered in the best possible fashion.

In addition to these issues, the psychologist can approach the channel to include information on the show's website and other publicity about sources of further help for people who are struggling with a particular issue.

Guest Professionals on Radio Shows

In the same way that psychologists are approached for quotes for articles, they may be approached for short interviews on the radio. Radio shows often discuss psychological topics, so the number of psychologists being invited to appear on radio is increasing. Radio interviews can cause anxiety as they are often broadcast live so one has to be both quick to respond and careful about what is said. There is an obvious time pressure as concise sound-bites are preferred, but the problem of mis-editing does not arise as the psychologist can have complete control over what they say and how they say it. Radio interviews can be done by telephone, at the studio or in booths at the broadcasting house. Phone and booth interviews have the disadvantage that the presenter is not physically present: the psychologist is talking into a handset or microphone and gazing at a wall. As most counselling psychologists do the vast majority of their work face-to-face, interaction while talking to a wall can be disconcerting and it may be difficult to engage with the warmth and empathy that is usually present in their work. Media training and practice can be beneficial.

As in the other areas discussed, the most important concern for the psychologist working on the radio should be the listener. There is an ethical obligation to communicate clinically sound information in an empathic, non-judgemental, non-exploitative and non-patronising manner. Even if we recognise that it is unlikely that all of the listeners will be struggling with the issue being discussed, some will be and they deserve respect. A psychologist must make an effort to remain psychological and not resort to entertaining. Although the two are not mutually exclusive, it is far more important to communicate in a client-centred style rather than a professional 'presenting' one. Roger's (1951) therapeutic elements of empathy, unconditional positive regard and congruence should underpin the tone and the content of the psychologist's contribution to the radio show, regardless of the rest of the item's tone.

One advantage radio has is that there is usually some preparation time, even if it is only 24 hours. A producer will often telephone or e-mail requesting the interview and then the content will be discussed between psychologist and producer and sample questions given. Radio presenters will not be tied to the sample questions but the overall tenor of the piece and subject matter will have been discussed and therefore reflected on prior to the interview.

In conclusion, the relationship between psychology and the media can have great benefits for all of those involved. However, it can also be an uneasy alliance, so careful reflection and considered practice is required. Like most things, when it goes wrong it can go terribly wrong, but when it goes well psychological involvement in the media can be very positive and rewarding for the continued development of psychology and its place within society.

In Summary

When working with the media
    Do:

- Become involved with projects that you feel passionate and knowledgeable about.

- Try to take psychology beyond the consulting room, making specialist knowledge accessible to all.
- Attend to the ethical complexities, using the therapeutic relationship as your indicator. In each instance be clear about who your client is and how you meet their therapeutic needs best.
- Work a statement into your contract about not deviating from professional bodies' code of ethics.
- Help people struggling in isolation through what they watch, hear or read.
- Be sure of yourself and your ability to promote your own professional development effectively and appropriately and implicitly that of counselling psychology as a whole.
- Remember that, ethically, you can only give your professional opinion and not speak for the whole discipline.

Don't:

- Prioritise entertainment over care.
- Set contributors up for ridicule.
- Set yourself or your profession up for ridicule or criticism.
- Contribute to television shows that are likely to be detrimental in some way to the contributors' wellbeing.
- Allow yourself to be edited in an unprofessional or uncaring light.
- Lose sight of your initial motivation.
- Be manipulated into abandoning your core values.
- Ignore any niggling doubts.

References

Clarkson, P. (1995). *The therapeutic relationship*. London: Whurr.

Gelso, C. & Carter, J. (1985). The relationship in counselling and psychotherapy: Components, consequences and theoretical antecedents. *The Counselling Psychologist, 13*(2): 143–155.

Norcross, J. & Grencavage, L. (1990). Eclecticism and integration in counselling and psychotherapy: Major themes and obstacles. In W. Dryden & J. Norcross (Eds.) *Eclecticism and Integration in counselling psychology and psychotherapy*. Loughton, Essex: Gale Centre.

Rogers, C. (1951). *Client-centred therapy: Its current practice, implications and theory*. Boston, MA: Houghton Mifflin.

Chapter 18

Coming Home to Roost: Counselling Psychology and the Natural World

Martin Milton

> The three cheetah brothers led us to the top of McKenzies Kopje. It was there we succumbed to the mesmerising effect of the vast plains of Southern Africa. As the sun sets it is as if the world is on fire and I am no more. 'I' have been absorbed into the enormity of the moment, of life itself. I am overwhelmed by the beauty and it is a struggle to hold back the tears.
>
> (Mashatu, April 2007)

We are wild beasts. Scratch our civilised surface and you soon find wildness – aspects that we love and parts we cannot abide. Qualities we claim as our own and those we project onto our primate cousins. This chapter looks at the relationship between humans and what is known as the 'natural world' and explores the ways in which counselling psychology engages with the natural world – in therapy and beyond. At a time when our disconnection from nature is increasingly obvious (Higley & Milton, 2008) and the related crises are receiving more attention (Gore, 2006, 2007; Uzzell, 2008), our attention to this relationship is becoming increasingly important (Randall, 2005; Spence *et al.*, 2009).

The notion of the 'natural world' is not unproblematic. Despite it feeling *as if* there are two different worlds – a human, urban environment and the

Therapy and Beyond: Counselling Psychology Contributions to Therapeutic and Social Issues
Edited by Martin Milton
© 2010 John Wiley & Sons, Ltd.

wilds as they evolved millennia ago – 'there are not two worlds – human and non-human – but one world, and we humans are in it, along with oak trees and lesser whitethroats and horses and nematode worms' (Barnes, 2007, p. 123). This is one of the complexities of this discussion: at times people refer to an experience of the natural and the manmade worlds feeling fragmented and disconnected from each other while recognising that the split is not total – it can't be (Deurzen & Arnold-Baker, 2005). It has been argued that this splitting is both a social and a psychological process. Despite the recognition of humanity's place in the web of life (Kovel, 2002), much contemporary discourse encourages a view of people as 'self-contained individuals' (Strawbridge & Woolfe, 2003), separate from each other and separate from the world we exist in. The reader is asked to keep these shades of meaning in mind when reading this chapter and to recognise the fact that despite any perceived separateness, both contexts relate by virtue of their coexistence and complete interdependence.

Being Human: A Natural World Perspective

We exist in the world and our interdependence is total. Deurzen notes that 'we cannot live good lives without constant contact with the natural world. We breathe air and eat and drink natural products. Our own bodies are therefore part of the natural world' (2008, p. 54). In addition to biological reality, the relationship is psychological. 'We make attachments with our *whole* environment and these relationships shape our psychic development along with human relationships' (Rust, 2005, p. 9); or, as Macfarlane puts it, 'our minds are shaped by the bodily experience of being in the world' (2007, p. 203). Macfarlane also notes that in humans' destruction of the environment 'it is not only unique species and habitats that disappear, but also unique memories, unique forms of thought. Woods, like other wild places, can kindle new ways of being or cognition in people, can urge their minds differently' (2007, p. 98).

When we focus on wellbeing, we know that among other things:

> living near nature has beneficial effects on wellbeing . . ., contact with animals has beneficial health effects . . . exposure to natural scenes has positive effects on physiological arousal and health . . . exposure to nature has a positive effect on cognitive functioning . . . spectacular nature is awe inspiring and can promote confidence and wellbeing . . .
>
> (Gaterslaben, 2008, pp. 24–35)

Studies show that 'populations in urban areas with gardens and green space have fewer mental health problems' (Sustainable Development

Commission, 2008, p. 8). This same review 'concluded that contact with nature specifically impacts positively on blood pressure, cholesterol, outlook on life and stress reduction' (Sustainable Development Commission, 2008, p. 9) and we know that the benefits include 'feelings of pleasure and interest and a reduction in anger and anxiety. Natural spaces have also been shown to have a restorative effect, helping people recover more quickly from attention demanding tasks' (Sustainable Development Commission, 2008, p. 9). Berman *et al.* (2008) outline the cognitive benefits of interacting with nature and Mabey notes that there are 'hundreds of studies that seem to prove that the merest glimpse of a growing thing does you good' (2006, p. 13).

Evolved Traits

It makes sense that we are suited to the natural world (Maller *et al.*, 2006) as 'we are descendants of a long lineage, only a fraction of which is human. We are far more than the traces that other humans have left in us. Our brains and spinal cords are encrypted with traces of far older worlds' (Gray, 2002, p. 79). Evolution is a long process, and while our intellect may help us with the contemporary aspects we encounter, our 'hardwired' capacities relate to the physical environment we evolved for. Thus 'both client and therapist each share the same ancestral heritage that goes back into the distant reaches of mammalian, primate, hominid and human evolution' (Bailey & Gilbert, 2000, p. 333; see also Dolley, 2008). Of course, *in situ*, the therapist and client might see themselves as a modern urban couple in the consulting room, but they remain two primeval beasts sniffing each other out as they explore their shared territory.

Contemporary Life

In a relatively short period of time, our industrial, technological and reproductive successes have meant that, to one degree or another, we have adjusted to living in large, heavily populated areas. This is very different from our early communities and has been an enormous adaptation to make. For millennia humans have lived in social groupings of approximately 150 people (Dunbar, 2004; Smith, 2007). Ulstrand suggests that

> [This figure] is the normal size for tribes or clans of people that live outside the influence of modern civilization today. Humans are adapted for living as hunter-gatherers and it is a lifestyle that presupposes small groups and low population densities.
>
> (2002, p. 230)

This expansion puts a strain on both the environment and our emotional systems. In the city our talents for guarding against threat (from other humans as much as anything else) are, metaphorically, working on overdrive. We are constantly on high alert. Uzzell (2008, 2008a) has suggested that these contexts are physically and emotionally stressful and complicit in the physical and psychological difficulties that people are experiencing. Our evolved traits and contemporary lives offer both advantages and disadvantages.

Advantages and Disadvantages

There are advantages to city life. We enjoy health benefits, medical assistance to cure many illnesses and recover more quickly from disease, live longer and our everyday exertions are limited. But modern life is not just physically 'advantageous'. There is much to delight in socially too. Material success means that people's lives have improved enormously – many people take time away from work so that we can be together, more people have money to enjoy and they are able to indulge in leisure activities. Freedom can mean that our intimate relations are enhanced as we enjoy our comforts and our travels with those we are closest to. We can treat ourselves and our loved ones to evenings out where others take care of the catering and the transport.

Paradoxically though, the advantages can also be disadvantages. Our comfort may be what is bad for us; few of us need to walk great distances to secure food or water – if we don't jump in the car to nip to the supermarket we can order online. Instead of using our bipedal legs to walk great distances across the savannah, we now utilise the comfortable technologies of the car, bus or train. Consequently, it is becoming harder to stay fit and we are suffering physical health problems.

In addition, the greater the population the more complex the social dimension is (James, 2007). Dunbar notes that:

> to survive in a large primate group (and so gain the ecological advantages of group size), an animal has to engage in a sophisticated balancing act in which other group members are kept at just sufficient distance to prevent them from imposing serious ecological and reproductive costs while at the same time not driving them away altogether.
>
> (2003, p. 171)

Our relationship to the natural world has come to the fore in recent years as a series of environmental crises have arisen. Pollutants in the food chain (see Carson, 1999), species extinction, the threat to the ozone layer and now global warming and climate change (IPCC, 2001). As well as these being cultural matters, we are seeing psychological reactions in the form of stress, anxiety, interpersonal conflict and post-traumatic stress disorder related to these events (Uzzell, 2008a).

Dislocation from the world we evolved for can mean that we lose access to trusted people. We become swamped by strangers and the potential threat they pose. One response is to try to dominate the world to assuage our anxieties. This gets played out in a number of ways. Some are discouraged (e.g. anti-social behaviour), while others, such as consumerism – with its ability to construct hierarchies through shopping – are constructed as desirable and the way to solve personal, social and even global economic problems. Where:

> traditionally the economic system was situated within and designed to serve the larger value system of the community and natural world. Today the situation is reversed: The consumerist economic system dominates, and everything else is situated within it, captivated by its reverence of (supposed) progress via technological domination of nature.
>
> (Adams, 2005, p. 279)

To a certain degree, urban living hoodwinks us into thinking that we have it good, all the while helping us forget – or ignore – that many of our needs are not being met (James, 2007). In our world of apparent abundance we are prone to wanting – and getting – things that in excess are toxic and literally do us harm. This is true physically where too much 'good living' leads to obesity, heart disease and increased rates of asthma (James, 2007; Louv, 2006). It is also true psychologically, with greater rates of mental health problems in urban and capitalist areas than in rural or traditional societies (Hamilton, 2004). Adams suggests that 'our estrangement is implicated in clinical and non-clinical forms of anxiety, depression, narcissism, addiction, emptiness, and acting-out, and in our confusion over existential concerns regarding meaning, value, purpose, identity, and responsibility' (2005, p. 271). Despite this awareness and the prevalence of these difficulties McCallum says 'this split between humans and nature . . . an Origins Deficit Disorder, is one of the most undiagnosed conditions in modern psychiatry' (McCallum & Milton, 2008, p. 63). The struggle to see the immediate and direct relevance of the natural world to our psychological state (individual and collective) is itself a symptom of our culture, which splits and fragments experience from its context. Increasingly, attention is being paid to the way in which specific difficulties, such as eating disorders, are closely linked to capitalism, urban living and a dislocation from both our bodies and the natural world (Rust, 2008). Rust argues that in traditional cultures eating problems and weight issues simply do not exist. The older women have dignity and pride in themselves and their bodies, whereas the younger generation are less able to make contact; they hold their bodies in a different way. Their sense of dignity has palpably changed.

(2005a, p. 13)

In the West, consumption – financial and of food - can be a way of managing the pain of dislocation from our bodies, the world and from each other (Baker, 2000; du Plock, 2002; Orbach, 2009; Randall, 2005).

Depression is a reaction to unsatisfactory aspects of our lives and can be both an individual and a communal experience. In depression, our modern mind can struggle to understand some of our emotional, more 'archaic' (Jung, 1990) responses, reliant as it has become on reason. Yet this deathly sense of depression speaks volumes and for some it is clearly related to a lack of contact with the natural world. Mabey related his depression to our dislocation from the natural world by saying: 'I had become an incomprehensible creature adrift in some insubstantial medium, out of kilter with the rest of creation. It didn't occur to me at the time, but maybe that is the way our whole species is moving' (2005, p. 4).

Despite the strength of the evidence that people and their wellbeing are intimately linked with the natural world, an anthropocentric bias remains in much psychological thinking. Many psychologists have 'stopped' at the boundary of the human body/personality (Higley & Milton, 2008), though some have explored this relationship. Rollo May noted 'in modern man's desire to conquer nature, man has not only become estranged from nature but also from himself resulting in the fragmentation of man' (May *et al.*, 1958, p. 35) and Harold Searles commented on the absurdity of this:

> the nonhuman environment is . . . considered entirely irrelevant to human personality development, and to the development of psychiatric illness, as though human life were lived out in a vacuum – as though the human race were alone in the universe, pursuing individual and collective destinies in a homogeneous matrix of nothingness, a background devoid of form, colour and substance.

(1960, p. 3)

These insights are supported by research from an attachment perspective which highlights that migrants 'maintain a strong emotionally charged bond or "residual link" to the non-human as well as human elements of their homeland' (Ward & Styles, 2007, p. 319).

Counselling psychologists are increasingly taking their place alongside philosophers, zoologists, conservationists, town planners and geologists when working with the emotional and behavioural consequences of our environmental struggles (Milton, 2007, 2009; Uzzell, 2008). This is a natural development related to one of the central identifying characteristics of counselling psychology – its focus on relational ways of understanding people and their contexts. Counselling psychology guidelines for professional practice prioritise this relational perspective, stating clearly that 'practitioners must consider all contexts that might affect a client's experience and incorporate it into the assessment process, formulation and planned intervention' (Division of Counselling Psychology, 2005, p. 7).

Counselling Psychology: The Consulting Room . . .

Assessment and Formulation

Sometimes there are clear aspects of a client's presentation that lead a counselling psychologist to explore the client's relationship with the natural world, for example when a client brings overt distress in relation to climate change and environmental devastation. In these circumstances, while the counselling psychologist will be mindful of the symbolic dimension, they will also consider the reality of these issues and the direct meanings they hold for the client. By considering *both* possibilities the counselling psychologist is informed more broadly about the client.

It is not always that straightforward. Counselling psychologists frequently work with clients who are at a loss as to the nature of their distress. In these circumstances, direct questions are not always fruitful. This may partly be because 'nothing comes to mind' for the client; sometimes it is because the person has yet to trust the relationship with the therapist; and sometimes the meanings are mysterious. In these circumstances it is as important to wait for things to emerge as it is to ask for information. Sensory, intuitive and embodied experiences are particular aspects that the process will illuminate. While traditional approaches to assessment and formulation offer important insights, they can also fail to consider the wider framework in which a client lives. When this occurs significant material is overlooked and we are none the wiser as to whether the wider relationship is a 'neglected yet vital' aspect of the client's experience (Higley & Milton, 2008).

What this chapter suggests, therefore, is not to *ignore* proven ways of gaining insight, but to become curious and to *extend* our engagement. The same way that a counselling psychologist may ponder a client's presentation with a variety of models in mind (e.g. What are the cognitive aspects of this presentation? What is going on consciously and unconsciously? How will the client respond to different styles of therapeutic response?), we can also ponder the nature of the client's embodied experience, their relationship to the wider political and natural aspects of their lives. In this way, traditional aspects of assessment and formulation are enriched when the client material (explicit and implicit, verbal and embodied) is explored in relation to the client's experience of the environment, of nature and of other species. Steyn suggests that as:

> there are so many similarities between humans and animals that a knowledge of the natural world, and especially the instinctive behaviour which seems so much more raw in nature ... might help one to understand the often suppressed instinctive behaviour of mankind.
>
> (2008, p. 60)

When working with an openness to the impact of the natural world, it is useful to ask a few more questions and to think of a few more possible ways to formulate the client's presenting issue. Requests such as 'Tell me about your politics/faith/relationship to the natural world' can be useful additions to any assessment repertoire and are easily included alongside the more traditional 'Tell me about your mum and dad'. An environmental awareness is simply an invitation to broaden our thinking. It is 'to bring the entire human history into the consulting room. It is to see ourselves and our patients as two-and-a-half-million-year-old survivors. It is an acknowledgement that our animal and human ancestors are alive and with us' (McCallum & Milton, 2008, p. 65). This perspective was illustrated with my work with Kyle (all identifying details have been altered to ensure that clients are offered confidentiality and anonymity):

> Kyle (pseudonym) approached me for assistance with what he felt was 'social anxiety'. He certainly fit the diagnostic criteria with marked and persistent fear of public scrutiny, anxiety and panic attacks which he felt were excessive and which interfered with his interpersonal interactions and professional tasks (APA, 1994, p. 205). He had identified patterns of thinking which led up to his distress and incapacitation, and together we had considered interpersonal difficulties that underpinned this experience. Despite this, Kyle had a nagging doubt that we were missing something he felt was important.
>
> A useful point came when he returned from a camping trip in Wales where he had 'only seen about two cars most afternoons ... and loved it'. He had been able to 'wander, forage and explore to my heart's content, just like the monkeys on the farm'. Kyle came from the Karoo, a wide expanse of scrubland in South Africa. The association and the strength of feeling allowed us to question whether the move to London, with its enormous population, packed underground trains and competitive work

environments was also a part of the stress. He had been to university in a large city and graduate school overseas, but somehow he felt that he didn't belong in London ('It isn't right for me'). Like those monkeys might experience, he was living in a world that he was not equipped for. He had underestimated the impact this would have and the support factors he would require to make a success of his migration to London.

Environmentally Aware Therapy

Environmentally aware therapy is not necessarily a different 'brand' of therapy; instead it is characterised by the fact that the natural world is taken seriously, whether the counselling psychologist is working humanistically, psychodynamically or from any other perspective. It recognises that 'our outer environment is never merely a geographical setting. From positive to negative, every environmental encounter evokes a particular feeling – pleasure, awe, fascination, disappointment, sadness, fear, panic, disgust, anger, indifference, etc.' (McCallum, 2007, p. 135). Environmentally aware therapy attends to evolutionary factors and questions contemporary assumptions about our urban lives. It attends to the significance that people give to their encounters with the natural world and respects these as experiences in their own right, and not simply as coded messages about human relationships. McCallum suggests that 'the patient needs a guide (someone who knows the terrain, the animals, the weather patterns and when it is appropriate to proceed or withdraw)' (McCallum & Milton, 2008, p. 65).

This *may* lead to innovative ways of working as the interdisciplinary consensus about the beneficial aspects of our relationship to the natural world (Gaterslaben, 2008; Hamilton, 2004; Maller *et al.*, 2006) allows counselling psychologists to question why therapists limit their practice to hour-long sessions behind closed doors away from nature. There is much to learn from those who work with people on the move (Priest, 2007) or out in nature (Jordan, 2005; Wright, 2009).

Ecotherapy

While there are concerns about the ever-increasing range of therapies that focus on 'bits of the puzzle' (Shillito-Clarke, 2008) and risk being as consumerist as many other aspects of our lives, it is worth noting the development of 'ecotherapy'. Ecotherapy 'is emerging as a clinically valid treatment option for mental distress, and a core component of an adequate public health strategy for Mental Health' (MIND, 2007, p. 4). Ecotherapy facilitates new, imaginative and embodied practices, while retaining a thoughtful and ethical stance – tenets at the heart of counselling psychology.

The starting point is to 'Stand still. Listen. Be patient. Try and make sure that the space between you and the other is safe and containing for you both. As practiced in analytical therapy, 'begin by giving a free-floating attention to the encounter' (McCallum, 2007, p. 188). Jordan has written that ecotherapy:

> can act as a very powerful mobilizer of fear and then a containing space in which the person can find their own sense of themselves. Rituals and exercises performed during the process can act as a way of managing the issues that arise and hold a potentially transformative power for the person engaging and marking a transition in their life.
>
> (2005, p. 2)

Ecotherapy is:

> especially effective when people have been on the receiving end of violence and torture . . . people who are so very badly hurt by other humans, as well as being dislocated from their homes and country, often find it easier to connect to nature first, before daring to risk human relationships again.
>
> (Rust, 2004, p. 1)

So whether in traditional or new forms, the natural world is being recognised as related to how we experience and understand wellbeing and distress and also the ways in which we work with people.

Beyond Therapy

Many responses to the environmental challenges we face are psychological processes such as 'anxiety, denial, splitting and projection, experienced and expressed at the social rather than at the individual level' (Randall, 2005, p. 3). Stern has suggested that 'by adding a psychologist's perspective to theories from elsewhere you can develop fresh insights' (2009, p. 184). Mabey notes that 'almost all the major ecological crises of the world need mathematicians, psychologists, philosophers and economists as well as biologists working on them' (BBC Books, 2006, p. 162). Similarly, Scott suggests that 'psychologists could be more engaged as professionals as to how we can actually make our message most listenable to, how we can capture people's attention' (Scott & Milton, 2008, p. 57).

The phenomenological stance that underpins counselling psychology allows us to contribute through research, direct experiences with nature, parenting and child development, psychotherapy, contemplative practices, ecological education and services to the natural world (Adams, 2005).

Counselling psychologists' research skills can be useful to the environmental debate as a way to explore the relationship between people and the natural world, the benefits thereof and the struggles that exist. This can be undertaken by way of a critique of the literature, empirical work and the overarching epistemological pressures that inform much policy. Empirical work by counselling psychologists explores the relationship between people and their place in the world (see Favali, 2008; Higley, 2008; Howard, 1993; Milton, 2003, 2008; Owen, 2008).

Counselling psychologists also contribute by way of their teaching, which can be as useful to non-governmental organisations and others involved in environmental projects as it has traditionally been to applied psychologists, nursing and care staff. Counselling psychologists have been involved in establishing training programmes that address 'the connections between personal action, social, industrial and agricultural systems and our planet's ecology' (Centre for Human Ecology, 2008).

Counselling psychologists also widen the scope of their work by collaborating with conservationists and environmental psychologists. These collaborations are enriched by attention to the human factors, environmental issues and most importantly their interrelationship. Working in this way means that we can go beyond 'tweaking' and engage in innovative research and consultation practices (Devine-Wright, 2009).

Warnings

As when working in other areas of human life, working in the environmental domain is unlikely to be easy (Randall, 2005). One danger is that the natural world becomes idealised and this can lead to *illusions* of nature rather than the *experience* of it. Mabey notes that 'having already become the new rock and roll, nature seems poised to become the new complementary medicine' (2006, p. 13). This risks leaving practitioners unprepared for the reality of work in this domain.

On the one hand, like our clients and communities, practitioners might struggle to find enough contact with the natural world and so feel the physical and psychological strain that modern life places on us. On the other, the wilder, natural world also challenges us physically and can be

a difficult environment (Milton, 2003, 2008). It is one we should prepare for. To underestimate this means we can be overwhelmed by our
limitations.

The difficulties are not just physical; environmental work can have a
painful psychological impact. The environmentalist Jonathan Porrit notes
that 'I've always felt a kind of deep, gut-wrenching sense of pain when I think
about the speed with which we're laying waste the planet; and it is a deep,
emotional response to what I see as horrifically irresponsible, unthinking,
unnecessary behaviour on our part' (BBC Books, 2006, p. 211). Former US
Vice President Al Gore also noted how 'an astonishing number of people go
straight from denial to despair, without pausing on the intermediate step of
saying, "We can do something about this"' (2006, p. 276).

While these dangers exist, counselling psychologists have developed ways
to monitor the impact of the traumatic stories we hear in our work and
the challenges of a range of contexts. For example, we use supervision and
our own personal therapy, training and other aspects of our lives to avoid
burnout and feeling impotent. To work in the natural domain does not
require us to start all over again but to transfer our learning from one
context to another. We may, of course, need to find ways to *tailor* our
sources of support in this domain.

Alongside the challenges, though, are the benefits – for the practitioner,
client and wider community. Engaging with important and meaningful
phenomena, the chance to process the feelings about them is 'the work
that reconnects' (Macy, 1995) and in our own reconnection we avoid/repair
some of the damage done by the disconnection from the natural world that
affects us all.

It seems fitting to end with a challenge.

> We suffer from a dangerous, yet potentially reversible state of ecological
> amnesia. At a huge cost to the natural environment and to ourselves, we
> have suppressed the evolutionary significance of our relationship to wilder-
> ness, to landscapes and rivers, to mountains, oceans and ice and to the wider
> community of animals that live in these areas. We have forgotten our origins
> and our common bloodline with all living mammals. Threatened by its fierce
> vitality, we are afraid of what is deepest in us – our wild nature.
>
> (McCallum, 2008, p. 90)

Let us hope that this is indeed reversible. Politicians have their role,
conservationists theirs and counselling psychology, with its insight into
relational matters and our experience of working to promote human
wellbeing, has an equally important contribution to make. If we can
embrace our own wild nature, reflect on it with our contemporary logic

and engage in collaborative practices, there is a potential of enhanced wellbeing – of both the planet and all its inhabitants.

References

Adams, W. W. (2005). Ecopsychology and phenomenology: Towards a collaborative engagement. *Existential Analysis*, *16*(2): 269–283.

American Psychiatric Association (1994). *Diagnostic and statistical manual of mental disorders.* (4th edn.). Washington, DC: American Psychiatric Association.

Bailey, K. & Gilbert, P. (2000). Evolutionary psychotherapy: Where to from here? In P. Gilbert & K. Bailey (Eds.) *Genes on the couch: Explorations in evolutionary psychotherapy*. Hove: Brunner-Routledge.

Baker, A. (2000). *Serious shopping: Essays in psychotherapy and consumerism*. London: Free Association Books.

Barnes, S. (2007). *How to be wild*. London: Short Books.

BBC Books (2006). *Planet earth: The future . . . what the experts say*. London: BBC Books.

Berman, M. G., Jonides, J. & Kaplan, S. (2008). The cognitive benefits of interacting with nature. *Psychological Science*, *19*(12): 1207–1212.

Carson, R. (1999). *Silent spring*. London: Penguin Books.

Centre for Human Ecology (2008). www.che.ac.uk/mambo/content/blogsection/20/188. Accessed 1 August 2008.

Deurzen, E. van (2008). Interview: Prof. Emmy van Deurzen. *Counselling Psychology Review*, *23*(2): 53–54.

Deurzen, E. van, & Arnold-Baker, C. (2005). *Existential perspectives on human issues: A handbook for therapeutic practice*. Basingstoke: Palgrave Macmillan.

Devine-Wright, P. (2009). An energetic approach. *The Psychologist*, *22*(2): 116–117.

Division of Counselling Psychology (2005). *Professional practice guidelines*. Leicester: British Psychological Society.

Dolley, T. (2008). Reclaiming our animal body. *Greenspirit Journal*, *10*(1): 9–11.

du Plock, S. (2002). Some reflections on an existential-phenomenological approach to working with addiction. *Existential Analysis*, *13*(1): 83–90.

Dunbar, R. I. M. (2003). The social brain: Mind, language and society in evolutionary perspective. *Annual Review of Anthropology*, *32*: 163–81.

Dunbar, R. (2004). *The human story: A new history of mankind's evolution*. London: Faber and Faber.

Favali, V. (2008). Disabled horse-rider's experience of horse-riding: Exploring the therapeutic benefits of contact with animals. Unpublished dissertation, University of Surrey.

Gaterslaben, B. (2008). Humans and nature: Ten useful findings from environmental psychology research. *Counselling Psychology Review*, *23*(2): 24–35.

Gore, A. (2006). *An inconvenient truth: The planetary emergency of global warming and what we can do about it*. London: Bloomsbury.

Gore, A. (2007). *Earth in the balance.* London: Earthscan.

Gray, J. (2002). *Straw dogs: Thoughts on humans and other animals.* London: Granta.

Hamilton, C. (2004). *Growth fetish.* London: Pluto Press.

Higley, N. (2008). *Connectedness to nature explored: An interpretative phenomeno-logical analysis of people's experiences of their ecological self.* Unpublished PsychD portfolio, University of Surrey.

Higley, N. & Milton, M. (2008). Our connection to the earth: A neglected relationship in counselling psychology. *Counselling Psychology Review, 23*(2): 10–23.

Howard, G. S. (1993). On certain blindness in human beings: Psychology and world overpopulation. *The Counseling Psychologist, 21*(4): 560–581.

Intergovernmental Panel on Climate Change (IPCC) (2001). *Climate change 2001: The scientific basis, contribution of Working Group 1 to the third assessment report of the IPCC.* In J. T. Houghton, Y. Ding, D. J. Griggs, M. Noguer, P. J. van der Linden & D. Xiasou (Eds.) Cambridge: Cambridge University Press.

James, O. (2007). *Affluenza.* London: Vermillion.

Jordan, M. (2005). The process of the Vision Fast: A (trans)personal journey. Paper presented at the Transpersonal Psychology Section of the British Psychological Society, 17 September 2005. www.ecotherapy.org.uk/files/ecotherapy/home/The_vision_fast_unmarked.doc. Accessed 2 April 2008.

Jung, C. G. (1990). *Memories, dreams and reflections.* London: Flamingo.

Kovel, J. (2002). *The enemy of nature: The end of capitalism or the end of the world.* London: Zed Books.

Louv, R. (2006). *Last child in the woods: Saving our children from nature-deficit disorder.* Chapel Hill, NC: Algonquin Books.

Mabey, R. (2005). *Nature cure.* London: Pimlico.

Mabey, R. (2006). A brush with nature. *BBC Wildlife Magazine,* September, *24*(9): 13.

Macfarlane, R. (2007). *The wild places.* London: Granta Books.

Macy, J. (1995). Working through environmental despair. In T. Roszak, M.E. Gomes & A. D. Kanner (Eds.) *Ecopsychology: Restoring the earth: Healing the mind.* San Francisco: Sierra Club Books.

Maller, C., Townsend, M. & Pryor, A. (2006). Healthy nature, healthy people: Contact with nature as an upstream health promotion intervention for populations. *Health Promotion International, 21*(1): 45–54.

May, R., Angel, E. & Ehlenberger, H. F. (Eds.) (1958). *Existence: A new dimension in psychiatry and psychology.* New York: Basic Books.

McCallum, I. (2007). *Ecological intelligence: Rediscovering ourselves in nature.* Cape Town: Africa Geographic.

McCallum, I. (2008). Wild at heart. *Africa Geographic, 16*(7): 90.

McCallum, I. & Milton, M. (2008). In conversation: Ian McCallum, Jungian analyst, ecopsychologist and author in conversation with Martin Milton. *Counselling Psychology Review, 23*(2): 62–67.

Milton, M. (2003). The call of the wild: Lessons from natural history. *Counselling Psychology Review, 18*(1): 3–11.

Milton, M. (2007). Life and our role in it. *Counselling Psychology Review*, 22(2): 37–40.

Milton, M. (2008). Wisdom from the wilderness. *Counselling Psychology Review*, 23(2): 36–46.

Milton, M. (2009). Waking up to nature: Exploring a new direction for psychological practice. *Ecopsychology*, 1(1): 1–6.

MIND (2007). *Ecotherapy: The green agenda for mental health: Executive summary.* London: MIND.

Orbach, S. (2009). *Bodies.* London: Picador.

Owen, J. (2008). A blue tit got me thinking: Reflections on the therapeutic aspects of human–animals relationships. *Counselling Psychology Review*, 23(2): 47–52.

Priest, P. (2007). The healing balm effect: Using a walking group to feel better. *Journal of Health Psychology*, 12(1): 36–52.

Randall, R. (2005). A new climate for psychotherapy? *Psychotherapy and Politics International*, 3(3): 165–179.

Rust, M. (2004). Creating a psychotherapy for a sustainable future. In *Resurgence.* www.mjrust.net/downloads/Seeking%20Health%20in%20an%20Ailing%20World.pdf. Accessed 2 February 2009.

Rust, M. (2005). Making the sea change: From chaos and inertia to creativity. Keynote speech for the PCSR Conference, 2005. www.mjrust.net/downloads/Making%20the%20Sea%20Change%20.pdf. Accessed 2 February 2009.

Rust, M. (2005a). Psychology for a change: From inertia to inspiration for action. Schumacher Lecture. www.mjrust.net/downloads/Psychology%20for%20a%20Change%202005.pdf. Accessed 2 February 2009.

Rust, M. J. (2008). Nature hunger: Eating problems and consuming the earth. *Counselling Psychology Review*, 23(2): 47–52.

Scott, J. & Milton, M. (2008). In conversation: Jonathan Scott, naturalist, author and television presenter in conversation with Martin Milton. *Counselling Psychology Review*, 23(2): 56–59.

Searles, H. (1960). *The non-human environment in normal development and in schizophrenia.* New York: International Universities Press.

Shillito-Clarke, C. (2008). Interview: Carol Shillito-Clarke. *Counselling Psychology Review*, 23(2): 5–6.

Smith, D. L. (2007). *The most dangerous animal: Human nature and the origins of war.* New York: St. Martin's Press.

Spence, A., Pidgeon, N. & Uzzell, D. (2009). Climate change: Psychology's contribution. *The Psychologist*, 22(2): 108–111.

Stern, P. (2009). One on one with Paul Stern. *The Psychologist*, 22(2): 184.

Steyn, V. (2008). Interview: Villiers Steyn. *Counselling Psychology Review*, 23(2): 60–61.

Strawbridge, S. & Woolfe, R. (2003). Counselling psychology in context. In R. Woolfe, W. Dryden & S. Strawbridge (Eds.) *Handbook of counselling psychology.* London: Sage.

Sustainable Development Commission (2008). *Health, place and nature: How outdoor environments influence health and well-being: A knowledge base.* www.sd-commission.org.uk/publications/downloads/Outdoor_environments_and_health .pdf. Accessed 16 April 2008.

Ulstrand, S. (2002). *Savannah lives: Animal life and human evolution in Africa.* Oxford: Oxford Press.

Uzzell, D. (2008). Challenging assumptions in the psychology of climate change. *InPsych: The Bulletin of the Australian Psychological Society, 30*(4): 10–13.

Uzzell, D. (2008a). The challenge of climate change: The challenge for psychology. Keynote paper presented at the 43rd Australian Psychological Society Annual Conference, Hobart, Tasmania, 23–27 September 2008.

Ward, C., & Styles, I. (2007). Evidence for the ecological self: English-speaking migrants' residual links to their homeland. *International Journal of Applied Psychoanalytic Studies, 4*(4): 319–332.

Wright, R. (2009). Conservation work: A therapeutic intervention? *The Psychologist, 22*(2): 108–111.

Epilogue

And Finally ...

Martin Milton

... there are more solutions, which are made by accommodation, by partnership, by symbiosis, by association, than there are by outright struggle, and I
think this is a good thing for us to understand.
                                    (Richard Mabey, cited in Beeley *et al.*, 2006)

In this book, the contributors and I have set out our own views of many
of the issues that counselling psychology currently faces and we hope that
in some small way the book will be a useful contribution to the reader's
exploration and interrogation of these subjects. We are under no illusion
that we have captured every meaning – indeed, many of us would be sceptical
of such a possibility at all. The recognition of difference and dialogue is
what makes counselling psychology such a vibrant and useful discipline.
Dialogue, development and evolution are processes counselling psychology
is familiar with, even in our relatively short existence.

It can be exhilarating to be a part of such evolution, but it can also be a
source of uncertainty. While confident in our arguments, we recognise that
our professional reality today may simply be a stepping-stone *en route* to a
variety of other future identities and practices – some we may welcome, the
idea of others might worry us enormously. So while we have tried to stay as
up to date as possible, it is only the test of time that will keep these views
fresh or make them old before their time.

At the time of writing we are into the reality of state regulation, National
Occupational Standards and the like and can only speculate what these will

Therapy and Beyond: Counselling Psychology Contributions to Therapeutic and Social Issues
Edited by Martin Milton
© 2010 John Wiley & Sons, Ltd.

bring. Indeed, after an extended period of lobbying by the British Psychological Society, the regulation of psychologists became a reality in 2009. But not quite in the way that had been envisaged and for many of us, not in a way that makes a great deal of sense. Instead of a regulatory body based within psychological models of practice, we suddenly all became health professionals whether or not our work is medical in nature. As readers will now be aware, the medical model and the assumptions it has about discrete entities (both in terms of pathologies and 'treatments') may be useful in some circumstances, but fails to capture the experience of people's values, struggles or ways of coping with the challenges they face.

The adoption of psychology into a health framework required an enormous amount of energy in translating psychological practice into a different language. There may be nothing wrong with that, of course, if it clarifies things while facilitating the range of contributions that psychology can make. However, a relational framework reminds us that language both allows and disallows certain thoughts, feelings and behaviours. The translation of our work into a different language is not without its difficulties; for we all know that meanings can be lost in translation. These new statements about the psychological professions set precedents, benchmarks that may not always be helpful. For example, the prioritising of an agenda of risk avoidance in the National Occupational Standards is just one oddity that we need to get to grips with. How do we live a life and guarantee that it is risk-free, let alone guarantee clients that life and relationships can be meaningful as well? These are just two of the challenges that the applied psychologies will faced as time moves on. The ways in which adjustments will be made are still to be seen, but there is no doubt that we shall attend to these pressures in the same way we do with these other challenges – with relational models, curiosity and creativity and a desire to work collaboratively, whether that be with clients, research participants or wider society. And we shall do this with an open mind but also an ability to critique and challenge too.

Meanwhile, the contributors and I are pleased to have the opportunity to offer a timely and contemporary account of the way in which counselling psychology, its values, knowledge base and practices, is proving a useful discipline, both within therapy and beyond.

Reference

Beeley, F., Colwell, M. and Stevens, J. (2006) *Planet earth: The future: What the experts say*. BBC Books, London.

Index

Therapy and Beyond: Counselling Psychology Contributions to Therapeutic and Social Issues
Edited by Martin Milton
© 2010 John Wiley & Sons, Ltd.